A·N·N·U·A·L E·D·I·T·I·O·N·S

Education

Thirtieth Edition

03/04

W9-DIF-974

EDITOR

Fred Schultz

University of Akron (Retired)

Fred Schultz, former professor of education at the Unive
University to earn a B.S. in social science education in
philosophy of education in 1966, and a Ph.D. in the histc
and American studies in 1969. His B.A. in Spanish was c
Akron in May 1985. He is actively involved in researc
tory of American education with a primary focus on the
losophy of education. He also likes to study languages.

608512547

McGraw-Hill/Dushkin

530 Old Whitfield Street, Guilford, Connecticut 06437

Visit us on the Internet
http://www.dushkin.com

Credits

1. **How Others See Us and How We See Ourselves**
   Unit photo—© 2003 by Sweet By & By/Cindy Brown.
2. **Rethinking and Changing the Educative Effort**
   Unit photo—© 2003 by Cleo Freelance Photography.
3. **Striving for Excellence: The Drive for Quality**
   Unit photo—© 2003 by Sweet By & By/Cindy Brown.
4. **Morality and Values in Education**
   Unit photo—© 2003 by Cleo Freelance Photography.
5. **Managing Life in Classrooms**
   Unit photo—© 2003 by PhotoDisc, Inc.
6. **Cultural Diversity and Schooling**
   Unit photo—© 2003 by Cleo Freelance Photography.
7. **Serving Special Needs and Concerns**
   Unit photo—© 2003 by Cleo Freelance Photography.
8. **The Profession of Teaching Today**
   Unit photo—Courtesy of Pamela Carley/McGraw-Hill/Dushkin.
9. **A Look to the Future**
   Unit photo—© 2003 by Cleo Freelance Photography.

Copyright

Cataloging in Publication Data
Main entry under title: Annual Editions: Education. 2003/2004.
1. Education—Periodicals. I. Schultz, Fred, *comp.* II. Title: Education.
ISBN 0–07–254841–X   658'.05   ISSN 0272–5010

Thirtieth Edition

Cover image © 2003 PhotoDisc, Inc.
Printed in the United States of America   1234567890BAHBAH543   Printed on Recycled Paper

Editors/Advisory Board

Members of the Advisory Board are instrumental in the final selection of articles for each edition of ANNUAL EDITIONS. Their review of articles for content, level, currency, and appropriateness provides critical direction to the editor and staff. We think that you will find their careful consideration well reflected in this volume.

Staff

To the Reader

In publishing ANNUAL EDITIONS we recognize the enormous role played by the magazines, newspapers, and journals of the public press in providing current, first-rate educational information in a broad spectrum of interest areas. Many of these articles are appropriate for students, researchers, and professionals seeking accurate, current material to help bridge the gap between principles and theories and the real world. These articles, however, become more useful for study when those of lasting value are carefully collected, organized, indexed, and reproduced in a low-cost format, which provides easy and permanent access when the material is needed. That is the role played by ANNUAL EDITIONS.

Issues regarding the purposes of education as well as the appropriate methods of educating have been debated throughout all generations of literate human culture. This is because the meaning of the word "educated" shifts within ideological realms of thought and cultural belief systems. There will always be debates over the purposes and the ends of "education" as it is understood in any time or place. This is because each generation must continuously reconstruct the definition of "education" based upon its understanding of "justice," "fairness," and "equity" in human relations, and each generation must locate and position their understanding of social and personal reality.

In the twenty-first century, educators are presented with many new challenges caused by many forces at work in human society. We must decide really what knowledge is of most worth and what basic skills and information each child, of whatever heritage, needs to know. We must face this question once and for all. It is no longer a choice; it is a duty if we are disciplined persons interested in the well-being of our children and adolescents. We have before us a great qualitative challenge, our response to which will determine the fate of future generations of our society.

The technological breakthroughs now developing in the information sciences will have an amazing impact on how people learn. The rates of change in how we learn and how we obtain information is already increasing at a very rapid pace that will assuredly continue.

The public conversation on the purposes and future directions of education is lively as ever. Alternative visions and voices regarding the broad social aims of schools and the preparation of teachers continue to be presented. *Annual Editions: Education 03/04* attempts to reflect current mainstream as well as alternative visions as to what education ought to be. Equity issues regarding what constitutes equal treatment of students in the schools continue to be addressed. This year's edition contains articles on gender issues in the field and on the application of research in multicultural education to the areas of teacher preparation and the staff development of teachers already in the schools. The debate over whether all public monies for education should go to the public schools or whether these funds should follow the student into either public or private schools has again intensified.

Communities are deeply interested in local school politics and school funding issues. There continues to be healthy dialogue about and competition for the support of the various "publics" involved in public schooling. The articles reflect spirited critique of our public schools. There are competing, and very differing, school reform agendas being discussed. All of this occurs as the United States continues to experience fundamentally important demographic shifts in its cultural makeup.

Compromise continues to be the order of the day. The many interest groups within the educational field reflect a broad spectrum of viewpoints ranging from various behaviorist and cognitive developmental perspectives to humanistic, postmodernist, and critical theoretical ones.

In assembling this volume, we make every effort to stay in touch with movements in educational studies and with the social forces at work in schools. Members of the advisory board contribute valuable insights, and the production and editorial staffs at the publisher, McGraw-Hill/Dushkin, coordinate our efforts. Through this process we collect a wide range of articles on a variety of topics relevant to education in North America.

The readings in *Annual Editions: Education 03/04* explore the social and academic goals of education, the current conditions of the nation's educational systems, the teaching profession, and the future of American education. In addition, these selections address the issues of change and the moral and ethical foundations of schooling. As always, we would like you to help us improve this volume. Please rate the material in this edition on the postage-paid article rating form provided at the back of this book and send it to us. We care about what you think. Give us the public feedback that we need.

Fred Schultz
Editor

Contents

UNIT 1
How Others See Us and How We See Ourselves

Three articles examine today's most significant educational issues: cultural development, education renewal, and the current public opinion about U.S. schools.

UNIT 2
Rethinking and Changing the Educative Effort

Four articles discuss the tension between ideals and socioeconomic reality at work in today's educational system.

The concepts in bold italics are developed in the article. For further expansion, please refer to the Topic Guide and the Index.

UNIT 3
Striving for Excellence: The Drive for Quality

Six selections examine the debate over achieving excellence in education by addressing issues relating to questions of how best to teach and how best to test.

The concepts in bold italics are developed in the article. For further expansion, please refer to the Topic Guide and the Index.

UNIT 4
Morality and Values in Education

Four articles examine the role of American schools in exploring humanistic and character education and in teaching morality and social values.

UNIT 5
Managing Life in Classrooms

Four selections consider the importance of building effective teacher-student and student-student relationships in the classroom.

The concepts in bold italics are developed in the article. For further expansion, please refer to the Topic Guide and the Index.

UNIT 6
Cultural Diversity and Schooling

Six articles discuss issues relating to fairness and justice for students from all cultural backgrounds and how curricula should respond to cultural pluralistic student populations.

The concepts in bold italics are developed in the article. For further expansion, please refer to the Topic Guide and the Index.

UNIT 7
Serving Special Needs and Concerns

Six articles examine some of the important aspects of special educational needs and building cooperative learning communities in the classroom setting.

UNIT 8
The Profession of Teaching Today

Four articles assess the current state of teaching in U.S. schools and how well today's teachers approach subject matter learning.

The concepts in bold italics are developed in the article. For further expansion, please refer to the Topic Guide and the Index.

UNIT 9
A Look to the Future

Three articles look at new forms of schooling that break from traditional conceptions of education in America.

The concepts in bold italics are developed in the article. For further expansion, please refer to the Topic Guide and the Index.

Topic Guide

This topic guide suggests how the selections in this book relate to the subjects covered in your course. You may want to use the topics listed on these pages to search the Web more easily.

On the following pages a number of Web sites have been gathered specifically for this book. They are arranged to reflect the units of this *Annual Edition.* You can link to these sites by going to the DUSHKIN ONLINE support site at *http://www.dushkin.com/online/.*

ALL THE ARTICLES THAT RELATE TO EACH TOPIC ARE LISTED BELOW THE BOLD-FACED TERM.

Accountability
2. An Overview of America's Education Agenda
7. The Dark Side of Nationwide Tests
8. The Human Face of the High-Stakes Testing Story
9. How and Why Standards Can Improve Student Achievement: A Conversation With Robert J. Marzano
10. Standards: Here Today, Here Tomorrow
12. Saving Standards
13. Welcome to Standardsville
31. Tales of Suburban High
35. Accountability: What's Worth Measuring?

Action research
6. Action Research for School Improvement
36. Early Childhood Education: Distance Learning for Teachers Adds a New Dimension

Aggression
18. Bullying Among Children

Character development
17. Humanistic Education to Character Education: An Ideological Journey

Children
18. Bullying Among Children

Classroom management
18. Bullying Among Children
19. Creating School Climates That Prevent School Violence
20. Discipline and the Special Education Student
21. E-Mentality: Is E-Learning Affecting Classroom Behavior?

Cultural diversity and schooling
22. Decisions That Have Shaped U.S. Education
23. Educating African American Children: Credibility at a Crossroads
24. The Evils of Public Schools
25. Can Every Child Learn?
26. School Vouchers Showdown
27. Meeting the Challenge of the Urban High School

Demographics
1. Beyond Census 2000: As a Nation, We Are the World

Discipline in schools
18. Bullying Among Children
19. Creating School Climates That Prevent School Violence
20. Discipline and the Special Education Student
21. E-Mentality: Is E-Learning Affecting Classroom Behavior?

Education, equity in
27. Meeting the Challenge of the Urban High School

Education, excellence in
8. The Human Face of the High-Stakes Testing Story

9. How and Why Standards Can Improve Student Achievement: A Conversation With Robert J. Marzano
10. Standards: Here Today, Here Tomorrow
11. Where's the Content? The Role of Content in Constructivist Teacher Education
12. Saving Standards
13. Welcome to Standardsville
40. The New Century: Is It Too Late for Transformational Leadership?

Education, future of
39. The World Is Your Classroom: Lessons in Self-Renewal
40. The New Century: Is It Too Late for Transformational Leadership?

Educational agenda
2. An Overview of America's Education Agenda

Educational leadership
38. The Kind of Schools We Need
40. The New Century: Is It Too Late for Transformational Leadership?

Emotional development
18. Bullying Among Children

How others see us
1. Beyond Census 2000: As a Nation, We Are the World
2. An Overview of America's Education Agenda
3. The 34th Annual Phi Delta Kappan/Gallup Poll of the Public Attitudes Toward the Public Schools
30. The Other Marriage War

Humanistic education
15. Inculcating a Passion for Truth and Learning
17. Humanistic Education to Character Education: An Ideological Journey

Learning environment
6. Action Research for School Improvement
19. Creating School Climates That Prevent School Violence
20. Discipline and the Special Education Student
29. Common Arguments About the Strengths and Limitations of Home Schooling
31. Tales of Suburban High

Literacy
11. Where's the Content? The Role of Content in Constructivist Teacher Education
13. Welcome to Standardsville
31. Tales of Suburban High
32. Learning With Jazz

Moral development
17. Humanistic Education to Character Education: An Ideological Journey

World Wide Web Sites

The following World Wide Web sites have been carefully researched and selected to support the articles found in this reader. The easiest way to access these selected sites is to go to our DUSHKIN ONLINE support site at *http://www.dushkin.com/online/*.

AE: Education 03/04

The following sites were available at the time of publication. Visit our Web site—we update DUSHKIN ONLINE regularly to reflect any changes.

General Sources

Education Week on the Web
http://www.edweek.org

At this *Education Week* home page, you will be able to open its archives, read special reports on education, keep up on current events in education, look at job opportunities, and access articles relevant to educators today.

Educational Resources Information Center
http://www.eric.ed.gov

This invaluable site provides links to all ERIC sites: clearinghouses, support components, and publishers of ERIC materials. You can search the ERIC database, find out what is new, and ask questions about ERIC.

Internet Resources for Education
http://web.hamline.edu/personal/kfmeyer/cla_education.html#hamline

This site, which aims for "educational collaboration," takes you to Internet links that examine virtual classrooms, trends, policy, and infrastructure development. It leads to information about school reform, multiculturalism, technology in education, and much more.

National Education Association
http://www.nea.org

Something about virtually every education-related topic can be accessed via this site of the 2.3-million-strong National Education Association.

National Parent Information Network/ERIC
http://npin.org

This is a clearinghouse of information on elementary and early childhood education as well as urban education. Browse through its links for information for parents and for people who work with parents.

U.S. Department of Education
http://www.ed.gov

Explore this government site for examination of institutional aspects of multicultural education. National goals, projects, grants, and other educational programs are listed here as well as many links to teacher services and resources.

UNIT 1: How Others See Us and How We See Ourselves

Charter Schools
http://www.edexcellence.net/topics/charters.html

Open this site for news about charter schools. It provides information about charter school research and issues, links to the U.S. Charter Schools Web site, and Best on the Web charter school sites.

Pathways to School Improvement
http://www.ncrel.org/sdrs/pathwayg.htm

This site of the North Central Regional Educational Laboratory leads to discussions and links about education, including the current state of education, reform issues, and goals and standards. Technology, professional development, and integrated services are a few of the subjects also discussed.

UNIT 2: Rethinking and Changing the Educative Effort

The Center for Innovation in Education
http://www.center.edu

The Center for Innovation in Education, self-described as a "not-for-profit, nonpartisan research organization" focuses on K–12 education reform strategies. Click on its links for information about and varying perspectives on school privatization and other reform initiatives.

Colorado Department of Education
http://www.cde.state.co.us/index_home.htm

This site's links will lead you to information about education-reform efforts, technology in education initiatives, and many documents of interest to educators, parents, and students.

National Council for Accreditation of Teacher Education
http://www.ncate.org

The NCATE is the professional accrediting organization for schools, colleges, and departments of education in the United States. Accessing this page will lead to information about teacher and school standards, state relations, and developmental projects.

Phi Delta Kappa International
http://www.pdkintl.org

This important organization publishes articles about all facets of education—from school vouchers and charter schools to "new dimensions" in learning.

UNIT 3: Striving for Excellence: The Drive for Quality

Awesome Library for Teachers
http://www.awesomelibrary.org/

Open this page for links and access to teacher information on everything from educational assessment to general child development topics.

Education World
http://www.education-world.com

Education World provides a database of literally thousands of sites that can be searched by grade level, plus education news, lesson plans, and professional-development resources.

EdWeb/Andy Carvin
http://edwebproject.org

The purpose of EdWeb is to explore the worlds of educational reform and information technology. Access educational resources around the world, learn about trends in education policy and

www.dushkin.com/online/

information infrastructure development, examine success stories of computers in the classroom, and much more.

Kathy Schrock's Guide for Educatiors
http://www.discoveryschool.com/schrockguide/

This is a classified list of sites on the Internet found to be useful for enhancing curriculum and teacher professional growth. It is updated daily.

Teacher's Guide to the U.S. Department of Education
http://www.ed.gov/pubs/TeachersGuide/

Government goals, projects, grants, and other educational programs are listed here as well as many links to teacher services and resources.

UNIT 4: Morality and Values in Education

Association for Moral Education
http://www.wittenberg.edu/ame/

AME is dedicated to fostering communication, cooperation, training, curriculum development, and research that links moral theory with educational practices. From here it is possible to connect to several sites on ethics, character building, and moral development.

Child Welfare League of America
http://www.cwla.org

The CWLA is the United States' oldest and largest organization devoted entirely to the well-being of vulnerable children and their families. This site provides links to information about issues related to morality and values in education.

Ethics Updates/Lawrence Hinman
http://ethics.acusd.edu

This site provides both simple concept definition and complex analysis of ethics, original treatises, and sophisticated search engine capability. Subject matter covers the gamut from ethical theory to applied ethical venues. There are many opportunities for user input.

The National Academy for Child Development
http://www.nacd.org

This international organization is dedicated to helping children and adults reach their full potential. Its home page presents links to various programs, research, and resources into such topics as ADD.

UNIT 5: Managing Life in Classrooms

Classroom Connect
http://www.classroom.com

This is a major Web site for K–12 teachers and students, with links to schools, teachers, and resources online. It includes discussion of the use of technology in the classroom.

Global SchoolNet Foundation
http://www.gsn.org

Access this site for multicultural educational information. The site includes news for teachers, students, and parents, as well as chat rooms, links to educational resources, programs, and contests and competitions.

Teacher Talk Forum
http://education.indiana.edu/cas/tt/tthmpg.html

Visit this site for access to a variety of articles discussing life in the classroom. Clicking on the various links will lead you to electronic lesson plans covering a variety of topic areas from Indiana University's Center for Adolescent Studies.

UNIT 6: Cultural Diversity and Schooling

American Scientist
http://www.amsci.org/amsci/amsci.html

Investigate this site to access a variety of articles and to explore issues and concepts related to race and gender.

American Studies Web
http://www.georgetown.edu/crossroads/asw/

This eclectic site provides links to a wealth of resources on the Internet related to American studies, from gender studies to race and ethnicity. It is of great help when doing research in demography and population studies.

Multicultural Publishing and Education Council
http://www.mpec.org/mpec.html

This is the home page of the MPEC, a networking and support organization for independent publishers, authors, educators, and librarians fostering authentic multicultural books and materials. It has excellent links to a vast array of resources related to multicultural education.

National Institute on the Education of At-Risk Students
http://www.ed.gov/offices/OERI/At-Risk/

The At-Risk Institute supports research and development activities designed to improve the education of students at risk of educational failure due to limited English proficiencey, race, geographic location, or economic disadvantage.

Prospects: The Congressionally Mandated Study of Educational Growth and Opportunity
http://www.ed.gov/pubs/Prospects/index.html

This report analyzes cross-sectional data on language-minority and LEP students in the United States and outlines what actions are needed to improve their educational performance. Family and economic situations are addressed. Information on related reports and sites is provided.

UNIT 7: Serving Special Needs and Concerns

Consortium on Inclusive Schooling Practices
http://www.asri.edu/cfsp/brochure/abtcons.htm

The Consortium represents a collaborative effort to build the capacity of state and local education agencies to provide inclusive educational services in school and community settings, focusing on systemic reform rather than on changes in special education only.

Constructivism: From Philosophy to Practice
http://www.stemnet.nf.ca/~elmurphy/emurphy/cle.html

Here is a thorough description of the history, philosophy, and practice of constructivism, including quotations from Socrates and others, epistemology, learning theory, characteristics, and a checklist.

Kenny Anthony's Gifted and Talented and General Educational Resources
http://www2.tsixroads.com/~kva/

In addition to definitions and characteristics of giftedness and needs of the gifted, an excellent list of education resources for the gifted can be found on this site.

National Association for Gifted Children
http://www.nagc.org/home00.htm

NAGC, a national nonprofit organization for gifted children, is dedicated to developing their high potential.

www.dushkin.com/online/

National Information Center for Children and Youth With Disabilities (NICHCY)
http://www.nichcy.org/index.html

NICHCY provides information and makes referrals in areas related to specific disabilities, early intervention, special education and related services, individualized education programs, and much more. The site also connects to a listing of Parent's Guides to resources for children and youth with disabilities.

UNIT 8: The Profession of Teaching Today

Canada's SchoolNet Staff Room
http://www.schoolnet.ca/home/e/

Here is a resource and link site for anyone involved in education, including special-needs educators, teachers, parents, volunteers, and administrators.

Teachers Helping Teachers
http://www.pacificnet.net/~mandel/

This site provides basic teaching tips, new teaching methodology ideas, and forums for teachers to share their experiences. Download software and participate in chat sessions. It features educational resources on the Web, and new ones are added each week.

The Teachers' Network
http://www.teachers.net/

Bulletin boards, classroom projects, online forums, and Web mentors are featured on this site, as well as the book *Teachers' Guide to Cyberspace* and an online, 4-week course on how to use the Internet.

Teaching with Electronic Technology
http://www.wam.umd.edu/~mlhall/teaching.html

Michael Hall's Web site leads to many resources of values to those contemplating the future of education, particularly regarding the role of technology in the classroom and beyond.

UNIT 9: A Look to the Future

Goals 2000: A Progress Report
http://www.ed.gov/pubs/goals/progrpt/index.html

Open this site to survey a progress report by the U.S. Department of Education on the Goals 2000 reform initiative. It provides a sense of what goals educators are reaching for as they look toward the future.

Mighty Media
http://www.mightymedia.com

The mission of this privately funded consortium is to empower youth, teachers, and organizations through the use of interactive communications technology. The site provides links to teacher talk forums, educator resources, networks for students, and more.

Online Internet Institute
http://www.oii.org

A collaborative project among Internet-using educators, proponents of systemic reform, content-area experts, and teachers who desire professional growth, this site provides a learning environment for integrating the Internet into educators' individual teaching styles.

We highly recommend that you review our Web site for expanded information and our other product lines. We are continually updating and adding links to our Web site in order to offer you the most usable and useful information that will support and expand the value of your Annual Editions. You can reach us at: *http://www.dushkin.com/annualeditions/*.

UNIT 1

How Others See Us and How We See Ourselves

Unit Selections

1. **Beyond Census 2000: As a Nation, We Are the World**, Kenneth Prewitt
2. **An Overview of America's Education Agenda**, Rod Paige
3. **The 34th Annual Phi Delta Kappan/Gallup Poll of the Public Attitudes Toward the Public Schools**, Lowell C. Rose and Alec M. Gallup

Key Points to Consider

- What has been the effect of an increasingly more multicultural population upon public school systems in the United States?

- Discuss the educational doctrine inherent in the phrase "no child left behind." Do you agree or disagree with this approach to education? Defend your answer.

- What are the most important problems blocking efforts to improve educational standards?

- How can we most accurately assess public perceptions of the educational system?

- What is the fundamental effect of public opinion on national public policy regarding educational development?

 **Links: www.dushkin.com/online/**
These sites are annotated in the World Wide Web pages.

Charter Schools
http://www.edexcellence.net/topics/charters.html
Pathways to School Improvement
http://www.ncrel.org/sdrs/pathwayg.htm

There are many ways in which children and youth are educated. The social, racial, and cultural landscape in the United States is becoming more and more diverse and multifaceted. How youth respond to current issues is a reflection of their perceptions as to how older citizens respond to social reality. How to improve the quality of educational services remains a concern of the general public. Public perceptions of the nation's efforts in the education of its youth are of great importance to those who work with children and youth. We must be attentive to the peoples' concerns; we cannot ignore them.

How the people served by a nation's schools perceive the quality of the education they received is of great interest, because public perceptions can translate into either increased or decreased levels of support for a nation's educational system. Achieving a public consensus as to what the aims or purposes of education ought to be can be difficult. Americans debate what the purposes of education should be in every generation. Many different sorts of schools exist at both the elementary and the secondary levels. Many different forms of "charter" schools are attracting the interest of parents; some of these charter schools are within public school systems and some are private ones. Parents wish to have choices as to the types of schools their children attend.

Schools need to be places where students and teachers feel safe, places that provide hope and that instill confidence in the prospects for a happier and better future for all. The safety of students and teachers in schools is a matter of concern to many persons due to tragic events in the recent past. Schools also need to be places where students can dream and hope and work to inform themselves in the process of building their futures. Schools need to help students learn to be inquiring persons.

There are several major policy issues regarding the content and form of schooling that are being debated. We are anticipating greater ranges of choice in the types and forms of schooling that will become available to our children and youth. The United States has great interest in policy issues related to increased accountability to the public for what goes on in schools. Also, we are possibly the most culturally pluralistic nation in the world, and we are becoming even more diverse.

We may be approaching a historic moment in our national history regarding the public funding of education and the options parents might be given for the education of their children. Some of these options and the lines of reasoning for them are explored in this volume. Financial as well as qualitative options are being debated. Scholars in many fields of study as well as journalists and legislators are asking how we can make our nation's schools more effective as well as how we might optimize parents' sense of control over how their children are to be educated.

Young people "read" certain adult behaviors well; they see it as hypocrisy when the adult community wants certain standards and values to be taught in schools but rewards other, often opposite behaviors in society. Dialogue regarding what it means to speak of "literacy" in democratic communities continues. Our students read much from our daily activities and our many information sources, and they form their own shrewd analyses of

what social values actually do prevail in society. How to help young people develop their intellectual potential and become perceptive students of and participants in democratic traditions are major public concerns.

There is serious business yet to be attended to by the social service and educational agencies that try to serve youth. People are impatient to see some fundamental efforts made to meet the basic educational needs of young people. The problems are the greatest in major cities and in more isolated rural areas. Public perceptions of the schools are affected by high levels of economic deprivation among large sectors of the population and by the economic pressures that our interdependent world economy produces as a result of international competition for the world's markets.

Studies conducted in the past few years, particularly the Carnegie Corporation's studies of adolescents in the United States, document the plight of millions of young persons in the United States. Some authors point out that although there was much talk about educational change in the 1990s, those changes were only marginal and cosmetic at best. States responded by demanding more course work and tougher exit standards from schools. With still more than 25 percent of schoolchildren in the United States living at or below the poverty level, and almost a third of them in more economically and socially vulnerable non-traditional family settings, the overall social situation for many young people continues to be difficult. The public wants more effective responses to public needs.

So, in the face of major demographic shifts and of the persistence of many long-term social problems, the public watches how schools respond to new as well as old challenges. In recent years, these challenges have aggravated rather than allayed much public concern about the efficacy of public schooling. Various political, cultural, corporate, and philanthropic interests continue to articulate alternative educational agendas. At the same time the incumbents in the system respond with their own educational agendas, which reflect their views from the inside.

Beyond Census 2000:

AS A NATION, WE ARE THE WORLD

In the year 2000, for the first time in its 200-year history, the U.S. census allowed people to state that they were of more than one race. Here, Kenneth Prewitt, who directed that census, comments on issues raised for the nation by the new "multiple-race" option.

by Kenneth Prewitt

How can we live together? How can we live together justly?

Haven't we, as Americans, already asked ourselves these questions—and answered them? They were forcefully addressed in the Constitutional amendments after the Civil War that abolished slavery, provided equal protection under the law and guaranteed all citizens, regardless of race, the right to vote. Although these principles were slow to be honored, and not seriously enforced until the advent of court rulings and legislation stimulated by the civil rights movement, it would seem that our nation has finally rejected discrimination based on race, ethnicity or national origin. Today we view ourselves as more tolerant, more welcoming of diversity than at any time in our history.

In fact, this nation has had a complicated relationship to diversity. We have prided ourselves on finding common ground in the midst of diversity; we have based our claim to being exceptional among nations on having established a nation rooted not in ties of blood, ancestry, nationality or religion but on the shared belief in an ideal: liberal democracy. There is some truth to this claim, but it is also true that at various moments in our history, significant numbers of Americans—black slaves, native Indians, Catholic immigrants, Chinese workers and Jewish tradesmen, to name just a few—were thought to be too "other" to join in the common enterprise. Diversity and discrimination have been linked throughout our history more, perhaps, than we care to admit. Perhaps this is unavoidable. There are inescapable political and philosophical tensions between, on the one hand, a belief in human unity and, on the other, the reality of differences and persistence of conflicts among multiple cultures, ethnicities, nationalities, religions and languages.

In this country, while we have lived together, it has not always been peacefully. It has not always been justly. And there

is no guarantee that we will do so in the coming decades. There are issues to be confronted, particularly those raised by the recently completed national census.

Census 2000 and Liberal Democracy

Since the nation's founding we have counted and classified ourselves every ten years—but it was not until the 2000 census that Americans were given the opportunity to declare themselves as being of more than one race. This may appear to be a technical adjustment in how we classify racial groups, but the "multiple-race" option on the census form goes to the core of the tension between unity and diversity. The multiple-race option, I suggest, has set off tremors that signal a political and social earthquake to come.

This earthquake will occur against a backdrop of far-reaching shifts in the nation's demography. We are in the early stages of diversifying our population in a manner historically unprecedented. We start with the fact that the foreign born cohort of our population is now ten percent. This may not seem significant: after all, as a frontier nation built upon immigration, we have always had high levels of foreign-born people living within our borders, with rates occasionally rising well above ten percent. Our liberal democracy has adjusted itself accordingly, embracing both assimilation and accommodation. Certainly there have been rough moments, yet we have generally found ways to work through them.

But something new is underway. The 19th and early 20th century immigration patterns transformed a nation initially based on a northern European population into one that became pan-European. A nation that started the 19th century as a Protestant stronghold ended it as an amalgam of Protestants, Catholics and Jews. This transformation, though consequential, was qualitatively different from the situation that we now face. The U.S. has become home to people from, literally, every civilization and of every nationality, and speaking almost every language. Not in recorded history has there been a nation so demographically complex. So it falls to us, the American citizens of the 21st century, to fashion, from this diversity, history's first "world nation."

If diversity and **discrimination** *have so often been joined together in American history, will the pairing* grow *weaker or stronger—as we become more diverse?*

Since the first census in 1790, which recognized only a few population categories—free whites, other free people and slaves—those who count and classify us have tried to keep up with changing demographic realities. But looking to the future, how will we deal with our extraordinary and ever-growing diversity? Will newly arriving groups be counted and sorted in some yet-to-be-designed racial and ethnic taxonomy? If so, the issues to be worked out are daunting: will Sudanese refugees, for example, be assigned to the same "race" as seventh-generation African Americans? Will Arab Americans become an independent racial group? Is "white" one race or a residual category for everyone not noticeably something else? Resolving these issues justly is a challenge for our fractious politics. Or perhaps we won't go this route at all. Perhaps there will be a movement toward dismantling racial and ethnic classifications altogether. That possibility also leaves a host of uncomfortable issues in its wake, not least of which is the future of civil rights. If diversity and discrimination have so often been joined together in American history, will the pairing grow weaker or stronger—will racism and nativism wax or wane—as we become more diverse?

It is the task of a liberal democracy to keep reflecting on the inescapable tension between unity and diversity, to ask, for each fresh set of conditions: *How can we live together? How can we live together justly?* A quick historical tour, focused on America's continuous demographic transformation, helps to frame these questions for today.

The Demographic Journey to Independence

It is tempting to think of our demographic history as one of self-selected immigration, starting with the first settlers and followed by successive waves of immigrants drawn by the promise of religious tolerance, political freedom and economic opportunity. As we are all aware, that's only part of the story. Our demographic history is also about conquest, purchase and the slave trade. Not everyone who became "American" did so voluntarily.

In 1500, the land mass that is today the U.S. was home to approximately 3.5 million native Indians belonging to 17 major language groups. Population densities were very low, with the largest population groups situated in the coastal areas of the Northwest. Once Europeans arrived, contact with their diseases, especially smallpox, began to reduce native populations, as did the fact that Europeans had guns, making settlers almost always the superior force in warring encounters. Indian groups along the Atlantic Coast, where the earliest settlers established themselves, were particularly vulnerable. By the time that the first U.S. census was taken in 1790, native Indians living in the 13 recently formed states comprised only 1.2 percent of the total population. Three centuries of imported diseases, colonization and genocide had reduced to a tiny fraction the Native Americans' share of the new nation's population.

Involuntary immigration—the slave trade—was a second factor in the nation's early demographic history. Slavery reached the Caribbean Islands in 1501 and was first recorded in the colonies in 1619 with the arrival of a single African American male, slave to a Jamestown family. Over the next 30 years, the slave population of the colonies grew to around 50,000, largely concentrated in Virginia and Massachusetts, and the numbers were still rising. Between 1670 and 1700, for instance, the black population increased five-fold while the white population only doubled. When the first census was taken, slaves were the second largest demographic group in the new nation, comprising 19% of the population.

The largest group counted in the 1790 census was, of course, from the British Isles. The English, Welsh, Scottish and Irish comprised nearly three million of the almost four million people counted in the first national census. Another ten percent of the population was northern European, primarily Dutch and German. (All of these groups also overwhelmingly shared the same Protestant faith.) But things were about to change.

The 19th Century as a Story of Immigration

Demographically, the 19th century started quietly. Social and political observers considered the new U.S. to be a stable society. Its population, now settled for several generations, had shared colonialism, independence and the birth of the republic. These shared experiences had, presumably, melded the population into one nation, one people—excepting, of course, the slaves and the native Indians.

The Census of 1790

(Demographic groups by percent of population)

British	70%
Other Northern European	10%
African	19%
Native Indian	1%

But the nation was less demographically formed, less finished than both its citizens and outside commentators may have thought. Immigrants—though that term was not yet in use—were beginning to crowd into cities on the eastern seaboard. Although the most astute of social commentators, Alexis de Tocqueville, did not focus on immigration, there is a telling passage in his classic treatise, *Democracy in America*. He noted that recent immigrants, mostly Irish, were, to his way of thinking, a lower class that brought the threat of mob rule to America. "Living in a country of which they are not citizens," de Tocqueville wrote, "they are ready to take advantage of all the passions that agitate it." He wrote that social order could best be preserved through a national military force that was "independent of the people of the cities and able to restrain their excesses."

De Tocqueville was giving early voice to nativist sentiments, in full cry by mid-century, which started from the premise that the first settlers were not themselves "immigrants" and were now the true Americans. Immigrants, by this view, were not only altogether different, they were something to be concerned about—particularly because of their ever-expanding numbers. Still, they kept coming, reducing the numerical domination of British stock and greatly contributing to the growth of the population. Fewer than four million people were counted in the first census; nearly 92 million were recorded in 1910, on the eve of World War I. And with growth came diversity, including a religious diversity not welcome to the country's original Protestant base.

In the early 19th century, Roman Catholics, especially from Ireland, began to arrive in large numbers, generally escaping economic deprivation more than religious persecution. Emigration was further stimulated by political turmoil in northern Europe, sending people from Germany, France, Belgium and Holland to the American shores. By 1850, the Roman Catholic Church was the largest denomination in the country, though Catholics were still less numerous than all the Protestant denominations combined.

It was in 1850 that the census first introduced the distinction between native- and foreign-born Americans. When the census results were tallied, they showed, then as now, that the foreign-born concentrated in urban areas: more than half of New York City's population was foreign born, with similar high proportions in Chicago, Milwaukee, Detroit, St. Louis and New Orleans.

Living together amidst all this diversity did not come easily. In the eastern U.S., the nativist Know-Nothing Party led an anti-

Catholic cry. "Romanism," it was feared, would undermine Protestant Puritanism on which the nation had constructed its moral and political identity. The effort by nativists to close down immigration was opposed by economic interests: factory owners needed workers, as did the railroads pushing across the country. The frontier was there to be settled, and shipping interests benefited from the huge cross-Atlantic traffic. Economic interests prevailed. Immigration continued, though naturalization was not made easy.

The middle of the 19th century also saw a sharp upsurge in the arrival of Asian immigrants on the West Coast. They were drawn to the "Mountain of Gold," where work in the mines and on the railroads offered economic returns unheard of in China and Japan. The "coolie" labor trade was beneficial to the American economy, but in the case of the Chinese, for example, only men and not women were allowed to come to the U.S. to work. This was to prevent Chinese from being born in America, thereby becoming citizens. In many additional ways, patterns of discrimination and anti-immigration sentiment directed at Catholics in the eastern U.S. repeated themselves on the West Coast. Asians, denied the protections of citizenship, were poorly paid, badly treated and sometimes violently attacked. In the first instance of closing our borders to immigrants, the Chinese Exclusion Act of 1882 and successor laws stopped Chinese immigration; the 1907 "Gentleman's Agreement" between the U.S. and Japan to discourage emigration had a similar effect on the flow of Japanese. These policies reflected both racist views and fears of wage competition in a mixture that came to dominate immigration policy for decades.

Even more dramatic population shifts resulted from the next wave of immigration, which began about 1880, peaking in the years before WW I. It was during this period that immigration from northern Europe fell sharply to be replaced by large numbers of arrivals from southern and Eastern Europe, including the first large wave of Jewish immigrants.

Across the 19th and into the 20th century, learning to live together did not proceed smoothly. Anti-Catholicism, anti-Semitism and anti-Asian views fit easily into the beliefs and practices of the descendents of the settlers who viewed the Mediterranean, Jewish, Negroid and Oriental races—the terms used during those years—as inferior to those of Anglo stock. These attitudes were fueled by psuedo-scientific racist theories such as Social Darwinism and eugenics, which came into vogue in this era; the former suggested that the poor were deservedly so while the latter would advance racial purity through selective reproduction. Racist quotas in the restrictive immigration laws passed in the 1920s were the culmination of four decades of efforts to legally control immigration and represented a last gasp effort to reestablish the dominance of the "better" race that had founded the Republic. But it was too late. The country had little choice but to try to figure out how it could become a pan-European nation.

Immigrants came to America voluntarily. The same cannot be said for groups added to the population through purchase or conquest. Even though the slave trade was terminated in the early 19th century, the slave population continued to grow through reproduction. The Civil War may have emancipated the

Census by Race Categories: A Sampling

YEAR	RACE CATEGORY		
1790	Free white males of 16 years and upward, including heads of families under 16 years		
	Free white females, including heads of families		
	All other free persons		
	Slaves		
1830 and 1840[a]	Free white persons: males divided into 13 age cohorts Free white persons: females, divided into 13 age cohorts		
	Slaves: males, divided into 6 age cohorts Slaves: females, divided into 6 age cohorts		
	Free colored persons: males, divided into 6 age cohorts Free colored persons: females, divided into 6 age cohorts		
1890	white	black	mulatto, quadroon, octoroon, Chinese, Japanese, Indian
1990	White	Black or Negro	Indian (Amer), Eskimo, Aleut, Chinese, Filipino, Hawaiian, Korean, Vietnamese, Japanese, Asian Indian, Samoan, Guamanian, Other API, Other race

Reprinted with permission from: *Who Counts?* by Margo J. Anderson and Stephen E. Feinberg ©1999 Russell Sage Foundation.
Source: Wright and Hunt 1900, passim; U.S. Bureau of the Census ©1979, 1993a
[a]The federal government used a two-sided schedule: in 1830, the age/sex breakdowns for Whites were on the front of the schedule and those for slaves and the free colored on the back; in 1840, the age/sex breakdowns for Whites and free colored were on the front of the schedule and those for slaves were on the back.
Note: The categories are given in the order they appeared on the schedule. If abbreviations were used, the abbreviation is listed. Otherwise, the full term is written out.

slaves but it did not extend full civic membership. Social segregation, economic discrimination, second-class citizenship, all sanctioned in law, continued a carefully tiered system of civic membership based on race.

Other wars of the 19th century played their part in demographic change. The Indian Wars that opened the West to European settlers further reduced and relocated the native Indian populations. Other military action added new lands in the Southwest and a new population group: by the end of the Mexican-American War in 1848, the U.S. had acquired its first large Mexican population—about 80,000 people. The Spanish-American War in 1889 added the Puerto Rican islands and their people. When Hawaii was annexed in 1898, its native Pacific Islander population also became "Americans."

Along with territorial wars, land purchase altered our demography. Thomas Jefferson's vast Louisiana Purchase in 1803 added a French settler population; William Henry Seward's purchase of the Russian colony of Alaska in 1867 added the Inuit, the Kodiak and other Alaskan natives.

While population increases resulting from conquest and purchase were not large, relatively speaking, they did add to the country's demographic diversity. In a pattern now familiar, this diversity provided new opportunities for discrimination in the labor market, in housing and in the educational system, which was as true for Hispanics as it was for the ex-slave population.

Native Alaskans and Pacific Islanders were given no more rights than were Native American Indians, who were denied citizenship until 1924.

Out of all the new racial and ethnic groups added to the U.S. population in the 19th century, only those of European origin were granted civic membership. Non-European peoples, though living and working in the U.S., were "stateless": they were without the right to have rights. It was not until well into the 20th century that the nation finally took up the issue of full civic membership for all social groups

The Civil Rights Movement: In the 20th Century, New Changes, New Definitions

We do not normally think of the civil rights movement (which is often seen as beginning in 1955, when Rosa Parks refused to give up her seat on a Montgomery, Alabama bus) as central to the nation's demographic narrative, but we should. In many ways, it is the 20th century result of forces rooted in 19th century immigration, both voluntary and forced. Under the banner of civil rights, African Americans mounted an offensive designed to bring about an alignment of demography with democracy. Courts and legislatures were enlisted in what became a campaign to end the injustice of exclusion. Thus, the civil

rights movement can be understood as arising from a desire for unity, rather than a celebration of diversity. Many believed that discrimination would be swept away when the principles of democracy were recognized by all and applied equally to all citizens.

Over the years, racial **categories** *have been added or dropped depending on prevailing political beliefs.*

But as it turned out, discrimination did not give way easily and, as a society, we were soon enmeshed in unfamiliar political and legal territory. Equal opportunity came to mean proportionate representation; the definition of individual rights expanded to include group rights; and the principles of nondiscrimination were translated into affirmative action. Discrimination, which many had thought of as simply the attitudes and actions of real estate agents or employers or college admissions officers or election clerks, proved also to be embedded in residential segregation patterns, wage rates, university enrollments and the shape of election districts. In other words, it was something that could be *measured*. The vocabulary of prejudice began to include definitions of institutional racism. In the 20th century, statistical proportionality—comparing the percentage of the population that is minority with the percentage of that minority working, for example, in the police force, or participating in higher education or living in desirable housing—became the weapon of choice in advancing the goals of the civil rights movement. This gave the census an even more central role to play in the nation's civic and political life because statistical proportionality cannot be assessed without a count of how many members of various racial and ethnic groups are living in the U.S. Thus the story of the census in the 20th century also becomes one of racial taxonomy.

Sorting by Race in the U.S. Census

In 1790, the census divided the resident population of the U.S. into three racial groups: free whites, slaves and all other free persons (native American Indians). No census since has been without a question on race, a distinction shared with only two other population characteristics: age and gender. How we have measured these two traits has been stable across two centuries—after all, we know what those traits mean. Not so with race; it has been measured dozens of different ways. Racial categories have been added or dropped depending on prevailing political beliefs. Over the years, this situation has led to a steady expansion in the number of racial categories listed on the census form, a pattern, as we shall shortly see, that repeats itself with a vengeance in the 2000 census.

In the 1820 census, for instance, we first added "free colored persons" to the racial classification scheme. After the Civil War, there was interest in "shades of color," and the census classified people as mulatto (the offspring of a black person and a white person), quadroon (one-quarter black ancestry) and octoroon (one-eighth black ancestry). In 1890, Asians were counted in the census, which listed separate categories for Chinese and Japanese. Filipinos, Koreans and Hindus (confusing a religion with a race) were counted in 1920. Hawaiian and Part Hawaiian appeared on the 1960 census form, as did Aleut and Eskimo, in each instance recognizing that the newest states in the Union had introduced further diversity. Mexican as a category appeared in 1930, then was dropped to be replaced by a question on Hispanic origin.

Why has the way we count and sort by race always been such a volatile issue? Because throughout American history, starting with the 1790 census, a classification of racial groups has been used to regulate relations among the races and to support discriminatory policies designed to protect the numerical and political supremacy of white Americans of European ancestry. Throughout the 19th and the first half of the 20th century, the racial classification system separated those entitled to full participation in national life from those whose race or national origin was cause for exclusion. Slavery itself, including the attempt to balance admission to the Union of slave and free states in the first half of the 19th century, is one such instance. So also—to give just a few other examples—were the forced relocation of native Americans to reservations; "Jim Crow" laws that discriminated against black Americans; racially motivated immigration quotas; and the interning of Japanese Americans in detention camps after the attack on Pearl Harbor.

Even today, as modern biology provides mounting evidence that race is not a scientifically meaningful way to sort and classify, we find it hard to let go of racial divisions. The civil rights legislation of the 1960s gave fresh momentum to racial measurement. In the latter part of the 20th century, using the same tool previously wielded to deny rights, groups historically discriminated against began to use racial measurement to achieve full civic membership. The nation was called upon to explain why there were—proportionately speaking—few members of minority groups heading major corporations, or at the helm of universities or being elected to political office; or why there were more people of color in prisons and receiving harsher sentences than their white counterparts committing similar offenses. The basic logic of racial taxonomy was easily extended—as it was for women's rights and the rights of the handicapped—to encompass the idea that disproportionate representation implied a glass ceiling or other racially based barriers to full access that had to be eliminated.

As far as the **government** *is concerned, race is a matter of "You are who you want to be."*

The racial taxonomy that gave rise to statistical proportionality as a tool of governance was based on a small number of discrete categories—white, black and Indian. Asians were then added and, in 1970, "Hispanic" was included as an ethnic category. By 1990, every resident of America, according to the census, could be sorted into one of five main racial groups: White, Black or Negro, Native Indian/Native Alaskan, Asian, or Other. There were Asian sub-groups, but these were combined as one Asian category. Importantly, being of Spanish/Hispanic origin was treated in 1990, and again in 2000, as an ethnic and not a racial distinction; a person of Hispanic origin could be of any race.

Census 2000 introduced a dramatic change in our racial classification system. It allowed Americans to define themselves as being of multiple race. From now on, as far as the government is concerned, you don't have to try to shoehorn yourself into one discrete racial group: you can belong to two, even three, four or five.

How did this happen? What does this mean for *how we live together?*

It happened because Americans who viewed themselves as being of more than one racial group, or who had married someone of a different race and had children, felt it was discriminatory to be forced to select only one identity. Black mothers married to white fathers, as well as many other interracial couples, sent photographs of their mixed race children to the Office of Federal Statistical Policy and Standards (where the decision would be made), pleading for the chance to count them for what they were—multiracial. The cause was right, the pressure was intense; eventually, the government agreed that Census 2000 would give Americans the right to check more than one racial category.

Where We Are Now

Although the race question on the 2000 census form seems to allow for as many as 15 separate groups, because of the number of Asian sub-groups listed, in fact the basic classification system recognizes only six categories: White, Black, Asian, Native Indian/Native Alaskan, Native Hawaiian/Pacific Islander, and Other Race. In terms of basic categories, one difference between 1990 and 2000 is that Native Hawaiian/Pacific Islander is treated as a separate racial group rather than as part of a more inclusive Asian group.

It is a second difference that leads to multiple-race responses. In permitting respondents to mark "one or more," the census sets up the possibility of 63 discrete racial groups. This is the number of permutations that occur when six categories can be combined in any way one chooses. Hispanic/non-Hispanic, an ethnic distinction for the purpose of the census, divides the entire population into two additional categories, allowing for 126 possible racial/ethnic groupings.

The instruction to "mark one or more races" is staggering in its implications. Though not that many persons identified as multiple-race—fewer than 7 million, or 2.4 percent of the population, did so and the rate was twice as high for children as it was for adults—demographers expect the numbers to continue to grow as interracial marriages occur and as people become more comfortable with the multiple-race option.

What is extraordinary is that the nation moved suddenly, and with only minimal public understanding of the consequences, from a limited and relatively closed racial taxonomy to one that has no limits. In the future, racial categories will no doubt become more numerous. And why not? What grounds does the government have to declare "enough is enough?" When there were only three or even four or five categories, maybe "enough is enough" was plausible. But how can we decide, as a nation, that what we allow for on the census form of today—63 racial groups or 126 racial/ ethnic ones—is the "right" number? It can't be, nor can any other number be "right." There is no political or scientifically defensible limit.

Moreover, given that there is no scientific basis to support racial divisions, the federal government correctly insists that one's race is what one decides it is. As far as the census is concerned—and by extension, this also goes for the entire official statistical system—race is a matter of "you are who you want to be." This invites the politics of identity based on race and ethnicity, or it does as long as benefits are distributed in terms of such identities. Surely, additional groups will soon demand separate recognition and accommodation. Leaders in the Arab-American community, for example, have expressed strong interest in becoming a "racial group" in the census.

The future of racial measurement is uncertain. The taxonomy based on Census 2000 has both too many and too few categories. There are too many to support race-based policies that use statistical proportionality but too few to accommodate the pressures of identity politics. Taxonomies with both too many and too few categories are inherently unstable. The full significance of this must be assessed in the context of the demographic transformation now underway in our country. To develop a picture of these trends, we must return, briefly, to our immigration narrative.

Late 20th Century Immigration

After the passage of restrictive immigration laws in the 1920s, immigration dropped off sharply; and those who were allowed into the U.S. were primarily from northern and western European countries. These patterns began to shift in the 1960s when, influenced by the civil rights movement, new and more liberal immigration laws were enacted, including those based on the moral claim of family reunification and the humanitarian cause of admitting political refugees. Immigrants from Southeast Asia and, later, from Central America, who owed their refugee status to American military action, began arriving in large numbers. Additional changes in immigration law, responding, in part, to the need for farm labor and service workers, offered legal status to significant numbers of undocumented aliens. Under pressure from universities and technology companies, Congress also increased selected categories of employment-based immigration to encourage hi-tech workers to come to this country.

Taken together, these new criteria have massively shifted the routes of world immigration flowing into the U.S. In 1850, more than nine-out-of-ten foreign-born residents were from Europe, and this pattern held well into the 20th century. As late as 1960, Europeans still comprised three-out-of-every-four foreign-born Americans. But by 1997, more than half of the foreign-born cohort of the U.S. population was from Latin America and more than a quarter from Asia. Foreign-born Europeans have dropped to fewer than one-in-five and will soon be a tiny fraction of the foreign born.

It is these census numbers that give rise to the recent flood of media stories announcing that by mid-century, America will be a minority-majority nation. As convoluted—and misleading—as that phrase is, it still points to the fact that the U.S. is now more demographically diverse than ever in its history.

This, I suggest, is why the nation must yet again confront the questions, *How can we live together? How can we live together justly?*

An Uncertain Future

Census 2000 marks a demographic turning point. A radical change in how we count and sort by race is interacting with immigration patterns that are producing escalating diversity. Either of these two factors taken by itself has large and uncertain consequences. For example:

• We rely upon local, state and federal government to lead the way in eliminating discrimination in areas such as education, employment, housing and health care; to protect voting rights; to stop racial profiling; and to safeguard our civil liberties in dozens of other ways. Equity in these areas, however, has often depended upon the use of statistical proportionality, a tool that is being weakened as racial groups are divided into more and more subcategories. What methodology will we use in its place?

• Until recently, the economy has been strong and unemployment low. Has this created a national optimism about the future that has outweighed the forces of nativistic politics, or has the concept of multiculturalism become so thoroughly entwined with our image of the U.S. that anti-immigration policies are now largely discredited? We may not know the answer to these questions until there is a significant economic downturn and increased competition for low-end employment opportunities.

• The nation's often celebrated religious tolerance was originally based on differences within Protestantism, and only grudgingly extended to include Catholics and Jews. There are now swiftly growing numbers of Muslims, Hindus, Buddhists and others. Will religious tolerance be easily extended, or will we repeat one of the darker chapters in our history?

• Historically, immigrants arrive from world regions that are poor or in turmoil. But with the advent of globalization and internationally interdependent economies, there are new reasons to emigrate and new needs on the part of the U.S. to welcome skilled immigrants. Might educated technology workers from more developed countries come to dominate immigration flows to the disadvantage of poorer workers from poorer countries? If so, there are implications not only for our economy but for the countries of origin which may educate and then lose their most skilled people.

• Americans of European ancestry are not reproducing at replacement levels; neither are the native populations of western European nations. If this trend continues, the competition among wealthier nations for foreign labor may be fierce; in the struggle to find workers to support growing economies, nations that are hospitable to immigrants will have an advantage. Under these conditions, might *how we can live together* turn out to be as much about gaining an economic edge as about social justice?

There are any number of such issues, but as complicated as they are they do not begin to tell the whole story. What makes the future much more challenging is our uncertainty about the interaction between the two transformations discussed in this essay—the radical change in racial measurement and classification and the displacement of a European immigrant stream with one that is Asian and Latin. There is no historical reference point for this dynamic. For example:

• The pressure on previous immigrant groups was to assimilate, to become "American," when that meant to accept that getting ahead depended on individual effort and merit—not group rights. Identity politics have now been put into the mix, primarily as a way to compensate for the fact that some groups, be-

cause of race or ethnicity, were denied the normal routes of upward mobility. Will new immigrants find that asserting group rights is an avenue to success, or will they assimilate in a manner that blurs rather than sharpens boundaries between different groups?

• More generally, as today's new immigrants gain citizenship and become politically active, will they want more or less to focus on their separate identities? If the former, they will expect to find their own place in the racial and ethnic classification that has marked our politics for two centuries. And that classification will get more fine-grained and less usable. But if they seek to escape being measured as separate groups, they risk antagonizing other groups that still rely on statistical proportionality as a tool to redress earlier wrongs. For example, will new African immigrants from Somalia or Ghana want to be separately measured, not measured at all, or be included as African Americans?

For such questions there is no crystal ball. We cannot know if the changes that are now inevitable will be marked by tolerance and social order or by turmoil and violence. History offers ample evidence for both possibilities, suggesting that we are likely to have some of each. *How can we live together justly?* is the question we again must ask.

A century hence, historians will record of the early 21st century whether churches showed moral leadership or retreated to dogma; whether universities provided intellectual clarity or argued about disciplinary turf; whether civic organizations went boldly into new territory or hewed to the safe and familiar; whether businesses recognized the claims of social justice or saw only the next quarter's earnings; whether foundations were visionary or irrelevant; whether the political class was courageous or succumbed to intimidation; and, mostly, whether the public demanded of itself and its leaders an honest go at figuring out how we can, in fact, live together—*justly*.

Kenneth Prewitt is currently dean of the Graduate Faculty of Political and Social Science at the New School University. He was previously director of the U.S. Census Bureau. He has also served as president of the Social Science Research Council, and was, for ten years, senior vice president of the Rockefeller Foundation, where he directed the international Science-Based Development Program involving activities in Asia, Africa and Latin America. He has taught at the University of Chicago, Stanford University, Columbia University, Washington University, the University of Nairobi, and Makerere University (Uganda).

An Overview of
AMERICA'S EDUCATION AGENDA

Creating good schools for our children is more than a matter of doing what is morally right, Mr. Paige asserts. It is a matter of maintaining our national security, building on our prosperity, preserving our democracy, and strengthening our great country.

Rod Paige

WHEN PRESIDENT Bush asked me to accompany him to Washington to help promote his principles of education reform, I accepted eagerly. I had worked with him in Texas for six years when I was superintendent of the Houston schools and he was governor. I knew he was dedicated to the needs of students and particularly concerned with improving the performance of and opportunities for disadvantaged children.

During those six years, I instituted then Gov. Bush's principles of education reform in my large urban school district, and I watched student achievement skyrocket. The results I observed were not unique to Houston. Across Texas, white students improved, black students improved, and Hispanic students improved. At the same time, the achievement gap between minority and disadvantaged students and their peers narrowed. The Education Trust heralded our success in closing the achievement gap with this comparison: "If African American eighth-graders everywhere wrote as well as their peers in Texas, the national achievement gap between White and African American eighth-graders would be cut in half." The Education Trust report concluded that the large achievement gaps of 1994 had shrunk substantially, from 36 percentage points to 21 percentage points for black students.

I knew then that Gov. Bush was a strong and talented leader, with an impressive knack for bipartisanship and the determination to accomplish great things for our students. He had the vision to see that the education system in Texas had lost its way, and he knew how to set it back on the right course: by committing it to achieving results for every child. He knew that if we harnessed the power of parents and communities, our schools could live up to our ideals. Under his leadership, practitioners, policy makers, parents, and leaders of business, government, and communities of every ideology in Texas united behind his plan for education reform and effected extraordinary change in our schools. I have been honored to help him bring his vision for education to every state in the nation.

Our task began on President Bush's second day in office, when he unveiled his No Child Left Behind plan. This plan sought to change the culture of education by using the same principles of reform that had already shown results in Texas: accountability for results, local control and flexibility, expanded parental options, and doing what works according to scientific research. We faced a formidable challenge. According to the National Assessment of Educational Progress, most of the progress in student performance in reading and math was made during the 1970s. Little has improved in terms of student performance since 1980. And while science scores declined in the 1970s and improved during the 1980s, they too were flat throughout the 1990s.

While these problems were evident, many school boards were enmeshed in arguments over such topics as budgets and work rules. The system was focused on itself, not on students.

The President designed his No Child Left Behind plan to guide Congress in reauthorizing the Elementary and Secondary Education Act (ESEA), the legislation that defines the federal role in education. It is the most sweeping reform of the federal role in education since ESEA was passed in 1965.

PRACTITIONER TO POLICY

One reason that President Bush chose me to be secretary of education was that he wanted someone with practical experience in improving achievement among those student populations often dismissed as "hard to teach." When I arrived in Washington last year, I was confident in my expertise and determined to put my experience as a practitioner to work in the policy debates. As a superintendent, I learned firsthand what works to improve student performance. I knew that a good accountability system was vital and that test scores could and should be used to track the progress of individual students, so that teachers could tailor their teaching to meet the specific needs of their children. As we worked to reauthorize ESEA this year, I was often the lone practitioner in a room filled with policy makers and legislators, and my practical experience and perspective as the former superintendent of a large urban school district proved invaluable.

BIPARTISANSHIP

Despite my expertise in education, I had a lot to learn about how Washington worked. My first year in office has led me to reconsider many of my long-held beliefs about politics and the federal government. One notion that was challenged almost immediately after I arrived here was my perception of Washington Democrats. At my very first meeting with Sen. Edward Kennedy (D-Mass.), we hit it off famously—much better than I, as a Republican, had expected. He was instrumental in my confirmation, and, throughout the reauthorization process of ESEA, we worked well together, as did the President and other Democrats, such as Rep. George Miller (D-Calif.).

I also learned some things about my fellow Republicans. Just a few years ago, after all, many of them had supported the abolition of the U.S. Department of Education. But by working with them, I came to understand that their goal was to restore local control of schools to the parents of America. The new No Child Left Behind law will do just that.

Before I got to Washington, I thought that Democrats adhered to entirely different ideals about education than Republicans did. To my surprise, I discovered that Democrats and Republicans have the same goal at heart when it comes to education: giving all children access to excellent schools. They may disagree on what is the best way to reach this goal, but they are always thinking about what is best for students.

Throughout the past year, Sen. Kennedy and Rep. Miller worked well with their Republican counterparts, Sen. Judd Gregg (R-N.H.) and Rep. John Boehner (R-Ohio), to turn the principles of No Child Left Behind into law. The dialogue spurred progress. The year before, members of Congress had struggled over positioning in education reform as well as in many other issues. Mired in partisan politics, they failed to reauthorize ESEA. This time, even after the attacks of September 11, Congress did not abandon its resolve to produce a good education bill that would improve schools for all students. While many sharp differences needed resolution, the members and their staffs worked with White House and Education Department staffs with great determination through the summer and fall and through anthrax and evacuations. In December, they sent the President the No Child Left Behind Act, which he signed on 8 January 2002, ushering in a new era in American education.

NO CHILD LEFT BEHIND

The No Child Left Behind law heralds a major change in direction for American schools. A river that had wandered sluggishly east suddenly shifted and began to flow west. Everyone involved in education—teachers and administrators, students and parents, business and community leaders—will notice the change, and the more they understand it, the more it will help them. The new westward current will flow swiftly, and it will carry everyone along. Boats that had run aground or been snagged in the shallows will be shaken loose and brought back to midstream. Most important, the river and everyone on it will flow toward success.

No Child Left Behind helps us look at schools, governance, and the federal role in education in the right way. It reminds us that the goal of schools is not diplomas, but educated citizens. It assures us that the responsibility for student performance lies not just with educators, but also with communities. Most important, it changes the federal role in education from funding to investing. When federal spending becomes an investment, it gives the federal government leverage to demand results.

With the No Child Left Behind law, education reform has grown up. No longer is reform about access or money. No longer is it about compliance or excuses. Instead, it is about improving student achievement by improving the quality of the education we offer our students. It is once again focused on the student, not the system.

Rep. Miller summed it up well when he said, "This bill will help return our school system to the original goals of the 1965 Elementary and Secondary Education Act—to ensure that all children have an opportunity to learn regardless of income, background, or racial or ethnic identity. But unlike the laws on the books over the past 35 years, we will back up our commitment with a set of unambiguous expectations, time lines, and resources."

ACHIEVEMENT GAP

There is no doubt that our system is in urgent need of repair. Half a century ago, had we known that America would make astonishing improvements in technology, put an end to government-enforced segregation, and spend more than $8 trillion on schools, we would have expected to finish the century with all our citizens—from business leaders to busboys—able to read, calculate, and understand American history. Instead, though our nation is blessed with many excellent schools and many excellent educators, our system is still failing too many children. According to the most recent National Assessment of Educational Progress (NAEP), only 32% of fourth-graders can read proficiently, and the proportion in urban areas is even lower. Twenty-six percent of urban fourth-graders are proficient readers, compared with 36% of suburban and 32% of rural fourth-graders. (If Americans in 1952 had known they would spend $8 trillion over 50 years, at the end of which time only about a third of children could read, they might have questioned that use of funds.)

There is also a persistent achievement gap between ethnic groups. While 40% of white fourth-graders read at or above the proficient level, only 12% of blacks and 16% of Hispanics perform as well. The situation is not better in high school. Our high school seniors scored lower on the 2000 NAEP math assessment than their predecessors in 1996. And, although more children are attending college, nearly a third of our college freshmen must take remedial courses. Minority students are taking more courses that will prepare them for college-level work. The performance of most minority groups is still measurably lower than that of whites, and an achievement gap between minority and disadvantaged students and their peers endures despite billions spent trying to close it.

ACCOUNTABILITY

In order to eliminate the achievement gap and improve student performance across the board, we must hold educators accountable to the bold proposition that every child can learn. This is a belief that President Bush takes very seriously, and he means *no child* left behind quite literally. He does not mean that, after you siphon off the children who have disabilities, or were never properly taught how to read, or never learned English, or disrupted their classrooms, then the rest can learn. He means that all of our students, even the ones our system calls "hard to teach," can learn.

There is no middle ground or room for excuses. Either educators believe that every child can learn, or they do not. When educators begin to make excuses for children based on race or socioeconomics, both those who make excuses and our children fall prey to what the President calls "the soft bigotry of low expectations."

The No Child Left Behind law places accountability squarely in the center of our education system. The law requires each state to enact a strong accountability structure based on clear and high standards and a system of annual assessments to measure student progress against those standards.

Testing is not designed to punish students or teachers; it is an integral part of determining whether or not students are learning what the state has decided they should know. When we have clear standards and tests that are aligned to them, testing allows us to make sure every child is making progress. Annual testing allows us to identify and correct problems quickly, so that schools can be held accountable for the progress of their students. For this reason, the No Child Left Behind law calls for states to test their students annually in grades 3 through 8 in the basic subjects of reading and math. Science assessments will be less frequent, but no less important in tracking student progress. Students should make substantial progress every year, in every class, and annual assessments will ensure that they do. Every time they do not, we are not just wasting time, money, and opportunities; we are making students more discouraged, despondent, and disenfranchised.

Every child's education should be a voyage of discovery, and the No Child Left Behind law is all about discovering and disseminating the information about student performance that assessments will provide. Test scores will be disaggregated by poverty, race, ethnicity, disability, and English proficiency so that we can see where the achievement gap exists and attack it so that no group is neglected. School districts and schools that fail to make adequate progress toward statewide goals will be identified for improvement and, over time, will be subject to corrective action and restructuring measures aimed at getting them back on course to meet state standards. Schools that meet or exceed adequate yearly progress objectives or close achievement gaps will be eligible for State Academic Achievement Awards.

Teachers will be able to use individual student data to tailor their teaching to the specific needs of each student. Principals will be able to use the data to make informed decisions about what their schools need in order to improve student performance. Parents will no longer wonder whether or not their children's schools are teaching them.

In the mystery of who is failing children, teachers blame parents, and parents blame teachers. Assessments will give us the evidence, class by class, child by child, and the data will allow parents to make informed, confident decisions about their children's education.

Under the plan, if a school is identified for improvement or corrective action, the district must give parents the option of enrolling their children in another public school, including a charter school. The district must pay for transportation, and it must also provide funds for low-income students in persistently failing schools to seek supplemental educational services, such as tutoring. There is no more powerful force for change than parents armed with information and options. The No Child Left Behind law provides both.

Test scores give us the information we need to find out what works, to find out who needs help, and to give more information and control to the people closest to the action: parents, teachers, administrators, and communities. Too often, the reason that schools have trouble is that the people who are the most invested in them are not the people in control. It is time to recognize that the people who know and care the most about neighborhood schools are the people of the neighborhood: the teachers, parents, administrators, and business and community leaders.

This year, the federal government will spend $387 million to assist states with the cost of developing a system of assessments, and the U.S. Department of Education will work with them to put solid, viable accountability systems in place. We will be a vigilant partner for states as they set high standards and institute annual assessments.

TEACHERS

Just as we empower parents with information and choices, we must equip teachers with the best teaching methods available. Schools should use instructional methods based on reality, not ideology. By now, for example, we have a big store of information on successful reading instruction. Research has confirmed that reading is the gateway to all learning and that learning to read is much easier before the third grade. We also know from research that even very young children can begin to develop pre-reading skills, and we have learned how valuable phonemic awareness is to developing language skills. President Bush's reforms are based on this research, and his Reading First Program promotes teaching methods that are scientifically proven to work. This year, Reading First commits $900 million to ensuring that every child learns to read by the third grade. After tripling federal funding for reading, the President has requested an additional increase of $100 million, which would bring next year's total to $1 billion.

More generally, the No Child Left Behind law supports and prepares teachers by providing almost $3 billion to improve teacher quality. This money will ensure that every classroom has a highly qualified teacher, and it gives states and school districts the flexibility to spend the money as they see fit. Local education leaders know better than Washington whether they need to focus on professional development, reducing class size, or other activities related to teacher quality. The law also includes funds for, among other things, math and science partnerships that can be used for professional development for math and science teachers, for the promotion of strong teaching skills based on scientific research and technology-based teaching methods, for the development of mentoring programs for teachers, and for recruiting qualified college students into teaching.

While we should elevate and support the teachers we have, we must encourage additional qualified students and professionals to pursue a career in teaching. The Troops to Teachers Program in the law assists members of the armed forces in becoming qualified to teach and helps them find jobs in high-need schools. Transition to Teaching will help to encourage highly qualified midcareer professionals and recent college graduates to become teachers by recruiting them and encouraging alternative certification routes.

We all know that teachers should be respected and celebrated more, but the only way to improve conditions for our teachers is to turn our children into educated adults every time. Success by some teachers, with some children, has not made teaching the honored career it ought to be. We must be courageous enough to say that some of our teachers are poorly trained and that, as a result, too many children slip through the cracks. If we can show the American people that we have accounted for every child—that every child is learning and growing and maturing—then more Americans will respect, honor, and dream of becoming teachers.

CHARACTER EDUCATION

We depend on teachers and schools to give our children knowledge. We should also expect them to teach our children character, because our children must have character to benefit from the knowledge they receive in school. While reading, math, and science can give our children strength of mind, character education is necessary to give them strength of heart. It is time for schools to return to teaching children that character, honesty, and integrity are important. Good character is not something you are born with; it is something you must learn from those who have it.

We need to make sure our children are on the path to respect, responsibility, honesty, and civic virtue. We must set our children on the path not only to academic achievement and professional success, but also to moral strength.

For President Bush, character education is a special priority. In turn, the No Child Left Behind law reflects the importance of character education programs. The law triples funding for character education grants to states and districts to $25 million. The grants can be used for such activities as developing character education curricula; implementing model character education programs that involve parents and community members, including private and nonprofit organizations; and training teachers to incorporate character-building lessons and activities into their classrooms. Students will be taught about the principles and values of good character through their regular curriculum.

The No Child Left Behind law gives schools and districts not only the money for these programs but also the freedom from government red tape to use that money to get the job done. The law allows schools and districts to form partnerships with private, nonprofit organizations in order to add a spirit of innovation and a special expertise to their character education programs. Those who receive funds under this program will be required to demonstrate results. In keeping with a guiding principle of the No Child Left Behind law, what matters in character education is product, not process.

IMPLEMENTATION

The No Child Left Behind law dramatically reshapes the federal role in education. It authorizes the federal government to demand results from our schools. Though responsibility for implementing the bill lies with the Department of Education, real change will occur at the state and local levels. To give states and school districts the flexibility to change, the federal department will relieve them of some burdensome federal requirements right away. We are also working to issue guidelines, establish grant requirements, and offer technical assistance to states and school districts in preparing for the requirements of the law.

The Department of Education wants to hear the needs, concerns, and suggestions of states as they implement the law. The No Child Left Behind law has addressed the shortcomings and loopholes of previous laws that allowed states to miss deadlines, and we will enforce the requirements of the law strictly. I will not let deadlines slip or see requirements forgotten. When students beg their teachers to extend deadlines, the choice between discipline and compassion can be very difficult. But if states ask me to extend deadlines, they will be asking me to make a choice between the needs of children and the flaws of the system. This will be an easy choice for me. I will choose the children.

One thing we learned from Congress last year is how productive we can be when we work together. The department has been working hard to build partnerships with states and school districts. We will be a vigilant partner and a steadfast source of support for states and districts as they implement the reforms of No Child Left Behind. However, for the spirit of progress to take root across states, school districts, and classrooms, we must follow Congress' lead and work together across ideological lines. Superintendents and teacher unions can blame one another until summer vacation and lose sight of the reason they are both there, which is to ensure that students learn.

Our children do not need adults who measure success in dollars or compliance. Our children don't need adults who make excuses for their failures. Our children need adults who focus on results. Our children deserve to learn promptly and well, and anything that distracts from their learning is a distraction from the schools' mission. I am quite serious about the partnership between the department and states and school districts, and I am very sincere in stating that we are, in fact, in this together. Our success is dependent upon one another.

The goal of leaving no child behind is a daunting challenge and an exhilarating prospect, and every American has a part to play. The students of today are the leaders, citizens, scholars, technicians, and parents of tomorrow, and they are relying on us to give them schools that prepare them for these roles. One day, we will depend on them to assume these roles with wisdom and confidence. Creating good schools for our children is more than a matter of doing what is morally right. It is a matter of maintaining our national security, building on our prosperity, preserving our democracy, and strengthening our great country.

ROD PAIGE was appointed secretary of education by President George W. Bush in 2001. He came to the post after serving as dean of the College of Education at Texas Southern University and as superintendent of the Houston Independent School District.

From *Phi Delta Kappan,* May 2002, pp. 708-713. © 2002 by Phi Delta Kappa International. Reprinted by permission of the author.

THE 34TH ANNUAL PHI DELTA KAPPA/GALLUP POLL OF THE PUBLIC'S ATTITUDES TOWARD THE PUBLIC SCHOOLS

BY LOWELL C. ROSE AND ALEC M. GALLUP

The 34th Annual Phi Delta Kappa/Gallup Poll of the Public's Attitudes Toward the Public Schools comes with K–12 education at the state and federal levels in flux. School improvement efforts that have been blossoming since the 1990s are threatened by financial realities. Public school educators find themselves pulled between the improvement demanded in the federal No Child Left Behind Act (NCLBA) and financial conditions at the state level that make simply maintaining the status quo a challenge. And, in continuing to lower the wall between church and state, the U.S. Supreme Court has given approval to vouchers that allow parents to direct public funds to private schools, including religious schools. This poll explores these and other issues in depth.

There is good news in the poll for public school advocates. Local schools continue to be regarded favorably, with 71% of public school parents giving the school their oldest child attends a grade of A or B. And, in what may be the best news for the public schools, when asked how states should adjust to the reduced revenues brought on by the weak economy, Americans reject cuts in education spending. Seventy-eight percent would avoid such cuts by reducing spending in other areas, while 58% would go so far as to raise taxes to avoid cutting education spending.

There is also good news in this poll for advocates of directing public funds to private schools. Although 52% of Americans still oppose allowing parents and students to "choose a private school to attend at public expense," support for this idea rises to 46% in this year's poll, after dropping to 34% last year. And, in the companion question, support for allowing parents to choose "any public,

private, or church-related school" with the government paying all or part of the tuition for parents who choose a "nonpublic school" rises eight points in this year's poll to 52%. This poll was conducted prior to the Supreme Court's decision, and we can expect these gains to have an impact on the public debate regarding vouchers that will doubtless arise as a result of that decision.

A major focus in this year's poll is the No Child Left Behind Act, signed into law on 8 January 2002. A bipartisan effort, the NCLBA represents the greatest federal incursion into K–12 education to date. The NCLBA initiatives will make the federal government a major player at the state and local levels—despite the fact that federal funding for K–12 education remains less than 8% of total expenditures. This year, the poll set out to determine how the public is reacting to the prospect of an increased federal role. The data suggest that the public welcomes the possibility.

Fifty-seven percent believe the federal government's increased involvement is a good thing; 68% of Americans would go beyond the requirements of the NCLBA and require all 50 states to use the same nationally standardized test to measure student achievement. Although not suggested by the NCLBA, 66% would go so far as to have a national curriculum. In response to specific provisions of the NCLBA, support among Americans is evident in a number of areas:

- 67% support mandated testing in grades 3 through 8;
- 96% support requiring teachers to be licensed in the subjects they teach;

• 96% believe that teachers should pass a competency test before being licensed; and

• for schools that fail to meet state standards, 86% support offering "in-district" choice for all students, 90% support offering tutoring by state-approved private providers; and 56% support termination of the principal and the teachers.

The one consequence the public rejects for a school that fails to meet state standards is closing the school. Seventy-seven percent are opposed to this action. And, perhaps in support of this opinion, 77% believe that additional money should be provided to such schools.

The public and educators do not see eye to eye on many of the details of the NCLBA. Many educators are concerned about the provision of the NCLBA that indicates that a school will be judged to be failing unless every student demonstrates proficiency on a "high-standards" test by the end of the 2013–14 school year. The public does not share this concern. Eighty percent believe the goal is likely to be met by their local schools. Educators are also concerned that the emphasis on reading and mathematics in both the NCLBA and state improvement efforts will mean reduced attention in other subject areas. Not the public! To the contrary, 56% believe this result would be a good thing.

Neither is the public concerned by the increase in testing involved in state improvement efforts and likely to be enhanced by the NCLBA. Forty-seven percent express the view that the amount of testing is just about right, a level of satisfaction that has not changed since 1997.

The public shows some disagreement with the NCLBA regarding the consequences for schools that fail to meet the NCLBA mandate that there be a "highly qualified teacher" in every classroom by 2005–06. A "highly qualified teacher" is, at a minimum, one with a degree and certification and demonstrated competency in the areas taught. The NCLBA, although silent on the consequences, excludes waivers in this area. Ninety-three percent of the public takes what may be a more realistic view, saying that, in the event that teacher supply makes compliance with the NCLBA impossible, schools should use the most qualified teachers available.

On a matter closely related to the NCLBA's emphasis on meeting the needs of students not currently being well served by the schools, last year's poll sought to determine the public's attitude toward the achievement gap between white students and black and Hispanic students. This year's poll revisited that issue. Results for the two years confirm that the public believes that there is a gap and that that gap must be closed. However, the public does not attribute the gap to the quality of schooling. Asked what causes the gap, the public lists, in order, factors related to home life, economic disadvantage, and poor community environment.

The 1983 report *A Nation at Risk* recommended increasing time-on-task by lengthening the school day or year as one way to improve student achievement. At the time, parents showed little support for this idea. Not much has changed. This year, 70% of respondents oppose lengthening the school day, and 59% oppose lengthening the school year. The public is, however, in favor of having formal school experience start earlier. Eighty-five percent favor making kindergarten mandatory, and 82% favor making prekindergarten available as part of the formal school program.

Regarding the problems that the public schools face, lack of financial support tops the list of public concerns (23%), with lack of discipline and overcrowded schools, which tied for second, lagging well behind at 17%. Asked about the seriousness of these problems, 76% say discipline is a very or somewhat serious problem, and 71% say likewise for overcrowding. It is worth mentioning that public school parents are less likely to point to discipline and more likely to point to financing and overcrowding as problems for the schools.

For the first time, this year's poll explored size of a school. The public believes that size is important and that smaller is better. Seventy-seven percent say the size of a school makes a difference in student achievement. And, regarding the desired size, 52% prefer elementary schools of less than 500, and 73% prefer middle schools of less than 1,000. Preferences for the size of high schools are less clear, with one method of grouping showing 50% preferring less than 1,000 and another showing 64% supporting high schools of 500 to 2,000.

These and other findings are presented in detail in the following pages. There are also examples of the interesting demographic data provided in the full cross tabulations of the poll, a complete reporting of which can be obtained from Phi Delta Kappa (see notes at the end of this report).

Attitudes Regarding the Public Schools

Grading the Public Schools

When asked to grade schools on the traditional A-to-F scale, respondents continue to assign high grades to the schools in their own community while downgrading schools nationally. Twenty-four percent give the nation's schools an A or a B. This rises to 47% for the schools in the community, to 58% when public school parents grade their local schools, and to 71% when public school parents are asked to grade the school their oldest child attends. The 47% is down four points from one year ago, while the 71% is up three points. Looking back 10 years to 1992, 41% of the total sample assigned an A or a B to community schools, while 66% of parents gave an A or a B to the school attended by their oldest child.

The first question:

Students are often given the grades A, B, C, D, and FAIL to denote the quality of their work. Suppose the public schools themselves, in this community, were graded in the same way. What grade would you give the public schools here—A, B, C, D, or FAIL?

	National Totals		No Children in School		Public School Parents	
	'02	'01	'02	'01	'02	'01
	%	%	%	%	%	%
A & B	47	51	44	47	58	62
A	10	11	9	8	16	19
B	37	40	35	39	42	43
C	34	30	35	33	30	25
D	10	8	10	8	8	8
FAIL	3	5	3	4	3	4
Don't know	6	6	8	8	1	1

• A's and B's awarded in the East are 51%; in the Midwest, 54%, in the South, 44%; and in the West, 40%

• A's and B's awarded by urbanites are 32%; by suburbanites, 51%; and by rural residents, 53%

The second question:

How about the public schools in the nation as a whole? What grade would you give the public schools nationally—A, B, C, D, or FAIL?

	National Totals		No Children in School		Public School Parents	
	'02	'01	'02	'01	'02	'01
	%	%	%	%	%	%
A & B	24	23	25	22	20	25
A	2	2	1	1	2	2
B	22	21	24	21	18	23
C	47	51	46	53	51	47
D	13	14	13	13	11	15
FAIL	3	5	3	5	3	4
Don't know	13	7	13	7	15	9

• 34% of 18- to 29-year-olds assign an A or a B; 20% of those 50 and older.
• 19% of Republicans assign an A or a B; 30% of Democrats.

The third question:

Using the A, B, C, D, FAIL scale again, what grade would you give the school your oldest child attends:

	Public School Parents	
	'02	'01
	%	%
A & B	71	68
A	27	28
B	44	40
C	20	22
D	6	6
FAIL	2	3
Don't know	1	1

Focus of School Improvement

Asked about the focus of school improvement, the public supports—by 69% to 27%—the option of "reforming existing system" over that of "finding an alternative system." In a follow-up question designed to probe the meaning of the response to the first question, 69% chose "improving and strengthening existing public schools," while 29% chose "providing vouchers." The percentages are little changed from last year.

The first question:

In order to improve public education in America, some people think the focus should be on reforming the existing public school system. Others believe the focus should be on finding an alternative to the existing public school system. Which approach do you think is preferable—reforming the existing public school system or finding an alternative to the existing public school system?

	National Totals					No Children In School					Public School Parents				
	'02	'01	'00	'99	'97	'02	'01	'00	'99	'97	'02	'01	'00	'99	'97
	%	%	%	%	%	%	%	%	%	%	%	%	%	%	%
Reforming existing system	69	72	59	71	71	69	73	59	73	70	69	73	60	68	72
Finding alternative system	27	24	34	27	23	26	23	34	24	23	27	25	34	30	24
Don't know	4	4	7	2	6	5	4	7	3	7	4	2	6	2	4

• 71% of whites would reform the existing system, as compared to 60% of nonwhites.

The second question:

Which one of these two plans would you prefer—improving and strengthening the existing public schools or providing vouchers for parents to use in selecting and paying for private and/or church-related schools?

	National Totals		No Children in School		Public School Parents	
	'02	'01	'02	'01	'02	'01
	%	%	%	%	%	%
Improving and strengthening existing public schools	69	71	69	71	72	73
Providing vouchers	29	27	28	26	27	25
Neither (volunteered)	—	—	—	—	—	2
Don't know	2	2	3	3	1	—

• 38% of Republicans select providing vouchers; 24% of Democrats.

Funding the Public Schools

In questions related to school funding, 88% of respondents expressed the view that funding should be the same for all public school students in the state. This finding, which varies little among the demographic groups, bears directly on the many state court actions designed to equalize funding. A second question explored public attitudes toward dealing with revenue shortages so severe that tax increases or spending cuts are necessary. Only 26% would reduce state spending for education. Seventy-eight percent would avoid such cuts by cutting in other areas, while 58% would do so by increasing state taxes. The public's view of the importance of funding and the priority it assigns to schools seem clear.

The first question:

Do you think the amount of money allocated to public education in this state from all sources should or should not

be the same for all students whether or not they live in wealthy or poor districts?

	National Totals			No Children in School			Public School Parents		
	'02	'93	'91	'02	'93	'91	'02	'93	'91
	%	%	%	%	%	%	%	%	%
Should be the same	88	88	80	89	87	78	86	89	84
Should not be the same	10	10	13	9	11	14	13	10	12
Don't know	2	2	7	2	2	8	1	1	4

The second question:

The current economy is forcing most states to reduce revenue shortages by either increasing revenues or reducing expenditures. As I read each of the following ways to fund education in your state, please tell me whether you would favor that action a great deal, a fair amount, not very much, or not at all.

	Great Deal and Fair Amount	Great Deal	Fair Amount	Not Very Much	Not At All	Don't Know
	%	%	%	%	%	%
Reduce state spending for education	26	10	16	18	55	1
Increase state taxes to produce enough funds to avoid education cuts	58	23	35	18	22	2
Use a combination of increased state taxes and spending cuts in education	53	17	36	21	24	2
Keep present level of education funding by making spending cuts in other areas	78	35	43	13	7	2

Approaches to School Improvement

The No Child Left Behind Act

The No Child Left Behind Act (NCLBA), signed into law on 8 January 2002, increases the federal government's decision-making role regarding K–12 schools. Using specific provisions from the NCLBA, this year's poll set out to determine how the public feels about this expansion of federal authority. Eight questions most directly related to the NCLBA are reported in this section; however, other questions in the poll touch directly and indirectly on its provisions. The first question dealt directly with the federal government's increased involvement; 57% said they believe it is a good thing.

The first question:

The new national education legislation will increase the federal government's involvement in local public school affairs to a greater extent than in the past. In your opinion, will this be a good thing or a bad thing for the public schools in your community?

	National Totals	No Children In School	Public School Parents
	%	%	%
A good thing	57	56	62
A bad thing	34	34	32
Don't know	9	10	6

- 55% of whites say a good thing; 70% of nonwhites.
- 72% of 18- to 29-year-olds say a good thing; just 46% of those 50 and older.
- 53% of Republicans say a good thing; 63% of Democrats.
- 65% in the East say a good thing; 49% in the Midwest; 61% in the South; and 53% in the West.

Two questions dealt with the NCLBA's testing program. In response to the first, 67% said they favor the use of an annual test to track student progress in grades 3 through 8. (In an independent Gallup poll conducted in 1997, 68% favored annual testing in grades 4 through 8.) In response to the second question, 68% said all 50 states should be required to use a nationally standardized test. The NCLBA currently leaves test selection to each state.

The second question:

The new national education legislation requires the tracking of student progress from grades 3 to 8 based on an annual test. Would you favor or oppose such a test in the public schools in your community?

	National Totals	No Children In School	Public School Parents
	%	%	%
Would favor	67	69	65
Would oppose	31	29	34
Don't know	2	2	1

The third question:

According to the new national education legislation, each of the 50 states can select the test it wishes to use for the grade 3 through 8 tracking. Which would you prefer—letting your state use its own test, or requiring all 50 states to use a single standardized test?

	National Totals	No Children In School	Public School Parents
	%	%	%
Letting your state use its own test	30	31	26
Requiring all 50 states to use a nationally standardized test	68	67	72
Don't know	2	2	2

The next question dealt with the NCLBA goal requiring that every student in a school demonstrate proficiency on a high-standards test by the end of the 2013–14 school year. Eighty percent said they believe achieving this goal in their local schools is either very likely or somewhat likely. The responses varied little across demographic groups.

The fourth question:

The new national legislation requires that a public school guarantee that every student in that school pass the state proficiency test by the end of the school year 2013–14.

How likely do you think it is that this goal could be achieved in the public schools in your community—very likely, somewhat likely, not very likely, or not at all likely?

	National Totals	No Children In School	Public School Parents
	%	%	%
Very and somewhat likely	80	81	77
Very likely	31	30	36
Somewhat likely	49	51	41
Not very likely	12	11	15
Not at all likely	6	5	6
Don't know	2	3	2

Three questions were directed at the NCLBA requirement that, by the 2005–06 school year, every teacher be highly qualified. Highly qualified, at the minimum, requires full certification, licensing in the area being taught, and demonstrated competency. The uncertainty of the teacher supply makes this a matter of concern. Ninety-six percent of respondents indicated that it is either very or somewhat important that teachers be licensed in the subject area in which they teach; 96% said they support requiring teachers to pass a statewide basic competency test before being licensed. In probing what a school should do if a highly qualified teacher cannot be found, 93% of respondents said the schools should use the best-qualified teachers available.

The fifth question:

How important do you think it is that public school teachers in the public schools in your community be licensed by the state in the subject areas in which they teach—very important, somewhat important, not very important, or not at all important?

	National Totals	No Children In School	Public School Parents
	%	%	%
Very and somewhat important	96	97	97
Very important	80	79	84
Somewhat important	16	18	13
Not very important	2	1	1
Not at all important	1	1	1
Don't know	1	1	1

The sixth question:

Before being licensed, do you think the teachers in the public schools in your community should or should not be required to take a statewide competency test in the subjects they will teach?

	National Totals	No Children in School	Public School Parents
	%	%	%
Yes, should	96	96	95
No, should not	4	3	5
Don't know	—	1	—

The seventh question:

The new national education legislation requires that the public schools have a "highly qualified teacher" in every classroom. If the current shortage of teachers makes this requirement impossible to achieve, would you favor or oppose each of the following alternatives in the public schools in your community?

	Favor	Oppose	Don't Know
	%	%	%
Increasing the number of students per class	21	78	1
Reducing the number of courses offered in the school	37	61	2
Using the most qualified teachers available	93	6	1

- 26% of Republicans say increase students per class; 17% of Democrats
- 26% of men say increase students per class; 16% of women.
- 25% of 18- to 29-year-olds say reduce the number of courses; 41% of those 50 and older.
- 27% of urbanites say reduce the number of courses; 38% of suburbanites; 43% of rural dwellers.

Finally, respondents were asked about what should be done if a school fails to meet state standards. Five of the six options were taken directly from the NCLBA. The public approves of all but one. Seventy-seven percent reject closing the school. The one option not mentioned in the NCLBA, obtaining additional money for the school, is supported by 77%. These two responses are similar to last year, when 66% rejected withholding federal funds from schools that did not meet state standards, and 65% favored awarding more money to the school.

The eighth question:

If a public school in your community does not show progress toward meeting state-approved standards for student learning, would you favor or oppose each of the following measures?

	Favor	Oppose	Don't Know
	%	%	%
Offering after-school tutoring by state-approved private providers	90	9	1
Offering students the opportunity to transfer to another school in the district	86	14	—
Obtaining additional money from the local district to address the school's problems	77	22	1
Not renewing the contract of the principal	56	40	4
Not renewing the contracts of the teachers	56	40	4
Closing the school	21	77	2

- 46% of the 18- to 29-year-olds would fire the principal; 56% of those 50 and older.
- 61% of urbanites would fire the principal; 56% of suburbanites; and 49% of urban dwellers.
- 58% of whites would fire the teachers; 41% of nonwhites.
- 40% of 18- to 29-year-olds would fire the teachers; 59% of those 50 and older.
- 62% of Republicans would fire the teachers; 47% of Democrats.

Choice, Public and Private

Private Schooling at Public Expense

These polls have used two questions to track the public's attitude toward funding private school attendance. The first deals simply with allowing "students and parents to choose a private school to attend at public expense." The second focuses on allowing parents "to send their school-age children to any public, private, or church-related school they choose." Responses to the two questions are frequently the subject of debate.

The question regarding allowing "students and parents to choose a private school to attend at public expense" was first asked in 1995, with 33% responding in favor. Support then rose, peaked at 44% in the late Nineties, and declined to 34% last year. The percentage in favor this year has jumped to 46%, with 52% opposed.

The picture on the second question is almost identical. When first asked in 1996, the proportion in favor was at 43%. It climbed, peaked at 51% in the late 1990s, and had dropped to 44% last year. This year, 52% are in favor of the proposal, and 46% opposed.

The first question:

Do you favor or oppose allowing students and parents to choose a private school to attend at public expense?

	National Totals							
	'02 %	'01 %	'00 %	'99 %	'98 %	'97 %	'96 %	'95 %
Favor	46	34	39	41	44	44	36	33
Oppose	52	62	56	55	50	52	61	65
Don't know	2	4	5	4	6	4	3	2

- 51% of men are in favor; 41% of women.
- 53% of 18- to 29-year-olds are in favor; 37% of those 50 and older.
- 52% of urbanites are in favor; 45% of suburbanites: 41%: of rural dwellers.

The second question:

A proposal has been made that would allow parents to send their school-age children to any public, private, or church-related school they choose. For those parents choosing nonpublic schools, the government would pay all or part of the tuition. Would you favor or oppose this proposal in your state?

	National Totals %	No Children In School %	Public School Parents %
Favor	52	51	51
Oppose	46	47	46
Don't know	2	2	3

- 49% of whites are in favor; 63% of nonwhites.
- 69% of 18- to 29-year-olds are in favor; 39% of those 50 and older.

	National Totals						Public School Parents					
	'01 %	'00 %	'99 %	'98 %	'97 %	'96 %	'01 %	'00 %	'99 %	'98 %	'97 %	'96 %
Favor	44	45	51	51	49	43	52	47	60	56	55	49
Oppose	54	52	47	45	48	54	47	51	38	40	43	49
Don't know	2	3	2	4	3	3	1	2	2	4	2	2

Charter Schools

This is the third year that the poll has explored charter schools, with three of the five questions having been asked in all three years. Awareness and opinions have changed little. In response to the first question, 56% said they have heard or read about charter schools. Given a brief definition, 44% said they are in favor of such schools, and 43% said they are opposed. And 77% said that charter schools should be accountable to the state in the same way public schools are accountable.

The first question:

Have you heard or read about so-called charter schools?:

	National Totals			No Children In School			Public School Parents		
	'02 %	'01 %	'00 %	'02 %	'01 %	'00 %	'02 %	'01 %	'00 %
Yes	56	55	49	55	57	49	58	50	44
No	43	44	50	45	42	49	41	49	55
Don't know	1	1	1	–	1	2	1	1	1

- 39% of 18- to 29-year-olds say yes; 69% of those 50 and older.
- 54% of urbanites say yes; 63% of suburbanites; and 45% of urban dwellers.

The second question:

As you may know, charter schools operate under a charter or contract that frees them from many of the state regulations imposed on public schools and permits them to operate independently. Do you favor or oppose the idea of charter schools?

	National Totals			No Children In School			Public School Parents		
	'02 %	'01 %	'00 %	'02 %	'01 %	'00 %	'02 %	'01 %	'00 %
Favor	44	42	42	44	40	42	44	43	40
Oppose	43	49	47	43	51	47	44	47	47
Don't know	13	9	11	13	9	11	12	10	13

- 57% of 18-to 29-year-olds are in favor; 36% of those 50 and older.
- 51% of Republicans are in favor; 33% of Democrats.
- 52% of urbanites are in favor; 44% of suburbanites; and 39% of rural dwellers.

The third question:

Do you think that charter schools should be accountable to the state in the way regular public schools are accountable?

	National Totals			No Children In School			Public School Parents		
	'02 %	'01 %	'00 %	'02 %	'01 %	'00 %	'02 %	'01 %	'00 %
Should be accountable	77	77	79	78	77	78	77	77	81
Should not	19	18	17	19	18	18	19	18	14
Don't know	4	5	4	3	5	4	4	5	5

Respondents were then asked whether they would favor charter schools if funding them meant reduced funds for the regular public schools. Sixty-five percent said no. A final question on charter schools asked about the appropriateness of offering all instruction over the Internet.

(continued)

POLICY IMPLICATIONS
OF THE 34TH ANNUAL PHI DELTA KAPPA/GALLUP POLL

It has always been the purpose of this annual poll to provide information for use by policy makers in shaping the decisions that guide the direction of the public schools. This special section captures much that is important in the poll but is inadequate to provide the understanding that will come through a thorough study of poll results. It is brought to you by the Phi Delta Kappa Educational Foundation in memory of Bessie F. Gabbard.

Conclusion 1: Public support for the public schools is strong and increases as people have more contact with the schools. It is logical, therefore, that the public expects improvement of education to come through the public school system.

FIGURE 1.
Public Support for and Reliance on Public Schools

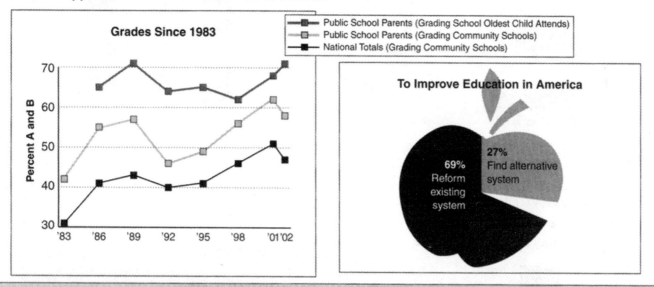

Conclusion 2: The jump in support for allowing students and parents to choose a private school to attend at public expense will fuel the debate over vouchers that is almost guaranteed by the recent Supreme Court decision on vouchers.

FIGURE 2.
Public Support for Using Public/Government Money for Private School Tuition

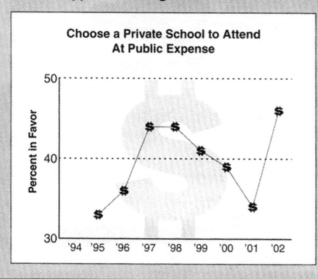
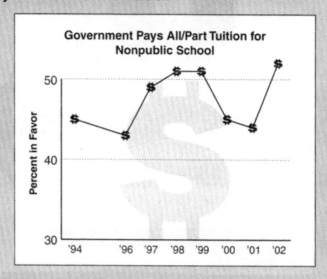

Conclusion 3: The public is not well informed on charter schools, is mixed in its support for them, and believes they should be accountable to the public in the same way public schools are accountable.

FIGURE 3.
Charter Schools

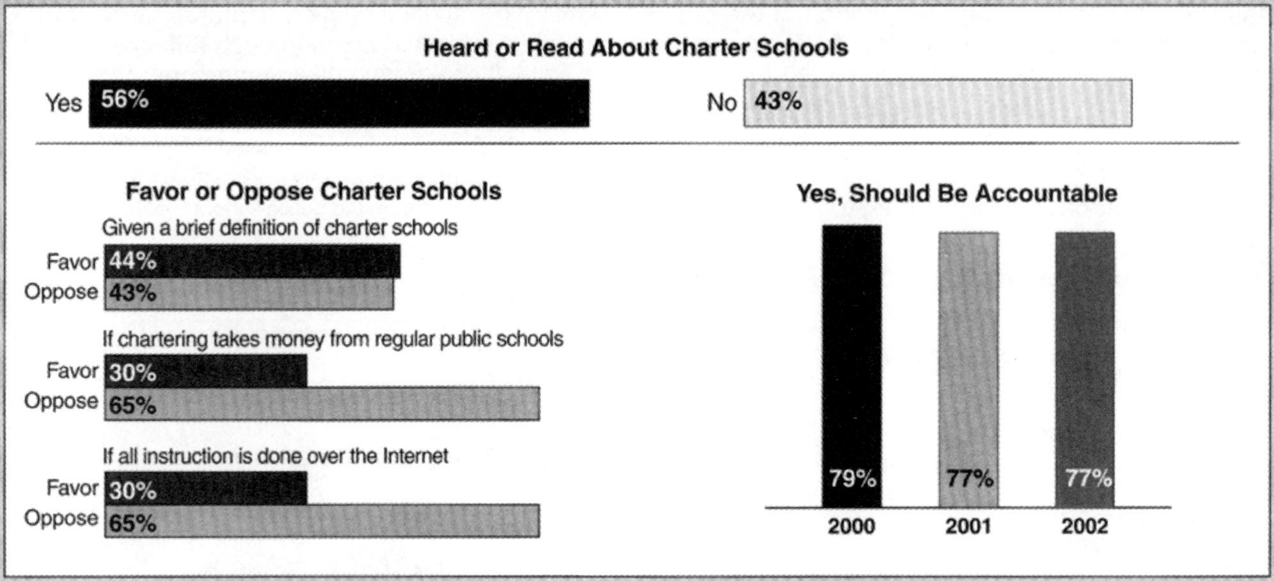

Heard or Read About Charter Schools

Yes 56%   No 43%

Favor or Oppose Charter Schools

Given a brief definition of charter schools
Favor 44%
Oppose 43%

If chartering takes money from regular public schools
Favor 30%
Oppose 65%

If all instruction is done over the Internet
Favor 30%
Oppose 65%

Yes, Should Be Accountable

2000: 79%
2001: 77%
2002: 77%

Conclusion 4: The public welcomes the possibility of an increased federal role in K-12 schools.

FIGURE 4.
Possibility of Increased Federal Role

Good thing 57%
Bad thing 34%

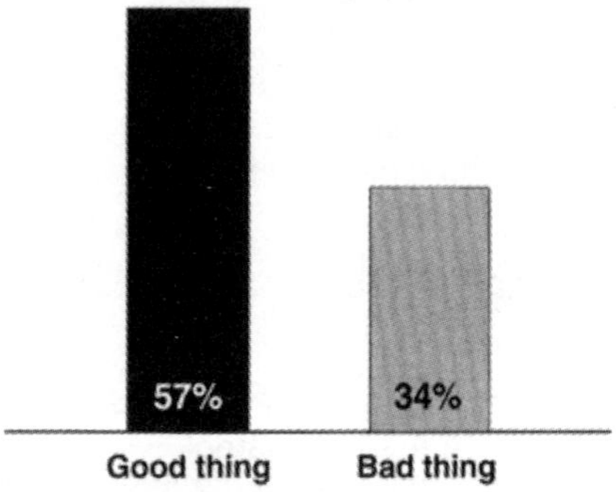

Conclusion 5: The sanctions in the federal No Child Left Behind Act (NCLBA) for schools not meeting state standards are generally supported.

FIGURE 5.
NCLBA Measures

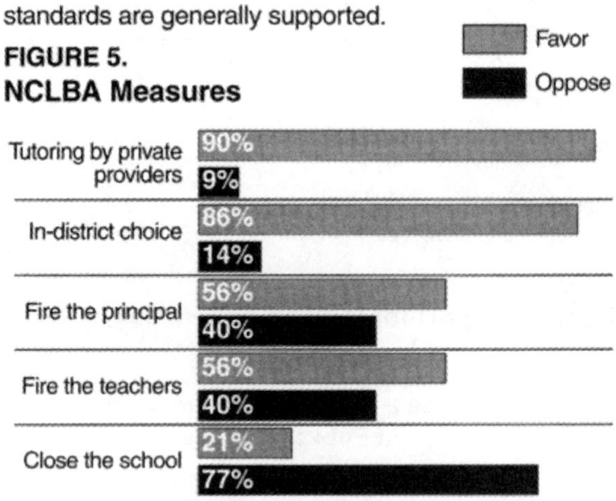

Favor
Oppose

Tutoring by private providers: Favor 90%, Oppose 9%
In-district choice: Favor 86%, Oppose 14%
Fire the principal: Favor 56%, Oppose 40%
Fire the teachers: Favor 56%, Oppose 40%
Close the school: Favor 21%, Oppose 77%

Conclusion 6: The public sends mixed signals that shed little light on the concern educators feel about the emphasis the NCLBA and state improvement efforts place on reading and math.

FIGURE 6.
Emphasis of the NCLBA

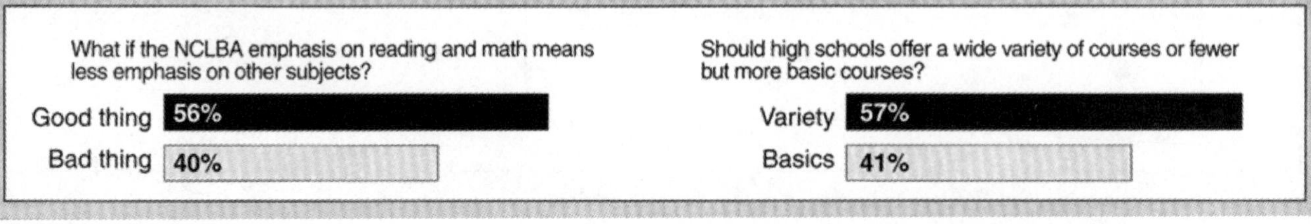

What if the NCLBA emphasis on reading and math means less emphasis on other subjects?
Good thing 56%
Bad thing 40%

Should high schools offer a wide variety of courses or fewer but more basic courses?
Variety 57%
Basics 41%

Conclusion 7: Preschool programs draw strong public support while the public continues to scorn other proposals for increasing time in school.

FIGURE 7.
Support for Selected Initiatives

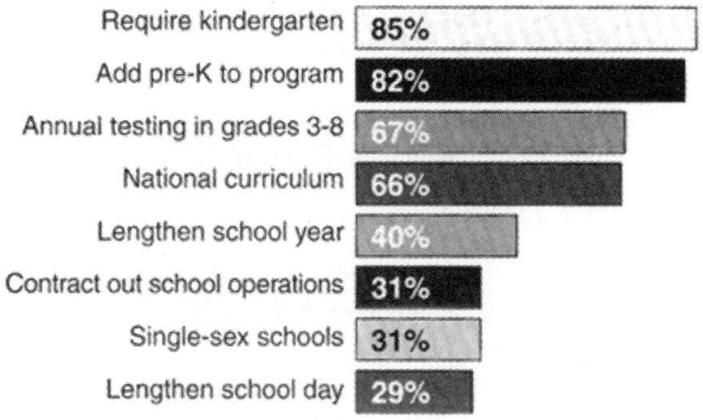

Require kindergarten	85%
Add pre-K to program	82%
Annual testing in grades 3-8	67%
National curriculum	66%
Lengthen school year	40%
Contract out school operations	31%
Single-sex schools	31%
Lengthen school day	29%

Conclusion 8: The public believes the size of a school is an important factor in student achievement and that "smaller is better" — especially for young children.

FIGURE 8.
Size of School

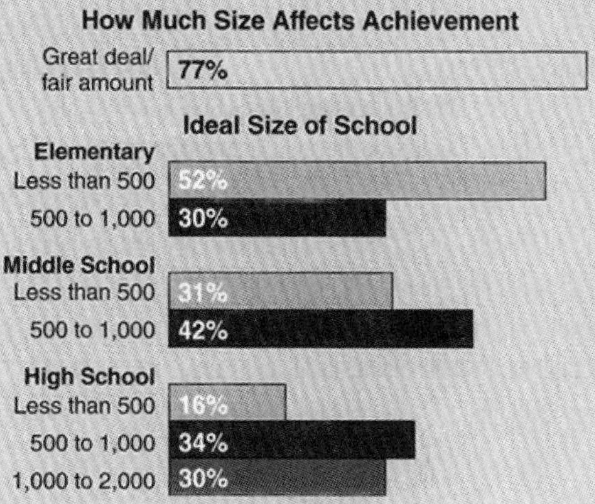

How Much Size Affects Achievement

Great deal/fair amount	77%

Ideal Size of School

Elementary
Less than 500	52%
500 to 1,000	30%

Middle School
Less than 500	31%
500 to 1,000	42%

High School
Less than 500	16%
500 to 1,000	34%
1,000 to 2,000	30%

Conclusion 9: The public attitude regarding the amount of testing remains remarkably stable at a time when there is likely to be an increase in the amount of testing and concerns about too much testing are frequently heard.

FIGURE 9.
Amount of Testing

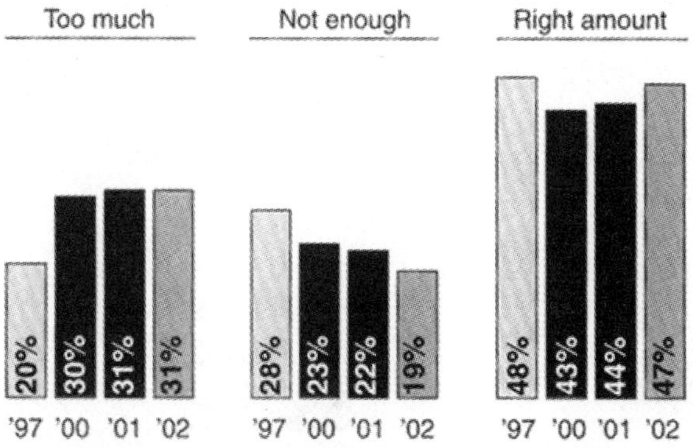

Too much				Not enough				Right amount			
20%	30%	31%	31%	28%	23%	22%	19%	48%	43%	44%	47%
'97	'00	'01	'02	'97	'00	'01	'02	'97	'00	'01	'02

Conclusion 10: The public does not want current economic problems to result in cuts in education spending.

FIGURE 10.
Handling Revenue Shortages

A great deal or fair amount of support

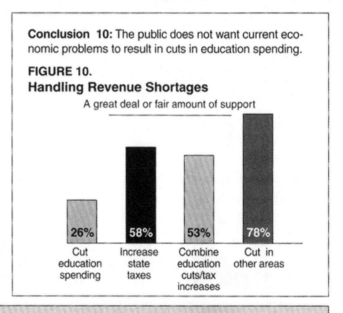

Cut education spending	Increase state taxes	Combine education cuts/tax increases	Cut in other areas
26%	58%	53%	78%

Conclusion 11: The public sees finance as the major problem facing public schools but is also concerned about discipline, overcrowding, drugs, gangs, and the difficulty of getting good teachers.

FIGURE 11.
Problems Facing Community Schools

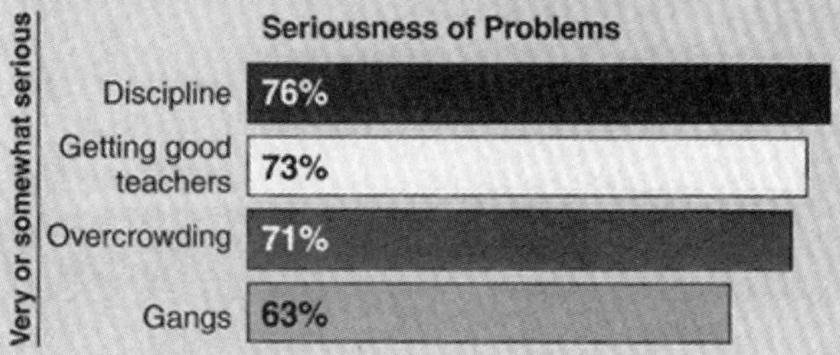

Seriousness of Problems

Very or somewhat serious

Discipline	76%
Getting good teachers	73%
Overcrowding	71%
Gangs	63%

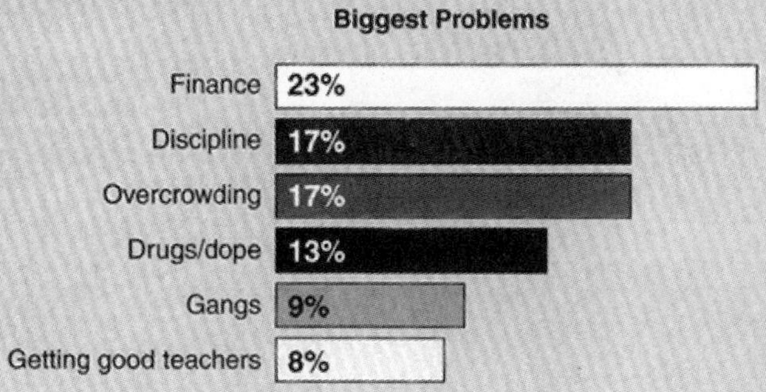

Biggest Problems

Finance	23%
Discipline	17%
Overcrowding	17%
Drugs/dope	13%
Gangs	9%
Getting good teachers	8%

Conclusion 12: The public believes there is a gap between the achievement of white and minority students, feels strongly that the gap must be closed, and (in a finding that suggests a more general effort than schools can mount) attributes the gap to factors not related to schooling.

FIGURE 12.
The Achievement Gap

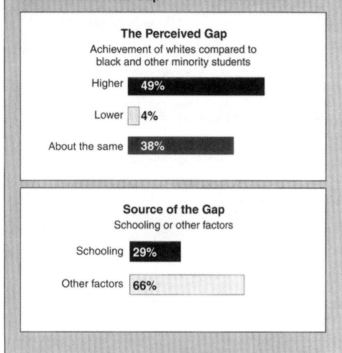

The Perceived Gap
Achievement of whites compared to black and other minority students
Higher 49%
Lower 4%
About the same 38%

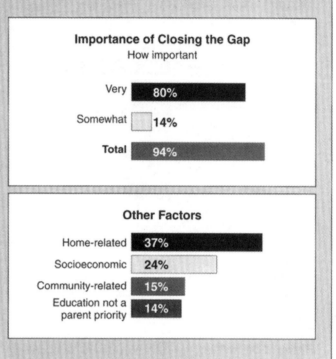

Importance of Closing the Gap
How important
Very 80%
Somewhat 14%
Total 94%

Source of the Gap
Schooling or other factors
Schooling 29%
Other factors 66%

Other Factors
Home-related 37%
Socioeconomic 24%
Community-related 15%
Education not a parent priority 14%

Conclusion 13: Opinion differences by age, race, and home location are so significant that they must be recognized and addressed.

FIGURE 13.
Examples of Opinion Differences by Age, Race, and Home Location

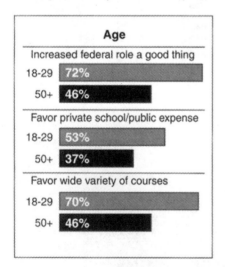

Age
Increased federal role a good thing
18-29 72%
50+ 46%
Favor private school/public expense
18-29 53%
50+ 37%
Favor wide variety of courses
18-29 70%
50+ 46%

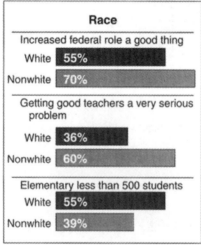

Race
Increased federal role a good thing
White 55%
Nonwhite 70%
Getting good teachers a very serious problem
White 36%
Nonwhite 60%
Elementary less than 500 students
White 55%
Nonwhite 39%

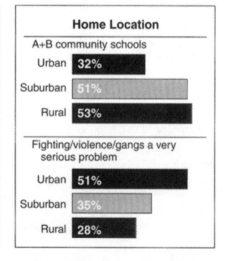

Home Location
A+B community schools
Urban 32%
Suburban 51%
Rural 53%
Fighting/violence/gangs a very serious problem
Urban 51%
Suburban 35%
Rural 28%

Sixty-five percent of respondents said they would oppose such schools in their community. The latter finding is similar to the 67% in last year's poll who said no to high school students' earning all credits over the Internet.

The fourth question:

Would you favor charter schools in your community if funding them meant reducing the amount of funds for the regular public schools—or not?

	National Totals %	No Children In School %	Public School Parents %
Would favor	30	31	25
Would oppose	65	64	70
Don't know	5	5	5

- 37% of men would still favor; 24% of women.
- 38% of Republicans would still favor; 26% of Democrats.
- 37% of urbanites would still favor; 29% of suburbanites; and 26% of rural dwellers.

The fifth question:

Some charter schools offer all instruction to students online over the Internet. Would you favor or oppose such schools in your own community?

	National Totals %	No Children In School %	Public School Parents %
Would favor	30	30	31
Would oppose	65	65	65
Don't know	5	5	4

- 27% of whites would favor; 45% of nonwhites
- 39% of 18- to 29-year-olds would favor; 21% of those 50 and older.
- 25% in the East would favor; 26% in the Midwest; 33% in the South; and 37% in the West.

Problems Facing the Public Schools

The one question repeated in all 33 previous Phi Delta Kappa/Gallup polls offers respondents the opportunity to identify the biggest problems facing local public schools. Lack of financial support has topped the list for the last two years and remains in first place this year. The percentage of mentions is higher this year (23%), with lack of discipline and overcrowded schools tied for second at 17%. Respondents were also asked to indicate how serious four of the problems identified last year are in their local schools. Percentages rating them very serious or somewhat serious range from 63% to 76%.

The first question:

What do you think are the biggest problems with which the public schools or your community must deal?

	National Totals			No Children In School			Public School Parents		
	'02 %	'01 %	'00 %	'02 %	'01 %	'00 %	'02 %	'01 %	'00 %
Lack of financial support/ funding/money	23	15	18	23	15	17	23	17	19
Lack of discipline, more control	17	15	15	18	17	17	13	10	9
Overcrowded schools	17	10	12	14	7	10	23	15	14
Use of drugs/dope	13	9	9	14	9	10	11	10	9
Fighting/violence/gangs	9	10	11	9	11	11	9	9	11
Difficulty getting good teachers/quality teachers	8	6	4	8	6	4	8	6	4

- Overcrowding at 25% ties for the head of the list among public school parents.

The second question:

I am going to read off several of the problems facing the public schools, nationally, one at a time. For each problem, please tell me how serious you think that problem is in the public schools in your community—is it very serious, somewhat serious, not too serious, or not at all serious?

	Very and Some- what Serious %	Very Serious %	Some- what Serious %	Not Too Serious %	Not At All Serious %	Don't Know %
Lack of student discipline	76	43	33	17	4	3
Getting good teachers	73	40	33	17	9	1
Overcrowding	71	38	33	16	10	3
Fighting, violence, gangs	63	37	26	24	12	1

- 33% of public school parents see discipline as a very serious problem; 46% of those with no children in school.
- 60% of nonwhites regard getting good teachers as a serious problem; 36% of whites.
- 60% of urbanites consider fighting, violence, and gangs a very serious problem; 35% of suburbanites; and 28% of rural dwellers.

Education and Minorities

The No Child Left Behind Act focuses the federal role in education on those students who are failing to achieve success in school. Minorities make up a disproportionate share of such students. The public is aware of the gap between white and minority students. Forty-nine percent said that achievement for whites is higher than that for black or Hispanic students. Last year, respondents were asked if closing the gap is important. Eighty-eight percent judged it to be very important or somewhat important; that percentage rises to 94% this year.

The first question:

Just your impression, is the academic achievement of white students nationally higher, lower, or about the same as black and Hispanic students?

	National Totals		No Children In School		Public School Parents	
	'02 %	'01 %	'02 %	'01 %	'02 %	'01 %
Higher	49	48	49	47	47	46
Lower	4	5	4	5	4	5
About the same	38	39	37	38	42	43
Don't know	9	8	10	10	7	6

The second question (asked of those who chose "higher"):

In your opinion, how important do you think it is to close the academic achievement gap between white students and black and Hispanic students—very important, somewhat important, not too important, or not important at all?

	National Totals		No Children In School		Public School Parents	
	'02 %	'01 %	'02 %	'01 %	'02 %	'01 %
Very and somewhat important	94	88	93	89	96	87
Very important	80	66	80	66	80	67
Somewhat important	14	22	13	23	16	20
Not too important	2	5	2	5	2	5
Not important at all	3	5	4	4	1	6
Don't know	1	2	1	2	1	2

• 69% of Republicans say very important; 82% of Democrats.

Respondents this year and last year were asked whether the perceived gap is related to the quality of schooling received or to other factors. Seventy-three percent responded "other factors" last year, and 66% did so this year. That being the case, poll planners this year deemed it important to determine the nature of the "other factors." Those who were asked the follow-up question this year mentioned home life/environment/upbringing, economic advantages/disadvantages, poor community environment, education not a priority for parents, and lack of parent involvement in that order. The factors are important since last year's respondents, though saying that the gap is not related to schooling, indicated that it is still the schools that must close the gap.

The third question:

In your opinion, is the achievement gap between white and black and Hispanic students mostly related to the quality of schooling received or mostly related to other factors?

	National Totals		No Children In School		Public School Parents	
	'02 %	'01 %	'02 %	'01 %	'02 %	'01 %
Related to the quality of schooling received	29	21	31	20	22	22
Related to other factors	66	73	64	72	75	74
Don't know	5	6	5	8	3	4

• 70% of whites say other factors; 53% of nonwhites.

• 75% of Republicans say other factors; 64% of Democrats.

• 56% of urbanites say other factors; 70% of suburbanites; and 71% of rural dwellers.

The fourth question (asked of those who chose "other factors"):

Just your opinion, what are some of the factors that cause the achievement gap between white students and black and Hispanic students?

	National Totals %	No Children In School %	Public School Parents %
Home life/environment/upbringing	37	36	38
Economic advantage/disadvantage	24	24	24
Poor community environment	15	15	15
Education not a priority for parents	14	16	11
Lack of parent involvement	12	11	12
Biased/racist attitudes	10	9	12
Student lack of interest	8	9	7

• 40% of whites mention home life/environment/upbringing; 23% of nonwhites.

• 34% of those in the East mention home life/environment/upbringing; 41% in the Midwest; 42% in the South; and 27% in the West.

Issues Related to the Operation of Schools

Curriculum

With the prospect of the federal government's increased role in local schools, it seemed logical to ask about a national curriculum. Sixty-six percent of respondents said they support such a move. This finding is little changed from the 68% that favored this choice in 1981 and the 69% that did so in 1991. In a repeat of a question first asked in 1979, 57% said they would favor a curriculum with a wide variety of courses, while 41% said they would favor one with fewer but more basic courses. Here, opinions have changed since 1979, when respondents favored concentration on a few basic courses by 49% to 44%. In a response that seems somewhat conflicting, 56% of respondents said it would be a good thing if the current emphasis on reading and math in federal and state improvement efforts resulted in less emphasis on other subjects.

The first question:

Would you favor or oppose requiring the schools in your community to use a standardized national curriculum?

	National Totals %	No Children In School %	Public School Parents %
Would favor	66	67	66
Would oppose	31	30	30
Don't know	3	3	4

• 64% of whites favor a national curriculum; 77% of nonwhites.

The second question:

Public high schools can offer students a wide variety of courses, or they can concentrate on fewer basic courses, such as English, mathematics, history, and science. Which

of these policies do you think the local high schools should follow in planning their curricula—a wide variety of courses or fewer but more basic courses?

	National Totals	No Children In School	Public School Parents
	%	%	%
Wide variety of courses	57	57	57
Basic courses	41	41	42
Don't know	2	2	1

• 55% of whites say a wide variety of courses; 65% of nonwhites.

• 70% of 18- to 29-year-olds say wide variety of courses; 46% of those 50 and older.

	National Totals			
	2002 %	2001 %	1993 %	1979 %
Wide variety of courses	57	54	48	44
Basic courses	41	44	51	49
Don't know	2	2	1	7

The third question:

Suppose the increased emphasis on reading and mathematics results in reduced emphasis on the other subjects in the curriculum. In your opinion, would this be a good thing or a bad thing?

	National Totals	No Children In School	Public School Parents
	%	%	%
A good thing	56	55	57
A bad thing	40	41	40
Don't know	4	4	3

Testing

Monitoring the reaction to testing is important because the NCLBA and other improvement efforts place great stress on test performance. Two questions explored the public response to testing. Forty-seven percent of respondents said that there is just the right amount of emphasis on testing, a finding that has changed little since the question was first asked in 1997. That Americans are satisfied with the amount of testing is interesting since, in response to the second question, they said that classroom work and homework are better ways to measure student achievement. This response was chosen by 53% of the respondents. Confusing the matter further is that 66% of last year's respondents indicated that tests should be used primarily to determine the instruction needed.

The first question:

Now, here are some questions about testing. In your opinion, is there too much emphasis on achievement testing in the public schools in this community, not enough emphasis on testing, or about the right amount?

	National Totals				No Children In School				Public School Parents			
	'02 %	'01 %	'00 %	'97 %	'02 %	'01 %	'00 %	'97 %	'02 %	'01 %	'00 %	'97 %
Too much emphasis	31	31	30	20	30	29	28	20	32	36	34	19
Not enough emphasis	19	22	23	28	20	22	26	28	14	20	19	26
Just the right amount of emphasis	47	44	43	48	46	45	41	46	54	43	46	54
Don't know	3	3	4	4	4	4	5	6	—	1	1	1

• 26% in the East indicate too much emphasis; 22% in the Midwest; 38% in the South; and 33% in the West.

The second question:

In your opinion, which is the best way to measure student academic achievement—by means of test scores, or by classroom work and homework?

	National Totals			No Children In School			Public School Parents		
	'02 %	'01 %	'00 %	'02 %	'01 %	'00 %	'02 %	'01 %	'00 %
By means of test scores	26	31	26	28	31	28	22	31	23
By classroom work and homework	53	65	68	50	65	66	61	66	71
Both combined (volunteered)	20	—	—	21	—	—	16	—	—
Don't know	1	4	6	1	4	6	1	3	6

• 64% of 18- to 29-year-olds indicate classroom work and homework; 48% of those 50 and older.

• 48% of Republicans indicate classroom work and homework; 57% of Democrats.

School Size

In an area new to the poll, respondents were asked about the importance of school size and the ideal size for schools. In response to the first question, 77% said that they believe size affects achievement a great deal or quite a lot. Then, in three additional questions, 82% specified less than 1,000 as the ideal size of an elementary school, 72% indicated less than 1,000 for a middle school, and 50% indicated less than 1,000 for a high school. The high school choice can be interpreted differently to indicate that 64% feel the ideal size is between 500 and 2,000. Nevertheless, the public is clear in its belief that smaller is better. Mean averages provide another way to look at desired school size. The Gallup Organization calculated the following mean averages: 520 for an elementary school, 711 for a middle school, and 1,033 for a high school.

The first question:

In your opinion, does the number of students in a school affect the level of achievement of its students a great deal, a fair amount, not very much, or not at all?

	National Totals %	No Children In School %	Public School Parents %
A great deal and a fair amount	77	75	81
A great deal	40	36	47
A fair amount	37	39	34
Not very much	13	13	13
Not at all	7	9	4
Don't know	3	3	2

The second question:

What do you consider the ideal number of students in an elementary school—less than 500 students, 500 to less than 1,000 students, 1,000 to less than 2,000 students, or 2,000 or more?

	National Totals %	No Children In School %	Public School Parents %
Less than 500 students	52	49	59
500 to less than 1,000	30	31	28
1,000 to less than 2,000	5	5	6
2,000 or more	1	2	1
Don't know	12	13	6
Mean average (calculated)	520	—	—

- 44% of men say less than 500; 60% of women.
- 55% of whites say less than 500; 39% of nonwhites.

The third question:

How about for a middle school? What do you consider the ideal number of students—less than 500 students, 500 to less than 1,000 students, 1,000 to less than 2,000 students, or 2,000 or more?

	National Totals %	No Children In School %	Public School Parents %
Less than 500 students	31	29	34
500 to less than 1,000	42	42	44
1,000 to less than 2,000	13	14	12
2,000 or more	2	1	3
Don't know	12	14	7
Mean average (calculated)	711	—	—

The fourth question:

How about for a high school? What do you consider the ideal number of students—less than 500 students, 500 to less than 1,000 students, 1,000 to less than 2,000 students, or 2,000 or more?

	National Totals %	No Children In School %	Public School Parents %
Less than 500 students	16	16	16
500 to less than 1,000	34	31	41
1,000 to less than 2,000	30	32	27
2,000 or more	8	8	9
Don't know	12	13	7
Mean average (calculated)	1,033	—	—

- 43% of men say less than 1,000; 56% of women.
- 53% of whites say less than 1,000; 39% of nonwhites.

Scope of School Responsibilities

Over the years public schools have taken on additional responsibilities, many of which are not directly related to academic purposes. Two questions in this poll were designed to determine public reaction to this trend. Fifty-four percent of respondents said that they believe the schools have taken on too many responsibilities. On the second and more difficult question, 69% said that the school's re-

sponsibilities in nonacademic areas should be reduced. One-fourth (25%) said that the responsibilities should be reduced in both academic and nonacademic areas.

The first question:

Over the years, public schools have taken on additional responsibilities in both academic and non-academic areas. In your opinion, have the public schools today taken on too many responsibilities beyond their original role or not?

	National Totals %	No Children In School %	Public School Parents %
Yes, have	54	55	49
No, have not	41	39	48
Don't know	5	6	3

- 57% of whites say yes; 44% of nonwhites.

The second question (asked of those who said "yes"):

Which of the following do you think would be the best solution to this problem?

	National Totals %	No Children In School %	Public School Parents %
Reduce the school's responsibilities in the academic area	3	4	3
Reduce the school's responsibilities in nonacademic areas	69	67	72
Reduce the school's responsibilities in both areas	25	26	23
Don't know	3	3	2

- 75% of Republicans say reduce in nonacademic areas; 65% of Democrats.
- 57% of 18- to 29-year-olds say reduce in nonacademic areas; 70% of those 50 and older.

Miscellaneous Questions

On three previous occasions, this poll sought to determine the sources the public relies on to get information about school quality. In 1973, students, newspapers, and parents of students were identified in that order. Newspapers moved into first place in 1983, stayed there in 1988, and remain there this year. Forty-three percent of respondents indicated that newspapers are their main source of information about schools. It should be noted that this is an open-ended question, with respondents mentioning whatever comes to mind. In that context, the 43% mentioning newspapers is impressive. It is interesting that only 10% of public school parents mention communications from school.

The question:

What are the sources of information you use to judge the quality of schools in your community—that is, where do you get your information about the schools?

	National Totals %	No Children In School %	Public School Parents %
Newspapers	43	46	36
Word of mouth/friends/relatives	35	35	30
Children/students	17	13	30
Television	16	17	11
Personal experience/observation	10	10	9
School employees	8	6	11
Media (not specified)	6	7	4
Communications from school	6	5	10

• 45% of whites say newspapers; 32% of nonwhites.

The NCLBA and the tracking of student progress create the possibility that teachers will be evaluated on the basis of the performance of their students on standardized tests. With this in mind, respondents were asked whether teacher salaries should be based on the results of the test selected by the state. Fifty-four percent of respondents indicated that they disapprove of this idea, while 43% expressed approval.

The question:

Do you approve or disapprove of a proposed plan that would base the salaries of public school classroom teachers on how well their students perform on the standardized test adopted by the state to track student progress?

	National Totals %	No Children In School %	Public School Parents %
Approve	43	42	46
Disapprove	54	54	52
Don't know	3	4	2

The public continues to be unwilling to lengthen the school day or year: 70% of respondents said they oppose lengthening the school day, and 59% said they oppose lengthening the school year. The public does, however, offer strong support for guaranteeing kindergarten participation (85% of respondents in favor) and providing prekindergarten experience (82% of respondents in favor).

The question:

Here are some plans that have been proposed for increasing the amount of time students spend in school. As I read each plan, please tell me whether you would favor or oppose that plan as a way of increasing the amount of time students spend in the public schools in your community?

	Favor %	Oppose %	Don't know %
Increasing the length of the school day	29	70	1
Increasing the length of the school year	40	59	1
Making kindergarten a requirement	85	14	1
Making prekindergarten available as part of the public school system	82	17	1

• 35% of men favor lengthening the school day; 23% of women.

• 25% of 18- to 29-year-olds say lengthen the school day; 33% of those 50 and older.

• 30% of 18- to 29-year-olds say lengthen the school year; 47% of those 50 and older.

The issue of single-sex schools has surfaced recently, with proponents claiming that some girls achieve better when separated from boys. Sixty-seven percent of respondents said they would oppose such schools.

The question:

One issue being debated currently is whether separate schools for boys and girls would help to improve academic achievement for some students. Would you favor or oppose single-sex schools as an option for parents and students in your community?

	National Totals %	No Children In School %	Public School Parents %
Would favor	31	32	25
Wold oppose	67	65	74
Don't know	2	3	1

• 39% of urbanites would favor; 30% of suburbanites; and 25% of rural dwellers.

Fifty-nine percent of respondents in 1996 and 72% in 2001 opposed allowing local businesses to run the entire school operation. The respondents to this poll confirmed that opinion, with 65% indicating they would oppose contracting out the operation of schools to private profit-making corporations.

The question:

Would you favor or oppose a plan in which your local school board would contract with private profit-making corporations to run the entire operations of the public schools in your community?

	National Totals %	No Children In School %	Public School Parents %
Would favor	31	31	30
Would oppose	65	64	67
Don't know	4	5	3

• 42% of 18- to 29-year-olds would favor; 21% of those 50 and older.

• 35% of Republicans would favor; 25% of Democrats.

• 42% of urbanites would favor; 30% of suburbanites; an 22% of rural dwellers.

Research Procedure

The Sample. The sample used in this survey embraced a total of 1,000 adults (18 years of age and older). A description of the sample and methodology can be found at the end of this report.

Time of Interviewing. The fieldwork for this study was conducted during the period of 5 June to 26 June 2002.

The Report. In the tables used in this report, "Nonpublic School Parents" includes parents of students who attend parochial schools and parents of students who attend secular private or independent schools.

Due allowance must be made for statistical variation, especially in the case of findings for groups consisting of relatively few respondents, e.g., nonpublic school parents.

The findings of this report apply only to the U.S. as a whole and not to individual communities. Local surveys, using the same questions, can be conducted to determine how local areas compare with the national norm.

Design of the Sample

For the 2002 survey the Gallup Organization used its standard national telephone sample, i.e., an unclustered, directory-assisted, random-digit telephone sample, based on a proportionate stratified sampling design.

The random-digit aspect of the sample was used to avoid "listing" bias. Numerous studies have shown that households with unlisted telephone numbers are different in important ways from listed households. "Unlistedness" is due to household mobility or to customer requests to prevent publication of the telephone number.

To avoid this source of bias, a random-digit procedure designed to provide representation of both listed and unlisted (including not-yet-listed) numbers was used.

Telephone numbers for the continental United States were stratified into four regions of the country and, within each region, further stratified into three size-of-community strata.

Only working banks of telephone numbers were selected. Eliminating non-working banks from the sample increased the likelihood that any sample telephone number would be associated with a residence.

The sample of telephone numbers produced by the described method is representative of all telephone households within the continental United States.

Within each contacted household, an interview was sought with the youngest man 18 years of age or older who was at home. If no man was home, an interview was sought with the oldest woman at home. This method of respondent selection within households produced an age distribution by sex that closely approximates the age distribution by sex of the total population.

Up to three calls were made to each selected telephone number to complete an interview. The time of day and the day of the week for callbacks were varied so as to maximize the chances of finding a respondent at home. All interviews were conducted on weekends or weekday evenings in order to contact potential respondents among the working population.

The final sample was weighted so that the distribution of the sample matched current estimates derived from the U.S. Census Bureau's Current Population Survey (CPS) for the adult population living in telephone households in the continental U.S.

Sampling Tolerances

In interpreting survey results, it should be borne in mind that all sample surveys are subject to sampling error, i.e., the extent to which the results may differ from what

would be obtained if the whole population surveyed had been interviewed. The size of such sampling error depends largely on the number of interviews. For details and tables showing the confidence intervals for the data cited in this boll, please visit the Phi Delta Kappa website at http://www.pdkintl.org/kappan/kpoll0209sample.htm.

Composition of the Sample

Adults	%		Education	
No children in school	71		Total college	60
Public school parents	26		College graduate	24
Nonpublic school parents	3		College incomplete	36
			Total high school	39
			High school graduate	33
			High school incomplete	6
Gender	%			
Men	47		Income	
Women	53		$50,000 and over	34
			$40,000-$49,999	11
Race			$30,000-$39,999	13
White	82		$20,000-$29,999	12
Nonwhite	16		Under $20,000	18
Black	11		Undesignated	12
Undesignated	1			
			Region	
Age			East	23
18-29 years	22		Midwest	23
30-49 years	21		South	32
50 and over	36		West	22
Undesignated	1			
			Community Size	
			Urban	25
			Suburban	29
			Rural	26

How to Order the Poll

The minimum order for reprints of the published version of the Phi Delta Kappa/Gallup education poll is 25 copies for $15. (Institutional purchase orders, cash, or MasterCard or VISA number required.) Additional copies are 50 cents each. This price includes postage for delivery (at the library rate). Where possible, enclose a check or money order. Address your order to Phi Delta Kappa International, P.O. Box 789, Bloomington, IN 47402-0789. Ph. 800/766-1156.

If faster delivery is desired, phone the Shipping Department at the number listed below. Persons who wish to order the 347-page document that is the basis of this report should contact Phi Delta Kappa International, P.O. Box 789, Bloomington, IN 47402-0789. Ph. 800/766-1156. The price is $95, postage included.

Conducting Your Own Poll

The Phi Delta Kappa Center for Professional Development and Services makes available PACE (Polling Attitudes of the Community on Education) materials to enable nonspecialists to conduct scientific polls of attitude and opinion on education. The PACE manual provides detailed information on constructing questionnaires, sampling, interviewing, and analyzing data. It also includes updated census figures and new material on conducting a telephone survey. The price is $6. For information about using PACE materials, write or phone Shari Bradley at Phi Delta Kappa International, P.O. Box 789, Bloomington, IN 47402-0789. Ph. 800/766-1156

LOWELL C. ROSE is executive director emeritus of Phi Delta Kappa International. ALEC M. GALLUP is co-chairman, with George Gallup, Jr., of the Gallup Organization, Princeton, N.J.

UNIT 2

Rethinking and Changing the Educative Effort

Unit Selections

4. **When Improvement Programs Collide**, Thomas Hatch
5. **Personalized Instruction**, James W. Keefe and John M. Jenkins
6. **Action Research for School Improvement**, Emily F. Calhoun
7. **The Dark Side of Nationwide Tests**, B. K. Eakman

Key Points to Consider

- What are some issues in the debate regarding educational reform?

- Describe the "renewal" approach to education. Do you believe it will result in "communities of learning?" Why or why not?

- Should the focus of educational reform be on changing the ways educators are prepared, on the changing needs of students, or on both of these concerns?

- Discuss nationwide testing. What are the ethical issues involved? What are the "psychographics" of testing? What are the psychological uses of testing?

 **Links: www.dushkin.com/online/**
These sites are annotated in the World Wide Web pages.

The Center for Innovation in Education
http://www.center.edu

Colorado Department of Education
http://www.cde.state.co.us/index_home.htm

National Council for Accreditation of Teacher Education
http://www.ncate.org

Phi Delta Kappa International
http://www.pdkintl.org

The dialogue regarding how to rethink and restructure the priorities of educational services is continuing; this is not surprising. There has been a similar dialogue in every generation of American history. Some of the debate centers on whether change and reform in education today should focus on restructuring how teachers are prepared or on research into the changing conditions of the lives of many American youth today and how to help them better meet the challenges in their lives.

The articles in this unit reflect a wide range of opinion about these concerns. Several new and exciting ideas are being proposed as to how we might reconceive the idea of school to encompass much more variety in school learning communities as well as to meet a broader range of the academic and social needs of today's youth.

American educators could have a much better sense of their own past as a profession, and the public could better understand the history of public education. In the United States, a fundamental cycle of similar ideas and practices reappears in school curricula every so many years. The decades of the 1970s and 1980s witnessed the rise of "behavioral objectives" and "management by objectives," and the 1990s brought us "outcome-based education" and "benchmarking" in educational discourse within the public school system's leadership. These are related behavioral concepts focusing on measurable ways to pinpoint and evaluate the results of educational efforts. Why do we seem to "reinvent the wheel" of educational thought and practice every few decades? This is an important question worth addressing. Many of our ideas about change and reform in educational practice have been wrongheaded. There is a focus on more qualitative, as opposed to empirical, means of assessing the outcomes of our educative efforts; yet many state departments of education still insist on objective assessments and verifications of students' mastery of academic skills. How does this affect the development of imaginative teaching in schools? All of us in the education system are concerned, and many of us believe that there really are some new and generative ideas to help students learn basic intellectual skills and content.

Our current realities in the field of education reflect differing conceptions of how schooling ought to change. It is difficult to generalize regarding school quality across decades because of several factors; high schools, for instance, were more selective in 1900, when only 7 percent of American youths graduated from them. Today we encourage as many students as possible to graduate. The social purposes of schooling have been broadened; now we want all youths to complete some form of higher education.

We have to consider the social and ideological differences among those representing opposing school reform agendas for change. The differences over how and in what directions change is to occur in our educational systems rest on which educational values are to prevail. These values form the bases for differing conceptions of the purposes of schooling. Thus the differing agendas for change in American education have to be positioned within the context of the different ideological value systems that underpin each alternative agenda for change.

There are several currently contending (and frequently conceptually conflicting) strategies for restructuring life in schools as well as options open to parents in choosing the schools that they want their children to attend. On the one hand, we have to find ways to empower students and teachers to improve the quality of academic life in classrooms. On the other hand, there appear to be powerful forces contending over whether control of educational services should be even more centralized or more decentralized (site-based). Those who favor greater parental and teacher control of schools support greater decentralized site management and community control conceptions of school governance. Yet the ratio of teachers to nonteaching personnel (administrators, counselors, school psychologists, and others) continues to decline as public school system bureaucracies become more and more "top heavy."

In this unit, we consider the efforts to reconceive, redefine, and reconstruct existing patterns of curriculum and instruction at the elementary and secondary levels of schooling and compare them with the efforts to reconceive existing conflicting patterns of teacher education. A broad spectrum of dialogue is developing in North America, the British Commonwealth, Russia, Central Eurasia, and other areas of the world about the redirecting of learning opportunities for all citizens.

Prospective teachers here are being encouraged to question their own individual educational experiences as part of this process. We must acknowledge that our values affect our ideas about curriculum content and the purpose of educating others. This is perceived as vitally important in the developing dialogue over liberating all students' capacities to function as independent inquirers. The dramatic economic and demographic changes in our society necessitate a fundamental reconceptualization of how schools ought to respond to the many social contexts in which they are located. This effort to reassess and reconceive the education of persons is a vital part of broader reform efforts in society as well as a dynamic dialectic in its own right. How can schools, for instance, better reflect the varied communities of interest that they serve? What must they do to become better perceived as just and equitable places in which all young people can seek to achieve learning and self-fulfillment?

Each of the essays in this unit relates to the tension involved in reconceiving how educational development should proceed in response to all the dramatic social and economic changes in society.

When Improvement Programs Collide

Efforts to implement and integrate various improvement efforts face a paradox, Mr. Hatch argues. Although many improvement initiatives can provide some of the inspiration, resources, and expertise that can help build schools' capacity to change, implementing those initiatives can bring new demands, requirements, and costs that schools do not always have the capacity to meet.

BY THOMAS HATCH

THE CENTURY that began with "the one best system"[1] is ending with concerns about whether there is any "system" at all. Teachers and schools today are besieged by a host of often-competing demands and responsibilities. While many new practices, policies, and reform efforts may make sense in their own right, teachers and schools are frequently left to try to integrate and coordinate these varied initiatives when they have neither the resources nor the time to do their work well in the first place. Unfortunately, the cumulative demands and resulting fragmentation and incoherence can undermine the capacity of schools to make the very improvements so many desire.

Among the responses to this problem have been initiatives to encourage schools to take advantage of the services and resources offered by organizations promoting "whole-school" reform programs or changes in the teaching of particular subjects such as English, mathematics, or science. Specifically, in 1998 Congress created the Comprehensive School Reform Demonstration (CSRD) program, in which $145 million was earmarked for schools that sought to work with one or more improvement programs or to create their own strategy for "comprehensive" reform. Many of the improvement programs mentioned in the CSRD legislation and guidance—such as Success for All/Roots and Wings, Accelerated Schools, High Schools That Work, and the Modern Red Schoolhouse—can point to affiliated schools that have made substantial improvements in operations and student performance. Furthermore, it is clear that these kinds of improvement programs can provide a variety of useful resources and services and can serve to motivate and inspire some staff members, students, and parents.[2] But it remains unclear whether efforts to increase the number of schools working with improvement programs will lead to more effective reforms on a larger scale and the kind of school-level coherence and capacity for increased student learning that so many desire. Too often, programs are simply added to the many initiatives already in place instead of being integrated into a focused effort.[3] In the process, rather than contribute to substantial improvements, the adoption of these programs may further sap the strength and spirit of schools and their communities.

Today, many schools may be trying to juggle the demands of implementing several improvement programs at the same time. For example, in a 1998–99 survey of the principals of schools in one district in the San Francisco Bay Area (with 77% responding), more than half of the respondents (52%) reported that they were involved with three or more programs or partnerships that were created by nationally known or local groups and organizations; 15% reported that they were involved with six or more different programs or partnerships. Surveys in three comparison districts in California and Texas showed that, of the responding schools in all districts, 63% were engaged in three or more improvement programs, and 27% were engaged in six or more. In one district, 18% of schools were working with nine or more different programs simultaneously.

The programs and partnerships with which schools were involved included whole-school reform programs, such as Success for All, the Coalition of Essential Schools, and AVID (Advancement via Individual Determination), and programs such as Reading Recovery and Connected Mathematics that focus on improving student performance in specific subjects. In the Bay Area district alluded to above, locally developed programs included the Bay Area School Reform Collaborative (BASRC), which provided funds, technical assistance, and network participation funds, technical assistance, and network participation to schools that passed through a portfolio appreciation procedure; Joint Venture Silicon Valley (JVSV), which offered funds and resources to schools interested in coordinating their curricula and assessments with other schools in their feeder pattern; and a local university that offered professional development school partnerships.

Of course, schools are attempting to put these programs in place at the same time that they are trying to respond to the rising standards and new demands of numerous state and district initiatives that have been established in the last few years. For example, in the Bay Area district, schools have had to deal with new district graduation requirements in mathematics, science, and foreign languages (in order to correspond with entrance requirements for the University of California system) and the development of exit exams in a number of subjects (with a requirement to be added in the coming years that high school students complete 40 hours of community service). In addition, schools have had to contend with major new policies from the state such as class-size reduction, elimination of many bilingual education programs, and the recent passage of the Public Schools Accountability Act, which has created a system of tests, incentives, and support to encourage schools to improve their performance.

Under these circumstances, it is not surprising that many teachers and administrators in the Bay Area district feel stretched to the limit. According to one assistant superintendent, frustration and anger at the school level have never been higher. Over and over again, he told us, principals and teachers are saying, "We don't want anything else. We're over our heads."

It is easy to blame the principals for getting involved in too many initiatives, the districts for failing to coordinate their own initiatives, and the improvement programs for making unrealistic demands. But the problems of fragmentation and overload experienced in the Bay Area district and elsewhere around the country may be a feature of an education "system" in which schools, districts, and improvement programs face numerous, often conflicting, demands from diverse constituencies, experience frequent changes in policies and personnel, and operate with significant constraints on the time, resources, and funding available to them.[4]

As a consequence, efforts to implement and integrate different initiatives face a basic paradox: creating new incentives for improvement and aligning some policies may motivate or smooth the way for some school reform efforts, but it takes capacity to build capacity at the school level. Ironically, although improvement programs can provide some of the inspiration, resources, services, and expertise that can help schools develop the capacity to change, the adoption of such programs can bring new demands, requirements, and costs that schools do not always have the capacity to meet. As a result, schools and improvement programs often have to figure out how to address a series of Catch-22s in order to make implementation successful.

- To select appropriate programs, schools have to have substantial knowledge of the programs' approaches and demands even before implementation begins.
- Implementing these programs often requires more time, resources, and flexibility than schools have readily available.
- And schools need to have a good understanding of their own approaches to learning and to school improvement in order to figure out how to integrate the improvement initiatives into their own work.

These issues can be addressed. But our conversations with a small number of principles, administrators, and improvement program staff members in the Bay Area district, as well as a review of the materials from 44 different improvement programs, provided a glimpse of the complexity of the problems.[5]

KNOWLEDGE FOR IMPROVEMENT

Without adequate knowledge of the approaches, requirements, resources, and expected outcomes of improvement programs, schools cannot make a wise choice about which ones are likely to meet their needs. Yet, given the time and resources that schools have available, it can be very difficult for schools to develop sufficient knowledge about different approaches before they make that choice.[6] As an elementary school principal described it, "A lot of times you just have to go on faith. You don't know exactly how it's going to work. So, in one case, when the opportunity came up in the district—'Hey, who wants to be a professional development school?' and 'This is vaguely the concept of it...'—I said, 'Hey, that's an opportunity that's not going to take a lot of paperwork,' so we went."

The problem of developing adequate knowledge about a program in order to determine whether or not it fits a school's needs is compounded by the fact that the more unusual and unconventional an approach, the harder it is to learn about it and the longer such learning will take. In fact, if members of a school community have relatively little knowledge about an approach, they may have considerable difficulty recognizing its value in the first place, and they may not be interested in learning more about it.[7] As a result, schools that truly want to change their curriculum or make comprehensive changes—not just minor modifications—have to make a substantial investment up front in exploring different improvement programs and building their knowledge about them.

In recognition of the importance of this preparation, many improvement programs try to ensure that schools are "ready" by requiring them to participate in exploration processes in which they study the philosophy and approach of the improvement program, to agree to a "memorandum of understanding," or to produce a school portfolio or other form of application. Such processes do have the potential to enable schools to develop some of the knowledge and commitment needed for successful implementation, but they can also take considerable time and effort with no guarantee of success. As one high school principal pointed out, her faculty has drafted their commitments for a Memorandum of Understanding with one organization five different times, but it has yet to be accepted. The principal of an elementary school finally gave up trying to work with an improvement program after her school portfolio failed to meet the appropriate criteria twice. "I can't afford to work on a portfolio that meets all the criteria and hire someone to do that when we can't teach our kids to read," she explained.

Furthermore, almost all exploration processes end with a vote in which the teachers, school staff members, or members of the larger school community are given a chance to decide whether or not to move ahead with the implementation of the program. But these "buy-in" votes are often little more than perfunctory exercises that can easily be manipulated by principals or other powerful members of the school community. As an elementary principal said, "You work with the school leadership and get their buy-in, and the rest of them will more or less come along." Thus, rather than demonstrate whether or not a school actually has learned enough about a program to make an informed choice, these votes may simply reflect the effectiveness of the campaign to support the program.

Adding to the complications, the more time and money a school invests in exploring one program, the less time and money it has to invest in examining alternative approaches and the more difficult it may be to choose *not* to pursue that approach. If a school abandons an approach, it will have spent considerable time and money but may be no closer to making significant changes. Given the considerable pressures many schools face to produce improvements in student performance in short periods of time, saying "no" may cost too much.

Under these conditions, both schools and improvement programs have to balance the time and money they have available for exploration with the depth of the knowledge needed to make implementation work. Too little time and money, and schools could adopt a program that will cost them far more than they bargained for and will end up contributing more to overload and fragmentation than to in-

creased performance. Too much time and money, and a school may not be able to afford the initial commitment.

As a result, for the implementation of improvement programs to work on a larger scale, many improvement programs—and their funders—have to recognize that their own success may rest as much on a school's capacity to select *other* programs as it does on the number of schools that adopt their program. If schools do not understand their options, they are more likely to base their selections on superficial features and factors such as availability, accessibility, and ease of use without developing the knowledge they need to implement the programs effectively. For their part, districts have to allow schools to spend the necessary time involved in exploring the options, and they have to be willing and able to support the many different plans and choices that may emerge, even if those choices do not match the districts' own beliefs about which ones will be successful.

THE TIME AND RESOURCES FOR IMPROVEMENT

Many initiatives, particularly in the early stages of implementation, involve far more time, effort, and resources than some schools have readily available.[8] For example, the principal of a middle school involved with two improvement programs explained that she has to consider carefully whether the school has the capacity to begin another partnership with a local technology company. "We want to be known as having the best technology and the best training in the district," the principal told us. "Having the computer company come in will keep us on that path." The company is offering $100,000 of equipment (including 60 computers), Internet access, and training that could be central to the schools' improvement efforts, but to take advantage of those resources the school has to have a "critical mass" of teachers willing to commit to 30 hours of training and to developing curriculum for the new technology. "So it looks like this wonderful gift," the principal explained. "But is it going to be more work than the gift is worth? A hundred thousand dollars would be nice, but we may not be able to handle the commitment."

Every time they consider a new initiative, principals and schools have to wrestle with this trade-off between the possible benefits of the resources, expertise, and positive publicity that can come from working with the improvement program and the possible costs in terms of time and commitments. Right now, the associate superintendent explained, some schools in the Bay Area district are caught in a double bind because they cannot afford to take on the extra work required in order to get the additional money and resources they need. "Principals need the money so they can hire people on their staff to do things," he told us. "The difference is now, unlike five or six years ago, they can't use the money to pay teachers in the afternoon to do teaming and to do professional development activities, because the teachers don't have time. They're too burned out trying to keep on top of what they're expected to do." One principal put it even more simply: "It reaches a point where it doesn't make any difference how much money there is. You don't have any more time and energy."

When schools do decide to commit to initiatives, they often have to expend considerable effort to try to "negotiate down" the demands and requirements of their partners in order to make the programs "doable." The principal of a middle school involved in a partnership with a local university had to tell staff members of that partnership that she could not adopt the governance structure that was central to their approach. "I told them, 'I can't do it. I've got a governance structure that I have to design for another program, a governance structure for the school, and a governance structure for the federal magnet program. I'm not going to do that. You want too much blood from us for this reform effort.'"

Even though many improvement programs try to make explicit the requirements and costs of implementation and to discourage schools from adopting them if they cannot meet these expectations, a close reading of the programs' introductory materials suggests that numerous requirements of successful implementation are either left implicit or left to schools to address largely on their own. In many cases, the programs stress that schools need to have in place many of the "baseline conditions" that are often cited as critical for successful implementation—such as the support and commitment of school staff, school leadership, and parents. Yet many programs themselves do not have the capacity to ensure that these conditions can be met. Even comprehensive, "whole-school" programs, such as the school designs supported by New American Schools, can be undermined if these conditions are not addressed, and few can provide the resources, services, and expertise to address all of these conditions equally effectively.

Finally, implementing an improvement program may involve a variety of hidden costs that come simply with the passage of time and the inevitable changes in funding, personnel, policies, and economics. Most obviously, schools that get grants to implement programs often have to expend considerable time and effort to raise more funds even before they can demonstrate the expected improvements. These kinds of concerns contributed to the principal's difficulty in deciding whether her middle school should participate in the new technology partnership. "What happens if they come in and work with us for a year," she wonders, "and put all those computers in? Can it be sustained after that year, or is it going to drain all of our funds to maintain the technology?"

Changes in the offerings and strategies of improvement programs can also wreak havoc on a school's efforts to implement and integrate initiatives. Although these changes often reflect the programs' efforts to increase their effectiveness, they may create confusion at the school level. For example, one high school had to deal with the fact that two of the improvement programs it was working with began to

emphasize the need to address equity issues in order to improve student achievement. From the programs' perspective, this new emphasis was a response to what was being learned in the partner schools about how to make implementation successful. But from the school's perspective, the new emphasis brought new demands that diverted attention from ongoing efforts instead of deepening them. "We've gotten mixed messages," the principal complained. "The initial idea of working on curriculum and student achievement and best teaching practices is now changed. On the larger scale it's just shifting people's focus, and it's confusing."

The hidden costs related to the staff turnover that takes place very year in many schools can also take their toll on efforts to sustain and deepen the implementation of any improvement program. Schools with substantial turnover run the risk of finding themselves constantly stuck in what amounts to the first year of implementation—having to rebuild commitment to the program, retrain teachers, and familiarize students with the relevant approaches before the available funding runs out. As a result, the more innovative and comprehensive that programs are, and the more initiatives a school has under way, the more difficult it may be to bring students and teachers "up to speed."

Teacher turnover at the high school struggling with competing program demands for equity has been particularly problematic. During a four-year period, 56 new staff members had to be hired, with almost one-quarter of the staff turning over every year. That means that a significant percentage of staff members each year are in what the principal calls the "survival mode" of the first two or three years of teaching. Many of these teachers do not stay long enough to become meaningfully involved in the improvement initiatives or in the long-term development of the school. With a district demand to reduce class sizes in math to a 20–1 student/teacher ratio (which has increased the need for new staff members) and as few as two days a year allotted by the state for staff development, it is not hard to understand why the school needs the money that comes with BASRC and other partnerships in order to pay teachers to participate in staff development activities in the summer or after school during the year.

Like toys and furniture that come stamped "Some assembly required," improvement programs almost always involve more work than seems evident at first glance. But it may be unreasonable to expect improvement programs to account for every cost or anticipate every requirement that schools have to meet to be successful. Furthermore, improvement programs have to deal with the problem that, if they describe too many of the costs, requirements, and inevitable challenges, they might discourage schools from taking advantage of the resources and expertise the programs can provide. In fact, those programs that are less explicit about their demands may be more attractive to schools. This problem is compounded by the fact that many improvement programs are under significant financial pressures, and few have substantial long-term funding. Those that have established workable financial models have to carefully match their level of service and of staffing to the number of schools with which staff work. Thus, while programs can be more explicit about what it really takes to make improvements, district administrators, policy makers, funders, and others also have to develop a more realistic understanding of the costs involved and of how long meaningful improvements can take.

THEORIES OF LEARNING, SCHOOLING, AND CHANGE

Every school improvement program reflects beliefs and assumptions about how students learn, how schools should be run, and how change takes place. These beliefs and assumptions are expressed in program descriptions and presentations, in the design of resources and strategies (curriculum requirements, strategic plans, professional development offerings), and in the activities and behaviors of staff members. Taken together, these beliefs and assumptions constitute a program's or organization's "theories of action"—implicit and explicit understanding of how a school or program can accomplish its goals.[9]

In order to develop the kind of focused, integrated approach that both school personnel and improvement programs see as essential to success, schools need to have a good understanding of both their own theories of action and those of the improvement programs that they choose to implement. If they do not, conflicts are an almost inevitable result. Furthermore, it can be very difficult to figure out how different initiatives and programs can fit together in mutually reinforcing ways.[10] Unfortunately, while many schools have goals, mission statements, and strategic plans, few have clearly articulated or well-examined theories of action. Similarly, although some improvement programs have tried to articulate their own theories of action, many of their beliefs and assumptions remain implicit.

Theories of learning are perhaps the best-articulated aspects of schools' and programs' approaches. Theories of learning encompass the assumptions and beliefs about how children develop, what they should be learning, and what kinds of outcomes they need to achieve. If initiatives within a school reflect substantially different theories of learning, controversy is a frequent result.[11] Consequently, some improvement programs (particularly those that are on one side or the other of debates over "progressive" or "basic-skills" approaches to learning and teaching) warn schools not to adopt their model if they prefer a different approach. At the same time, school members need to have a shared understanding of their own theories of learning in order to make that kind of decision.

While conflicts among people and initiatives with different theories of learning are well known, differences in *theories of schooling* can also be problematic. Theories of schooling reflect assumptions and beliefs about how schools should be organized and who—parents, teachers,

administrators, educational experts, students, or some combination—can make the most effective decisions about how to educate students. Thus a high school can be pushed in different directions by such programs as the Coalition of Essential Schools and the Bay Area School Reform Collaborative, which give schools considerable flexibility in how they organize themselves and design their curricula, and those such as Joint Venture Silicon Valley, which may have more requirements or ask principals or school leaders to act in a more hierarchical fashion. At the same time, schools that are used to operating in a more conventional, hierarchical way may find programs that ask teachers and community members to take on more decision-making responsibility to be too vague, or they may be uncomfortable with the amount of time that needs to be devoted to planning and developing curricula.[12] Ultimately, if a school undertakes initiatives with conflicting theories of schooling, the result is likely to be confusion about who is in charge and how much the ideas of teachers, parents, students, and community members are valued.

Intertwined with theories of learning and theories of school are *theories of change*: the beliefs and assumptions about how innovation and improvement can take place. In particular, different initiatives within a school may reflect different views about the key problems that need to be addressed and the mechanisms and strategies that will make improvements possible. In many cases, schools may have to deal with multiple types of assessments, each reflecting a particular theory of change. For example, some schools in the Bay Area district are evaluated by the "review of progress" that the Bay Area School Reform Collaborative uses as a focus for reflection and a guide to the refinement of improvement strategies. They also have to use performance assessments, which Joint Venture Silicon Valley views as crucial to the collection of appropriate data on student learning. And they are required to administer the SAT 9, which the state uses as a critical lever to motivate schools to improve.

In many ways, theories of change may be the most problematic aspects of schools' and programs' theories of action. For one thing, it may be much more difficult to coordinate theories of change than to identify and employ improvement programs and other initiatives with compatible theories of learning. Even implementing improvement programs and initiatives with *similar* theories of change can be extremely difficult. In particular, many improvement programs and district and state initiatives assume that changes in classroom practice can be made most effectively by providing teachers with new resources and professional development experiences; yet, as the principals at many schools point out, teachers barely have enough time to take advantage of the offerings of a single new initiative, let alone several.

At the same time, if school staffs negotiate the demands of a program or initiative down into something "doable," they may also be dismantling the initiative's theory of change. For example, the theory of change of the Joint Venture Silicon Valley initiatives suggested that improvements in student performance depended on involving *all* teachers in the development of integrated curricula that focused on either science, language arts, or math. However, several of the schools in the Bay Area district implemented the JVSV program solely in their science classes. While the schools may have made this choice largely on practical grounds—not enough time or training for everyone, for example—they effectively rejected the JVSV theory of change. In such cases, the question becomes, What (and whose) theory of action is guiding the initiative?

In short, both schools and improvement programs may benefit from paying more attention to their theories of action, particularly their theories of change. But doing so will bring new challenges. While leaving these theories implicit can contribute to conflicts in philosophy and practice, making them explicit also creates the real possibility of polarizing those with different views and creating further fragmentation and incoherence. Leaving theories ambiguous, like the broad language of a diplomatic agreement, can make it easier for those with different views to believe that they share common ground and to support and rally behind the same improvement effort. Correspondingly, the need for schools to serve the interests of all their parents and students and the need for improvement programs to work with a range of schools and communities may also encourage them to craft their theories to appeal to the widest possible audience.

BACK TO BASIC QUESTIONS

Despite the challenges outlined in this article, some schools can select, implement, and even integrate improvement programs in effective reform efforts. Some schools do have the capacity to change and others manage to acquire it with the help of charismatic principals, superhuman efforts from teachers, or exceptionally strong leadership and support from the community. Furthermore, improvement programs and many district administrators are striving to make it easier for schools to get the information and support they need to implement those programs and to coordinate them with other initiatives. To make the adoption of these improvement programs successful in a larger number of schools and a part of a large-scale strategy of school reform, however, much more needs to be done. Creating exploration and selection processes that build the knowledge and expertise of school communities, developing more realistic approaches to the costs and requirements of effective implementation, and making the theories of action of both improvement programs and schools more explicit may all be steps in that direction.

At the same time, the experiences of the Bay Area district and the analysis of the approaches of many different improvement programs suggest that it is unrealistic to expect improvement programs—whatever their focus—to provide schools with everything they need to change. These pro-

grams can, under the right conditions, help schools to change, but implementing them cannot solve the problem that, for many schools, the local conditions are not right. Under these circumstances, it is not surprising that schools have difficulty meeting the demands and requirements of so many initiatives from so many different quarters, nor is it hard to understand why so many improvement programs have trouble "scaling up."

From this perspective, improvement has to begin with efforts to enable school communities to develop and exercise the knowledge, theories, and flexibility they need to implement improvement programs or to develop their own approaches to improving their schools. Establishing such local capacity may depend on figuring out how, within the time and resources that can reasonably be expected to be available, schools can develop theories of action that take into account—not ignore—the many different, and legitimate, perspectives about how learning can take place, schools can be run, and change can occur. As Michael Fullan puts it, "School systems need integration, wholeness, and at least periods of coherence. The paradox is that greater coherence in complex societies can only be achieved by grappling with differences and combining strategies that have hitherto been pursued independently from each other."[13]

In this view, a variety of theories of action will always be at work in schools, and those theories will be evolving and changing. Schools do not have to develop a single theory of action and make sure that all their initiatives reflect it, but there is no substitute for articulating and examining the theories of action at work in their own initiatives and in those of the programs they seek to adopt. In Fullan's terms, these steps will help schools to become "selectively innovative," identifying and taking advantage of whatever people, programs, and resources they need to build their capacity and improve their performance.

In a final paradox, however, while strong leadership and community support are key "baseline" conditions for successful implementation, the demands and requirements of improvement programs may undermine the very authority the school community needs to adapt and integrate programs and initiatives and to articulate its own theories of action. Thus schools may choose among different improvement programs, but, whatever program they choose, they have to implement it in ways that are consistent with the philosophy and goals of the program or risk losing its support.[14] Similarly, while building support among school leaders and among parents and community members is one thing, enabling the school community to develop the capacity to craft and examine its own theories of action and sustain its own approach to improvement is another. Ironically, the true measure of whether a school has the capacity to take advantage of an improvement program may be whether the school community has the power to say "no" and the knowledge, flexibility, and theories to pursue another approach.

If we accept the idea that school communities and improvement programs should be able to pursue theories of action that are truly different, then we have to come to terms with the fact that no single strategy for large-scale education reform or single set of measures will support each one of these approaches equally. Some schools may choose to adopt the theories of action of an improvement program whose approach is relatively consistent with predominant policies, standards, and assessments, and these schools may benefit from detailed materials and plans that can be scaled up across many different contexts and communities. But some schools may choose to work with the theories of action of improvement programs that depart significantly from current policies and assessment practices, and these schools may benefit more from relief from district and state requirements and opportunities to affiliate with like-minded schools. Still other schools may develop their own theories of action, and these schools may benefit from conditions and policies that enable them to exercise their authority and that ensure that resources and services—whether they come from districts, improvement programs, or other sources—conform to their demands. All will benefit from the opportunity to use meaningful—and multiple—measures of progress and performance that are consistent with the theories behind their approaches.[15]

In the end, the education system can be viewed as a mechanical system in which policies and practices can be aligned to produce a narrow set of outcomes. This view may be particularly appropriate in contexts where the beliefs and expectations of school communities, the initiatives they undertake, and the beliefs and expectations reflected in state standards and accountability systems are all consistent. It can also be useful to view the education system as a democratic political system in which diverse interests are constantly expressed. From this standpoint, establishing processes that schools can use to examine and negotiate diverse interests seems particularly important.

But it may also be useful to view schools as part of an ecosystem in which many different entities are trying to coexist.[16] Viewed in this way, the initiatives of improvement programs, districts, and states cannot be considered as the "start" of change efforts. Changes are constantly under way. In this context, new initiatives, whether from the district, the state, improvement programs, or others, have to be carefully examined in the same way that we have to consider how new species and new developments will affect the ecosystems into which they are introduced. Is there sufficient capacity to absorb and carry out the new initiatives? Do they extend and deepen efforts already at work? Are there high demands and hidden costs that can contribute to harmful, not just beneficial, effects? In ecosystems vastly different approaches can be accommodated, but they cannot be pursued independently. Learning to deal with forces far beyond human control and becoming more aware of the interaction among the many initiatives and programs currently at work in schools may be more than a step in the right direction; it may be part of a movement that embraces the complexity of schooling and the diversity of approaches to it.

Notes

1. David Tyack, *The One Best System: A History of American Urban Education* (Cambridge, Mass.: Harvard University Press, 1974).
2. Anthony S. Bryk et al., *Charting Chicago School Reform: Democratic Localism as a Lever for Change* (Boulder, Colo.: Westview Press, 1998); Joseph P. McDonald, "When Outsiders Try to Change Schools from the Inside," *Phi Delta Kappan*, November 1989, pp. 206–12; and Olatokunbo S. Fashola and Robert E. Slavin, "Schoolwide Reform Models: What Works?," *Phi Delta Kappan*, January 1998, pp. 370–79.
3. Bryk et al., op.cit.; *CSRD in the Field: Fall 1999 Update* (Washington, D.C.: U.S. Department of Education, 1999); Chester E. Finn, Jr., "The Politics of Change," in Diane Ravitch and Joseph Viteritti, eds., *New Schools for a New Century: The Redesign of Urban Education* (New Haven, Conn.: Yale University Press, 1997), pp. 226–50; Michael Fullan, *Change Forces: The Sequel* (London: Falmer Press, 1999); Thomas R. Guskey, "Integrating Innovations," *Educational Leadership*, February 1990, pp. 11–15; Frederick M. Hess, *Spinning Wheels: The Politics of Urban School Reform* (Washington, D.C.: Brookings Institution, 1999); and Paul T. Hill, Lawrence C. Pierce, and James W. Guthrie, *Reinventing Public Education: How Contracting Can Transform America's Schools* (Chicago: University of Chicago Press, 1997).
4. Hess, op. cit.; and Frederick M. Wirt and Michael W. Kirst, *The Politics of Education: Schools in Conflict* (Berkeley, Calif.: McCutchan, 1989).
5. It is worth keeping in mind that the programs reviewed for this study differ substantially in the demands they place on schools and how much capacity a school may need to carry them out. However, when these programs attempt to promote comprehensive changes or are used as a part of a comprehensive improvement, these issues of school capacity become particularly critical.
6. For discussions of the importance and difficulty of selecting programs that fit the needs and interests of schools, see Samuel Stringfield, Steven Ross, and Lana Smith, *Bold Plans for School Restructuring: The New American Schools Development Corporation Designs* (Mahwah, N.J.: Erlbaum, 1996); Susan Bodilly, *Lessons from New American Schools' Scale-Up Phase: Prospects for Bringing Designs to Multiple Schools* (Santa Monica, Calif.: RAND Corporation, 1998); Amanda Datnow, "Implementing an Externally Developed School Restructuring Design: Enablers, Constraints, and Tensions," paper presented at the annual meeting of the American Educational Research Association, San Diego, 1998; and Samuel Stringfield et al., "Scaling Up School Restructuring in Multicultural, Multilingual Contexts: Early Observations from Sunland Country," *Education and Urban Society*, vol. 30, 1998, pp. 326–57.
7. Wesley M. Cohen and Daniel A. Levinthal, "Absorptive Capacity: A New Perspective on Learning and Innovation," *Administrative Science Quarterly*, vol. 35, 1990, pp. 128–52; Raghu Garud, Praveen Rattan Nayyar, and Zur Baruch Shapira, eds., *Technological Innovation: Oversights and Foresights* (New York: Cambridge University Press, 1997); Thomas Hatch, "What Does It Take to Break the Mold? Rhetoric and Reality in New American Schools," *Teachers College Record*, vol. 102, 2000, pp. 561–89; Mariann Jelinek, "Organizational Entrepreneurship in Mature-Industry Firms: Foresight, Oversight, and Invisibility," in Garud, Nayyar, and Shapira, pp. 181–213; and James March, "Exploration and

Exploitation in Organizational Learning," *Organization Science*, vol. 2, 1991, pp. 71–87.

8. For an analysis of the financial costs of implementing the initiatives of one comprehensive reform program at a time, see Allan Odden, "The Costs of Sustaining Educational Change Through Comprehensive School Reform," *Phi Delta Kappan*, February 2000, pp. 433–38.

9. See, for example, Donald A. Schön and Joseph P. McDonald, *Doing What You Mean to Do in School Reform* (Providence, R.I.: Brown University, 1998); Carol H. Weiss, "Nothing as Practical as Good Theory," in James P. Connell et al., eds., *New Approaches to Evaluating Community Initiatives* (Aspen, Colo.: Aspen Institute, 1995), pp. 65–92; and Milbrey McLaughlin, "Supporting Teachers' Learning and Community: Theories of Action in Four Reform Movements," paper presented at the annual meeting of the American Educational Research Association, Chicago, 1997.

10. Bryk et al., op. cit.; Fullan, op. cit.; Thomas Hatch, "Differences in Theory That Matter in the Practice of School Improvement," *American Educational Research Journal*, vol. 35, 1998, pp. 3–32; and Joseph P. McDonald et al., *School Reform Behind the Scenes* (New York: Teachers College Press, 1999).

11. Liane Brouillette, *A Geology of School Reform: The Successive Restructurings of a School District* (Albany: State University of New York Press, 1996); Donna Muncey and Patrick McQuillan, "The Dangers of Assuming Consensus for Change," in G. Alfred Hess, Jr., ed., *Empowering Teachers and Parents: School Restructuring Through the Eyes of Anthropologists* (Westport, Conn.: Greenwood, 1992), pp. 47–69; and Diana Tittle, *Welcome to Heights High: The Crippling Politics of Restructuring America's Public Schools* (Columbus: Ohio State University Press, 1995).

12. Donna Muncey, Joyce Payne, and Noel White, "Making Curriculum and Instructional Reform Happen: A Case Study," *Peabody Journal of Education*, vol. 74, 1999, pp. 68–110; and John A. Nunnery et al., "Teachers' Initial Reaction to Their Pre-Implementation and Early Restructuring Experiences," *School Effectiveness and School Improvement*, vol. 8, 1997, pp. 72–94.

13. Fullan, op. cit.

14. Even many improvement programs that have relatively few constraints and requirements can choose to stop working with schools that they feel are not making enough progress or are not making an adequate effort to make changes that are consistent with their goals or philosophies.

15. For diverse perspectives on how schools should be run and how school change can take place, see *Governing America's Schools: Changing the Rules* (Denver, Colo.: Education Commission of the States, 1999); and Hill, Pierce, and Guthrie, op. cit.

16. For related discussions, see John I. Goodlad, *Educational Renewal: Better Teachers, Better Schools* (San Francisco: Jossey-Bass, 1994); and Guskey, op. cit.

THOMAS HATCH is a senior scholar at the Carnegie Foundation for the Advancement of Teaching, Menlo Park, Calif. He would like to thank Noel White, Shannon K'doah Range, Karen Herbert, Judy Baldwin, Ruby Kerawalla, Lee Shulman, John Barcroft, and Ann Lieberman for their assistance and support. He also acknowledges the support of the Carnegie Foundation for the Advancement of Teaching and the contributions and comments of his colleagues there. However, the conclusions expressed in this article are the author's own.

Article 5

A Special Section on

Personalized Instruction

In the final analysis, personalized instruction reflects deep concern for learners and the willingness to search for ways to adjust the teaching/learning environment to meet the learning needs of individual students, Mr. Keefe and Mr. Jenkins point out.

BY JAMES W. KEEFE AND JOHN M. JENKINS

KENNETH Sirotnik and John Goodlad caution us to think in terms of school "renewal" rather than "reform." Sirotnik tells us that reform is usually preoccupied with accountability rather than evaluation. Much high-stakes reform, for example, is aimed at rewarding or punishing schools and educators. Renewal, on the other hand, urges a new accountability that is more akin to "responsibility."[1] Goodlad points out:

> The language of reform carries with it the traditional connotations of things gone wrong that need to be corrected, as with delinquent boys or girls incarcerated in reform schools. This language is not uplifting. It says little or nothing about the nature of education, the self, or the human community.... School renewal is a much different game.... The language and the ethos of renewal have to do with the people in and around schools improving their practice and developing the collaborative mechanisms necessary to better their schools.[2]

Renewal is concerned primarily with what Seymour Sarason has called "creating new settings" that reflect critical inquiry about educational practice. Renewal is all about how a learner's growth in knowledge and self-awareness leads to wisdom, personal happiness, and collective responsibility. But only a minority of schools achieve such high levels of reflection. Most schools are average and are satisfied with maintaining or perhaps fine-tuning traditional patterns of school organization and pedagogy.

THE BASIC ELEMENTS OF PERSONALIZED INSTRUCTION

Personalization of instruction and learning is the effort on the part of a school to organize the learning environment to take into account individual student characteristics and needs and to make use of flexible instructional practices. Teachers committed to personalizing instruction help their students develop personal learning plans, assist in diagnosing their cognitive strengths and weaknesses, help adapt the learning environment and instruction to learner needs and interests, and mentor authentic and reflective learning experiences for their students.

In the past, personalization has been known under different names: nongraded education, continuous-progress education, individualized instruction, individually guided or prescribed education, and so forth. Each of these concepts is concerned with personalized education, but in a limited way. Personalization is broader in scope, more systematic in organization, and more authentic in its goals and strategies.

Several current systematic approaches to instructional improvement, such as instruction based on learning styles and differentiated instruction, do border on the truly personalized. The former typically draws on individualized instruction for its roots, and the latter tends to restrict itself to the individual classroom, but both can be highly personalized when implemented in a comprehensive, organic, and dynamic fashion.

What, then, are the basic elements of a personalized approach to instruction? If we consider the implications of historical efforts to renew schooling and take into account the most flexible of recent efforts to individualize learning, a direction begins to emerge. Linda Darling-Hammond has argued that we must put students first, that all children have a right to learn. She cites four factors that are important for powerful teaching and learning:

- structures for caring and structures for serious learning, structures that enable teachers to know students well and to work with them intensely;
- shared exhibitions of student work that make it clear what the school values and how students are doing;
- structures, such as teacher teams, that support teacher collaboration focused on student learning; and
- structures for shared decision making and dialogue about teaching and learning with other teachers, students, and parents.[3]

These structures are not a model to be imposed on schools but rather a broad blueprint for ongoing improvement in school organization and practice. With this important caveat in mind, we propose *six basic elements of personalized instruction* that should be present if a school wishes to develop powerful teaching and learning for student success. These elements or structures produce a challenging, integrative, but child-centered learning environment, one that is interactive and meaningful, but one that also features reasonably structured learning activities, flexible use of time and space, and authentic, performance-based assessment of student progress.

We think of these six basic elements as constituting the culture and context of personalized instruction. The cultural components—teacher role, student learning characteristics, and collegial relationships—establish the foundation of personalization and ensure that the school prizes a caring and collaborative environment, student diversity, and individual development. The contextual factors—interactivity, flexible scheduling, and authentic assessment—promote and support student engagement, thoughtful growth, and proficient performance.

DUAL TEACHER ROLE

The indispensable catalyst in the personalized instructional environment is the teacher, the instructional specialist closest to the learning situation who best understands the needs and interests of students as well as the policies of the school and the district. Personalized instruction demands that the teacher assume dual roles: teacher-coach and teacher-advisor. As a learning coach, the teacher collaborates with other teachers, with student peer tutors, and with community resource persons to guide student learning. As an advisor, the teacher provides advice,

counsel, and guidance to from 15 to 20 students on academic and school-adjustment issues.

Teacher-coach. Teacher-coaches offer the same kind of instruction, demonstration, practice, and feedback to their students as athletic coaches and student activity advisors have modeled in successful programs. The needs of today's students are quite different from those of their counterparts two or three generations ago. The world has experienced several social revolutions and a knowledge explosion that makes it almost impossible to "cover" more than a small part of what students need to know for a reasonably successful life. Cognitive and problem-solving skills—what some call metacognitive skills—are more important today than any particular piece of knowledge. The teacher-coach in the school environment must be a facilitator of learning, a guide who helps students find appropriate resources and engage in suitable learning activities.

Members of the Learning Environments Consortium International describe such a teacher as "not so much educational broadcaster as academic troubleshooter. He devotes fewer hours to lecturing in front of a class and more to working with students individually and in small groups."[4]

Teacher-advisor. Teacher-advisors are the first line of offense and defense in a school guidance program geared to student success. Advising is the other facet of the new job description for teachers. Teachers and other qualified adults join professional counselors in helping students plan and achieve appropriate career, personal, and social goals. Teachers, counselors, and other adults work as a team to promote students' adjustment to and success in school. Professional counselors serve as advisors to a group of teacher-advisors and help them to learn their role and its functions.

Over the years, advisement programs have gone under a variety of names, including expanded homeroom, advisory period, home base, advisory base, student assistance, teacher-advisor, advisor/advisee, and personal adult advocate. The programs have varied from place to place, but typically call for a teacher to assume guidance functions that are narrowly limited to planning academic programs, dispensing information about careers and colleges, addressing school adjustment issues, and offering personal/social guidance.

In middle schools, many advisor programs take on the character of group guidance, but these applications are usually limited in scope and often in success as well. The most successful advisement programs emphasize personal contact between students and advisors along with continuing support of the student in his or her academic program and personal adjustment to school. *Breaking Ranks*, a 1996 report from the National Association of Secondary School Principals (NASSP), specifically mentions the role of the "personal adult advocate" in helping the student personalize the education experience.

DIAGNOSIS OF STUDENT LEARNING CHARACTERISTICS

If the goal is to build a learning environment suited to the aptitudes, needs, and interests of each student, personalized instruction must begin with knowledge of the learner. The foundation of any personalized approach to instruction is some form of diagnosis—determining what are the learning-related characteristics of individual learners. Direct observation and various types of diagnostic assessments are among the principal tools available to teachers who view instruction as coaching, mentoring, facilitating, and advising. Diagnosis is concerned with discovering such student learning traits as developmental level, learning style, and learning history.

Developmental characteristics. Developmental characteristics are those specific stages in individual maturation when certain capacities for learned behavior appear (e.g., visual perception, language pronunciation, and cognitive thinking skills). Examining these characteristics of students can tell us *when* they are developmentally ready to learn something. They describe individual readiness for learning. Certain capabilities appear only after the appropriate stage in individual development occurs and need to be developed at that time. If teachers are to personalize student instruction, they must have a good understanding of learner developmental traits.

Darling-Hammond calls for "developmentally attentive schools," starting with the presumption that schools should be user friendly.[5] School organization and student work must build on developmental consideration. Learning activities should be based on student needs and legitimate interests rather than arbitrarily on generic curriculum guides or the contents of approved textbooks. Particularly in the lower grades, students need hands-on learning with active and concrete learning activities. Nor should developmental attentiveness end with primary schooling. Jomills Braddock and James McPartland argue that many problems that teenagers have in school are a result of the notable mismatch between their developmental needs and the learning environments of most junior and senior high schools.[6] When teenagers most need close relationships, they get large, impersonal schools. When they most need to experience increasing autonomy, they get rigid rules, curricular tracking, and large doses of memorization.

Student learning style. The second broadest diagnostic element is student learning style, which encompasses information-processing habits, attitudinal tendencies, and biologically based responses that are typical of the ways a given student learns and prefers to learn. There are three broad categories of learning style characteristics.

- *Cognitive styles* are preferred ways of perception, organization, and retention. For example, perceptual modality preferences—whether a student prefers visual, auditory, or psychomotor learning—are basic to cognitive style diagnosis.

- *Affective styles* include those dimensions of the learning personality that have to do with attention, emotion, and valuing. Each learner has a personal motivational approach.

- *Physiological styles* are individual traits deriving from a person's gender, health, nutrition, and reaction to the physical surroundings, such as preferences for levels of light, sound, and temperature in the learning environment.

Learning style is a gestalt that tells us *how* a student learns and prefers to learn. Learning styles can be measured by a variety of assessment techniques. The *Learning Style Profile,* for example, assesses 24 independent scales representing four factors: perceptual responses, cognitive styles, study preferences, and instructional preferences. Seven cognitive skills are profiled, including sequential and simultaneous processing skills. The *Learning Style Profile* and other comprehensive instruments help teachers identify students' strengths and weaknesses and organize instruction more efficiently and effectively. Learning style diagnosis is a key element in any attempt to make instruction more personalized.

Student learning history. "Student learning history" is a term coined by Benjamin Bloom and his colleagues in their mastery learning research to describe the aggregate of personal learning that each student brings to a particular course, class, or school program. A learner's history characterizes his or her instructional readiness or "entering behavior." Learning history is the third broad area of diagnosis. In fact, existing student knowledge, skills, and attitudes define the fertile ground for student success in subsequent learning.

Learning history tells us *what* a student knows and can do at a given point in his or her learning career. Diagnosis of learning history involves the determination of what has occurred as a basis for what should occur. Observation, surveys, inventories, and curriculum-referenced tests best assess these levels of knowledge or skill. Information about student learning history is also available to teachers in cumulative record folders, in teacher and counselor reports, and from student questionnaires, inventories, and various diagnostic tests.

CULTURE OF COLLEGIALITY

Another essential ingredient of personalized instruction is a school culture of collaboration, in which teachers and students work together in a cooperative social environment to develop meaningful learning activities for all students. Choice theory proposes that all behavior is an attempt to satisfy basic needs that are hardwired into us. We always choose to do what best satisfies our needs.

William Glasser, the originator of choice theory, tells us that "if what is being taught does not satisfy the needs about which a student is currently most concerned, it will make little difference how brilliantly the teacher teaches—the student will not work to learn.… Teachers are well aware that hungry students think of food, lonely students look for friends, and powerless students seek attention far more than they look for knowledge."[7] A constructivist environment and collaborative learning arrangements characterize a collegial culture.

Constructivist environment. Many educators today have adopted a constructivist view of learning. Constructivism holds that individual learners construct knowledge by giving meaning to their current experiences in light of their prior knowledge. Time and opportunity for reflective dialogue are critical elements of such a learning environment. Constructivist teachers build instruction on student learning styles and skills, and they encourage students to seek out personal knowledge of a topic. Students work with their teacher-coaches to improve their cognitive skills and to expand their current experience through reflection, seminars, and long-term projects. Constructivist teachers look for opportunities to encourage reflection, problem solving, and initiative.

Collaborative learning arrangements. The task of personalized instruction is to create learning communities in which students can confront important ideas and apply their learning to real-world experiences that they can understand and use. Collaborative learning arrangements provide an opportunity for students and teachers to work together to talk about their ideas and to sharpen their thinking. Considerable evidence exists, for example, that students learn better in cooperative groups than when alone.[8] Small cooperative groups encourage collaboration and better socialization than traditional classrooms, yet produce solid achievement gains.

Glasser believes that small learning teams offer a good chance of motivating almost all students, for several reasons. Students gain a sense of belonging by working in teams of two to five, and a sense of belonging provides the initial motivator for students to do the work. As they achieve some success, the students will want to work even harder. Stronger students, Glasser argues, find it need-fulfilling to help weaker students, and weaker students fine it need-fulfilling to contribute to the team effort. Students learn to depend not only on the teacher but on their teammates and on their own creativity. Collaborative learning arrangements are necessary for a personalized learning environment because they promote interaction, dialogue, and thoughtful reflection.

INTERACTIVE LEARNING ENVIRONMENTS

Interactive learning environments are designed to foster collaborative learning and reflective conversation. Recent studies have found that high schools which are restructured to provide interactive learning arrangements produce higher achievement gains that are also more equitably distributed among socioeconomic subgroups.[9] These studies found that collective responsibility for student learning, an academic emphasis, and high morale are important features of a good school learning community. Successful practices included school-within-school units, interdisciplinary teaching teams, and common planning time for teachers. Interactive learning environments are characterized by small school or group size, by thoughtful classrooms, by active learning experiences, and by authentic student achievement. Let us explore these characteristics.

School or group size. Darling-Hammond has reported that more than 30 years of studies on school organization "have consistently found that small schools (with enrollments of roughly 300 to 600) promote higher student achievement, higher attendance, lower dropout rates, greater participation in school activities, more positive feelings toward self and school, more positive behavior, less violence and vandalism and greater post-school success." These outcomes, she continues, "are also found in settings where students have close sustained relationships with a smaller than average number of teachers throughout their school careers."[10] The 1996 NASSP report *Breaking Ranks* also recommended that high schools not exceed 600 students.

Unfortunately, earlier studies of class size were inconclusive or at best debatable. Smaller class size is invariably the better choice when the group is 20 or smaller, but in the range from 20 to 40 students, class size makes little or no difference.[11] Class size studies are difficult to conduct because so many other socioeconomic, organizational, and instructional variables can intervene. The issue becomes moot, however, when one approaches the issue of class or group size from the learner's point of view. The question then is, How do we best meet the learner's needs? What kind of grouping (large, medium, or small) best serves the target content or the activity? A choir or a band usually benefits from being larger. Skill learning, discussion, and reflective conversation demand small groups. Research and reading are often best done alone. The size of the group should be a function of its purpose. Having said this, however, we should reiterate that most school-based learning benefits from smaller groups because they encourage collaboration, interaction, and shared satisfaction.

Thoughtful environments. Smaller schools and smaller groups can better support thoughtful conversation, learning by doing, apprenticeship experiences, and authentic student achievement. Francis Schrag has argued for more "thoughtfulness" in classrooms.[12] And researchers at the National Center on Effective Secondary Schools at the University of Wisconsin developed a set of rating scales for "thoughtful lessons" in social studies based on Schrag's conception of good thinking. The University of Wisconsin research found that social studies classes in 16 schools showed more thoughtfulness when school principals and department chairs promoted thinking as a central goal.[13]

Instruction is thoughtful when it focuses on a few important topics with coherence and continuity, provides plenty of time for investigation and interactive dialogue, raises challenging issues that require students to produce new knowledge, and stresses the quality of supporting explanations and reasons over the need for "right" answers. Barry Beyer argues that at least four elements must be present for a thoughtful learning environment:

- a classroom layout that invites thinking—not in traditional rows, but students facing each other in groups, working in learning centers or in meaningful clusters;
- classroom interactions that involve information processing, rather than information receiving or repeating—posing and solving problems, seeking out evidence, and judging the quality of supporting reasons;
- the use of precise, thoughtful language rather than vague terminology or generalizations—hypothesizing, sifting evidence, questioning inferences and assumptions, making predictions, drawing conclusions; and
- the organization of classroom study and courses around thoughtful questions—inquiry built on questions of real interest to students themselves.[14]

Active learning experiences. Susan Kovalik and Karen Olsen contend that prior learning experiences are critical to the success of active forms of learning.[15] The human brain continuously searches for patterns in incoming information as it attempts to find meaning in the data. The more active the learning experience, the more likely that the input will be rich in meaning. Kovalik and Olsen suggest two rules of thumb for enhancing learning:

- Provide real-life richness and context in all learning situations. The less the input, the harder the learner will struggle to find meaning.
- Curriculum and instruction must try to use all of a learner's prior experience and to maximize the amount of sensory input during learning. Human learning is rarely linear or neat or orderly or typically logical, but rather multilinear, multisensory, and seemingly illogical until the learner perceives clear patterns in the information that are personally meaningful.

At Central Park East Secondary School in New York City, all classes are organized in seminar style. The objective is to encourage a more active and interactive learning environment. Central Park East students spend their classroom time "building replicas, writing books, tran-scribing interviews, constructing mathematical models, creating dramas, developing photos, writing lab reports, or debating a class decision." In the field, they spend their time "collecting samples, interviewing contacts, sketching and drawing, looking for tracks, measuring, recording, searching, or just asking why. The point is that they are 'learning through doing, through genuine experience.'"[16] Teachers who are concerned about personalizing the learning process believe in teaching through genuine experiences and thoughtful reflection.

Authentic student achievement. Instruction is authentic when it focuses on the kind of mastery found in successful adults, and personalized instruction must be authentic. Authentic human achievement is concerned with what is significant, worthwhile, and meaningful in the lives of successful adults from all walks of life—from artists and electricians to laborers and scientists. Authentic academic achievement, then, must be concerned with accomplishments that are significant, worthwhile, and meaningful for learners preparing for adulthood.[17]

Fred Newmann, Walter Secada, and Gary Wehlage, researchers at the Center on Organization and Restructuring of Schools at the University of Wisconsin, Madison, devoted five years of research to the formulation and study of criteria and standards for authentic academic achievement, authentic instruction, authentic assessment tasks, and authentic performance.[18] They characterized authentic academic achievement in terms of three criteria: 1) construction (not production) of knowledge, 2) disciplined inquiry (mastery of a field), and 3) value beyond school.

Human cognition is complex, but the need for "authenticity" in learning is straightforward. All learners need to feel competent and capable if they are to understand and accomplish real-world tasks. Newmann, Secada, and Wehlage argue that "the kind of mastery required for students to earn school credits, grades, and high scores on tests is often considered trivial, contrived, and meaningless—by both students and adults. This absence of meaning breeds low engagement in schoolwork and inhibits transfer of school learning to issues and problems faced outside the school."[19] Engagement is the key word here. Without engagement, much of schooling is meaningless and unproductive. It is difficult to envision a personalized instructional environment without authenticity.

FLEXIBLE SCHEDULING AND PACING

The schedule of a school makes the educational philosophy of the school evident and visible. If the philosophy is traditional, the schedule is likely to be very structured, even rigid. If the philosophy is constructivist or learner-centered, the schedule will almost necessarily be personalized or at lease very flexible.

Two ingredients seem necessary to the development of a more personalized school schedule for students. First, both students and teachers need to have input into the way time is used. Teachers can accomplish this by making requests through team leaders, department chairs, or other representatives. This information can then be communicated to teacher-advisors, who meet with individual students to guide their scheduling decisions and to monitor their progress. Obviously, state and local mandates must be acknowledged, but waiver processes now in effect in most states permit some latitude in redefining credits and time. Second, achievement should be judged on the basis of performance. Placing the emphasis on performance rather than time increases opportunities for students to make choices in curriculum and instruction. (See the discussion of authentic assessment below for more on performance-based assessment.)

In *Horace's School: Redesigning the American High School*, Theodore Sizer proposes a sample high school schedule designed to tailor school practices to the needs of every group of adolescents.[20] The first, third, and sixth periods are 105 minutes each; the third, fourth, and fifth periods share two hours for lunch, advisories, and tutorials by the teaching team. Team members decide on group and individual activities, and advisors schedule tutorials for individual students. Between the first long period and the second, there is a 10-minute passing period; between all the others, there is just five minutes. Subjects are scheduled on a four-day rotation to provide opportunities for teachers and students to meet at different times of the day.

The longer periods in this version of a block schedule permit students to take part in community service and other extended experiences. Teachers have time to plan with colleagues; to serve as advisors to a prescribed number of students; to work on curriculum, instruction, and assessment; and to contact parents. That the schedule accommodates these priories shows the relationship of scheduling to the purposes of the school.

AUTHENTIC ASSESSMENT

Authentic assessment is the sixth defining element of personalized instruction. Assessment is the process of gathering information about students. The improvement of student learning, not sorting or grading, should be the primary purpose of assessment. Assessment is authentic when it focuses on real performance and mastery of a field of knowledge. The words assessment and testing are often used interchangeably. Tests, however, are only one form of assessment. Assessment goes beyond testing and includes such activities as demonstrations, oral and written presentations, performances, contests, projects, and problem-solving activities. Athletic competitions are assessments of how well a team or an individual has prepared for a contest. Similarly, a dramatic performance is an assessment of the cast's talents and readiness. The response of the audience is one measure of the quality of the performance.

In all cases, the method of assessment should fit the purpose of instruction. If students are expected to learn to write well, the competency can hardly be measured by multiple-choice questions about grammar. Having students actually write or develop responses to open-ended questions seems a more suitable assessment device. Even better is to give them time to write and then revise their writing. The various types of authentic assessment can be grouped under the headings of naturalistic assessment, performance assessment, and portfolio assessment.[21]

Naturalistic assessment is the kind of appraisal that takes place during normal learning activities. Naturalistic assessment involves the teacher as a "participant observer," a technique long used in anthropology. The teacher systematically collects information about students and records it for later analysis and summation.

Performance assessment is an umbrella term that refers to evaluating what students can do by watching them in the process of demonstrating some skill or performing a specified task or by examining a product that students construct and develop in response to a set of directions.[22] The object of this kind of assessment is a student performance or a student-developed product. Performance assessment can be used in such diverse activities as conducting a science experiment, using or programming a computer, debating, manufacturing or repairing an object, playing a musical instrument, speaking a foreign language, and writing a script or story. The merit badge system used in scouting is a form of performance assessment. Some educators call the more formal versions of these performance assessments "exhibitions," which are comprehensive demonstrations that enable students to present their academic efforts for review and discussion and to certify their competencies in specific areas.

Portfolio assessment involves both students as compilers and teachers as supervisors. Students collect and select pieces of their own work over a period of time as evidence that they have met their learning objectives. Usually, students also write a rationale explaining why they think the selected pieces are their best work. Portfolio assessment has its origin in the practices of artists, architects, and designers who assemble key examples of their work for prospective employers.

THE BIG PICTURE

George Wood characterizes the quintessential personalized instructional environment in his description of the learning community at Hubbard Woods Elementary School in Winnetka, Illinois. Wood writes:

> "A community of learners." This is the watchword of the Winnetka school district. It graces the cover of the most recent district curriculum report, appears frequently in newsletters home, and is often referred to by the staff as a guiding

principle. It is not mere rhetoric. The notion of the school as a learning community directs virtually all aspects of the school—from the length of the school day, to teaching, to staff relations, to the very layout of the buildings....

Most tasks are taken on collaboratively, with students working in teams to solve problems, create large-scale displays, or write plays, for example. Much of this is possible because the curriculum is geared to the developmental needs of children.

Rather than workbooks and worksheets, which require only the ability to manipulate a pencil and to copy, most classroom tasks involve a hands-on experience. Math games, tools for measuring or counting, costumes for plays, plants and animals all fill the rooms so that students can touch, feel, and experiment as they learn. Such learning does not require that students memorize "correct" answers, compiling enough of them to earn a grade; in fact, letter grades are not given. Rather, students learn through collaboration how to help one another find out, how to ask good questions, in short, how to learn. The notion of competitiveness on abstract tasks only hinders learning, and so these teachers break away from that orientation.[23]

In the final analysis, personalized instruction reflects deep concern for learners and the willingness to search for ways to adjust the teaching/learning environment to meet the learning needs of individual students.

Notes

1. Kenneth A. Sirotnik, "Making Sense of Educational Renewal," *Phi Delta Kappan*, April 1999, pp. 606–10.

2. John I. Goodlad, "Flow, Eros, and Ethos in Educational Renewal," *Phi Delta Kappan*, April 1999, pp. 574–75.

3. Linda Darling-Hammond, "The Right to Learn and the Advancement of Teaching: Research, Policy, and Practice for Democratic Education," *Educational Researcher*, August/September 1996, pp. 5–17; and idem, *The Right to Learn: A Blueprint for Creating Schools That Work* (San Francisco: Jossey-Bass, 1997).

4. William D. Georgiades et al., *Take Five: A Methodology for the Humane School* (Los Angeles: Parker and Son, 1979), p. 43.

5. Darling-Hammond, *The Right to Learn*.

6. Jomills H. Braddock and James M. McPartland, "The Education of Early Adolescents," in Linda Darling-Hammond, ed., *Review of Research in Education*, vol. 19 (Washington, D.C.: American Educational Research Association, 1993), pp. 135–70.

7. William Glasser, *Choice Theory in the Classroom* (New York: Harper Perennial, 1986), pp. 21–22.

8. See, for example, Robert E. Slavin, "Synthesis of Research on Cooperative Learning," *Educational Leadership*, February 1991, pp. 71–82; and idem, *Cooperative Learning: Theory, Research, and Practice*, 2nd ed. (Needham Heights, Mass.: Allyn and Bacon, 1995).

9. Valerie E. Lee and Janice B. Smith, *Effects of High School Restructuring and Size on Gains in Achievement and Engagement for Early Secondary Students* (Madison: Wisconsin Center for Educational Research, University of Wisconsin, 1995).

10. Darling-Hammond, *The Right to Learn*, p. 136.

11. Gene V. Glass and Mary L. Smith, "Meta-Analysis of Research on the Relationship of Class Size and Achievement," *Educational Evaluation and Policy Analysis*, vol. 1, 1978, pp. 2–16.

12. Francis Schrag, "Nurturing Thoughtfulness," in James W. Keefe and Herbert J. Walberg, eds., *Teaching for Thinking* (Reston, Va.: National Association of Secondary School Principals, 1992), pp. 27–34.

13. Fred M. Newmann, Walter G. Secada, and Gary G. Wehlage, *A Guide to Authentic Instruction and Assessment: Vision, Standards, and Scoring* (Madison: Wisconsin Center for Educational Research, University of Wisconsin, 1995), pp. 98–101.

14. Barry K. Beyer, "Teaching Thinking: An Integrated Approach," in Keefe and Walberg, pp. 94–95.

15. Susan Kovalik and Karen D. Olsen, "The Physiology of Learning—Just What Does Go On in There?," *Schools in the Middle*, March/April 1998, pp. 32–37.

16. George H. Wood, *Schools That Work* (New York: Plume, 1992), p. 158.

17. James W. Keefe and John M. Jenkins, *Instruction and the Learning Environment* (Larchmont, N.Y.: Eye On Education, 1997).

18. Newman, Secada, and Wehlage, op. cit.

19. Ibid., p. 7.

20. Theodore R. Sizer, *Horace's School: Redesigning the American High School* (Boston: Houghton Mifflin, 1992), p. 226.

21. Roland Case, "On the Need to Assess Authentically," *Holistic Education Review*, Winter 1992, pp. 14–23.

22. Joseph M. Ryan and Jeanne R. Miyasaka, "Current Practice in Testing and Assessments: What Is Driving the Changes?," *NASSP Bulletin*, October 1995, pp. 1–10.

23. Wood, pp. 27–29.

JAMES W. KEEFE, retired director of research for the National Association of Secondary School Principals, is president of the Learning Environments Consortium International, Reston, Va. JOHN M. JENKINS served as the director of the P. K. Yonge Developmental Research School at the University of Florida, Gainesville, where he now teaches graduate courses in educational leadership. This article is adapted from their recent book, Personalized Instruction: Changing Classroom Practice (Eye On Education Publishers, 2000), and is used with permission. To order, phone 914/833-0551 or visit the website at www.eyeoneducation.com. The price is $29.95. © 2002, Eye on Education.

From *Phi Delta Kappan*, February 2002, pp. 440-448. © 2002 by Eye on Education, 6 Depot Way West, Larchmont, NY 10538, 914-833-0551, www.eyeoneducation.com. Reprinted by permission of James W. Keefe and John M. Jenkins.

Action Research for School Improvement

*Action research is continual professional development–
a direct route to improving teaching and learning.*

Emily F. Calhoun

Seeking to understand and acting on the best we know. That describes how most educators hope to live and grow as professionals. It also describes action research. For the past 10 years, I have used that statement to introduce action research to school teams, administrators, and other educators in central offices, intermediate service agencies, and departments of education.

A more formal definition of action research is continual disciplined inquiry conducted to inform and improve our practice as educators. Action research asks educators to study their practice and its context, explore the research base for ideas, compare what they find to their current practice, participate in training to support needed changes, and study the effects on themselves and their students and colleagues.

For 60 years, action research has been an avenue for creating professional learning communities whose members engage in problem solving and for attaining individual and collective goals. As Lewin (1946) wrote, action research can

> transform... a multitude of unrelated individuals frequently opposed in their outlook and their interests, into cooperative teams, not on the basis of sweetness but on the basis of readiness to face difficulties realistically, to apply hon-

est fact-finding, and to work together to overcome them. (p. 211)

My experience with action research has convinced me of its potential to transform professional development. Action research can change the social system in schools and other education organizations so that continual formal learning is both expected and supported. It can replace superficial coverage with depth of knowledge. And it can generate data to measure the effects of various programs and methods on student and staff learning.

> **Action research can change the social system in schools and other education organizations so that continual formal learning is both expected and supported.**

Action Research at Work: A Teacher's Story

Katie's school was involved in an initiative called "Every Child Reads." Sponsored by the Iowa state department of education, the initiative aimed to change the context in which participants engaged in professional development, help them become more closely connected to scholarship in reading, and support them in generating knowledge and increasing their capacity as learners and leaders. Over

a three-year period, participating school facilitation teams (composed of teachers, the principal, and, when possible, district office and intermediate service agency staff responsible for supporting school improvement) became a statewide professional learning community engaged in the study of literacy.

Participants attended 14 days of workshops and received additional technical assistance at their school sites. They studied current practices in their schools and classrooms; examined research related to literacy development; selected and used evaluative instruments to assess literacy; organized and used data to make decisions about effectiveness; learned how to implement new practices; and learned to provide staff development to colleagues as they engaged in these same actions.

Katie implemented the picture word inductive model (PWIM), a new teaching strategy for her, and studied her kindergarten students' vocabulary development as a part of learning to use this model. The picture word inductive model is an inquiry-oriented language arts approach that uses pictures containing familiar objects and actions to elicit words from students' own vocabularies. Teachers use it to lead their students into inquiring about word properties, adding words to their sight-reading and writing vocabularies, discovering phonetic and structural principles, and using observation and analysis in their study of reading, writing, comprehending, and composing. The picture word cycles (inquiries into the pictures) generally take from four to six weeks at the kindergarten level (Calhoun, 1999).

At first, Katie thought the learning tasks might be too demanding for her students. But as she tried the model and studied what her students did in response, she changed her mind. Katie's data collection showed that her students had achieved a mean gain of 16 sight vocabulary words during their third PWIM unit (ending in mid-March). These results confirmed for Katie the effectiveness of the picture word inductive model.

Katie also collected detailed data on each student's word knowledge as he or she began the unit and again at the end of the unit. The data allowed her to analyze the word-reading strategies that individual students were using: sight vocabulary, decoding, analogies, common spelling patterns, and context clues (Ehri, 1999). As she analyzed the data for each student and across students, Katie made many instructional decisions, such as which phonics principles needed additional explicit instruction, when more modeling was needed to support using context clues, which students needed small-group work on phonemic analysis, and who needed special attention to encourage independent decoding.

Studying specific domains of student performance and her own instructional practice has become a way of life for Katie.

The Power of Organization-Wide Support

Katie's use of action research occurred as part of a structured initiative sponsored by a state department of education. This initiative illustrates how education leaders in states, districts, and schools are attempting to make action research a dominant way of doing business—building an organization context that supports inquiry by school staffs working as a whole and by smaller groups and individuals pursuing their particular avenues of study. The development of inquiring communities is what distinguishes action research from school improve-

ment approaches that focus on the implementation of specific initiatives, such as a new curriculum or a new mode of assessment.

Although I am an advocate of carefully conducted action research whether it is individual, collaborative, or organization-wide, I put my professional energy and time into supporting schoolwide and organization-wide action research (Calhoun, 1994; Joyce, Calhoun, & Hopkins, 1999). This action research option has the power to transform the organization into a learning community.

My experience is that regular use of multiple sources of data to inform us about student performance or our own performance is often threatening at first, because it requires that we juxtapose our practices and our students' performance against exemplary research-based practices and high levels of student performance attained in similar settings. The resulting confrontation and social turmoil, however, may be natural accompaniments to substantive change.

> **Regular use of multiple sources of data to inform us about student performance requires that we juxtapose our practices against exemplary research-based practices.**

The good news is that when groups have adequate organization support in using data as a source of information to guide practice, leadership generally surfaces within the group. These leaders provide examples of using classroom data to make instructional and curriculum changes and model informed decision making and problem solving in action. Their schools begin to use on-site data and the external knowledge base as sources for continually assessing the effectiveness of actions and current practices.

This emerging leadership often signals a change in the social system of the school. It doesn't come easily in most settings, but with opportunity and leadership from school and district administrators, it happens. Along with benefits for students, educators feel more professional.

Using a Structured Action Research Model

Educators who wish to use action research for professional development or school improvement should select a structured process to use in the school, district, or region. Many resources are available. Although all action research approaches encourage disciplined inquiry, reflection, and the improvement of practice or expansion of knowledge, they do vary in purposes and emphases.

My own approach (Calhoun, 1994) focuses on the schoolwide or district-wide pursuit of student learning goals. It emphasizes using action research to change how the organization works so that educators study student and staff learning continually and pour information from the external knowledge base into the collective study and action-taking process. Glanz (1998) provides a number of tools useful for administrators and leadership teams as they study school effectiveness and student performance. Sagor (1992) emphasizes the development of collaborative action research teams who identify issues or problems, study the context of those problems, collect data, take actions, and engage in discourse and reflection around the results of those actions. And Hopkins (in press) emphasizes changes in classroom practice through careful study by individual teachers as researchers.

> **When groups have adequate organization support in using data as a source of information to guide practice, leadership generally surfaces within the group.**

After selecting a resource or action research model, those leading the effort need to learn to use it in their work and determine how to support its use within their organization. If no one in the initiating group has experience and skill in using action research, perhaps faculty members at the local college or university can provide technical assistance.

If the group wishes to use action research to support school improvement as well as individual professional development, the chief

The Schoolwide Action Research Matrix—One Example

School Focus: *To improve reading comprehension*

(Academic student learning goal in a curriculum area)

	Learners (Students)		Learning Environment (District/School)	
ON-SITE INFORMATION: (Information at the district/school level)	**1. Current student information** Gates-MacGinitie scores, grade 9: Only 25% of students scored at GLE 9.0 or higher **State Tests:** Matched comparisons, student performance decreased from grade 8 to 10: 1998–1999, 12% 1999–2000, 10% 2000–2001, 14% Teacher, parent, and business leader perceptions: Consensus that students are not prepared	**3. Student performance and response we would like to see** ■ Students able to comprehend and learn from the texts being used in courses ■ No loss from 8th to 10th grade on state curriculum tests ■ More benchmarks will be developed	**4. Information about the current learning environment in our district/school** ■ Summer school ■ Tutorials ■ Buddy program ■ Special education ■ Reading aloud ■ Group work ■ Extra time for assignments ■ Computer tutorials	**6. Learning environment we would like to see** ■ Increased staff development on designing classroom activities and homework assignments ■ Increased student access to tradebooks ■ More tutors ■ A course for accelerating literacy for struggling students
EXTERNAL INFORMATION: (Study of literature, standards, & best practices)	**2. External information about learners/students** ■ Data from the state testing program from other high schools with similar demographics; found 3 schools with better performance ■ NAEP Executive Summary and test items ■ District curriculum standards		**5. External information about the learning environment** Collective study of four selected texts: ■ Moore et al. (1999). *Adolescent Literacy: A Position Statement* ■ Stahl (1999). *Vocabulary Development* (pp. 8–13) ■ Richardson (2000). *Read It Aloud: Using Literature in the Secondary Content Classroom* ■ Showers et al. (1998). "A Second Chance to Learn to Read"	

administrators in the school or district need to be on board—preferably as members of the initiating group. In most settings, school or district staff members will need to change the way they use data, study student and staff learning, and use the external research base. These changes are unlikely to occur if principals, district office staff members, and the superintendent do not participate and help lead the effort.

The Schoolwide Action Research Matrix

Figure 1 provides an example of how schools might structure their action research around a common student learning goal. In providing technical assistance to sites working to implement action research focused on student achievement, I often recommend that they use this Schoolwide Action Research Matrix as a guide for structuring collective inquiry and

action. The matrix includes a place to identify the student learning goal that a staff selects for its current collective focus and six sections to describe the content of collective study and action. Educators build their school or district action plans and staff development plans around the actions outlined in each of the six matrix sections.

In the example shown in Figure 1, a high school staff focused on improving reading comprehension because staff members felt that many of their students could not read and write well enough to succeed in the core academic curriculum subjects. Here are some of the major action research tasks that they engaged in during the first year, led by their action research facilitation team.

Current Student Information

Scores on both norm-referenced tests and state curriculum exams told the staff that their students were performing below expected levels. For example, the staff reviewed data comparing their students' reading performance on the state curriculum tests in 8th grade with the performance of the same cohort in 10th grade. In the three years studied, the mean percentiles in reading had decreased 12 percent, 10 percent, and 14 percent from their 8th grade levels.

Staff members also collected data about perceptions. Teachers identified many instances where students would have been able to manage the assignments from their courses had they had better literacy skills. And according to data from the past three years of school climate questionnaires, dissatisfaction with students' reading and writing performance had been a persistent problem identified by parents (42 percent), the business community (60 percent), and school staff members (75 percent).

External Information About Learners

The staff reviewed data on student reading performance in high schools with demographics similar to theirs. Out of 21 high schools studied, they found three where students were performing at much higher levels in reading and writing on state tests administered in 10th grade. The principal had insisted that the staff look at these data because he wanted teachers to recognize that some schools with similar student populations were achieving better results.

To gather information about the literacy standards that students should be achieving, the staff also reviewed their district's new curriculum standards document and the executive summary and sample items from the National Assessment

of Education Progress in Reading (Donahue, Voelkl, Campbell, & Mazzeo, 1999).

Student Performance Goals

Staff members decided that they wanted to improve the reading performance of all their students to the point where students could at least manage the secondary education that was planned for them—the basic high school curriculum.

Using the state tests, they set one of their first targets: Students would not lose ground in their scores on these tests between 8th and 10th grade. Staff members, however, were not ready to set other benchmarks or indicators of performance. The facilitators agreed that it might be useful to begin by studying what worked to improve reading performance and how much could be improved in a semester or year. Then, the staff would set further benchmarks for improvement.

Internal Information About the Learning Environment

Next, the facilitation team organized the teachers to identify the programs, initiatives, and instructional practices that they were currently using to address the literacy problem. Organization efforts already in place included summer school programs, after-school and lunchtime tutorials, a "buddy program" in which high school students read with elementary students once a week, and special education programs. In addition, individual teachers identified what they were already doing to help struggling students, such as reading materials aloud, using computer programs, giving students extra time for assignments, and using cooperative learning. The teachers agreed, however, that they had no systematic program or plan for accelerating the reading and literacy development of the struggling readers and writers.

External Information About the Learning Environment

The facilitation team had a resource collection of about 20 articles and chapters and four books. From this, the team selected four items for in-depth study by the staff. At staff

meetings during the next two months, the teachers worked in cross-department groups to discuss and analyze each item. Using structured response sheets (Sparks, 1999), they identified curriculum ideas, instructional strategies, and assessment techniques that would be applicable in their courses, as well as ideas about organizing the learning environment more effectively in terms of staff deployment, class size, changes in course availability, and scheduling. A facilitation team member worked with each group.

Learning Environment Goals

The facilitation team studied what groups had derived from their analyses and put together a tentative action plan for the staff to review. The plan included actions at the school level, actions all teachers would take, and actions for departments. Actions included

- Providing a series of staff development sessions on designing classroom activities and homework assignments, including modeling and discussing successful strategies for gaining meaning from text.

- Increasing student access to high-quality, non-fiction tradebooks at a range of reading levels (in classrooms, the school library, and community libraries).

- Recruiting more tutors, providing a better support system for them, and increasing the amount of time tutoring is available before and after school.

- Developing a course for accelerating literacy for those students who are reading two or more grade levels below their placement. The course would be 90 minutes per day, replace elective courses, and focus primarily on the reading and writing of informative prose. Both teachers and students would study progress assiduously.

Some Results

A group of teachers volunteered to teach the literacy course. A consultant helped the group design it and learn the new teaching strategies that were needed. The teachers selected students for the course on the basis of a combination of standardized test scores and teacher judgment, serving the poorest readers first. During the first semester, the teachers enlisted the students in the formative evaluation process. For example, each student kept a "word box" that contained cards with vocabulary words that he or she was learning.

It became immediately apparent that the standardized test scores were *over-estimates* of the actual reading levels of many of the students. About half of them were not even sure of the "high-frequency, useful little words" that are often learned in the first year of school.

At the end of the first semester, a re-administration of the standardized test indicated that about half of the student scores had risen about two grade level equivalents, and by the end of the second semester, most of the students were making gains and had learned how to learn more effectively. Teachers and students are continuing to refine and improve the class.

The Potential for Change

As with other types of school improvement efforts, school and district staff members who attempt to make effective use of action research will encounter barriers to change. They may have difficulty providing time for the staff to work together, finding and supporting staff members who are willing to lead such work, and designing collective work that improves student learning, professional expertise, and staff leadership capacity simultaneously.

It's a challenging task to help staff structure action research into their work and the work of the organization. Yet we know that improvement in education requires us to change

the typical, ineffective practice of professional development.

The good news is that we have options and models. When used as an organization-wide process for school improvement, action research changes the context and provides a way of organizing collective work so that professional expertise is tended and extended, helping to build a strong professional learning community. Whether action research is used as a school improvement tool or as an individual professional development option, staff members who draw on the current research base, add to their current knowledge, and create new knowledge-in-action can make instruction in the school or in the classroom more intentional and effective for student learning.

References

Calhoun, E.F. (1994). *How to use action research in the self-renewing school.* Alexandria, VA: ASCD.

Calhoun, E.F. (1999). *Teaching beginning reading and writing with the picture word inductive model.* Alexandria, VA: ASCD.

Donahue, P. L., Voelke, K. E., Campbell, J. R., & Mazzeo, J. (1999). *NAEP 1998 reading report card for the nation and states.* Washington, DC: U.S. Department of Education.

Ehri, L. C. (1999, April). Phases of acquisition in learning to read words and instructional implications. Paper presented to the annual meeting of the American Educational Research Association, Montreal, Canada.

Glanz, J. (1998). *Action research: An educational leader's guide to school improvement.* Norwood, MA: Christopher-Gordon.

Hopkins, D. (In press). *A teacher's guide to classroom research* (3rd ed.). Buckingham, England: Open University Press.

Joyce, B., Calhoun, E. F., & Hopkins, D. (1999). *The new structure of school improvement: Inquiring schools and achieving students.* Buckingham, England: Open University Press.

Lewin, K. (1946). Action research and minority problems, In K. Lewin, *Resolving social conflicts: Selected papers on group dynamics* (compiled in 1948). New York: Harper & Row.

Moore, D. W., Bean, T. W., Birdyshaw, D., & Rycik, J. A. (1999). *Adolescent literacy: A position statement.* Newark, DE: International Reading Association.

Richardson, J. S. (2000). *Read it aloud! Using literature in the secondary content classroom.* Newark, DE: International Reading Association.

Sagor, R. (1992). *How to conduct collaborative action research.* Alexandria, VA: ASCD.

Showers, B. Joyce, B., Scanlon, M., & Schaubelt, C. (1998). A second chance to learn to read. *Educational leadership,* 55(6), 27–30.

Sparks, D. (1999). The singular power of one goal: An interview with Emily Calhoun. *Journal of Staff Development,* 20(1), 54–58.

Stahl, S. A. (1999). *Vocabulary development.* Cambridge, MA: Brookline Books.

Emily F. Calhoun is Director of The Phoenix Alliance, 624 Demere Way, Saint Simons Island, GA 31522; (912) 638-0685; efcphoenix@aol.com.

The Dark Side of Nationwide Tests

President Bush's education initiative calls for the testing of every student in the nation, but these 'assessments' in the past involved Big Brother-style psychological profiling.

By B.K. Eakman

The proponents of President George W. Bush's education initiative, called "No Child Left Behind," believe that they can make schools accountable to parents as well as taxpayers. The centerpiece of this, as it appears in the amendments to the Elementary and Secondary School Act, still in House-Senate conference as **Insight** goes to press, is a massive nationwide program designed to test every student in grades three to eight in reading and math. Both House and Senate bills propose some $400 million in federal funds to be sent to the states to devise and administer the tests on a state-by-state basis.

By giving tax money to each state to devise its own tests, supporters hope to mollify conservatives on the one hand, who fear national indoctrination by the U.S. Department of Education, and liberals on the other, who dread the consequences of holding educators personally accountable for whether the children they teach actually learn. The language of the House bill, HR1, for example, states in an unresolved contradiction that each state shall demonstrate that it has adopted "challenging academic standards and challenging academic-achievement standards." In the same breath, the bill says that "a state shall not be required to submit such standards to the Secretary."

The problem is that "academic standards" as defined by common sense and by lawmakers tend to be meaningless when defined by educators. The bill calls for "challenging academic-content standards in academic subjects that specify what children are expected to know and be able to do" and contain "coherent and rigorous content... and encourage the teaching of advanced skills." Yet both House and Senate bills shy away from using the term "tests" and substitute the edu-speak word "assessments."

The reason is that public education during the last 30 years has tended against testing for knowledge of content, instead emphasizing a psychological assessment of a child's needs, background and ability to conform to the group. A "test" is an objective measure of a child's ability to solve a problem; an "assessment" is a social scientist's speculation about the environmental conditioning of the child.

Thus the "assessment" of a child's ability to read or to do math in the current testing already in use has more to do with probing the child's psyche and teaching him or her to conform to group values than with testing ability to add two plus two. The leading educational experts will read the bill's language as a license to invade the privacy of every child in the country rather than hold failing schools accountable. And since the bill necessarily honors the principle of local control, it is likely the local educational bureaucracies doing the controlling will welcome the bill as a $400 million slush fund to do exactly what they have been doing to thwart educational reform.

The trouble with school tests begins with the increasing inclusion of sophisticated "behavioral" components that encompass a wide variety of lifestyle and opinion data, nailing down student proclivities, social attitudes and parent-inculcated worldviews. Combined with the plethora of "health" (sex and drug) surveys, mental-health screenings, diary/journal-keeping and other miscellaneous questionnaires— mostly taking place in the classroom under cover of academics—testing has become more equated with personality inventories than proficiency exams. In that context, what passes for testing even may undermine the accountability President Bush advocates.

The case against standardized tests hinges on the quantum leap in data-gathering, cross-matching and information-sharing capabilities, with all the accompanying problems associated with data-trafficking, invasion of privacy and consumer profiling. Barely a week goes by that a publication somewhere doesn't carry a story detailing a new affront to what used to be considered "nobody's business."

One of the earliest examples of psychological data-gathering under the cover of academics occurred in the pivotal 1980s, when enormous breakthroughs in computer technology were being piloted with federal funds in selected localities. One of those was in Allegheny County, Pa., initiated under the eight-state Cooperative Accountability Project. A handful of parents—among them, Gen Yvette Sutton, Anita Hoge and Francine D'Alonzo—got wind of a standardized academic test "no one could possibly study for" being disseminated in the McGuffey School District: the Educational Quality Assessment (EQA). After several unsuccessful attempts to gain access, a trip to the state education agency in Harrisburg finally yielded the facts. Not only did more than one-half the questions not relate to factual knowledge, but numerical codes next to the questions as printed on the administrative version of the test turned out to correlate with specific "remediating" curricula. It included questions such as:

"I get upset easily at home: [a] very true of me; [b] mostly true of me; [c] mostly untrue of me; [d] very untrue of me.

"You are asked to dinner at the home of a classmate having a religion much different from yours. In this situation I would feel: [a] very comfortable; [b] comfortable; [c] slightly uncomfortable; [d] very uncomfortable.

"There is a secret club at school called the Midnight Artists. They go out late at night and paint funny sayings and pictures on buildings. I would JOIN THE CLUB when I knew … [a] my best friend had asked me to join; [b] most of the popular students in school were in the club; [c] my parents would ground me if they found out I joined."

This last question, in particular, got parents' attention. It presumes that the child will join the club under some circumstances, including the desire to provoke parents. They thought the question more or less asked: "How can we get this kid to vandalize property?"

The EQA had 375 questions covering attitudes, worldviews and opinions—mostly hypothetical situations and self-reports. There were 30 questions on math and another 30 covering verbal analogies—just enough academic questions to appear credible.

Every such test is distributed with professional literature for the educators—which is strictly off-limits to the parents. The EQA told educators it was testing for: the student's "locus of control," his "willingness to receive stimuli," his "amenability to change" and whether he would "conform to group goals." In lay terms, these translate to: Where's the child coming from? Is he easily influenced? Are his views firm or flexible? Is he a team player who will accede to group consensus? Choice "b," then, was the preferred response to the Midnight Artists question because it reflects a willingness to "conform to group goals."

Today, such testing is more sophisticated. A fascinating aspect of a recent Michigan Assessment, for example, was that regardless of the section—reading, science, geography—the questions all sounded like social studies. For example, there was nothing about topography in the geography section; it covered "global issues"—overpopulation, colonial victimization and redistribution of resources to Third World countries. The writing-sample topic? "Coping With Change."

Five science questions for fifth-graders concerned universal child fingerprinting, but involved no science. The multiple choices, even the "incorrect" ones, seemed more like endorsements than questions: "fingerprinting doesn't hurt," "lost children can be identified," etc. Not a single "down side" was offered. The one question that sounded like a question was so simple that one could reasonably have asked whether this were the reading or the science section: "Fingerprinting is MOST useful in which of the following jobs: [a] police work, to help in crime fighting; [b] window washing, to help clean windows; [c] auto mechanics, to help cars run better; [d] teaching, to help kids learn to multiply."

Task I from the history section—on women in combat—was "Interpreting Information." Prefaced in small print was, "Directions: Read the following hypothetical information about a public policy issue. Use it with what you already know to complete the tasks that follow."

Parent activists Deborah DeBacker of Troy, Mich., and Joan Grindel of Bloom-field, Mich., say it's doubtful fifth-graders either understood or acted upon the term "hypothetical." In any case, the only interpretation one could draw from the data provided is that women should be in combat. Despite assurances in the essay instructions that the student's views per se don't matter, it's clear that any view not supported by those "hypothetical facts" in the data section will be judged insufficient to warrant a top grade. In the example, testers actually begin the paragraph for the pupil: "I think that women members of the military should definitely be allowed to participate.…"

Questionnaires, curricula and activities that target the belief system are called "affective devices." Psychology texts describe the belief system as made up of attitudes, values and worldviews existing below the level of conscious awareness. Affective means "noncognitive," "dealing with emotions and feelings" rather than the intellect. Using affective-questioning techniques makes it easier to test the subject's belief system. Some go so far as to test for "psychological threshold." The teacher's guide to Pennsylvania's 1986 citizenship curriculum defined this threshold as "the severity of stimulus tolerated before a change of behavior occurs." The manual explained that "it is possible to assess not only the students' predisposition [toward certain reactions]… but also to provide some measure of the intensity of that predisposition across a wide spectrum of situations."

Some profiling instruments are explicit and blatant, such as Pennsylvania's and Michigan's, while others are more subtle. Most states label them "assessments" rather than "tests," further confusing the issue for parents. Regardless of the label, opponents claim that personality testing in the context of an academic setting, and the psychotherapeutic sales packages (curricula) that typically ensue, portend a high-tech threat not only to privacy but to a child's future employability and freedom of conscience.

Then there are the student-identification methods applied to "confidential" tests and surveys the testers say are not "individually identifiable." This doesn't mean, however, that students are not "individually identified." Confused? *The National Center for Education Statistics 1993 Field Restricted Use Data Procedures Manual* explains this semantic sleight of hand. Techniques range from simple barcoding and "slugging" to more-complicated exercises such as "sticky-labeling" and inserting "embedded identifiers."

To the testers, however, the term "confidential" means "need to know." The "confidential" label casually applied by officials to modern testing and survey devices invariably is taken for anonymity, thereby masking the fact that: (1) higher scores are accorded "preferred" viewpoints, (2) curriculum is modified and targeted to specific groups of children to correct "inappropriate" attitudes and, more ominously, (3) certain views that once were considered "principled" now are deemed "rigid" and associated with mental illness or psychological defects.

Among the at-risk "indicators" are viewpoints and behaviors deemed by the testers to be what they call "indicative of a rigid or underdeveloped belief system." Pupils are referred to psychologists for "remediation" to render their attitudes and responses more "realistic." Several professional papers, beginning with the acclaimed 1969 Behavioral Science Teacher Education Project (BSTEP), place "firm religious belief" in the "rigid/inflexible" category. BSTEP also projected a world "so saturated with ideas and information [by the 1990s that] few will be able to maintain control over their opinions."

So far is all this testing and evaluation from confidential that today's burgeoning computer cross-matching capability of public and private records has launched an information industry of data traffickers and information brokers. Some are licit and others black-market, but they cater to the needs of employers, credit bureaus, universities, corporate spies and government agencies.

Of course, evidence of serious peril to our American presumption of "personal affairs" was being debated among high-ranking educators as far back as 1969, when Wolcott Beatty wrote his seminal work, *Improving Educational Assessment and an Inventory of Measures of Affective Behavior*. Dozens of related publications followed, documenting a slippery slope from conceptual design of a test that would evaluate and compare effectiveness of learning programs to a federal-funding carrot that would ensure massive personal-data collection with automatic-transfer capability to federal and international databases.

In 1970, L.J. Chronbach's *Essentials of Scientific Testing* sounded the first alarm: "Coding of records is not a full safeguard. Identity can be detected by matching facts from the coded questionnaire with other facts that are openly recorded."

By that time Dustin Heuston of the renowned World Institute of Computer-Assisted Technology (WICAT) in Utah uttered his prophetic assertion: "We've been staggered by realizing that the computer has the capability to act as if it were 10 of the top psychologists working with one student.... Won't it be wonderful when no one can get between that child and that curriculum?" Behavioral-science gurus Richard Wolf (Teachers College, Columbia University) and his colleague, Ralph Tyler, openly were advocating a need for surreptitious methods of data collection and student identification as early as 1974 in their coedited book, *Crucial Issues in Testing*. They called for unified coding and standardized definitions to enhance cross-matching and data-sharing—from elementary schools on into the workplace.

Wolf supported the 'permissibility of deception' in school-testing based on 'rights of an institution to obtain information necessary to achieve its goals.'

Wolf supported "the permissibility of deception" in school-testing based on "the rights of an institution to obtain information necessary to achieve its goals." He stated that, danger or not, there "are occasions in which the test constructor [finds it necessary] to outwit the subject so that he cannot guess what information he is revealing. From the constructor's point of view this is necessary since he wishes to ascertain information that the individual might not... furnish if it were sought directly. A number of personality tests fall into this category."

Despite admonitions, the lure of computerized cross-matching proved too enticing. In 1981, the first education databanks were launched: the Common Core of Data, the Universe Files and the Longitudinal Studies. In what is perhaps the most evidential document on the subject, "Measuring the Quality of Education" by Willard Wirtz and Archie LaPointe, the writers outline the U.S. Education Department's (ED's) intention to ignore the legal and ethical warnings against privacy invasion:

"Getting into the students' personal characteristics and situations invariably prompts warnings that the NAEP [National Assessment of Educational Programs] purpose is not to analyze human development, and injunctions against confusing the measurement of educational results (outcomes) and the analysis of cause (inputs). But it is being recognized increasingly that the measurement of achievement is incomplete without the accompanying identification of whatever educational circumstances may affect these results."

More prophetically, Wirtz and LaPointe wrote: "A different kind of assessment would help correct the tilt in the educational-standards concept toward functional literacy and away from excellence."

Direct education away from excellence? That's right. The authors detailed how a clearinghouse-style database incorporating demographic and psychological-profiling data would help steer schools toward what these "experts" deemed a more realistic ideal: mere functional literacy.

Policymakers at the ED quickly moved to shelve concerns about student and family privacy. For example, James P. Shaver wrote a detailed monograph, *National Assessment of Values and Attitudes for Social Studies*, published through the Office of Educational Research and Instruction (OERI), a division of the U.S. Department of Education. But by then there was no need to hide intent because OERI already had brought in four computer experts from Utah's WICAT to prepare a working paper for the first consolidated education database.

In 1986, "A Plan for the Redesign of the Elementary and Secondary Data Collection Program" was finalized, incorporating attitudinal, lifestyle and value information. It fell to the federally funded Council of Chief State School Officers (CCSSO) to ensure state/federal compatibility of computer systems and promote collection of data at the local level. In a 1985 speech, CCSSO Director Ramsey Seldon placed "coordination of educational assessment and evaluation" on the highest priority, promoting the exchange of information about private citizens and their children in the name of comparing educational achievement.

Today, the three original education databases are part of a mammoth data-tracking/sharing system called the SPEEDE/ ExPRESS. Among other capabilities, data can be transmitted to universities and prospective employers via WORKLINK, a system set up by the Educational Testing Service.

In 1988, the National Center for Education Statistics named 29 organizations, some with no clear ties to education, that were given automatic access to national assessment data —among them the Census Bureau, the office of the Montana State Attorney General, the Rand Corp. and the Economic Policy Institute. Then technology took another quantum leap—more storage capability in less space, ultraso-

phisticated search engines, intricate cross-matching methods.

And critics of all this are saying that puts President Bush's national-testing initiative in a different light. And it cuts left and right. After all, if one faction can target a child's belief system and keep records, so can another.

The basic dilemmas remain: If the use of psychographic instruments is legal and ethical, without informed, written, parental consent; if behavior-modification curricula can be brought into the classroom as legitimate learning material; if teachers, or even bona fide mental-health workers, can

use the schools to "treat" youngsters for real or imagined psychological problems—then are schools really educational institutions or day-care clinics?

B.K. Eakman, a former teacher and executive director of the National Education Consortium, is the author of Cloning of the American Mind: Eradicating Morality Through Education.

UNIT 3

Striving for Excellence: The Drive for Quality

Unit Selections

Key Points to Consider

- Identify some of the different points of view on achieving excellence in education. What value conflicts can be defined?

- Do public school teachers see educational reform in the same light as governmental, philanthropic, and corporate-based reform groups? On what matters would they agree or disagree?

- What are some assumptions about achieving excellence in student achievement that you would challenge? Why?

- What can educators do to improve the quality of student learning?

- Have there been flaws in American school reform efforts in the past 30 years? If so, what are they?

- Do standardized tests accurately measure a student's aptitude, in your opinion?

 **Links: www.dushkin.com/online/**
These sites are annotated in the World Wide Web pages.

Awesome Library for Teachers
http://www.awesomelibrary.org/
Education World
http://www.education-world.com
EdWeb/Andy Carvin
http://edwebproject.org
Kathy Schrock's Guide for Educatiors
http://www.discoveryschool.com/schrockguide/
Teacher's Guide to the U.S. Department of Education
http://www.ed.gov/pubs/TeachersGuide/

The debate continues over which academic standards are most appropriate for elementary and secondary school students. Discussion regarding the impact on students and teachers of state proficiency examinations goes on in those states or provinces where such examinations are mandated. We are still dealing with how best to assess student academic performance. Some very interesting proposals on how to do this have emerged.

There are several incisive analyses of why American educators' efforts to achieve excellence in schooling have frequently failed. Today, some interesting proposals are being offered as to how we might improve the academic achievement of students. The current debate regarding excellence in education clearly reflects parents' concerns for more choices in how they school their children.

Many authors of recent essays and reports believe that excellence can be achieved best by creating new models of schooling that give both parents and students more control over the types of school environments available to them. Many believe that more money is not a guarantor of quality in schooling. Imaginative academic programming and greater citizen choice can guarantee at least a greater variety of options open to parents who are concerned about their children's academic progress in school.

We each wish the best quality of life that we can attain, and we each desire the opportunity for an education that will optimize our chances to achieve our objectives. The rhetoric on excellence and quality in schooling has been heated, and numerous opposing concepts of how schools can reach these goals have been presented for public consideration in recent years. Some progress has been realized on the part of students as well as some major changes in how teacher education programs are structured.

In the decades of the 1980s and 1990s, those reforms instituted to encourage qualitative growth in the conduct of schooling tended to be what education historian David Tyack once referred to as "structural" reforms. Structural reforms consist of demands for standardized testing of students and teaching, reorganization of teacher education programs, legalized actions to provide alternative routes into the teaching profession, efforts to recruit more people into teaching, and laws to enable greater parental choice as to where their children may attend school. These structural reforms cannot, however, in and of themselves produce higher levels of student achievement. We need to explore a broader range of the essential purposes of schooling, which will require our redefining what it means to be a literate person. We need also to reconsider what we mean by the "quality" of education and to reassess the essential purposes of schooling.

When we speak of quality and excellence as aims of education, we must remember that these terms encompass aesthetic and affective as well as cognitive processes. Young people cannot achieve the full range of intellectual capacity to solve problems on their own simply by being obedient and by memorizing data. How students encounter their teachers in classrooms and how teachers interact with their students are concerns that encompass both aesthetic and cognitive dimensions.

There is a real need to enforce intellectual standards and yet also to make schools more creative places in which to learn, places where students will yearn to explore, to imagine, and to hope. Compared to those in the United States, students in European nations appear to score higher in assessments of skills in mathematics and the sciences, in written essay examinations in the humanities and social sciences, and in the routine oral examinations given by committees of teachers to students as they exit secondary schools.

What forms of teacher education and in-service reeducation are needed? Who pays for these programmatic options? Where and how will funds be raised or redirected from other priorities to pay for this? Will the "streaming and tracking" model of secondary school student placement that exists in Europe be adopted? How can we best assess academic performance? Can we commit to a more heterogeneous grouping of students and to full inclusion of handicapped students in our schools? Many individual, private, and governmental reform efforts did not address these questions.

Other industrialized nations champion the need for alternative secondary schools to prepare their young people for varied life goals and civic work. The American dream of the common school translated into what has become the comprehensive high school of the twentieth century. But does it provide all the people with alternative diploma options? If not, what is the next step? What must be changed? For one, concepts related to our educational goals must be clarified and political motivation must be separated from the realities of student performance.

Policy development for schooling needs to be tempered by even more "bottom-up," grassroots efforts to improve the quality of schools that are now under way in many communities in North America. New and imaginative inquiry and assessment strategies need to be developed by teachers working in their classrooms, and they must nurture the support of professional colleagues and parents.

Excellence is the goal; the means to achieve it is what is in dispute. There is a new dimension to the debate over assessment of academic achievement of elementary and secondary school students. In addition, the struggle continues of conflicting academic (as well as political) interests in the quest to improve the quality of preparation of our future teachers, and we also need to sort these issues out.

No conscientious educator would oppose the idea of excellence in education. The problem in gaining consensus over how to attain it is that the assessment of excellence of both teacher and student performance is always based on some preset standards. Which standards of assessment should prevail?

The Human Face of the High-Stakes Testing Story

Schools like the Boston Arts Academy are desperately trying to keep the Massachusetts Comprehensive Assessment System from destroying their very fabric, Ms. Nathan says. She intends to make it through the MCAS mania by continuing to fight for a rich and rigorous arts and academic curriculum, taught by highly qualified and committed teachers in an atmosphere of respect and high expectations.

BY LINDA NATHAN

THE NEWS stories, editorials, and academic debates about high-stakes tests deal mostly in ideologies, generalizations, and statistics. What's easily lost in the palaver is the reality of school for the people who have the most to gain or lose—the students.

In Massachusetts, the reality that faces students now includes the imminent threat that they will not receive a high school diploma unless they pass the 10th-grade exams in the Massachusetts Comprehensive Assessment System (MCAS). The numbers are grim, even with this year's much-heralded improvement in scores: close to half of the students in urban high schools are still failing the test; among black and Latino students, the failure rate is between 60% and 70%. But who are these students, really? What do they know and not know? What are their strengths and weaknesses, and what are their possible futures?

I know some of these young people very well. They are students at my school, the Boston Arts Academy (BAA), a three-year-old public high school of visual and performing arts. They are products of the Boston Public Schools. They are typical, yet each one is unique. And their stories shed a different light on high-stakes testing. Let me introduce you to two of them.

TONY'S STORY

Tony first caught my attention by standing over me in the school cafeteria one day as I ate lunch with some students and teachers. He glared at me, put his hands on his hips, and stomped his foot a little. I turned to him. "This school isn't teaching real science, Ms. Nathan," he said. "You need to do something about it."

The other students looked up from their tater tots and turkey nuggets, glancing back and forth from me to Tony. The teachers stopped eating too. This was during the fall of the Boston Arts Academy's first year. We'd been open

for all of two months, and no one had challenged me in quite this way before.

I was acutely aware that my response would have long-lasting significance. "What is it you object to, Tony?" I asked, trying to stay calm.

"First of all," he said, "there are no textbooks. The teachers give us these readings—novels and stuff. What is that? And I'm in a class with freshmen and sophomores. I've already *done* my freshman year. I don't get why I'm in a class with freshmen. Don't I know more science than them? Anyway, we're just not doing science. I mean, how is building an energy-efficient house *science*? And then there's this *humanities* stuff. What is that? Where's English? Where's history? My friends at Central High aren't studying *China* like we are. And the math. Come *on*, Ms. Nathan. Where are the problems? It's all reading! I used to be an honor-roll student and get 90s or 100s on all the tests. I haven't even *had* a test here!"

Tony paused for breath, and I took a deep one, too. "Wow, you have a lot of issues," I said, with a voice as steady as I could muster. I asked Tony to sit with me. Then I asked him a little about the classes at his previous high school. He described them pretty much the way I thought he would.

Each week the teacher would assign a new chapter from the textbook, and the students would answer the questions at the end. The technique was the same for all subjects. Tony had never experienced what might be called active, hands-on, or open-ended learning. He had certainly never had to read primary-source documents as he was now doing in his humanities class (English and history) at the Arts Academy. He had probably never heard anything about ancient China before. And the notion of learning physics through building an energy-efficient house was also alien to him.

The Interactive Math Program we were using was a shock to most students, not just Tony. They were used to doing 20 rote problems in math, getting a check mark or an X on each one, and moving on. Tony was confounded by having to write a detailed explanation of each "problem of the week" or developing a math portfolio.

Most classes at the Boston Arts Academy use, in addition to traditional tests and quizzes, some form of authentic assessment. What do I mean by "authentic"? I mean judging students on their ability to perform complex tasks. For example, in a math, science, or world language class, students might be asked to research a topic and then present it to an audience of students, teachers, and community members. A student would then be evaluated not only on her knowledge and understanding of the material, but also on her ability to make connections to other situations, to describe the perspective of the original author, and to analyze and articulate her own perspective.

In such exhibitions of mastery, students are often asked to make suppositions and to explain why the topic has relevance; most important, they are expected to use evidence persuasively. This authentic assessment process is not unlike the coaching doctoral students get in writing their dissertations. It represents a different way of awarding a high school diploma. None of this was familiar terrain for Tony.

I acknowledged Tony's frustration and advised him to give BAA a chance. I told him to ask for help when he was confused and to work hard. "You can always come see me if you get really frustrated," I said. "I know you'll be on the honor roll again."

Then we talked a bit about his theater project, an adaptation of cartoonist Art Spiegelman's *Maus*. Tony was playing the father. Before turning to ancient China, Tony's class had studied World War II and the Nazi murder of two-thirds of European Jewry and other groups. I wondered how he had responded to the challenge of adapting a book-length comic about the Holocaust for the stage. "Oh, that was cool," he said breezily.

Later I sat in on a rehearsal of *Maus*. Tony's performance was captivating. He understood just how to portray both the pain and the anger of Vladek Spiegelman. He even added a touch of comic timing to the role, which I wouldn't have imagined would work. But Tony convinced me that he had made the right choices for the character.

Throughout that first year and the next, Tony would find me in the cafeteria or in my office, stomp his foot, and complain about some aspect of the curriculum or some teacher who "wasn't fair." After one of these outbursts, I reminded him that he'd just gotten honorable mention (all A's and B's and just one C), and I said that I still thought he could make the honor roll. I asked if he might be expending more energy avoiding certain tasks than actually doing them. "Well, Ms. Garcia is unfair," he repeated. Then he walked away.

Tony's experience is not unlike that of other students at BAA. He went to public elementary and middle schools in Boston, dreamed of becoming an actor, auditioned for our theater program, and got in. He took regular academic classes—science, math, writing/advisory, humanities, Spanish. In addition, he took approximately 12 hours a week of theater classes, including acting, directing, playwriting, technical theater (including set design, costume and makeup design, and lighting design), theater history, movement, voice, and musical theater.

In spite of his outbursts, Tony missed the honor roll at BAA for only one term. Before graduating, he wrote the following in his self-assessment:

> I had a difficult time fitting in with the curriculum and the environment around me.... I felt as if I was in a foreign land and I had never before experienced the feeling of being lost. In addition, I felt as if I was the only individual who had not a clue to what was being taught in class.... I wanted to leave the school! During this time, I met often with the headmaster, Ms. Nathan. She repeatedly told me that I would be faced with the challenge of having new environments in life, where I would be introduced to new things. I hate to say it, but she was right!

As Tony approached graduation, he worried about college entrance exams. He had never done well on standardized tests. Even after taking a Princeton Review prep course, his combined verbal and math SAT score was below 800. Nevertheless, Tony was accepted to the BFA program of a prestigious four-year liberal arts college, with a generous financial aid package.

I was not surprised by Tony's low SAT scores. Over my 20 years as an educator, I have seen dozens of young men and women with very low test scores attend college and do well there. It is a widely held but patently false assumption that smart students always do well on standardized tests. The SAT is not a good indicator of intelligence or even of success in college beyond the first year.

What would have happened to Tony if he were just two years younger and a member of the first class required to pass the MCAS? Given his testing record, it seems certain that he would have been denied a high school diploma. Yet he writes well and is articulate, passionate, and extremely bright.

Watching Tony play Septimus Hodge in BAA's production of Tom Stoppard's *Arcadia* was a riveting experience. He clearly understood not only the subtleties of the character he was playing but also the complexities of the entire play, which poses difficult questions about historical truth, human passion, and physics. *Arcadia* is one of the most demanding plays I have ever seen, and it is rarely done by high school students. Tony took on his role with tremendous vigor.

In our newly emerging high-stakes world, Tony would have had to take test-prep classes and forgo Spanish, or science, or theater. He would have had to forfeit many other rigorous academic and artistic challenges in order to play the MCAS game.

MARINELA'S STORY

Marinela, two years younger than Tony, is another gifted student at the Boston Arts Academy. She wants to go to college. She wants to use her bilingual skills and has been pestering me to offer a course in reading, writing, and grammar skills for Spanish speakers. Although Marinela is not an outstanding actress, she is dedicated, hard working, a great ensemble member, and always positive about her work and the work of her colleagues. She has been on the honor roll since she arrived at BAA. Marinela does her homework on time, she stays after school to work with teachers when she doesn't understand a subject, and she has worked hard on her writing. She needs lots of coaching, especially with grammar and paragraph structure. She never gets a good grade until she has done three or four drafts of an assignment. She has begun to ask peers to help her review drafts so that she doesn't have to rely so much on her teachers. Her writing has improved greatly in the last two years.

Marinela's MCAS scores in writing are very low. Nevertheless, Marinela can write. She simply doesn't write well without lots of time and supervision. The MCAS allows for one draft and then a rewrite, but without any consultation. For some students, this is sufficient; for Marinela, it is not.

It doesn't bother me that Marinela needs help with her writing. It does bother me, though, that she might be denied a diploma because of one test. She understands the fundamentals of writing, but, as a bilingual student, she needs more time, assistance, and structure to work on her skills. Given the developmental nature of learning, Marinela needs to be encouraged to keep working on her weaknesses and developing her strengths.

In the high-stakes environment the state has created, Marinela will now be forced to make choices that are detrimental to her growth. She will need MCAS prep courses in order to pass the test. Thus she won't have time to take Spanish for Native Speakers, the very course she has lobbied for since coming to BAA. She may even have to leave the school, where she focuses on theater, and go to a regular school that places a much greater emphasis on MCAS preparation.

The state seems determined to label Marinela a failure because of one test and to cut off her chance to grow in other areas. What message does this treatment send her? It is that being bilingual is a liability and that needing more time or help to learn well is a mark of failure.

What do our educational leaders have to say about students like Tony and Marinela? "There will be some casualties," says the state commissioner of education in defending the MCAS graduation requirement. In such a get-tough climate, there is no room for students to work through "blockages" or bad attitudes. There is no room

for schools to develop alternative assessments. There will be some casualties. Why must education be a war?

Tony and Marinela represent only two of the many students whose lives will be dramatically altered in the brave new world of high-stakes testing. Schools like ours will be forced to make decisions that we know are educationally unsound just to get students through these tests. Arts courses will be canceled. Some academic courses will be replaced by test-prep courses because the day is only so long. And to what end? The students may pass these tests. But will they love science? Will they enter the job market with highly coveted bilingual skills? Will they pursue careers or college degrees in the arts? Or will their natural curiosity and love of learning be squashed?

THE UNMET PROMISE OF EDUCATION REFORM

Few educators imagined that the MCAS would become the sole method for assessing and validating student achievement. The Massachusetts Education Reform Act of 1993 promised improved schools that would fully develop the talents and skills of every child in the commonwealth. This legislation was a response to serious inequities in funding and performance in school districts across the state. The sponsors of the act promised the public "accountability" and clear benchmarks for student achievement. No longer would students be passed through school systems without acquiring basic academic skills.

No one could disagree with such goals. Moreover, the legislation promised principals more direct control of their schools, and parents were to have more involvement in school councils. Finally, the new law talked about the importance of multiple measures for assessing student learning. Many of us thought that our hard-won knowledge about authentic ways of assessing student achievement would finally be recognized by policy makers. We were wrong.

In some ways, it is easy to see why the MCAS quickly became the only game in town. It promised the carrot and stick that politicians, school administrators, and even some teachers wished for. A high-stakes test would force students (and their parents) to take education seriously. The test results, when made public, would make it very easy to rank individual schools and districts and so expose the slackers. And, of course, some real estate agents would be pleased. Furthermore, each child (and family) would receive individual scores that revealed the student's weaknesses, thus providing an opportunity for teachers to address them. A high-stakes test would also require a clear statewide curriculum, so that students in inner-city Boston and in its wealthy suburbs would be taught the same material (and then given the same test). Thus, the argument goes, the inequities in students' opportunity to learn would finally be eradicated. Besides creating the promised curriculum and new tests, the state promised a significant infusion of money for low-performing and poor districts to "level the playing field."

Finally, a high-stakes test would allow for intervention, presumably by the state, when a school produced persistently low test scores. If a school is given the appropriate resources, isn't it reasonable to assume that students should learn the required material? And isn't it also reasonable to think that taxpayers have the right to expect results from those students and teachers and to intervene when results aren't forthcoming?

But this way of thinking about teaching and learning, for all its superficial logic, is fundamentally flawed. First, research shows that high-stakes tests discourage and demoralize at least as many students and teachers as they motivate to work harder. The notion that threats of punishment (e.g., withholding a diploma) will create a positive learning environment and radically transform our most beleaguered educational institutions is not only discredited by research but is also grotesquely wrong-headed and cruel. High-stakes environments push dropout rates up, particularly for the most vulnerable students. The state's current policy will hurt most grievously the very students who are supposed to benefit most from it.

Even if we believed, as the testing proponents argue, that high-stakes tests will create conditions that force schools to change for the better, the withholding of diplomas is a flawed strategy. A one-size-fits-all test that determines every student's future takes the most important decisions about teaching and learning away from those closest to students: their teachers and families. That students like Tony or Marinela might actually do well in high school and perform adequately in reading, writing, math, and science but still get low scores on standardized tests is inconceivable to the high-stakes enthusiasts. Common sense and common experience prove that their idea of school reform is a fantasy—a war game in which young people are the expendable pawns.

THE PARADOX OF THE LATEST MCAS RESULTS

The MCAS results for the class of 2003 at the Boston Arts Academy have just been reported, and I am faced with a paradox. Our students did well. Like many other schools across the state, we had a dramatic reduction in the number of failing students. Colleagues are congratulating me. "Good for you, Linda," they say. "You put your personal opinions about the test aside and got your students to take it seriously."

It is true that we got our students to take the test seriously. Our theater students presented dramatic scenes about how to relieve test-prep stress; I spoke with students and parents about how we would be able to change the state's policy more easily from a position of strength (that is, passing) than from a position of weakness (that is, failing); and I continued to use scarce resources to bolster the students' math and literacy skills. We hired an extra math teacher rather than an administrative manager or a music teacher. Our music department badly needs another full-time teacher, but we cannot justify hiring one while our students' math scores (and skills) are still so far

behind those of their suburban peers. (Sadly, our students' music skills are also falling behind, but the state tells us that there is no contest between math and music: math must win.)

Our students did better on this year's MCAS for a number of reasons. First, we hired the Princeton Review to give them an MCAS prep course. The irony here is that the MCAS is touted by the policy makers as a test that cannot be studied for. It is supposed to measure students' accumulated mastery of 11 years of rigorous curricula from kindergarten through grade 10. That's why the policy makers say it's fair that the test carry high stakes.

Nevertheless, coaching helped our students pass the test. I am not sure that coaching helped them grapple with ideas, but I do think it made them much more comfortable with testing procedures and with what to expect on this particular test. Through coaching, our students learned how to sniff out good and bad answers to multiple-choice questions; they learned to skip down and read the questions before reading the literary passage or problem that preceded them; they learned about educated guessing.

Another reason that our students fared better this year is that the MCAS cut score was lowered. Last year, test-takers had to get 23 correct answers on the math test to pass; this year they needed only 20. The testing companies call this "scaled scoring." Whatever one calls it, it helped our students: 67% of them passed both the English and math tests. The district average was 40%; the state average was 68%. Only 18% of our students failed both tests. The district average was 43%; the state average, 19%.

Here's my dilemma, then. I can't help feeling good that our curriculum and test-prep strategies worked. But does teaching students how to take these tests merit such an enormous allocation of time and resources? Does knowing how to take a test make a student a better reader? Does it make him appreciate literature in a deeper way? Does it make her want to travel into the world of fiction or nonfiction or history? Do test-taking skills help sustain energy, organization, interest, and hard work for long-term projects?

Maybe I'm just a hard case. I was asked to leave the only prep course I ever took (for the Graduate Record Examination) because I challenged too many of the questions in the analogy section. I never scored particularly well on any standardized test, but I have been successful in school and professionally. I'm stubborn—like Tony and Marinela. And so I must ask again, What do these tests really measure?

The improvements in our students' MCAS scores this year reflect what we already know about the history of testing. As schools get to know a particular test, scores on that test go up year by year. Eventually that test is either abandoned for a "better" one or "recalibrated." There is no research that I'm aware of that shows sustained academic improvement driven by high-stakes testing.

I suspect that the tests students took this year were considerably less difficult than last year's. Certainly, the cut score—or passing bar—was lowered, and the tests may also have been revised to make them easier. The size of the improvement in scores in just one year has made testing experts very skeptical. If the MCAS were really forcing poor schools to do a better job, as the state would have us believe, then the gap between poor and minority students and white students would have shrunk. But it did not.

THERE IS AN ALTERNATIVE

In my ideal world, MCAS would be a minimum-competency test in English language arts and mathematics, and schools and districts would be able to develop their own accountability systems for other courses. At the Boston Arts Academy, our Humanities 3 benchmark is much higher than the MCAS standard, and we are in the first stages of developing numeracy benchmarks. Both the Massachusetts Teachers Association and the Coalition for Authentic Reform in Education (CARE) have put forward proposals that could be workable alternatives to MCAS-izing education. They call for limited tests in numeracy and literacy, with local assessments in other academic and arts areas, together with reviews of school quality based on the work of the British inspectorate system, the experience of the Boston pilot schools, and the school reviews that the state does for charter schools. It is imperative that the public be given an opportunity to review these alternative proposals.

It is tempting to simply congratulate ourselves on getting so many students over the MCAS hurdle. But let us think about what passing the test really means. A student can pass the MCAS and still have lousy math skills. Has the MCAS helped us deepen our understanding of what numeracy really means or how to help students acquire it? Will it bring teachers together to look at student work and help us ask hard questions about what constitutes good work? Will it provide the sustained professional development that teachers so desperately need and want? Will it support a commitment to literacy and numeracy coordinators and programs in all schools; high-quality instructional materials; and functioning, fully staffed libraries, arts, and sports programs?

Will the MCAS encourage our most intelligent and gifted college students to enter the teaching profession? Will it help the state figure out a way to staff summer schools so that students who need the extra time can be in rigorous programs with highly qualified teachers?

I fear MCAS will do none of these things. I fear that money will be spent on test-prep workbooks and Princeton Review-type courses, but not on lowering class size, providing professional development, or helping students learn the skills necessary to complete complex, long-term projects.

We have learned that we can get our students to pass this test through intensive coaching, double math classes, and a massive effort at emotional support (food, drinks, reminding students to relax and focus). All of this has paid off in the short term. In the long term, however, the test will change, and the positive results will last only a few years. Then the cycle will begin again.

Meanwhile, schools like the Boston Arts Academy are desperately trying to keep the MCAS from destroying their very fabric. I want Marinela and the many students like her to have the advantages and opportunities that helped Tony succeed so memorably. I don't want to create MCAS classes, steal time from arts instruction, and make good teachers abandon what they do best: develop innovative curricula and teach to a wide range of learners.

Why is it that the politicians who created the MCAS for public schools mostly send their own children to private schools, which rarely if ever use standardized tests to make important decisions about students? I want what the best private schools in the country have: small classes and assessment of students' actual achievements—their writing, their oral presentations, their science projects, their ways of attacking real-world problems, their artwork, their music, their ability to work with others.

Of our first graduating class of 52 seniors, 46 are now in two-year or four-year colleges, four are in career training programs, and two are still undecided. It baffles me that the philosophy, structure, and curriculum that undergird the Boston Arts Academy and that have created the conditions for this success are so rarely considered as serious solutions in the education reform debates. The current dialogue focuses solely on one-size-fits-all "accountability," measured by standardized tests, rather than on the success stories right in our midst.

What are we to do? For me, there is only one choice. I will continue to fight for a rich and rigorous arts and academic curriculum, taught by highly qualified and committed teachers in an atmosphere of respect and high expectations. If we can keep our eyes on these goals—and not on test scores alone—we can make it through this MCAS mania without destroying our students and our schools.

LINDA NATHAN is headmaster of the Boston Arts Academy.

How and Why Standards Can Improve
STUDENT ACHIEVEMENT

A Conversation with Robert J. Marzano

Marge Scherer

As Senior Fellow at the Mid-continent Research for Education and Learning (McREL) Institute in Aurora, Colorado, for the past 20 years, Robert J. Marzano has been responsible for translating research and theory into classroom practice. His most recent book for ASCD is the best-selling Classroom Instruction That Works, *which he coauthored with Debra J. Pickering and Jane E. Pollock.*

Recent efforts that address standards include coauthoring A Comprehensive Guide to Designing Standards-Based Districts, Schools, and Classrooms *(Alexandria, VA: ASCD and Aurora, CO: McREL, 1996) and authoring* Transforming Classroom Grading *(Alexandria, VA: ASCD, 2000). He is currently researching student-level variables related to academic achievement. In this interview, Marzano talks to* Educational Leadership *readers about the potential of standards-based education. He gives a progress report on the standards movement: the potential for reform, the challenges to overcome, and the direction to move in the future.*

What is the most compelling argument in favor of standards?

Standards hold the greatest hope for significantly improving student achievement. Every other policy mandate we've tried hasn't done so. For example, right after *A Nation at Risk* (Washington, DC: U.S. Department of Education, 1983) was published, we tried to increase academic achievement by making graduation requirements more rigorous. That was the first wave of reform, but it didn't have much of an effect.

The creation of standards documents by national subject matter organizations, such as the National Council of Teachers of Mathematics, set the stage for implementing standards. But we have yet to systematically enforce or implement standards.

Has the standards movement thus far had more positive or more negative effects on teachers and students?

I'd have to say it has had more positive effects. Even though the process of identifying standards has been clumsy, it has started a conversation across the United States about what students should know in different subject areas. Perhaps that's all it has done. But that's a huge step forward. The debate about whether or not academic achievement is important is over. Ten years ago, you wouldn't have had agreement that academic achievement was the central focus of public education. Today the standards movement has made this a foregone conclusion.

What conditions are necessary to implement standards effectively?

Cut the number of standards and the content within standards dramatically. If you look at all the national and state documents that McREL has organized on its Web site (www.mcrel.org), you'll find approximately 130 across some 14 different subject areas. The knowledge and skills that these documents describe represent about 3,500 benchmarks. To cover all this content, you would have to change schooling from K–12 to K–22. Even if you look at a specific state document and start calculating how much time it would take to cover all the content it contains, there's just not enough time to do it. So step one toward implementing standards is to cut the amount of content addressed within standards. By my reckoning, we would have to cut content by about two-thirds. The sheer number of standards is the biggest impediment to implementing standards.

Knowledge keeps expanding. Isn't it an impossible task to cut the standards by two-thirds?

It is a hard task, but not impossible. So far the people we've asked to articulate standards have been subject matter specialists. If I teach music and my life is devoted to that, of course I'm going to believe that all of what's identified in the national documents is important. Subject matter experts were certainly the ones to answer the question, What's important in your content area? To answer the question, What's absolutely essential? you have to broaden that population dramatically to include all constituents—those with and without college degrees.

In addition to trimming the standards, what else do we need to do to make standards-based education effective?

We need a monitoring system that allows us to track student progress on specific standards. State tests aren't effective feedback mechanisms. Those tests are given once a year. Schools and teachers don't get the results back for months. Effective feedback has to be timely; schools need to examine multiple data waves throughout the year, at least one data wave every grading period.

The only way to create an effective monitoring system is to change our grading practices to standards-based grading. We have the vehicle—grades. But the way we use our grading systems now tells us nothing about whether students have met standards. It will require major changes in thinking and record keeping to do this. But the good news is that people are starting to make those changes.

Talk more about what it means to use standards-based grading.

Grades—whether letter grades or percentage grades or a combination of both—don't tell us much unless we know the criteria on which they are based. Was the grade based on knowledge plus effort and behavior, and how was each factor weighted? In standards-based grading, you might still have, but not necessarily need, an overall score or letter grade. What you would have are rubric scores or percentage scores on specific standards that were covered in that course.

Over time you could plot the progress of students on specific standards. If all the math teachers scored students on the math standards, over the years you could see the pattern of scores for a student on a given standard. Those patterns are more reliable and valid than a single score on a test given at the end of the year.

As much as parents and the public have come to rely on national test results, will they ever have as much confidence in multiple teacher-made or school-made tests?

That's been a topic of study for me for the past five years. If kept track of appropriately and scored appropriately, classroom assessments can be very reliable. Five years from now, there will be enough research to ensure that standards-based classroom tests can be at least as precise as external tests. The two kinds of feedback—external assessments and internal classroom assessments—will balance each other and will lessen the need for a single high-stakes test. Using external and internal assessments will also decrease the chances of making incorrect decisions about students' achievement.

Some surveys suggest that the general public supports standards. Are teachers adapting to the new demands for accountability?

This is going to sound negative, but I don't think that teachers across the United States are implementing standards. Surveys about standards implementation usually boil down to asking teachers to verify whether or not they cover content that is specified in the state documents.

Districts often use a checklist—a surface-level approach to determining whether standards are implemented. They assume that the standards that teachers have checked off have been covered, but that might not be the case. A teacher might misinterpret the content stated in a standard or misjudge the depth to which the content must be covered for students to master it.

Some teachers don't take seriously the task of covering all the content. To get their students to do well on the state test, they teach to the test's topics. No matter how good the state tests are, they can never cover all the content in the standards, not even the essential content.

Should classroom teachers be responsible for selecting content?

Classroom teachers can't do it by themselves. Right now, the district or the school says, "Okay, teachers, here are the standards; you figure them out." And it's an impossible task. Someone at the district or school level has to cut the content down: get lean and mean and identify the bare-bones, essential content. Administrators have to set up a record-keeping and monitoring system that's easy for teachers to use. Only then can they expect teachers to implement standards. If teachers are given the tools and resources to complete the task, they will do a fine job of implementing standards.

Have states made any progress in helping teachers coordinate priorities in curriculum choices?

There's a funny dynamic that occurs. The schools and teachers are looking to the state departments of education for guidance about which content is important and essential. But the state departments, in an effort not to be too directive, are reluctant to provide guidance. They want to be flexible, but in fact they aren't giving the guidance that the schools and districts so desperately need. It's a very labor-intensive process to identify what's important and what's not.

Coordinating standards with curriculum is an easy task for teachers if they know what's essential and what's not. They are quite capable of making decisions about which parts of the textbook to use, which parts to supplement, which resources and instructional strategies to use.

You mentioned that some teachers misinterpret the standards. Are we making progress in drafting clearly stated, rigorous standards?

From my perspective, not enough. Even though state standards have become more specific, many statements at the benchmark level are still packed with too much content and too many activities. A single sentence within a benchmark might address two or three processes and several major generalizations. And as you read through the different benchmarks, you see incredible redundancies. And you can't easily translate the statements into learning goals. Part of the process of making standards lean and mean is not just cutting their numbers, but also making them specific and non-redundant. And no one at the state or national level is doing that.

The process of identifying standards has started a conversation about what students should know in different subject areas.

Would you single out one place where it's being done well?

No, but a number of states are trying.

Should we be working toward national content standards? For example, the southern states are identifying regional standards in algebra. Is this a positive development?

In general, yes, but let's qualify what we mean by national standards. If having national standards means having explicit goals—targets of knowledge and skill—yes, absolutely, we should have national standards, at least for certain subject areas. Algebra should address the same content, no matter whether it's taught in southern California or Maine. That's not necessarily the case with social studies, though, which is more values-driven.

But we must make the distinction between identifying the knowledge and skills that a student needs to know to be considered knowledgeable in a certain subject area and mandating the level of knowledge and skills that all students must achieve. These are two separate issues. On one side, you do education a great service by identifying the knowledge and skills that represent mastering a subject. But decisions about what students are held accountable for should be made at the local level.

A criticism of the standards movement is that having standards narrows the curriculum. Don't students get fewer choices in what they study if they have a standards-based education?

Remember, if you cut the standards down by two-thirds, you've made it possible for teachers to cover the essential knowledge in the time allotted. But you also have left a lot of room for teachers to supplement that content.

If I'm teaching a 7th grade math course and covering the mandated standards will take up one-third or even one-half of my instructional time, I still have the other half of the time to address content of my choosing. We should ensure that within a given school or state, all students are exposed to the same content. But we also must give teachers enough freedom to supplement this content and take advantage of serendipitous learning opportunities.

> ## To cover all the content in the standards identified thus far, you would have to change schooling from K-12 to K-22.

Will the new mandate to test students every year inspire a more thoughtful approach to standards and assessment or will it create more chaos?

The mandate for testing is a function of the need for more frequent feedback. Getting feedback on student progress as often as possible, at least once a year, is absolutely essential to the teaching and learning process. Using an external test, however, comes with built-in problems. The tests are narrow, and they narrow the curriculum if they are our only form of feedback. Results from external tests are gathered at one point in time, and data gathered at one point in time never truly indicate how students are doing. The place to go for the best feedback is the classroom. If we could make classroom assessment and classroom reporting a better feedback mechanism, we wouldn't have to rely on external tests. We'd have valid assessment information built into our system.

Some teachers feel that the emphasis on high-stakes testing stops them from being creative and from using good teaching strategies. What would you say to a teacher who expressed that point of view?

High-stakes testing does put negative pressure on teachers. If students don't do well on the test, the students can suffer severe consequences. Some may not receive a diploma or may only receive a certificate of attendance.

But I don't see how standards-based education hurts instructional creativity. Policymakers are not telling teachers how to teach; they're just saying that we must produce results relative to specific content. Using standards-based report cards would alleviate the pressure of the high-stakes tests because decisions could be made about students on the basis of patterns of scores obtained over time.

Even if teachers were given a more manageable number of standards to address and had a good record-keeping system that didn't increase their clerical work, they would still need a repertoire of instructional strategies to increase student learning.

In research we recently completed, we identified classroom practices that generally increase achievement: identifying similarities and differences; summarizing and note taking; receiving reinforcement for effort and recognition for achievement; doing homework and practicing; using nonlinguistic representations; learning cooperatively; setting objectives and receiving feedback; generating and testing hypotheses; and using cues, questions, and advance organizers. Regardless of whether or not you teach to standards, these classroom practices work well.

Where will the standards movement be in the next five years? Are standards here to stay?

In the next five years, we'll identify what's essential knowledge and what's not, and we will get very specific in terms of developmental expectations at different levels. And we'll develop a record-keeping system to help teachers provide valid classroom assessments. Researchers will do the technical work to show that classroom assessments can validly and reliably be used to judge students' performance on specific standards.

The biggest indicators that standards are here to stay are the public's demand for accountability and the dramatic increase in the public's access to information about students. With the national and state data available on the Internet, you can find out how students in specific schools are performing. Whether standards endure or not, what will remain is the demand for accountability. That means that we're going to have to be specific about what students know and are able to do. Whether we focus on standards or not, we're entering an era of accountability that has been created by technology and the information explosion.

Robert J. Marzano is Senior Fellow at the Mid-continent Research for Education and Learning (McREL) Institute, 2550 S. Parker Rd., Ste. 500, Aurora, CO 80014; robertjmarzano@aol.com. **Marge Scherer** is Editor in Chief of *Educational Leadership*; el@ascd.org.

STANDARDS:
Here Today, Here Tomorrow

Successful standards-based reform depends on clear standards, well-crafted tests, and fair accountability. Several strategies can help educators put those critical pieces in place.

Matthew Gandal and Jennifer Vranek

With which of these three propositions do you agree?

• Students, teachers, and parents need a clear idea of what students should learn each year, and those goals should be reasonable, rigorous, and the same for all children.

• Adults need to know whether students are reaching those targets, and to do so, we need a consistent way of measuring progress.

• Because it matters that students reach the goals, the system should connect incentives and supports with results.

We suspect that most adults in the United States agree with all these statements. But when we refer to these statements using the shorthand of *standards, assessment,* and *accountability,* we risk losing sight of the fundamental arguments that started us on this course of school improvement.

Every state and thousands of school districts have embraced the standards agenda for the same reason that Horace Mann, who championed the "common school" in the 19th century, used assessments to compare the quality of schools: This sort of comparison shines the spotlight on inequity and helps raise the achievement of all students. The public supports this agenda, with good reason. Parents and teachers know intuitively that the more we expect from children, the more they will achieve.

And most agree that our expectations have been too low for too long.

What Parents, Educators, and the Public Want

We don't have to guess how teachers, parents, or the general public feel about standards. Three recent opinion surveys paint an unmistakable picture of support for this direction of school improvement.

In an August 2000 national poll of both parents and nonparents conducted for the Business Round-table—an association of chief executive officers of leading U.S. corporations—8 of every 10 people said that raising academic standards is a move in the right direction (Business Roundtable, 2001). Three-quarters of parents and nonparents agree that students should have to pass reading and math tests to be promoted from 4th grade, even if they have passing grades in all their classes. Two-thirds agree that students should have to pass a test to earn a high school diploma, even if they have passed all their courses. Roughly 8 of 10 support such tests if students who initially fail the test receive extra help and more than one opportunity to pass. These sentiments are consistent even though those taking the poll also acknowledged that some students may have trouble passing tests and that the

tests may not measure every important skill that students are learning.

Last October, Public Agenda—a nonprofit, nonpartisan policy research organization—surveyed public school parents and found that only 2 percent favor abandoning standards (Public Agenda, 2000). A majority of respondents want their schools to continue implementing standards rather than go back to the way things were before those reforms began. The support was as strong in five large cities in the midst of standards-based reform efforts—Boston, Chicago, Cleveland, Los Angeles, and New York—as it was nationally.

When they are poorly devised and implemented, standards and assessments can become a distraction and a source of frustration.

More than 7 of 10 parents believe that tests are useful in several ways: to help identify students who need extra attention, to cause students to pay more attention to what is being taught, and to hold schools accountable for raising achievement. Only one parent in 10 believes that teachers put too much academic pressure on students, that schools require too many standardized tests, or that the test questions are too difficult.

In January 2001, *Education Week* released the results of a national survey that had probed U.S. teachers' views of standards, testing, and accountability. Eighty-seven percent of surveyed teachers agree that raising standards is "very much" or "somewhat" a "move in the right direction," and 74 percent say the level of standards in their states is "about right." This survey offers strong evidence that standards-based reforms are working, with a majority of teachers reporting more students reading, writing, and meeting more challenging expectations in the classroom.

These surveys are valuable because they go beyond simple yes-or-no questions about whether raising standards is a good idea. Many teachers and parents have legitimate concerns about the focus on testing in schools. We believe that these concerns have more to do with specific issues in specific states than with a wide disagreement about using higher standards to drive school improvement. Even when pressed, teachers and the public still believe that standards, assessment, and accountability will lead to the kind of schools that we want and need.

Still, anyone who has studied education reform in this country during the past century knows that good ideas and strong public support do not guarantee successful and widespread improvement. The key is in the execution—the translation of the broad aims upon which we agree into policies and practices that play out in classrooms.

Getting Standards and Tests Right

When they are well devised and implemented, academic standards and tests, and the accountability provisions tied to them, can change the nature of teaching and learning. They can lead to a richer, more challenging curriculum. They can foster conversation and collaboration among teachers within and across schools. They can create a more productive dialogue among teachers and parents. And they can help focus everyone's attention on raising student achievement. When they are poorly devised and implemented, standards, assessments, and accountability can become a distraction and a source of frustration in schools.

The independent, bipartisan, non-profit organization Achieve was created by U.S. governors and business leaders to help states determine the difference between high-quality and poor-quality standards, assessment, and accountability policies. During the past three years, we have worked with nearly half the states to examine their policies, compare them with the best examples from other states and nations, and offer suggestions for improvement.

We have drawn a number of conclusions from this work, which can best be expressed in terms of ongoing challenges that states face if standards are to bring about lasting improvements in U.S. classrooms.

Teachable Standards

For standards to have an impact on what goes on in the classroom, they must be teachable. Two qualities stand out in this regard: clarity and parsimony.

Clarity requires that the standards contain enough detail and precision to allow teachers, parents, and students to know what the students need to learn. Standards that are vague or unclear can be misunderstood or ignored altogether. Teachers may feel forced to turn to something else besides the standards to guide their instruction, and often they turn to the tests—thus fueling concerns that schools are teaching to the test rather than teaching a rigorous curriculum. If the standards are ambiguous, they also offer no assurance that every student is learning challenging material.

Even when pressed, teachers and the public still believe that standards, assessment, and accountability will lead to the kind of schools we want and need.

In our work with states, Achieve has found the clarity glass half full. Nearly all the standards that we have reviewed are clear and jargon-free. They avoid including expectations that cannot be measured, such as students' "enjoyment of reading," a pitfall of many earlier versions of standards.

But too often, the standards that we have reviewed tend to be impre-

cise and all-encompassing. Stating that students should "read literally, inferentially, and critically" gives little guidance to teachers trying to build lessons. Those standards could refer to Shakespeare's sonnets or to Julia Child's cookbooks. Such imprecision is a recipe for uneven teaching and unequal learning. Oregon, for example, is drafting new English standards in response to Achieve's benchmarking work. One of the new 4th grade standards requires students to use knowledge of the situation and setting and of a character's traits and motivation to determine the causes for that character's action. This standard focuses attention on the analysis of literary elements in a way that enriches instruction. The same is not true of standards that require students to identify the setting or to understand character motivation.

Five years ago, standards may have been left vague in deference to local control of the curriculum: Let the state set the broad goals, but leave the curriculum to local schools and educators. But that has not turned out to be very practical. As schools and students have begun to be held accountable for results, educators have demanded more specific guidance and teaching tools, and so far demand has outstripped supply.

In response, some states are getting creative. Indiana clarified its statewide standards in the 1999–2000 school year to provide more detail and guidance and is building aligned curriculum frameworks, complete with embedded assessments that districts can choose to implement. Vermont uses technology to help teachers align classroom teaching and assessment with the state standards. The state's system includes instructional planning and assessment management tools, an online teacher forum, and a database of its standards. In New York City, the United Federation of Teachers has launched a $2 million effort to help align standards and provide teachers time off to develop a bank of student work and lesson plans tied to standards.

Of course, states can go too far in providing clarity and specificity. Making standards more specific only helps if they become more focused as a result. Educators must make tough choices about the most important knowledge for all students to learn; a laundry list helps no one. Although politically expedient, the approach some states have taken—to include everything students could learn in a subject to avoid offending anyone— simply does not work. The end result of a glut of standards is the same as when the standards are ambiguous— they fail to define what all students should learn. Moreover, too many standards undermine the power of standards as common expectations and leave teachers feeling over- whelmed by the sheer volume of what needs to be taught. Many teachers will be more apt simply to cover the material rather than give it the in-depth treatment that we know benefits students.

Rigorous, Reasonable Standards

The public will continue to support standards so long as the students who reach them are prepared to suc- ceed in the next grade, in college, and in meaningful careers. These are the tangible outcomes that parents want for their children. The kinds of liter- acy, math, science, and problem-solv- ing skills that we once expected of only some students are needed by all to succeed in a fast-moving, technol- ogy-driven world.

So how high is high enough? The answer is murky, in part because lit- tle conclusive research pinpoints what all students need to learn to be prepared for life after high school. We do know, however, that most high school students aspire to attend col- lege and that most parents expect a high school diploma to signify readi- ness to do college-level work. Unfor- tunately, the Education Trust estimates that although as many as 80 percent of today's 8th graders will attend some form of college immedi- ately after they finish high school, on average one-third of those students (and as many as 50 percent of stu- dents from high-poverty areas) will need remediation in basic reading, writing, and math before they are ready to undertake college-level work (Haycock & Huang, 2001).

It is reasonable to expect that stu- dents who have met state standards are prepared to do college-level work without remediation, so we must en- sure that standards are rigorous at every grade level. In Achieve's analy- sis of state standards, we have found that although some states have im- proved the rigor of their standards, others still have not raised standards high enough to prepare all students for college-level work or for high-skilled jobs (Education Week, 2001).

Another way to determine where to set the bar is to look at what other countries expect of their students. When compared with the standards of high-performing nations, many state standards don't match the rigor or depth of content that other nations routinely expect their students to master. In Japan, for example, stu- dents are asked to know place values to 10,000 by 3rd grade and place val- ues up to 100 million, 1 billion, and 1 trillion by 4th grade. In some U.S. states, these expectations—met by Japanese students in two years—are spread over six years of math.

Parents and teachers know intuitively that the more we expect from children, the more they will achieve.

We recognize that many schools are already working hard to prepare students for the rigors of postsecond- ary life and that many students are struggling to meet those high expec- tations. That's why the pace at which states phase in these expectations needs to be reasonable and responsi- ble. Texas and New York, for exam- ple, both set the initial passing standard on their tests low and are slowly raising it as schools and stu- dents adjust to higher standards.

Tests That Measure the Standards

Although most states are trying to align their tests with their stan- dards, our experience shows that it is more difficult than many originally thought. We encourage states to con- sider three key principles.

If it's not in the standards, it shouldn't be on the test. Achieve has found that most states that have de- veloped their own tests have done a good job of ensuring that nearly ev- erything found in the tests can be found in the standards. The tests should offer no surprises for teachers and students and should provide a clear path for teaching and learning. The same is not true when states use off-the-shelf standardized tests. Al- though generic tests will probably measure a small portion of a state's standards, these tests are general enough to use in many states with varying standards. They cannot mea- sure the breadth and depth of each state's standards. Even more trou- bling, such tests may measure con- tent that is not specified in some states' standards, sending mixed mes- sages about what students should be learning. Tests based on standards that are clear, rigorous, and public are the fairest, most effective way to measure school and student perfor- mance. Tests not based on the stan- dards are neither fair nor particularly helpful to schools or parents.

When the standards are rich and rigorous, the tests must be as well. The most common problem Achieve has uncovered in our analysis of assess- ments is that even though the stan- dards may include high-level concepts and skills, the tests often don't (Educa- tion Week, 2001). Most states use some combination of multiple-choice, open-ended, and essay questions, and we have found weak and outstanding examples of every kind of question. For example, some open-ended questions on math assessments that purport to measure problem solving require only that students plug numbers into a for- mula, rather than asking them to de- termine how to solve the problem and show how they arrived at that solu- tion. We have also found that test makers underutilize multiple-choice questions—an important and straight- forward measure of student knowl- edge. Tests don't need to measure only the most rudimentary skills and knowledge, but they often do.

Regardless of the choice of ques- tion format, standards-based tests must tap both the breadth and the depth of content and skills in the standards. Otherwise, we risk nar- rowing the curriculum to only those concepts that are tested. In one state, for example, the mathematics as- sessments skirt nearly all of the more challenging concepts from the middle and high school standards, including slope; similarity; the Pythagorean Theorem; circles; sur- face area; volume; coordinate geome- try; spatial relationships; symmetry;

congruence; transformations; vectors; and measurement formulas for volumes, surface areas, or areas of polygons other than rectangles and triangles. What's left? Basic arithmetic, statistics, and other concepts that altogether account for only a portion of what we found in the standards are the topics of the tests.

In another state, the English standards typically ask students to "identify and analyze." But the tests almost exclusively focus on the easier skill—identify. Again, such high-level skills as analysis and interpretation can and must be measured by assessments if the assessments are to provide the type of information that teachers and parents need. Although the test format is a factor, multiple-choice questions can measure more than simple concepts. We have seen numerous examples of rigorous and meaningful multiple-choice questions that probe both students' understanding of characters, story events, and themes in literature and their ability to follow directions, extract meaning, and synthesize information from nonfiction materials. For example, an item on the 10th grade English exam in Massachusetts asked, "What do 'shadows' represent throughout this essay?" The correct answer—inherited instincts—required interpretation of a symbol rather than simple recall. On Michigan's English tests, students are sometimes asked to analyze a passage on the basis of what they have read in another passage: "The character in The 'Open Window' who best fits the description of a storyteller by the author of 'The Importance of Fiction' is…" Tests that pay short shrift to such critical concepts and skills may inadvertently encourage schools to narrow the curriculum.

Tests should become more challenging in each succeeding grade. If the standards grow more challenging as students move through school, it only makes sense that the tests should, too. The solid foundation of basic skills and knowledge for younger students should evolve into more complex skills for older students. Perhaps the most intriguing finding in our work has been that elementary and middle school tests, for the most part, are appropriately rigorous, yet the high school tests are often well below the level of challenge

that we would expect of all students. In a few cases, the high school tests are less rigorous than the 8th grade tests. Sometimes this situation occurs because the tests omit the more challenging concepts, and sometimes the test questions are simply too easy for high school students.

The public will continue to support standards so long as the students who reach them are prepared to succeed in the next grade, in college, and in meaningful careers.

Just what content should be measured and how rigorous the high school tests should be are difficult issues that most states are grappling with, particularly when students will be asked to pass the tests as a graduation requirement. It's easy to see why states may de-emphasize the more challenging concepts and skills on tests that all students are asked to pass. Yet, far too many high school graduates are bound for college but academically under-prepared. We are doing them no favors by lowering the standards.

Tools Teachers Need

Common sense dictates that teachers will be asked to do more if students are asked to do more. That's undoubtedly the case with standards, assessment, and accountability. One of the biggest challenges in advancing standards-based reform is providing teachers with the training, tools, and supports they need to help all students reach high standards.

Education Week's survey (2001) reveals that teachers believe that they are not getting enough help. Fewer than half of teachers in the United States say that they have plenty of access to curriculum guides, textbooks, or other teaching materials or to specific training connected to state standards. Barely a third say that they have plenty of access to lessons or teaching units that match standards, and fewer than a fifth say that they have had plenty of training on using state test results to diagnose learning gaps. In fact, only four states let teachers know how each student performed on every multiple-choice item, and only nine states

send teachers their own students' scored work on essay questions.

The report's analysis of professional development opportunities in the United States reveals that teacher training is not closely linked to standards. In our benchmarking work, we map each test question back to the standard that it is intended to measure as a starting point for evaluating that question's effectiveness. We would argue that the same should be possible for the college preparation that prospective teachers undergo and the professional development that practicing teachers experience. If we are to hold educators accountable for their work in helping students reach high standards, we have to know how the training those educators have received connects to the standards. *Education Week* reported, however, that whereas 38 states require teachers to participate in professional development to renew their teaching licenses, only seven of them require that some of the training be in the teachers' subject areas. Training in content areas is the least we should expect.

Some states are making professional development a priority. California has created professional development institutes for teachers of reading, English, and mathematics, with an emphasis on the subject matter covered in the state standards. The institutes provide intensive instruction to both beginning and veteran teachers, with priority going to teachers in low-performing schools.

A Fighting Chance for Students

If the standards represent the skills and knowledge that we agree are essential, we need to give students whatever assistance they need to reach them, whether it be more time, extra help, or a more focused curriculum. Inaction on this front could undermine the promise of standards-based reform.

The first question that schools need to ask is whether their curriculum is aligned with the state standards. If the standards are clear and rigorous, it will be easier to make this determination; if they are too broad or vague, any curriculum could be said to match. Growing evidence suggests that exposure to rigorous material pays off. Students who take a full set of college preparatory courses perform better on the National Assessment of Educational Progress (NEAP) tests in math and science and on the SAT than students who take two years or less of math (Haycock & Huang, 2001). The University of Massachusetts at Boston found that minority students in that state are underrepresented in the math classes that prepare students for the state's high school test. Such disparities explain much of the achievement gap between minority and white students on the state test (Coleman, 2001). Although a few states are responding to the cry for help, not enough is being done to identify or produce curriculum materials tied to standards.

In addition to a strong curriculum, all schools need an intervention and support system for students who fall behind. States and districts are beginning to put such programs in place, but the pace in many places is too slow. Maryland, for example, has recognized the importance of this challenge and has made addressing it a top priority. A new initiative will require schools to provide additional help to students who fall behind in reading and math, either in school, after school, on weekends, or over the summer. The state will supply the financial resources to carry out this mandate. The state will also help districts train their teachers to diagnose learning problems and provide the right help.

As for the tests, they shouldn't come at a moment's notice or be a single make-or-break experience. Students and schools should have adequate time to prepare before the tests count. Many states have followed the approach of allowing several years before stakes are attached to test results. Students should also have multiple opportunities to retake tests if they don't succeed on the first try, preferably after receiving additional targeted help.

Staying the Course

None of our observations about needed improvements in states' standards, assessment, or accountability policies should be confused with the chorus from critics who question the need for testing and accountability altogether. Some would have us abandon testing or put accountability on hold indefinitely until the tests are perfect. That would be a mistake. Standards and tests are better today than they have ever been. They can get better, but we shouldn't let the ideal be the enemy of what's very good and effective. Students have told us that they can do more if schools expect it of them. Teachers have told us that standards, assessment, and accountability are leading them to ask more from their students and that students are stepping up to the new demands. Although shortcomings still need to be addressed, we are already seeing meaningful improvements.

Standards and tests are better today than they have ever been.

It is no surprise that the states making the greatest gains in reading and mathematics on the NAEP in the 1990s—such as Connecticut, Kentucky, North Carolina, and Texas—also were early and consistent supporters of state standards and tests. They have stayed the course over time, making adaptations and improvements as necessary.

Educators praise the impact of standards, particularly in high-poverty schools. When Virginia began its state tests, fewer than 10 percent of students at Tidewater Park Elementary School in Norfolk passed the math, science, or history tests. Three years later, about 8 of 10 Tidewater Park students pass the tests. And there are many other examples of high-poverty schools and districts that are using standards and achieving both equity and excellence.

But we must move from the isolated pockets of excellence to excellence for all. If educators and policymakers can address the issues above, we will see schools improve in unprecedented ways. We owe it to our children to get this right.

References

Business Roundtable. (2001, Spring). *Assessing and addressing the "testing backlash."* Washington, DC: Author.

Coleman, S. (2001, April 12). Racial course disparities found. *The Boston Globe*, p. B5.

Education Week. (2001). *Quality counts 2001—A better balance: Standards, tests, and the tools to succeed.* Bethesda, MD: Editorial Projects in Education.

Haycock, K., & Huang, S. (2001, Winter). Are today's high school graduates ready? *Thinking K–16, 5*, 3–17.

Public Agenda. (2000, October 5). Survey finds little sign of backlash against academic standards or standardized tests [Press release].

Matthew Gandal is Vice President and **Jennifer Vranek** is Director of Benchmarking and State Services at Achieve; http://www.achieve.org.

Where's the Content? The Role of Content in Constructivist Teacher Education

by Sam Hausfather

Constructivism has become the reigning paradigm in teacher education in America today. More and more teacher education programs portray themselves as following a constructivist approach (Richardson, 1997), but there remains limited understanding among teachers and the public of the meaning of constructivism. Recently constructivism has come under attack from conservative elements who view it as too focused on empowerment, and from educators who view it as soft on content (Baines and Stanley, 2000). A deeper understanding of constructivism and the role of content in constructivist teaching is needed by both teacher educators and K–12 teachers in order to fulfill the constructivist promise of improved student learning.

What is Constructivism?

One aspect of constructivism that challenges easy understanding is the fact that there is not just one constructivist theory but a multiplicity of them (see, e.g., Fosnot, 1996; Phillips, 1995; Prawat, 1996). Steffe and Gale (1995) note six different constructivist paradigms: social constructivism, radical constructivism; social constructionism; information-processing constructivism; cybernetic systems; and sociocultural approaches to mediated action. Constructivism is often used as an umbrella term (Larochelle, Bednarz, and Garrison, 1998, p. vii) for a range of theories that offer various alternatives to the empiricist view that knowledge comes to us from the world "out there" and to the nativist view that knowledge is inborn.

In contrast with both empiricism and nativism, constructivism proposes that knowledge emerges from human activity as people interact with each other and with the physical world, using their minds and bodies as well as the material and symbolic tools made available to them by their cultures (Newman, Griffin, and Cole, 1989). Thus we actively construct our knowledge and do not passively receive it from experience or heredity. To be sure, experience and heredity make important contributions, but they do not constitute our knowledge in and of themselves. What is missing from such accounts is the crucial role of our *activity*, both as individuals and with others. Our own activity transforms what comes from within and from without; it results in the construction of something that cannot be reduced to either (Staver, 1998). What we construct at one time may later be reconstructed, and then reconstructed again, in the light of future experience and (sometimes) maturation. Most important, though, it is what we have already constructed that gives us a basis for using the resources given by nature and experience in the further construction of knowledge.

Constructivist Approaches to Learning Content

Constructivism is based on a firm knowledge base of learning theory derived from cognitive psychology. Research in cognitive science has supported constructivist theory and progressed to the point that clear implications are apparent in educational practice. Gaea Leinhardt (1992) has synthesized the cognitive research that supports constructivism and summarized the implications around three fundamental aspects: multiple forms of knowledge, the role of prior knowledge, and the social nature of knowledge and its acquisition.

Multiple Forms of Knowledge

Research on learning has led to the understanding that there are both different types and amounts of knowledge. Declarative knowledge of content concepts and principles becomes powerful for students when it is connected with procedural knowledge of actions and skills (Best, 1995).

Knowledge varies as we examine the different arrangements of facts, notations, and reasoning that are used in different subject areas. Documentation, arguments, and explanations are structured in distinctive ways in different disciplines. In addition, metaknowledge—knowing what and how well one knows—is seen as a powerful factor in developing understanding (Schoenfeld, 1987).

These multiple forms of knowledge highlight the complexity of learning. Knowledge is seen not just as information, but as an active process, retained when embedded in some organizing structure (Bereiter, 1985). When students interact with information, using it in solving problems, answering questions, or discussing interpretations, the information becomes their knowledge, tied to their unique understandings. This points toward teaching that integrates knowing content with using content, dissolving the line between content and process (Leinhardt, 1992). An active, problem-solving approach should be an element of any content approach taken. Because knowledge also does not exist in isolation, it must be connected to student prior knowledge and larger contexts in order to be incorporated into deep understanding. Interdisciplinary approaches can connect the richness of separate disciplines while acknowledging their interrelationships and modes of inquiry (Martinello and Cook, 2000).

In mathematics, students come to class with effective but alternative routes to mathematics processes that are often confounded by teaching.

The separation of schools of education from schools of arts and sciences within the university often disconnects content courses from courses on teaching methods and learning (NCTAF, 1996). Although teacher education has sought more integration of content with process, the content prospective teachers learn in their arts and sciences courses is generally left separate and inactive through the teacher education sequence. Teacher education students often take 50 percent to 85 percent of their course work in the arts and sciences (Gollnick, 1996).

Many large arts and sciences courses seldom challenge students' prior knowledge and often reinforce a transmission view of knowledge. A compilation of broad knowledge is emphasized over in-depth study that would challenge student misconceptions. Teacher education faculty should work closely with arts and sciences faculty to plan and implement courses linking strong disciplinary preparation with the methods and content of pedagogical studies. Brooklyn College of the City University of New York has developed a teacher education program in which students take several three-course sequences made up of a liberal arts course, an education "bridging" course, and a pedagogy course (Grumet, 1992). The mixed faculty teaching these courses plans syllabi, readings, and discussions together. All teacher education programs should closely examine their own curricula to determine the extent to which they model interdisciplinary integration of content and pedagogy.

Role of Prior Knowledge

Learning involves continually connecting prior knowledge with new information (Leinhardt, 1992). This prior knowledge can facilitate, inhibit, or transform learning. In reading, comprehension has been shown to depend on what one already knows or wants to know (Smith, 1988). Research into the nature of "children's science," the ideas and experiences students bring into class with them (Driver, Guesne, and Tiberghien, 1985; West and Pines, 1985), shows students hold tenaciously to their prior ideas. These alternative conceptions or misconceptions, which grow out of students' prior experiences, can interfere considerably with attempts to foster learning. In mathematics, students come to class with effective but alternative routes to mathematics processes that are often confounded by teaching (Carpenter et al., 1989). Research on history reveals students' tendency to see historical events in terms of individuals' intentions and interactions and to ignore the role of societal institutions (Barton, 1997).

Teacher educators are caught in the bind of informing teacher candidates about the importance of prior experiences and misconceptions while also having to deal with these candidates' own prior experiences and misconceptions. The "apprenticeship of observation" (Lortie, 1975) through lengthy personal experience with schooling prevents preservice teachers from searching beyond what they already know and from questioning the practices they see (Feiman-Nemser and Buchmann, 1987). On the other hand, some teacher education programs promote conceptual change in their students toward viewing schools as they could be, not merely as they are. Experiences that challenge student conceptions of schooling include provocative readings and discussion (such as Kozol, 1991, etc.), simulations, and experiences in experimental schools that can provide different visions of education. In their content studies, preservice teachers' misconceptions can also be challenged. Teacher education programs that work with faculty in arts and sciences to understand student preconceptions can promote approaches that will challenge these preconceptions. Through having their own conceptions challenged and through learning about the prior knowledge of their students, teacher candidates will be better prepared to provide their students content knowledge linked with student prior knowledge.

Social nature of knowledge

Finally, the social aspect of knowledge provides clear implications in practice. As outlined above, learning is an active process of knowledge construction and sense making. Beyond that, knowledge is understood as a cultural artifact. It is created and transformed by each individual and by groups of people (Vygotsky, 1978). As a result, learning should involve talk, public reasoning, and shared problem solving. Too often the social environment of schools is counterproductive to learning (Hausfather,

1996). Instead of a focus on individual achievement, learning should involve social interaction that supports thinking, brings prior knowledge to the surface, and allows skills to be used in the context of content knowledge. Participating in communities of discourse allows students to clarify, defend, elaborate, evaluate, and argue over the knowledge constructed (Brown, 1994). Many teachers use cooperative learning as a powerful route to building communities of discourse in their classrooms and to improving learning outcomes (Slavin, 1996).

Teacher education has a clear role in focusing a vision of a social environment supportive of learning. Preservice methods courses can model collaboration between and among the teacher and students. College teaching has traditionally stressed individual processes over social processes in learning. Teacher education needs to provide opportunities in which college students learn within cooperative or discourse groups while analyzing their own experiences, as a guide to their teaching. Instructional conversations can occur within the classic Socratic seminar, where instructor and students together explore problems as a small community of learners. Pairing students for field experience placements in schools helps foster deeper understandings of classroom situations (Hausfather, Outlaw, and Strehle, 1996). Pairing allows preservice teachers to see the value of collegial reflection in contrast to the individuality prevalent in schools.

Too often the social environment of schools is counterproductive to learning

Pedagogical content knowledge

Research in teaching has identified the linking of content with the process of teaching; such links occur as the teacher continually restructures subject matter knowledge (Cochran, DeRuiter, and King, 1993). Termed "pedagogical content knowledge" (PCK)—"the ways of representing and formulating the subject that make it comprehensible to others" (Shulman, 1986, p. 9)—this concept connects research on teaching with research on learning, helping determine constructivist approaches to learning content for teaching. This goes beyond knowledge of the content *per se* to include issues of teaching, including curricular choices, powerful ideas, common learning difficulties, and student conceptions. Teachers derive PCK from their understandings of content, their teaching practice, and their own school experience (Shulman, 1987). Although scholars have different conceptualizations of PCK, all agree it differs considerably from content knowledge, and that it is developed through an integrative process during classroom practice (Van Driel, Verloop, and De Vos, 1998). Cochran, DeRuiter, and King (1993) renamed PCK as pedagogical content *knowing* (PCKg), based on constructivist views. Their model includes subject matter content and specific pedagogical

knowledge but adds teachers' understanding of students and environment. Understanding students includes student abilities and learning strategies, developmental levels, attitudes, motivations, and prior conceptions. Context includes teachers' understandings of the social, political, cultural, and physical environment.

Research in PCK reinforces cognitive science (Cochran, DeRuiter, and King, 1993) and many of the implications listed above (Ashton, 1990). Programs can enhance the development of PCK in candidates by modeling and sharing teaching decisions and strategies with students, both by education and content-area faculty. Faculty should have opportunities to demonstrate and reflect on how they use PCK in their own teaching (Cochran, DeRuiter, and King, 1993). Contexts that promote active simultaneous learning about the many components of teaching within the content area promote the development of PCK. These contexts should be similar to classroom environments, which suggests the incorporation of multiple field-based opportunities. Early, continued, and authentic field experiences include real teaching, much contact with experienced teachers, reflection, and feedback (Hausfather, Outlaw, and Strehle, 1996).

It appears that a thorough and coherent understanding of content is necessary for effective PCK (Van Driel, Verloop, and De Vos, 1998). Teacher education programs can help preservice teachers construct a deep understanding of disciplinary content from a teaching perspective so it can be used to help specific students understand specific concepts (Cochran, DeRuiter, and King, 1993). This involves working closely with arts and sciences faculty to understand pedagogical perspectives and integrating methods courses with or alongside content courses.

Teacher education needs to provide opportunities in which college students learn within cooperative or discourse groups while analyzing their own experiences, as a guide to their teaching.

A teacher education program that balances attention to the process of learning with the content of what is being learned can help teachers to better understand both their content and the learning of their students. Too often content is taught without any attention to process, or process is taught without a deep understanding of content. Constructivist approaches seek to balance the process with the content. Content does not disappear but in fact is deepened!

Where's the Content?

Educators early in their career, and especially teacher education students, tend to focus on the hands-on aspect of teaching. Constructivism is often interpreted as making learning fun and active. Sometimes activity is misunderstood as physical activity only. Either through a desire to find alternatives to schooling as it exists or through less-than-complete presentations of constructivist theory from teacher educators, too many teachers are learning misinterpretations of constructivism. Teacher educators should continually emphasize the minds-on aspect of constructivist approaches to teaching. Mental activity is of primary importance, and, depending on developmental level, physical activity merely leads us to that end. The content and concepts that students must learn have to be at the center of constructivist teaching. Content, however, does not come first. Students' experiences, ideas, and prior knowledge come first. Content knowledge is then built upon student knowledge through the active involvement of students. The goal of our teaching must always be building an understanding of the current accepted knowledge within a particular discipline in ways that impact student understanding.

Constructivism is not a method. It is a theory of knowledge and learning that should inform practice but not prescribe practice. By its very nature, constructivism emphasizes the importance of the teaching context, student prior knowledge, and active interaction between the learner and the content to be learned. There is no teaching technique that should be prescribed or forbidden based solely on its constructivist "fit." Some teacher educators view lecturing solely as transmission of information. Yet there are effective ways to lecture that make use of constructivist principles. Lecturers can begin from a group's prior experiences and concerns. They can use stories to set and create contexts for understandings. They can make us think! The key is to move a mentally active audience toward deeper understandings of a particular content. Constructivism should be able to explain all instances of learning.

Conclusions

Constructivist approaches to teacher education must acknowledge the vital link between content and its acquisition. Constructivism challenges some basic understandings of content knowledge. Research supporting constructivist approaches can bring to teacher education practice insights that make for more powerful teaching, as long as student understanding of content remains paramount. An understanding of the nature of pedagogical content knowledge should lead teacher educators to work more closely with arts and sciences faculty.

Teacher education provides a multiplier effect. Teacher educators must first model approaches that lead their students to understand content deeply and to view content and process as inseparable aspects of knowledge construction. These new teachers then gain the perspectives and abilities to move their own students to deeper understandings of content. A constructivist approach shows us that content and process are not dichotomous.

References

Ashton, P.T. (1990). Editorial: Theme issue on pedagogical content knowledge. *Journal of Teacher Education* 41(3), 2.

Baines, L. A., and Stanley, G. (2000). 'We want to see the teacher' : Constructivism and the rage against expertise. *Phi Delta Kappan* 82(4), 327–330.

Barton, K. C. (1997). "Bossed around by the queen": Elementary students' understanding of individuals and institutions in history. *Journal of Curriculum and Supervision* 12 (4), 290–314.

Bereiter, C. (1985). Toward a solution of the learning paradox. *Review of Educational Research* 55, 201–226.

Best, J. B. (1995). *Cognitive psychology.* 4th ed. St. Paul, Minn.: West Publishing Co.

Brown, A. L. (1994). The advancement of learning. *Educational Researcher* 23(8), 4–12.

Carpenter, T. P., Fennema, E., Peterson, P. L., Chiang, C. P., and Loef, M. (1989). Using knowledge of children's mathematics thinking in classroom teaching: an experimental study. *American Educational Research Journal* 26(4), 499–531.

Cochran, K. F., DeRuiter, J. A., and King, R. A. (1993). Pedagogical content knowing: an integrative model for teacher preparation. *Journal of Teacher Education* 44(4), 263–272.

Driver, R., Guesne, E. and Tiberghien, A., eds. (1985). *Children's ideas in science.* Philadelphia, Pa.: Open University Press.

Feiman-Nemser, S., and Buchmann, M. (1987). When is student teaching teacher education? *Teaching and Teacher Education* 3(4), 255–273.

Fosnot, C., ed. (1996). *Constructivism: Theory, perspectives, and practice.* New York: Teachers College Press.

Gollnick, D. (1996). Can arts and sciences faculty prepare quality teachers? *American Behavioral Scientist* 40(3), 233–241.

Grumet, M. (1992). The language in the middle: Bridging the liberal arts and teacher education. *Liberal Education* 78(3), 2–7.

Hausfather, S. J. (1996). Vygotsky and schooling: creating a social context for learning. *Action in Teacher Education* 18(2), 1–10.

Hausfather, S. J., Outlaw, M. E., and Strehle, E. L. (1996). Relationships as a foundation: emerging field experiences within multiple college-school partnerships. In T. Warren, ed. *Partnerships in teacher education: schools and colleges working together*, 27–41. Lanham, Md.: University Press of America.

Kozol, J. (1991). *Savage inequalities: children in America's schools.* New York: Crown Publications.

Larochelle, M., Bednarz, N., and Garrison, J., eds. (1998). *Constructivism and education.* New York: Cambridge University Press.

Leinhardt, G. (1992). What research on learning tells us about teaching. *Educational Leadership* 49(7), 20–25.

Lortie, D. (1975). *Schoolteacher: A sociological study.* Chicago: University of Chicago Press.

Martinello, M. L. and Cook, G. E. (2000). *Interdisciplinary inquiry in teaching and learning.* 2nd ed. Upper Saddle River, N.J.: Prentice-Hall.

Newman, D., Griffin, P., and Cole, M. (1989). *The construction zone: Working for cognitive change in schools.* Cambridge, U.K.: Cambridge University Press.

NCTAF (1996). *What matters most: Teaching for America's future.* New York: National Commission on Teaching and America's Future.

Phillips, D. C. (1995). The good, the bad, and the ugly: The many faces of constructivism. *Educational Researcher* 24, 5–12.

Prawat, R. S. (1996). Constructivisms, modern and postmodern. *Educational Psychologist* 31(3/4), 215–225.

Richardson, V., ed. (1997). *Constructivist teacher education: Building new understandings.* Washington, D.C.: Falmer Press.

Schoenfeld, A. H. (1987). What's all the fuss about metacognition? In A. H. Schoenfeld, ed., *Cognitive science and mathematics education*, 189–253. New York: W. H. Freeman.

Shulman, L. S. (1986). Those who understand: knowledge growth in teaching. *Educational Researcher* 15, 4–14.

Shulman, L. S. (1987). Knowledge and teaching: foundations of the new reform. *Harvard Educational Review* 57, 1–22.

Slavin, R. E. (1996). Research on cooperative learning and achievement: What we know, what we need to know. *Contemporary Educational Psychology* 21(1), 43–69.

Smith, F. (1988). *Understanding reading: A psycholinguistic analysis of reading and learning to read.* Hillsdale, N.J.: Erlbaum.

Staver, J. R. (1998). Constructivism: Sound theory for explicating the practice of science and science teaching. *Journal of Research in Science Teaching* 35(5), 501–520.

Steffe, L. P., and Gale, J., eds. (1995). *Constructivism in education.* Hillsdale, N.J.: Erlbaum.

Van Driel, J. H., Verloop, N., and De Vos, W. (1998). Developing science teachers' pedagogical content knowledge. *Journal of Research in Science Teaching* 35(6), 673–695.

Vygotsky, L. S. (1978). *Mind in society: The development of higher psychological processes.* Cambridge, Mass.: Harvard University Press.

West, L. H., and Pines, A. L., eds. (1985). *Cognitive structure and conceptual change.* Orlando, Fla.: Academic Press.

Sam Hausfather, Ph.D., is dean of the School of Professional Studies, East Stroudsburg University of Pennsylvania.

From *Educational Horizons,* Fall 2001, pp. 15-19. © 2001 by Educational Horizons. Reprinted with permission of the author.

Saving Standards

Mr. Nevi wonders whether we have set standards that are unreasonable and that are becoming a form of punishment for students rather than a means of improving the quality of education. He also suggests a method for finding out.

BY CHARLES NEVI

THE RETURNS on the investment in standards-based education are beginning to come in, and they do not look good. Most of the results available so far are more than a little discouraging. Across the country, significant percentages of students are not reaching the standards that have been set for them, whether they are state standards, the standards of the National Assessment of Educational Progress (NAEP), or even benchmarks established for standardized achievement tests. In Washington, the state with which I am most familiar, about 60% of the 10th-grade students have failed to meet one or more of the standards that have been set for them by educators and legislators. And because the ultimate plan in the state is to link the standards with high school graduation, at current levels of performance roughly 40% to 50% of the students in the state will not graduate from high school once the standards are fully implemented.

And the bad news is not limited to the results of student performance on the tests. Teachers in New York and California have been caught cheating on tests, trying to help their students improve their performance. Parents have complained that the tests are too difficult and that the consequences for not reaching the standards are too severe. Some parents are exploring ways to excuse their children from taking the tests. There are even concerns that many of the states' standards are not well aligned with college expectations and that

the necessary teaching to the state standards is interfering with teachers' ability to prepare students effectively for college.

Reactions to the failures of students to meet the standards are varied, ranging from blaming the teachers for poor preparation and inadequate instructional strategies, to blaming the principals for inadequate or inappropriate instructional leadership, to blaming the parents for improper child-rearing strategies and lack of involvement with the schools, to blaming the students for lack of motivation and watching too much television, to blaming the publishing companies for inadequate textbooks, to blaming the school systems for poorly developed and articulated curricula and ineffective school governance strategies.

What has been strangely missing from the blaming and the hand wringing is a critical examination of the expectations that have been established in relation to the standards. Might it be possible that in their zeal to develop "rigorous" educational standards, educators and especially legislators have developed expectations that are simply too high? That the standards for students, a politically disenfranchised group, are unrealistic, higher than any comparable standards the educators and legislators would ever set for themselves or for anyone else? In our rush to improve the quality of education through rigorous standards, have we set standards that are unreasonable and that are becoming a form

of punishment for students rather than a means of improving the quality of education?

A somewhat similar situation has developed with regard to the national education goals established by then-President Bush and the nation's governors in 1990 as part of America 2000, now Goals 2000. None of the goals was accomplished in the 10-year period. Unrealistic goals create unrealistic expectations. The failure to reach the goals—or to reach standards—provides ammunition for critics of education, proof that the schools are failing and that educators are not doing their jobs. The criticism is frequently followed by new commissions and new sets of goals, similarly unrealistic. And the impression that schools are failing continues.

There is a relatively easy way to determine if the newly developed state standards and the NAEP standards have gone the way of Goals 2000. There is an approach that would be fairly easy to implement and that would answer the questions about the reasonableness and value of the standards. In fact, the results would be especially beneficial to the standards movement and could save it from eventual collapse.

As a means of assessing the reasonableness of any state's standards, take the standards-based test that is currently given to students and administer the test to the state's legislators, the state's school board members, and the state's teachers and administrators. In other words, determine if the standards expected of our young people have been reached by our adults. And not by just any adults, but by those who have promulgated the standards movement—the educators, the school board members, and the legislators.

Are we willing to walk our talk, put our money where our mouths are, put up or shut up?

Reactions to such a proposal are easily anticipated. It would be too time-consuming. It wouldn't prove anything. It might even be embarrassing for some. But students are entitled to exhibit the same reactions. They can and do legitimately raise these same concerns of too much time spent taking tests, content that has no meaningful relationship to their college or career ambitions, or results that are not only embarrassing but may even be harmful. So again the troubling question arises: Are we holding our students to too high a standard, a standard much higher than we are willing to hold ourselves to as adults? A series of street clichés suddenly leap to mind. Are we willing to walk our talk, put

our money where our mouths are, put up or shut up? In other words, are we willing to demonstrate that the standards are realistic?

Testing the adults is not as outlandish as it may at first seem. The tests would have to be given only every four years or so. Annual results would not be needed, since the groups being tested remain somewhat stable from year to year. And testing only every four years would help alleviate the concern that testing the adults would take too much of their valuable time. Other concerns could be similarly alleviated by keeping the individual test results confidential. No one would be required to have his or her individual scores made public, although, of course, anyone who wanted to make his or her own scores public would be free to do so.

Individuals who wanted to make their scores public could create some interesting situations. Imagine an election for a legislative seat or a school board position in which the candidates' scores are an issue. Does exceeding the standards make someone a better candidate than just meeting the standards? Do we want to select only those candidates who have clearly demonstrated proficiency? Should we elect someone who only approaches proficiency? These are the kinds of questions we ask about our

students, so it seems not unreasonable to ask them about adults.

One of the special advantages of testing adults is that new standards for proficiency could be established. Currently, most tests use rather bland benchmarks—such terms as "proficient," "exceeds proficient," and "approaches proficient." Under this new system, the scores of the adults could be used to establish standards for the students. The scoring categories would then have more significance, and the students could be categorized in more meaningful ways. Categories might include "scores at the school board proficiency level" or "scores at the legislator proficiency level" or—what would presumably be the equivalent of "exceeds proficiency"—"scores at the teacher/administrator proficiency level."

The ultimate value of such an approach is that it will bring meaning to state standards. And in doing so it may save the standards movement from collapse as significant numbers of students across the country continue to fail to reach the unreasonably high standards that have been set for them.

CHARLES NEVI is a retired public school teacher and district administrator living in Newcastle, Wash.

From *Phi Delta Kappan*, February 2001, Vol. 82, No. 6, pp. 460-461. © 2001 by Phi Delta Kappan. Reprinted by permission of the magazine and Charles Nevi who is a retired educator.

Welcome to Standardsville

Mr. Jones, a secondary school principal, feels it is time for a practitioner to provide the "real" reasons that standards will not work in this country. He lists a dozen such reasons and suggests some ways to get started on genuine school reform.

BY ALAN C. JONES

INTUITIVELY I have known that the term *educational standards* is an oxymoron. My feelings are based on years of sitting in classrooms with teachers who brought unique insights and styles into the classroom and with teachers who merely prepared us for taking tests. One type of teacher inspired me; the other, in the words of John Dewey, induced passivity.

Until now, I did not feel compelled to share my feelings about standards. Deep down I felt that this new reform idea, "too, shall pass." Then I went to see the movie Pleasantville. The film recounts the experiences of two teenagers who find themselves trapped in a fictional Fifties town called *Pleasantville*—a community that prides itself on conformity and whose landscape is restricted to black and white. Throughout the movie a series of questions kept running through my mind: What if my community were Standardsville? What would a school look like in Standardsville? Could a faceless state bureaucracy impose its will by paper standards? Would an army of state officials descend on schools to ferret out educators who tried to add any color to an already gray landscape of lectures, worksheets, and test preparation programs?

Fortunately, I know the answers to all these questions. No single reform or state agency has ever had the ability to disturb the routines and structures of public schools. Why will the standards movement ultimately fail to affect the way schools do business in our country? The simple answer is that the United States is not Pleasantville. The more complex answer lies in the practical realities of schooling, which defy grand designs for change. Although many academics have already provided their lists of reasons for opposing standards, I felt it was time for a practitioner to provide the "real" reasons that standards will not work in this country.

1. *Schools are systems.* State legislatures and state boards of education keep assuming that schools are *not* systems. These well-intentioned policy makers pass mandates that focus on what teachers and students do from 8 a.m. to 3 p.m. They forget about the issues a child faces before and after school. They do not understand how a school staff and a community manage to resolve conflicts over heartfelt issues. Teachers and administrators know very well that, for any reform to succeed in schools, all components of the "school system" must be addressed at once. Bureaucrats will continue to be frustrated with any efforts at reform that do not include the "village" and the system.

2. *We don't understand the standards.* I will not spend much space on this reason. The most recent issues of any education journal document the problems educators and scholars are having with the interpretation of their state's standards. Suffice it to say, when schoolpeople do not understand a reform, it's dead on arrival.

3. *Where are the standards?* I know that every state superintendent of schools has implemented an elaborate process for the development and ratification of standards for his or her state. And I can guess that, in most states (if they are like Illinois), teachers and administrators have been permitted only a token presence in the development of the standards. I can also guess that administrators have responded in one of two ways when the standards have arrived at their doors: 1) they have placed the standards in the learning resource center, or 2) they have sent teachers the following memo: "Attached are the new state standards." At this point in time, the standards are far away from the classroom.

4. *We already have standards*. Teachers already have standards. They are called textbooks. For most teachers, the state standards will be viewed as an unnecessary duplication of what they already use.

5. *There isn't enough time*. For all the standards to be taught, much less learned, all students in this country would have to enroll in four years of English, four years of social studies, four years of mathematics, four years of science, four years of physical education and health, and four years of fine arts. I predict that, within the next few years, all the disciplines that were left out of the original standards movement will jump in with their own required standards. I also predict that state legislators will respond to the pressure of these interest groups as they did with all the others—"What's the harm in another four years of something?" If you have been keeping count, students who desire to meet all state standards will be enrolled in "core" academic courses for seven periods a day. Schools in Standardsville will begin early and end late, they will have no electives, and gifted students will have no lunch. I can't wait for my first meeting with the football coach and the band director.

6. *Teachers don't agree with the standards*. I always wonder if state legislators have ever attended a social studies department meeting. If they did, they would spend hours listening to teachers argue about the number of weeks allocated to studying the Civil War or whether to waste time studying whatever another teacher feels is important. Recently, I attended a math department meeting during which a huge argument broke out over factoring. Factoring—can you imagine that? Although I view these discussions as healthy, the standards movement does not. Teachers will not be given the freedom to select or modify the standards for their disciplines. We already know what happened to the teacher-proof curricula of the Sixties and Seventies. Here we go again.

7. *Teachers have too many kids*. Although overall class sizes have declined in the last five years, the reductions have not compensated for the increase in the diversity of students entering most classrooms in America. Teachers just have too many students, too many demands on their time, and too few hours to focus on world-class standards.

8. *The standards aren't even on my list*. When I get in my car in the morning, I am thinking about students who could bring a gun to school. I am thinking about students who could be selling drugs to other students. I am thinking about what to do with the student who might be harassed because of a change in sexual preference. I am thinking about the teacher who is battling cancer. State standards aren't even on the list. Based on my reading of the latest statistics on the health of children in the United States, I suspect that most principals enter their cars every morning with a similar list of priorities.

9. *The kids don't speak English*. Jerome Bruner made the observation that in highly symbolic cultures there will always be some group that will have the power to make decisions on what symbols are valued in the culture. It is clear from reading the standards what groups have made the decisions on what symbols will be valued in our schools. Unfortunately, these groups do not represent or understand the diverse backgrounds of the students who are now entering our schools. This reality poses a serious challenge to teachers who must teach representations of symbol systems that make no sense to the majority of students seated in their classes. Teachers are survivors. They will close their classroom doors and do whatever it takes to make things work. There is no bigger obstacle to making things work than subject-matter content that does not make sense to their students.

10. *What's a big idea?* One redeeming quality of the standards is their attempt to develop units of instruction around big ideas, major themes, and important questions. This approach is part of the reason that many of the standards appear to be vague. To implement such an approach to curriculum organization, teachers must have a deep understanding of their disciplines. Unfortunately, the research would indicate that most teachers lack the content background to organize units of instruction based on the "big picture." Remember what occurred with "modern math" in the Sixties. However, this is where standards or curriculum frameworks could serve as an important foundation for beginning discussions about how to bring meaning to the maze of facts and skills that students are expected to navigate on a daily basis. These discussions will never take place because of the next reason.

11. *Embarrass them in public—they remember it longer*. A former boss gave me this management hint. I will not divulge the source of the quote. Most states, however, have adopted this management strategy as a means of gaining compliance with their mandates. "Publish test scores in the newspapers—they will remember it longer." Educators respond to this attempt at public embarrassment in a predictable fashion: they play defense. The last behavior we need to see from teachers who are facing tremendous challenges in their classrooms is *defense*.

12. *The workers need prodding*. I am sure that a state superintendent or legislator will be upset with this article. I can predict the response: "Just another example of a school bureaucrat who does not want to be held accountable for his performance." This strong belief—held by state legislators, state superintendents, and the business community—is, in the words of W. Edwards Deming, "a path to ruination." The originator of Total Quality Management saw more clearly than his contemporaries in business—even some of those who bow to his shrine—the damage done by imposing grading systems in schools, merit systems, incentive pay, and numerical goals without a method. In Deming's words, these approaches "rob people and the nation of innovation." What is needed instead is "management that will restore the power of the individual."

The teachers and administrators I have worked with for 30 years are "willing workers." They are trying to do the best job they can. Could all of us in education be doing a better job? Absolutely. Do we get better by regulation, inspection, standardization, and public embarrassment? Absolutely not.

IF STANDARDS are not the answer, then what is? Speaking from the trenches, I feel like a Christmas tree being decorated by one group after another with one idea after another. At this point in the reform cycle, the branches are hanging pretty low, and the lights have gone out. We need, first, to take the tree out of the house and start over again. Where do we begin?

We must begin with the experiences children are having in schools. Forget about test scores; forget about the economy; forget about Japan. What do students think about their experiences? Do they feel safe? Do they like their teachers? Do they talk at the dinner table about the interesting day they had at school? Before dismissing these comments as naive, remember that there are schools that students genuinely like to attend. These schools are typically small, they employ teachers who are comfortable with loosely structured environments, and they permit students to follow their interests for most or part of their day. These schools certainly do not resemble what I call the "aircraft-carrier high schools"—cost-efficient behemoths that possess many levels, many departments, and many ranks, but no heart.

We must begin by creating an environment of trust between educators and public policy makers. Unfortunately, a variety of political and economic agendas have polarized the conversation about what makes a school good. We cannot hope to transform the experiences children are having in schools when teachers and administrators are spending valuable energy defending themselves against the latest reform cycle. The quickest way to build trust among educators is to permit their voices to be heard and to let them be involved in the decisions about the schools they teach in.

We must begin to pay more attention to theory instead of to what we think would work. So much of the reform agenda is based on wrong understandings about human behavior and learning. State policy makers continue to pass mandates that ignore the latest theories about human motivation, how the brain functions, how children learn, how adults learn, and how organizations become learning communities. As Deming put it, "Experience teaches nothing without theory."

Finally, we must begin to remove the obstacles that prevent teachers and administrators from doing their jobs well. These obstacles range from state mandates that generate mountains of paperwork to a lack of basic resources—access to a telephone, a computer, a room in which to talk alone with a colleague. Creating learning experiences that are meaningful and engaging requires an enormous amount of thought and energy. Right now, teachers are spending too much time and energy taking attendance and worrying about when the copy machine will be repaired.

Tomorrow I will return to school and continue the complex work of bringing some color to the learning experiences of the students of our community. I am thankful that the community I work in is not Standardsville. My hope is that state policy makers will begin spending more time on helping schools develop more color in their programs than on preserving a landscape of black and white.

ALAN C. JONES *is principal of Community High School, District 94, West Chicago, Ill.*

UNIT 4
Morality and Values in Education

Unit Selections

14. **Is the Supreme Court's Ruling "Good News" for Public Schools?** Martha M. McCarthy
15. **Inculcating a Passion for Truth and Learning**, Stephen Goode
16. **My Morals, Myself**, John Leo
17. **Humanistic Education to Character Education: An Ideological Journey**, E. H. Robinson III, Karyn Dayle Jones, and B. Grant Hayes

Key Points to Consider

- What is the significance of the Supreme Court's rullings on church-state relations as they affect the public schools?

- What is moral education? Why do so many people wish to see a form of moral education in schools?

- Are there certain values about which most of us can agree? Should they be taught in schools? Why, or why not?

- Is there a national consensus concerning the form that moral education should take in schools? Is such a consensus likely if it does not now exist?

- What attitudes and skills are most important for a responsible approach to moral decision making?

- What can teachers do to help students become caring, morally responsible persons?

- Finally, can virtue be taught (Plato's question)? If so, how?

 **Links: www.dushkin.com/online/**
These sites are annotated in the World Wide Web pages.

Association for Moral Education
http://www.wittenberg.edu/ame/
Child Welfare League of America
http://www.cwla.org
Ethics Updates/Lawrence Hinman
http://ethics.acusd.edu
The National Academy for Child Development
http://www.nacd.org

Morality has always been a concern of educators. There has possibly not been a more appropriate time to focus attention on ethics, on standards of principled conduct, in our schools. The many changes in American family structures in past years make this an important public concern, especially in the United States. We are told that all nations share concern for their cherished values. In addition to discerning how best to deal with moral and ethical educational issues, there are also substantive values controversies regarding curriculum content, such as the dialogue over how to infuse multicultural values into school curricula. On the one hand, educators need to help students learn how to reason and how to determine what principles should guide them in making decisions in situations where their own well-being and/or the well-being of another is at stake. On the other hand, educators need to develop reasoned and fair standards for resolving the substantive values issues to be faced in dealing with questions about what should or should not be taught.

There is frustration and anger among some American youth, and we must address how educators can teach moral standards and ethical decision-making skills. This is no longer simply something desirable that we might do; it has become something that we must do. How it is to be done is the subject of a national dialogue that is now occurring.

Students need to develop a sense of genuine caring both for themselves and others. They need to learn alternatives to violence and human exploitation. Teachers need to be examples of responsible and caring persons who use reason and compassion in solving problems in school.

Some teachers voice their concerns that students need to develop a stronger sense of character that is rooted in a more defensible system of values. Other teachers express concerns that they cannot do everything and are hesitant to instruct on morality and values. Most believe that they must do something to help students become reasoning and ethical decision makers.

What teachers perceive to be worthwhile and defensible behavior informs our reflections on what we as educators should teach. We are conscious immediately of some of the values that affect our behavior, but we may not be as aware of what informs our preferences. Values that we hold without being conscious of them are referred to as tacit values—values derived indirectly after reasoned reflection on our thoughts about teaching and learning. Much of our knowledge about teaching is tacit knowledge, which we need to bring into conscious cognition by analyzing the concepts that drive our practice. We need to acknowledge how all our values inform, and influence, our thoughts about teaching.

Teachers need to help students develop within themselves a sense of critical social consciousness and a genuine concern for social justice. Insight into the nature of moral decision making should be taught in the context of real current and past social problems and should lead students to develop their own skills in social analysis relating to the ethical dilemmas of human beings.

There is a need for teachers to develop principles of professional practice that will enable them to respond reasonably to the many ethical dilemmas that they now face. Knowledge of how teachers derive their sense of professional ethics is developing; further study of how teachers' values shape their professional practice is very important. Schooling should not only transmit national and cultural heritages, including our intellectual heritage, but it should also be a fundamentally moral enterprise in which students learn how to develop tenable moral standards in the contexts of their own world visions.

The controversy over teaching morality deals with more than the tensions between secular and religious interests in society. We argue that the construction of educational processes and the decisions about the substantive content of school curricula involve moral issues as well.

One of the most compelling responsibilities of schools is that of preparing young people for their moral duties as free citizens of free nations. Governments have always wanted schools to teach the principles of civic morality based on their respective constitutional traditions. Indeed when the public school movement began in the 1830s and 1840s, the concept of universal public schooling as a mechanism for instilling a sense of national identity and civic morality was supported. In every nation, school curricula have certain value preferences embedded in them.

For whom do the schools exist? Is a teacher's primary responsibility to his or her client, the student, or to the student's parents? Do secondary school students have the right to study and to inquire into subjects not in officially sanctioned curricula? What are the moral issues surrounding censorship of student reading material? What ethical questions are raised by arbitrarily withholding information regarding alternative viewpoints on controversial topics?

Teachers cannot hide all of their moral preferences. They can, however, learn to conduct just and open discussions of moral topics without succumbing to the temptation to indoctrinate students with their own views.

Teaching students to respect all people, to revere the sanctity of life, to uphold the right of every citizen to dissent, to believe in the equality of all people before the law, to cherish freedom to learn, and to respect the right of all people to their own convictions—these are principles of democracy and ideals worthy of being cherished. An understanding of the processes of ethical decision making is needed by the citizens of any free nation; thus, this process should be taught in a free nation's schools.

What part ought the schooling experience to play in the formation of such things as character, informed compassion, conscience, honor, and respect for self and others? The issue of public morality and the question of how best to educate to achieve responsible social behavior, individually and collectively, are matters of great significance today.

Legal Update

Is the Supreme Court's Ruling "Good News" for Public Schools?

Martha M. McCarthy

In June 2001 the U.S. Supreme Court delivered a significant decision, *Good News Club v. Milford Central School*, allowing a private Christian organization to hold its meetings in a New York public school after school hours.[1] The Good News Club is affiliated with a national organization, Child Evangelism Fellowship, that teaches Christian values to children ages six to twelve. Nationwide, there are more than 4,500 of these clubs, and about 500 currently meet in public schools.[2]

The Milford decision encourages sectarian groups to seek greater religious accommodations in public schools.

The Milford School District had denied the Good News Club's request under its community-use policy that allows various civic and recreational groups to use the school, but not for religious purposes. The district contended that the club was engaging in religious worship and instruction that must be barred from public school facilities, and the federal district court and Second Circuit Court of Appeals agreed. The appeals court reasoned that the club's activities were "quintessentially religious," which would violate the Establishment Clause of the First Amendment if allowed in public education.[3] The court held that the policy's prohibition of subject matter involving religious purposes in the school's limited forum was a permissible restriction on categories of content rather than unconstitutional viewpoint discrimination.

The Fifth Circuit Court of Appeals had ruled similarly in a Louisiana case in which it upheld the exclusion of religious services from a school district's limited forum created for community use during nonschool time.[4] However, in an earlier case, the Eighth Circuit reached an opposite conclusion, upholding the right of the parent-led Good News/Good Sports Club to hold its meetings in a public school after school hours.[5] Thus, the Supreme Court was faced with conflicting appellate decisions when it agreed to review the *Milford* case.

Supreme Court Decision

Reversing the Second Circuit, the Supreme Court in *Milford* held that the school district discriminated against religious viewpoints in violation of the Free Speech Clause. The Court majority relied heavily on its 1993 decision, *Lamb's Chapel v. Center Moriches Union Free School District*, in which it held that another New York school district could not discriminate against a local church that wanted to use the public school to show a film series depicting family life from a Christian perspective.[6] Milford school authorities attempted to distinguish the Good News Club's activities, which target children under twelve and involve religious instruction and prayer, from the showing of films primarily to adults that was upheld in *Lamb's Chapel*. But the Supreme Court did not find the distinction significant, noting that whether moral lessons are taught through live storytelling and prayers or through films is inconsequential from a constitutional standpoint.[7] The majority reasoned that the Good News Club was merely seeking access to school facilities like other community groups and that it could not be disadvantaged based on the religious content of its meetings.

The Supreme Court found no Establishment Clause violation because the meetings were held after school and were not sponsored by the public school.[8] The majority also rejected the contention that elementary children would feel coerced to participate in the club's activities, declaring that the Court has never barred private religious conduct during nonschool hours simply because elementary children might be present. The Court majority did not refute Justice Souter's contention in his dissent that the clergy-led club's meetings were "evangelical worship services."[9] Instead, the majority relied on its conclusion that religious viewpoints, protected by the Free Speech Clause, were expressed during the club's devotional meetings. The majority emphasized that the Good News Club merely wanted to be treated neutrally, like other community groups, which is what the First Amendment demands.[10]

Implications

The Court's *Milford* decision seems to have erased the distinction between religious viewpoints and worship that some lower courts had drawn in condoning the use of public school facilities for community groups to discuss topics from sectarian perspectives, while not allowing use of public schools for religious worship.[11] Under the *Milford* ruling, if a public school establishes a limited forum for community meetings it cannot bar religious groups, even if students attending the school are the central participants in the devotional activities. The Court found no danger that the community would perceive the Good News Club's access as representing school endorsement of religion.

The *Milford* decision encourages sectarian groups to seek greater religious accommodations in public schools. Some churches will likely argue that they can hold weekly services in public school facilities if other community groups are allowed school access for meetings, because church services include the expression of religious viewpoints. Although meetings of community groups were at issue in *Milford,* some commentators, including George Will in his *Newsweek* column, have concluded that this ruling has far broader implications in terms of condoning religious activities in public schools.[12] It may portend the Supreme Court's expansion of what is considered *private* religious expression protected by the Free Speech Clause in contrast to *government-sponsored* religious expression prohibited by the Establishment Clause. A hierarchy of First Amendment rights seems to be emerging, with Free Speech Clause protections trumping Establishment Clause restrictions.

Milford is definitely an accommodationist ruling, augmenting the recent Supreme Court trend to allow more governmental aid to flow to religious schools.[13] The Supreme Court's pattern pertaining to devotional activities in public education is not as clear as it is regarding state aid to sectarian schools. The Court has protected the private expression of religious views in limited government fora[14] but also has struck down some efforts to return religious activities to public schools.[15] The *Milford* ruling will encourage legislative bodies to test the limits of the Establishment Clause, and these enactments will generate a steady stream of litigation.

Recent developments raise significant questions about the continued vitality of the Establishment Clause, suggesting that the "wall of separation between church and state" metaphor is being replaced by an emphasis on equal access and equal treatment of religious groups and expression. This once-high wall may indeed have some major cracks.

Editor's note: This piece was written prior to the September 11 terrorist attack. Given the centrality of prayer in local and national responses, including a period for prayer and remembrance in many public schools, there has been increased interest in school-sanctioned prayer since this national tragedy. Thus, the author has asked us to note that in light of recent events, the Milford decision addressed in this article may take on even more significance in efforts to expand religious observances in public education.

References

1. 121 A. Ct. 2093 (2001).
2. Mark Walsh, "Religious Club Seeks 'Good News' from Court," *Education Week,* February 21, 2001, pp. 1, 20.
3. 202 F.3d 502, 510 (2d Cir. 2000).
4. Campbell v. St. Tammany Parish Sch. Bd., 206 F.3d 482 (5th Cir. 2000), *vacated and remanded,* 121 S. Ct. 2518 (2001).
5. Good News/Good Sports Club v. Sch. Dist. of Ladue, 28 F.3d 1501 (8th Cir. 1994).
6. Lamb's Chapel v. Center Moriches Union Free Sch. Dist. 508 U.S. 384 (1993).
7. Good News Club v. Milford Central Sch., 121 S. Ct. 2093, 2101 (2001).
8. The three dissenting justices and one concurring justice argued that the Court should not have addressed the Establishment Clause issue because this was not addressed by the lower courts in granting the school district's request for summary judgment. These justices contended that the case should have been remanded for a full hearing on the Establishment Clause question. *See* 121 S. Ct. at 2112 (Stevens, J., dissenting); 121 S. Ct. at 2115 (Souter, J., joined by Ginsburg, J., dissenting); 121 S. Ct. at 2111 (Breyer, J., concurring in part).
9. 121 S. Ct. at 2117 (Souter, J., dissenting).
10. It is important to keep in mind that the controversy in *Milford* is not covered by the Equal Access Act (EAA), which pertains to student-initiated expression, 20 U.S.C. § 4071 (1984). *See* Board of Educ. of Westside Community Schs. v. Mergens, 496 U.S. 226 (1990) (rejecting an Establishment Clause challenge to the EAA). While the EAA provides substantial protection to student-initiated expression in federally assisted secondary schools that have created a limited forum for student groups to meet during noninstructional time, this law does not govern community access to public schools.
11. *See* Campbell v. St. Tammany Parish Sch. Bd., 206 F.3d 482 (5th Cir. 2000); Bronx Household of Faith v. Community

Sch. Dist., 127 F.3d 207 (2d Cir. 1997) (finding constitutional the school district's ban on religious services and instruction in its limited forum).

12. George F. Will, "The Last Word—'Good News' from the Court," *Newsweek,* June 25, 2001, p. 96.

13. *See,* e.g., Mitchell v. Helms, 530 U.S. 1296 (2000) (upholding use of federal funds to supply computers and other instructional equipment and materials for parochial school students); Agostini v. Felton, 521 U.S. 203 (1997) (upholding the use of public school personnel to provide remedial services in religious schools); Zobrest v. Catalina Foothills Sch. Dist., 509 U.S. 1 (1993) (finding no Establishment Clause violation in the use of public funds to support sign language interpreters for students attending religious schools).

14. *See* Rosenberger v. Rector and Visitors of Univ. of Virginia, 515 U.S. 819 (1995) (invalidating state university's policy that entailed discrimination against religious viewpoints in distributing student activity funds for student publications); Lamb's Chapel v. Center Moriches Union Free Sch. Dist., 508 U.S. 384 (1993); Good News Club v. Milford Central Sch., 121 S. Ct. 2093 (2001). Some federal appellate courts also have broadly interpreted First Amendment protection of students' private religious expression in public schools, e.g., Adler v. Duval County Sch. Bd., 250 F.3d 1330 (11th Cir. 2001); Chandler v. Siegelman, 230 F.3d 1313 (11th Cir. 2000).

15. See Santa Fe Independent Sch. Dist. v. Doe, 530 U.S. 290 (2000) (striking down student elections to authorize student-led invocations before public school football games); Lee v. Weisman, 505 U.S. 577 (1992) (striking down clergy-led prayers in public school graduation ceremonies).

Martha M. McCarthy is Chancellor Professor in the School of Education, Indiana University, Bloomington, Indiana.

From *Educational Horizons,* Winter 2002, pp. 66-68. © 2002 by Educational Horizons. Reprinted with permission of the author.

Inculcating a Passion for Truth and Learning

Christendom College President Timothy O'Donnell is committed to educating students with authentic grounding in the great Western intellectual tradition.

Text by Stephen Goode

Timothy T. O'Donnell is Christendom College's third president. He's an able defender of traditional Christian education. But he's also a man who with infectious enthusiasm will talk about the "sense of festivity" that comes with genuine learning and wisdom that are part of a liberal-arts education.

"How do young people get together and really enjoy themselves now that the art of making good conversation has been lost?" he asks rhetorically. "There has to be an effort to recapture the lost art of conversation and festivity."

If that sounds like the idle talk of an idealistic educator, there's a surprise. It is that at tiny Christendom, amid all the other things undergrads are prone to do, from drinking beer to daydreaming on a grand scale, students are very likely to be found talking passionately—and to care deeply about—what they learn from their college's traditional curriculum.

Insight: Take a quick look at the ad brochures produced by any American college or university today and you're very likely to come across the boast that "we prepare our students for the real world," as though other institutions of higher learning don't do any such thing. What do you think they mean by the real world?

Timothy T. O'Donnell: Putting the best spin on what they say, I think what they mean by training for the real world is getting a job. But, if that's the case, I think traditional liberal-arts colleges are doing a better job because we don't overspecialize. We aim at educating the whole person intel-

lectually and spiritually while being attentive to character formation and morality.

What you end up with are people who can think clearly, who have a sense of moral integrity. And aren't those the things that every employer is looking for? We put a strong emphasis on writing and on research papers, and those, too, are marketable skills, no matter what job our students go into. We have noticed indications that some of the Ivy League business schools, all factors being equal, actually prefer a graduate of a liberal-arts college over someone who's gone and majored in business. If they've studied business, they may know certain things about business, but they've been impoverished in many other areas.

In studying the liberal arts, what you're really pursuing is an arduous good.

Insight: Indeed. Sometimes very impoverished. But doesn't the boast about training students for the real world seem to be, at times, nothing more than code that says, "We don't waste students' time with liberal-arts courses," thereby justifying the impoverishment you're talking about?

TTO: If what passes as college education at most institutions is preparing students for the real world, then I think that claim is a joke. I would maintain that the real world is found in places like Christendom College where we introduce students

to the great questions with which men and women have struggled through millennia and about which they always have thought.

Of course, the fundamental problem is that as Americans we tend to be very practical, and liberal arts are not merely practical. In studying the liberal arts, what you're really pursuing is an arduous good—and an arduous good is by definition a very difficult thing to pursue.

But education is primarily not about getting a job. It's about learning. It's about coming to understand the great tradition of wisdom that has characterized so much of Western education down through history. One of the fruits of this is that you will be able to get a good job—but that's not the purpose.

Insight: It's not just secular and Protestant colleges that have given up the Great Tradition. Haven't Catholic schools also been plagued by this development?

TTO: I remember growing up in the 1950s with the strong sense of Catholic identity that I received from my Catholic grammar-school education. There was a strong sense of discipline and achievement, and that's why many of us who grew up then were appalled when we saw the chaos of the 1960s and 1970s. An institution that was really quite effective, Catholic higher education, was beginning to be dismantled and was aping what I think were many of the mistakes that were made by a lot of the Protestant colleges and universities.

When the Catholic schools began to pursue a brutal form of secularization, it badly upset many parents. They had sent their young people to Catholic colleges thinking they were going to be instructed in the faith. Many times that's not what they got at all, which meant in turn that there was no adult-level deepening of such study. While young people were progressing intellectually in the other disciplines, they were remaining at an infant level when it came to the Catholic faith.

They never were challenged intellectually to see the reasons why Catholics believe the way we do and to examine the strong reasons for our faith. That intellectual challenge is what we provide at Christendom.

Personal Bio

Timothy T. O'Donnell: *An educator with a traditional vision in search of wisdom.*

Currently: President, Christendom College, Front Royal, Va.

Born: Dec. 13, 1951; San Jose, Calif.

Family: Wife, Catherine; nine children, ranging in age from 23 years to 18 months. "God has been good and obviously has a sense of humor."

Education: Bachelor of arts in philosophy and history and master's degree in church history from Loyola Marymount University, Los Angeles. Doctorate in sacred theology from the Pontifical University of St. Thomas Aquinas in Rome, better known as the Angelicum; the first layman to receive both his licentiate and doctoral degrees in ascetical and mystical theology from that school.

Other work: Author of *Heart of the Redeemer*, and has done programs for Eternal Word Television Network.

Favorite book: G. K. Chesterton's *The Everlasting Man.* "I teach it every year as part of the freshman opening history course."

Insight: Christendom College is a Roman Catholic institution, and one of the "givens" of the modern secular world is that education should be a "liberation" from religion and its demands, a learning to "think freely."

TTO: Yes, a freeing from the "shackles of dogma"! The faith commitment was the one thing that inspired and brought the college into existence. Pope John Paul II in *Ex Corde Ecclesiae*, "Out of the Heart of the Church," makes the point that the university came out of the union of faith and reason that epitomized Christianity during the Middle Ages. Oxford University, Cambridge [University], the University of Paris and the University of Bologna were all church-related organizations that were the product of the fundamental Christian belief that there can be no real conflict between faith and reason.

Faith comes from God, reason comes from God, and they're meant to work in a harmonious fashion. So rather than seeing the Catholic faith as something that's unintellectual, as though you have to set your reason aside if you're going to be a Catholic, we say that's nonsense, that reason can give faith a deeper insight into the mysteries of the Christian religion. We believe that students are getting a greater understanding of reality by studying philosophy, by studying theology and history and by being exposed to the Great Tradition [of Judeo-Christian thought and history] than they can get from some alleged "real world" out there.

Insight: Christendom College has a core curriculum that provides this background in the Western tradition?

TTO: Yes. The lay Catholics who founded the college were opposed to the stripping down of the Western canon and the abandonment of the core curriculum that used to characterize all education, not just Catholic education, in this country. If you went to Yale, Harvard, Princeton and other famous colleges and universities, you were exposed to a solid core of learning. You would read Homer. You would read the great classics. So what the founders of Christendom College did was to establish a three-year core.

We don't want people to overspecialize. At other institutions today if you're a psychology major you will have a couple of courses of general education, but the rest will be taken up with psychology. You may come to know psychology fairly well, but you will not know how to integrate that discipline with the general purpose of education, which is to acquire wisdom.

At Christendom, you don't select your major until your junior year. Everyone who comes here will take three years of philosophy, three years of theology and three years of literature. They will study language, science and math, and everything is ordered within a historical matrix. The result is that when they finally do select a major they already will have this great foundation built up in the first two years.

Students can get a greater understanding of reality by studying philosophy, theology and history than they can get from some alleged 'real world' out there.

They will have a sense of what they like, of what they don't like and of their strengths and weaknesses. Then the professor, as he discusses the major with the student he's working with, will know that student has gone through all this stuff and can understand historical allusions and references to certain philosophies without betraying total ignorance. Because of the foundation that's been laid the first two years, the learning of the second two has more depth.

Insight: The core also provides all the students at Christendom with material they can talk about with one another outside class. Rather than being divided into countless majors, taking an enormous variety of courses, like students at big secular universities, Christendom's students have a common fund of information?

TTO: Absolutely. They speak a common language in discussions that take place in the lunchroom or late into the evenings in the dormitories. And this habit of conversation means that when they choose their particular majors there still will be discussions about what they're learning. This common foundation for the introduction of the wisdom, I think, is one of the things that makes Christendom unique.

ON SOCIETY

My morals, myself

Personal rules mean trying to have it both ways

By John Leo

Alan Wolfe thinks that the United States, like other Western nations, is undergoing a radical revolution in morals, and is now "morally speaking, a new society." This is a familiar argument, made bitterly by conservatives such as William Bennett and Robert Bork. But Wolfe is no prophet of despair. He is a sociologist and an upbeat public intellectual who has spent many years examining the moral condition of middle-class Americans. Americans are as morally serious as ever, Wolfe says, but they are no longer willing to follow old rules. Besides, he says, the revolution is irreversible. There's no going back, so we might as well get used to it. "Americans are not going to lead 21st-century lives based on 18th- and 19th-century moral ideals," he writes in his new book, *Moral Freedom: The Search for Virtue in a World of Choice.*

Wolfe thinks the traditional sources of moral authority (churches, families, neighborhoods, civic leaders) have lost the ability to influence people. In part, this is the result of appalling behavior by so many authority figures (lying presidents, pedophile priests, corrupt corporate executives, etc.). And as more and more areas of American life have become democratized and open to consumer "choice," people have come

to assume that they have the right to determine for themselves what it means to lead a good and virtuous life.

Waning war. Wolfe, a moderate and centrist by inclination, tends to see moderate behavior in the people he studies. In his previous book, *One Nation, After All,* he argued that the culture war is dead or dying and that America has evolved a strong consensus on political and social issues. This is a highly debatable thesis for all who remember the stark red and blue electoral map of Bush versus Gore, but Wolfe is surely right that Americans today are reasonably well united. *Moral Freedom* continues this genial, middle-of-the-road analysis. Wolfe finds San Francisco gays and militant feminists who speak for self-restraint and Bible Belt conservatives who argue for more self-expression. Americans, he says, are not caught up in the liberation-versus-oppression battles left over from the 1960s. Based on a *New York Times* survey he helped design, Wolfe concludes that Americans don't spend time pondering a culture war. Instead, they are caught up in an effort to bridge the old and the new, holding on to traditional standards, but refusing to accept them as absolutes. "Any form of higher authority has to

tailor its demands to the needs of real people," he writes.

Hovering over the new moral universe is the great cloud of nonjudgmentalism. Wolfe has qualms, but true to his approach, he sees the nonjudgmental ethic in generally positive terms. Americans are now unwilling to tell others how to live. By refraining from judgment, Wolfe thinks, Americans express a sense of humility and respect for the moral freedom of others. Nonjudgmentalism pushes us to interpret immoral behavior as a result of medical or genetic problems. The perpetrator is not at fault; he is the helpless victim of bad genes or a medical-psychiatric problem. A lot of moral concern is smuggled into the national conversation disguised as a scientific discussion of public health or addiction.

Much of the book analyzes various virtues and argues that Americans uphold the old virtues in principle while in practice turning them into personal "options." Americans prize loyalty, but in an age of easy divorce and mass corporate layoffs, loyalty is now seen as conditional. The same is true of honesty. Success today, Wolfe writes, often depends on managing the impressions of other people—a form of dissimulation. Honesty is no longer the best policy. It is a general mandate, strategically applied.

Wolfe offers the good news: Americans share a common moral philosophy "broad and inclusive enough to incorporate people whose views of the actual issues of the day are at loggerheads." But he doesn't spend much time lamenting the downside. Americans have strong principles, but they reserve the right not to apply them in difficult situations. Subscribers to the new moral order can have it both ways—strong principles with a built-in escape hatch.

This would explain much of the gap between polls on moral issues and actual behavior. One *L.A. Times* poll, for instance, shows that 57 percent of Americans think abortion is a form of murder. An annual survey of college freshmen consistently shows that about half of those polled think abortion should be illegal. Yet the prevalence of abortion points to a more relaxed moral standard when the chips are down.

Is this the future: Strong standards casually applied or simply ignored under stress? Could be. In his book *After Virtue*, philosopher Alasdair MacIntyre lamented that today "all moral judgments are nothing but expression of preference, expressions of attitudes or feelings." But moral codes are supposed to rein in many feelings and desires, not to offer them all free expression under cover of alleged moral seriousness. Wolfe's "moral freedom" seems to whisk away duty and obligation, relieving us all of the burden of doing anything costly. If this is the future, let's have more of the past.

From *U.S. News & World Report,* August 13, 2001, p. 10. © 2001 by U.S. News & World Report, L.P. Reprinted by permission.

Humanistic Education to Character Education: An Ideological Journey

Given the recent attention to character education in the public schools, it is important for educators and counselors to be aware of the philosophical underpinnings of the character education movement, particularly how it relates to humanistic education. This article presents information on character education, humanistic education, and the relationship between the 2 concepts.

E.H. Robinson III
Karyn Dayle Jones
B. Grant Hayes

Perhaps one of the fastest growing movements in education today is character education (Leming, 1996). Five years ago, states did not emphasize character education in their curriculum. Today, 15 states require character education programs in their schools, and most states require what might be considered aspects of character education to be taught in their schools (Robinson & Hayes, 1999; Ryan & Bohlin, 1999). The federal government is supporting this movement through grants from the Department of Education, and in the 4 years since its inception the program has funded almost 20 state initiatives (Character Education Partnership, 1999).

In a broad sense, the phrase character education refers to almost anything that schools might try to provide outside of academics, especially when the purpose is to help children become good people. In a narrow sense, the term denotes a particular style of moral training, one that promotes instruction and indoctrination of specific values (Kohn, 1996, p. 429). Character education can be thought of as relating to or developing from humanistic education. More than any other single principle of character education, the concept of caring for another human being for no other reason than his or her existence is central to humanistic thought.

Although *humanistic education* may be very closely related to *character education*, there are differences between the two terms. This article presents information about humanistic education and character education, and the relationship between the two concepts.

HUMANISTIC EDUCATION

To understand the relationship between humanistic education and character education it is necessary to first explore the popular concepts of the term *humanistic* within the education field. The Association for Humanistic Education and Development (AHEAD) committed a task force in 1982 to develop a position paper on humanistic education. The paper noted that the term *humanistic education* has been used to describe many different approaches to education, making agreement on a specific definition difficult. Because a single definition could not address all of the aspects of humanistic education, several basic tenets of humanistic education were identified. These tenets hold that humanistic education includes (a) the development of basic skills needed to function effectively in a complex world; is (b) a humane approach that "helps students believe in themselves and their potential, that fosters self-respect and respect for the worth and dignity of others, and that promotes skills in conflict resolution; is (c) an approach that deals with issues of concern to people trying to improve the 'quality of life'—to pursue knowledge, to grow, to love, to find meaning for one's existence"; and includes (d) the establishment of a particular atmosphere for traditional learning—"a challenging yet supportive environment, where the learner's needs and goals are considered, and where experiences are planned in light of the unique nature of each child" (AHEAD, 1982, p. 3).

Simpson (1976) described humanistic education as descended from the integrative tradition of the humanities:

> The search for the good life with balance among the experience of feelings, the explanation of reason, and the implementation of action… affect and cognition, feelings and intellect, emotion and behavior blend in an affirmative framework of nature derived from the humanistic and from [the] positive conception of mental health. (p. 16)

Perhaps Adam Smith best described the term *humanistic*. Although best known for his work titled *The Wealth of Nations*, it was his work on moral philosophy that he and his critics believed to be his best.

> How selfish soever man may be supposed, there are evidently some principles in his nature, which interest him in the fortune of others, and render this happiness necessary to him, though he derives nothing from it except the pleasure of seeing it. (Smith, 1759/ 1976, p. 5)

CHARACTER EDUCATION

At the heart of character education is a belief that there are specific virtues that should be a part of education for all students. From this point, the field begins to spread in different directions. Kohn (1996) emphasized the need for character education to broadly address the desire to help children become good people. He denounced character education programs that drill students in specific behaviors rather than "engaging them in deep, critical reflection about certain ways of being" (p. 429). He concluded that narrowly focused programs are extrinsic, have a "fix-the-kids" orientation, and emphasize distinctly conservative values.

In contrast, Doyle (1997) believed that children, as well as adults, have the potential for dreadful behavior as well as good behavior: "Just as children must learn to read, they must learn to be good" (p. 441). He believed that character education is about rote learning of specific values typically defined through religion. Good character education consists of three elements: example, study, and practice. Doyle believed that just as you would practice the piano to achieve success as a pianist, you must practice values to learn them. Eventually, practice will become habit.

Kirschenbaum (1995) believed that the heart of the character education movement is teaching values and moral virtues. He suggested that the term *character* is less controversial than such terms as *morals* and *values* and brings a more "old-fashioned concept to mind which evokes a set of internal qualities that have always been admired as hallmarks of goodness, virtue, and moral maturity" (p. 21). Character educators such as Ryan, La-

cons, and Vassels often paraphrase Plato's *The Republic* as they distinguish character education in a humanistic manner and have described it as "knowing the good, loving the good, and doing the good" (Ryan & Bohlin, 1999).

Some of the critics of character education see it as being indoctrinating at worst and simplistic at best (Kohn, 1996). The criticisms may be best understood by examining the humanistic foundation of knowing the good, loving the good, and doing the good. Plato's theory of Forms emphasized the *good*—the supreme values from which all else is understood. This truth is absolute. Plato looked for this universal truth believing that it surpassed the individual examples and incongruence of people (Allen, 1957).

Alternatively, Aristotle emphasized humans' individual differences and characteristics through a more empiricist approach. Whereas Plato was more concerned with the solution to all problems and with the one answer that could make all things understood beyond the observable, his student Aristotle looked more to reconcile the observable differences. Aristotle stated the following: "Neither by nature, then, nor contrary to nature do virtues arise in us; rather we are adapted by nature to receive them, and are made perfect by habit" (Ross, 1927, p. 38). Good character, then, is a matter of practice and the development of habits. Some people develop good habits and others develop bad ones.

Kant (as cited in Kaufman, 1956) later introduced the concepts of motive and character. Kant, similar to Plato, believed there was a good. However, in contrast, Kant believed that we are under an obligation to obey moral laws such as "I ought, therefore I can." Kant also maintained that we do the good because we impose it on ourselves; the command of an external authority, be it God himself, is binding on us only as it wins the recognition of our conscience.

Last, Kierkegaard (as cited in Kaufman, 1956) disputed the concept that the good can be understood in a universal way:

> The truth can neither be communicated nor be received except as it were under God's eyes, not without God's help, not without God being involved as the middle term, because it's God, He Himself being the truth. It can therefore only be communicated by and received by the 'individual' which as a matter of fact can be every living man. (p. 27)

As Kierkegaard suggested, the good may be understood solely by the individual in a relationship with the source of the good. In Kierkegaard's case, the good was God. For some existentialists, the source of understanding may be different.

Even philosophers run the gamut from believing in one universal good and that moral behavior is formed by habit to believing that the good can only be understood individually, through one's personal relationship with the source of the good. The argument holds true today. Educators may believe that good character is made up of good behavior, defined through conservatism, and learned through practice and habit (Doyle, 1997). Others may believe students must learn to intrinsically define moral behavior and be self-motivated to choose their way of being (Kohn, 1996). From each philosophical position develops a potential basis for a particular approach to and a particular criticism of character education.

HUMANISTIC EDUCATION AND CHARACTER EDUCATION

Humanistic education and character education show several commonalities. Like humanistic education, character education is fast becoming an umbrella term used to include such specific programs as service learning, citizenship education, and law-related education. Some approaches initially described as a part of humanistic education, such as moral education, values education, and conflict resolution, are now frequently lumped together in character education programs. Certainly character education and humanistic education share the goal of affecting the individual in a more holistic way than is common in the educational strategies in many of today's schools.

What then are the differences between humanistic education and character education? The differences, like the ideological bases, can be small or great. Because both terms are used to describe a variety of practices, the comparisons are different at best.

If we believe as Doyle (1997) believed from the view of Aristotle that character is developed through practice and indoctrination, then the gulf between character education and humanistic education is vast. Kohn (1996) described a more humanistic approach to character education. Rather than simply indoctrinating or inducing mere conformity of values, character education programs can help children grow into good people by transforming educational structures so they allow children to reflect on moral issues. Character education can be humanistic, and certainly humanistic education involves the development of character. The main difference may be where each emphasizes the importance of the individual in the process.

CONCLUSION

Character education has gained much emphasis in public schools in the last several years. In the broad sense, character education includes any program or activity that schools engage in to help children become good people. A narrow focus defines character education as indoctrinating students with specific values, typically conservative ones. On the whole, character education is closely related to humanistic education. The ultimate goal of both is to affect children in a more holistic way to help them function effectively in this world.

REFERENCES

Allen, E. (1957). *From Plato to Nietzsche*. London: University Press.

Association for Humanistic Education and Development. (1982). *A position paper on humanistic education* [Brochure]. Washington, DC: Author.

Character Education Partnership. (1999). *US Department of Education grant opportunities* [Online]. Available: http://www.character.org/involved/index.cgi?detail:grants.

Doyle, D. P. (1997). Education and Character: A conservative view. *Phi Delta Kappan*, 78, 440–443.

Kaufman, S. (1956). *Existentialism from Dostoevsky to Sartre*. New York: Meridian.

Kirschenbaum, H. (1995). *One hundred ways to enhance values and morality*. Needham Heights, MA: Allyn & Bacon.

Kohn, A. (1996). *Beyond discipline: From compliance to community*. Alexandria, VA: Association for Supervision and Curriculum Development.

Leming, J. S. (1996). Civic virtue: Common ground for character education and law-related education professional. *Update on Law-Related Education*, 20(1), 29–32.

Robinson, E. H. (1982). *Humanistic education: An appropriate part of public education*. Saganaw, NY: Coalition for Democracy in Education.

Robinson, E. H., & Hayes, B. G. (1999). *The counselor's role in character education*. Unpublished manuscript.

Ross, W. (1927). *Aristotle selections*. London: Cambridge University Press.

Ryan, K., & Bohlin, K. E. (1999). *Building character in schools: Practical ways to bring moral instruction to life*. San Francisco: Jossey-Bass.

Simpson, E. (1976). *Humanistic education: An interpretation*. Cambridge, MA: Ballinger.

Smith, A. (1976). *The theory of moral sentiments* (D. D. Raphael & A. L. Macfie, Eds.). Oxford: Oxford University. (Original work published 1759)

E. H. Robinson III is a professor of counselor education, and Karyn Dayle Jones and B. Grant Hayes are both assistant professors of counselor education, all at the University of Central Florida in Orlando. Correspondence regarding this article should be sent to E. H. Robinson, Department of Human Services and Wellness, University of Central Florida 32816-1250.

UNIT 5
Managing Life in Classrooms

Unit Selections

Key Points to Consider

- What are some things that can be done to help students and teachers to feel safe in school?

- What is a good technique for learning self-control?

- What should be the behavioral standards in schools? On what factors should they be based?

- What ethical issues may be raised in the management of student behavior in school settings?

- What are some strategies for improving discipline in schools and preventing violent situations? Discuss what might be appropriate school disciplinary codes that would include special education students.

- How is e-learning affecting classroom behavior? What should be an instructor's response? Discuss.

 **Links: www.dushkin.com/online/**
These sites are annotated in the World Wide Web pages.

Classroom Connect
http://www.classroom.com
Global SchoolNet Foundation
http://www.gsn.org
Teacher Talk Forum
http://education.indiana.edu/cas/tt/tthmpg.html

All teachers have concerns regarding the "quality of life" in classroom settings. All teachers and students want to feel safe and accepted when they are in school. There exists today a reliable, effective knowledge base on classroom management and the prevention of disorder in schools. This knowledge base has been developed from hundreds of studies of teacher/student interaction and student/student interaction that have been conducted in schools in North America and Europe. We speak of managing life in classrooms because we now know that there are many factors that go into building effective teacher/student and student/student relationships. The traditional term, "discipline," is too narrow and refers primarily to teachers' reactions to undesired student behavior. We can better understand methods of managing student behavior when we look at the totality of what goes on in classrooms, with teachers' responses to student behavior as a part of that totality. Teachers have tremendous responsibility for the emotional climate that is set in a classroom. Whether students feel secure and safe and whether they want to learn depend to an enormous extent on the psychological frame of mind of the teacher. Teachers must be able to manage their own selves first in order to effectively manage the development of a humane and caring classroom environment.

Teachers bear moral and ethical responsibilities for being witnesses to and examples of responsible social behavior in the classroom. There are many models of observing life in classrooms. Arranging the total physical environment of the room is a very important part of the teacher's planning for learning activities. Teachers need to expect from students the best work and behavior that they are capable of achieving. Respect and caring are attitudes that a teacher must communicate to receive them in return. Open lines of communication between teachers and students enhance the possibility for congenial, fair dialogical resolution of problems as they occur.

Developing a high level of task orientation among students and encouraging cooperative learning and shared task achievement will foster camaraderie and self-confidence among students. Shared decision making will build an *esprit de corps*, a sense of pride and confidence, which will feed on itself and blossom into high-quality performance. Good class morale, well managed, never hurts academic achievement. The importance of emphasizing quality, helping students to achieve levels of performance that they can feel proud of having attained, and encouraging positive dialogue among them leads them to take ownership in their individual educative efforts. When that happens, they literally empower themselves to do their best.

When teachers (and prospective teachers) discuss what concerns them about their roles (and prospective roles) in the classroom, the issue of discipline—how to manage student behavior—will usually rank near or at the top of their lists. A teacher needs a clear understanding of what kinds of learning environments are most appropriate for the subject matter and ages of the students. Any person who wants to teach must also want his or her students to learn well, to acquire basic values of respect for others, and to become more effective citizens.

There is considerable debate among educators regarding certain approaches used in schools to achieve a form of order in classrooms that also develops respect for self and others. The dialogue about this point is spirited and informative. The bottom line for any effective and humane approach to discipline in the classroom, the necessary starting point, is the teacher's emotional balance and capacity for self-control. This precondition creates a further one—that the teacher wants to be in the classroom with his or her students in the first place. Unmotivated teachers cannot motivate students.

Helping young people learn the skills of self-control and motivation to become productive, contributing, and knowledgeable adult participants in society is one of the most important tasks that good teachers undertake. These are teachable and learnable skills; they do not relate to heredity or social conditions. They can be learned by any human being who wants to learn them and who is cognitively able to learn them. There is a large knowledge base on how teachers can help students learn self-control. All that is required is the willingness of teachers to learn these skills themselves and to teach them to their students. There are many sound techniques that new teachers can use to achieve success in managing students' classroom behavior, and they should not be afraid to ask colleagues questions and to develop peer support groups with whom they can work with confidence and trust.

Teachers' core ethical principles come into play when deciding what constitutes defensible and desirable standards of student conduct. Teachers need to realize that before they can control behavior, they must identify what student behaviors are desired in their classrooms. They need to reflect, as well, on the emotional tone and ethical principles implied by their own behaviors. To optimize their chances of achieving the classroom atmosphere that they wish, teachers must strive for emotional balance within themselves, they must learn to be accurate observers, and they must develop just, fair strategies of intervention to aid students in learning self-control and good behavior. A teacher should be a good model of courtesy, respect, tact, and discretion. Children learn by observing how other persons behave and not just by being told how they are to behave. There is no substitute for positive, assertive teacher interaction with students in class.

This unit addresses many of the topics covered in basic foundations courses. The selections shed light on classroom management issues, teacher leadership skills, and the rights and responsibilities of teachers and students. In addition, the articles can be discussed in foundations courses involving curricula and instruction. This unit falls between the units on moral education and equal opportunity because it can be directly related to either or both of them.

Bullying Among Children

Most teachers are aware that bullying begins early, yet many appear to believe the myth that children "picking on" or teasing one another is a "normal" part of childhood.

Janis R. Bullock

Six-year-old Sam is barely eating. When asked by his dad what is wrong, he bursts into tears. "The kids at school keep calling me a nerd, and they poke and push me," he sobs.

"There's a kid at school no one likes," 7-year-old Anika shares with her parents. "We all tease her a lot. She is a total dork. I would never invite her to my birthday party."

Bullying is a very old phenomenon; European researchers have studied its effects for decades (Olweus, 1991). Until recently, however, the issue has received less attention from researchers in the United States, perhaps because of the prevailing belief that bullying among children is inevitable. Considering that bullying often is a sign that aggressive or violent behavior is present elsewhere in children's lives—young children may be acting out at school what they have observed and learned in the home—and the fact that bullying among primary school-age children is now recognized as an antecedent to progressively more violent behavior in later grades (Saufler & Gagne, 2000), it behooves teachers to take notice.

Unfortunately, teachers have differing attitudes toward children who bully. Most teachers are aware that bullying begins early, yet many appear to believe the myth that children "picking on" or teasing one another is a "normal" part of childhood. They also may believe that these conflicts are best resolved by the children themselves. Consequently, some teachers do not intervene.

CHARACTERISTICS OF BULLIES AND THEIR VICTIMS

Bullying refers to repeated, unprovoked, harmful actions by one child or children against another. The acts may be physical or psychological. Physical, or direct, bullying includes hitting, kicking, pushing, grabbing toys from other children, and engaging in very rough and intimidating play. Psychological bullying includes name calling, making faces, teasing, taunting, and making threats. Indirect, or less obvious and less visible, bullying includes exclusion and rejection of children from a group (Olweus, 1991).

Children who bully are impulsive, dominate others, and show little empathy. They display what Olweus (1991) defines as an "aggressive personality pattern combined with physical strength" (p. 425). Without intervention, the frequency and severity of the bullying behaviors may increase. Even more disturbing, it appears that the patterns of bullying learned in the early years can set children on a course of violence later in life (Batsche & Knoff, 1994; Baumeister, 2001).

Although a longstanding characterization of children who bully points to their low self-esteem, there is little empirical evidence to support this view. In fact, more recent research (Baumeister, 2001; Bushman & Baumeister, 1998) suggests that an inflated self-esteem increases the odds of aggressive behavior. When a bully's self-regard is seriously threatened by insults or criticisms, for example, his or her response will be more aggressive than normal. Furthermore, bullies often report that they feel powerful and superior, and justified in their actions.

Research on family dynamics suggests that many children already have learned to bully others by preschool age. Many young children who bully lack empathy and problem-solving skills, and learn from their parents to hit back in response to problems (Loeber & Dishion, 1984; Vladimir & Brubach, 2000).

Children who are bullied, on the other hand, are often younger, weaker, and more passive than the bully. They appear anxious, insecure, cautious, sensitive and quiet, and often react by crying and withdrawing. They are often lonely and lack close friendships at school. Without adult intervention, these children are likely to be bullied repeatedly, putting them at-risk for continued social rejection, depression, and impaired self-esteem (Schwartz, Dodge, & Coie, 1994). A smaller subset of these children, known as "provocative victims," have learned to respond aggressively to perceived threats by retaliating not only against the aggressor, but also against others (Olweus, 1993).

INCIDENCES OF BULLYING AMONG CHILDREN

Evidence suggests that, in the United States, the incidence of bullying among children is increasing and becoming a nationwide problem. One out of five children admits to being a bully (Noll & Carter, 1997). In general, boys engage in more physical, direct means of bullying, whereas girls engage in the more psychological and indirect bullying, such as exclusion. Roland (1989) reported that girls may be involved in bullying as much as boys, but are less willing to acknowledge their involvement. In addition, because indirect bullying is often less apparent, girls' bullying may be underestimated. Girls tend to bully less as they get older. The percentage of boys who bully, however, is similar at different age levels (Smith & Sharp, 1994).

Twenty-five to 50 percent of children report being bullied. The great majority of boys are bullied by other boys, while 60 percent of girls report being bullied by boys. Eight percent of children report staying away from school one day per month because they fear being bullied. Forty-three percent of children have a fear of being harassed in the school bathroom (Noll & Carter, 1997). Children report that many incidents of bullying occur in situations that are difficult for the teacher to monitor, such as during playground activity.

THE EFFECTS OF BULLYING ON CHILDREN

To succeed in school, children must perceive their environment as being safe, secure, and comfortable. Yet, for many children, bullying and teasing begins as soon as children first form peer groups. For some children, this is a time when patterns of victimizing and victimization become established. Consequently, the victims perceive school as a threatening place and experience adjustment difficulties, feelings of loneliness, and a desire to avoid school. These feelings may linger even when bullying ceases (Kochenderfer & Ladd, 1996).

Children desire and need interaction with peers, physical activity, and time outdoors. Consequently, they often consider outside recess to be their favorite part of the school day. Sadly, however, many children who are bullied report that problems occur on the playground and view the playground as a lonely, unhappy, and unsafe environment.

If children are fearful or feel intimidated, they cannot learn effectively. They may react by skipping school, avoiding certain areas of the school (the bathroom or the playground), or, in extreme, yet increasingly common, cases, they may bring weapons to school (Noll & Carter, 1997). Olweus (1991) reminds us that "every individual should have the right to be spared oppression and repeated, intentional humiliation in school, as in society at large" (p. 427). As early exposure to bullying can produce both immediate and delayed effects in children's ability to adjust to school, school staff need to intervene as soon as problems are detected.

RECOMMENDATIONS FOR TEACHERS TO SUPPORT CHILDREN

A comprehensive plan to address the problems of bullying and teasing must involve school personnel, teachers, children, and families. Intervention must occur on three levels: school-wide, in specific classrooms, and with individuals.

School-wide Intervention

School personnel must recognize the pervasiveness of bullying and teasing and its detrimental effects on children's development. Inservice training can be developed that outlines a clear policy statement against bullying and intervention strategies for addressing it. The school also can develop a comprehensive plan geared to teach children prosocial behaviors and skills. The children may be involved in the development of such policies and strategies, providing their input on what behavior is appropriate and identifying sanctions against bullies (Lickona, 2000; Olweus, 1997).

School personnel could enlist families' support and involvement by sharing details of the policy through parent-teacher conferences and newsletters. Families need to be aware of the specific sanctions that will be imposed on children who bully, and they need opportunities to offer feedback and suggestions. It is important to encourage parents to talk with their children about bullying. Children who are bullied often believe that their parents are unaware of the situation, and that their concerns are not being addressed or discussed. Children *do* want adults to intervene, however (Gropper & Froschl, 1999). If families are kept informed, they can work as a "team member" with school counselors and teachers to change the school environment.

Additional sources of school-wide support for children who are bullied and teased may be developed, including mentoring programs. Teachers can identify children who need support, and find them a mentor. Children may feel more at ease and less anxious when they have a "buddy," such as an older student, who can help intervene (Noll & Carter, 1997). Counselors at one elementary school selected, trained, and supervised high school students to teach the younger children how to deal with bullying and harassment. After implementation of this program, the teachers observed a decline in reports of harassment (Frieman & Frieman, 2000).

Bullying frequently occurs on the playground (Whitney, Rivers, Smith, & Sharp, 1994), yet many children believe that teachers do little to stop it. Consequently, "play-time… is more of a prison sentence than an opportunity to play and socialize" (Slee, 1995, p. 326). Therefore, school personnel may need to review playground design and space, children's access to these spaces, teacher supervision, and the role of the school in early intervention on the playground (Lambert, 1999). Yard monitors and lunch time supervisors can be trained to watch for signs of bullying. In addition, children can be asked to identify those places where bullying most frequently occurs.

Intervention in Specific Classrooms

Clearly, bullying and hurtful teasing affects children's ability to learn and enjoy play, as well as the teacher's ability to teach. Within the classroom, teachers can begin addressing the problem by creating times for children to talk about their concerns. Interestingly, one study showed that when children ages 5 to 7 years of age were asked about assisting someone who was being bullied, 37 percent replied that it was none of their business to help (Slee & Rigby, 1994).

Teachers can ask children to talk about what makes them feel unsafe or unwelcome in school. The teacher then can make a list of the children's responses, discuss them (e.g., "I don't like it when someone hits me or calls me a name"), and create corresponding rules (e.g., "Hitting and name calling are not allowed in the classroom"). When necessary, the discussions can be continued during class meetings so that the rules can be reviewed, revised, and updated. The teacher can also show children what to do to help themselves or other children, and remind them of the consequences of breaking the rules. Teachers can reduce children's anxiety by setting firm limits on unacceptable behavior (Froschl & Sprung, 1999).

If the bullying continues, teachers may need to make referrals to school counselors who will work with children, either individually or in groups, to talk about concerns, discuss solutions and options, and give suggestions on how to form friendships. Children without close friends are more likely to be victimized and may benefit from specific suggestions for building friendships (e.g., invite a friend to your house, work together on a school project, share a common interest, play a favorite game together).

Certain types of curricula, especially those that provide opportunities for cooperative learning experiences, may make bullying less likely to flourish. Children need to be engaged in worthwhile, authentic learning activities that encourage their interests and abilities (Katz, 1993). When they are intellectually motivated, they are less likely to bully. For example, project work (Katz & Chard, 2000) involves children's in-depth investigations into topics of their own choosing. As they explore events and objects around them in the classroom, in the school yard, in the neighborhood, and in the community, they learn to cooperate, collaborate, and share responsibilities. Project work can be complemented by noncompetitive games, role playing, and dramatization to raise awareness of bullying and increase empathy for those who experience it. Some teachers use children's literature to help create caring and peaceful classrooms (Morris, Taylor, & Wilson, 2000).

Intervention With Individuals

Developing both immediate and long-term strategies for identifying and working with bullies may be necessary. When teachers observe an incident of bullying, they can intervene by asking the bully to consider the consequences of his or her actions and think about how others feel. By talking calmly, yet firmly, to the bully, the teacher can make it clear that such behavior is unacceptable. Teachers can show the bully alternate ways to talk, interact, and negotiate; at the same time, they can encourage victims to assert themselves. By doing so, the teacher is showing the bully and the victim that action is being taken to stop the bullying. Acting promptly can prevent the bullying from escalating.

When interacting with children on a one-on-one basis, teachers should provide encouragement that acknowledges specific attributes, rather than dispensing general praise, approval, or admiration ("I am so glad that you have done a great job; it is wonderful; yours is one of the best projects") that may appear to be contrived. Expressions of specific encouragement ("You seem to be pleased and very interested in your project, and it appears you have worked on it for many days and used many resources to find answers to your questions"), as opposed to general praise, are descriptive, sincere, take place in private, focus on the process, and help children to develop an appreciation for their efforts and work. While developing children's self-esteem is a worthwhile goal, false praise may instead promote narcissism and unrealistic self-regard. Teachers should avoid encouraging children to think highly of themselves when they have not earned it (Baumeister, 2001; Hitz & Driscoll, 1988).

Additional long-term strategies may include encouraging children to resolve their own problems and using peers to mediate between bullies and their targets. Furthermore, teachers can spend time helping children to form ties with peers who can offer protection, support, security, and safety, thus helping to reduce children's exposure to bullying (Kochenderfer & Ladd, 1997; Ladd, Kochenderfer, & Coleman, 1996).

SUMMARY

Bullying and teasing are an unfortunate part of too many children's lives, leading to trouble for both bullies and their victims. Children who are bullied come to believe that school is unsafe and that children are mean. They may develop low self-esteem and experience loneliness. Children who continue to bully will have difficulty developing and maintaining positive relationships. A comprehensive intervention plan that addresses the needs of the school, the classroom, teachers, children, and families can be developed and implemented to ensure that all children learn in a supportive and safe environment.

References

Batsche, G. M., & Knoff, H. M. (1994). Bullies and their victims: Understanding a pervasive problem in the schools. *School Psychology Review, 23*, 165–174.

Baumeister, R. (2001). Violent pride: Do people turn violent because of self-hate, or self-love? *Scientific American, 284*, 96–101.

Bushman, B. J., & Baumeister, R. F. (1998). Threatened egotism, narcissism, self-esteem, and direct and displaced aggression: Does self-love or self-hate lead to violence? *Journal of Personality and Social Psychology, 75*, 219–229.

Frieman, M., & Frieman, B. B. (2000). *Reducing harassment in elementary school classrooms using high school mentors.* (ERIC Document Reproduction Service No. ED 439 797).

Froschl, M., & Sprung, B. (1999). On purpose: Addressing teasing and bullying in early childhood. *Young Children, 54*, 70–72.

Gropper, N., & Froschl, M. (1999). The role of gender in young children's teasing and bullying behavior. Montreal, Canada. (ERIC Document Reproduction Service No. ED 431 162).

Hitz, R., & Driscoll, A. (1988). Praise or encouragement? New insights into praise: Implications for early childhood teachers. *Young Children, 42*, 6–13.

Katz, L. G. (1993). *Distinctions between self-esteem and narcissism: Implications for practice.* Urbana, IL: ERIC Clearinghouse on Elementary and Early Childhood Education.

Katz, L., & Chard, S. (2000). *Engaging children's minds: The project approach* (2nd ed.). Stamford, CT: Ablex.

Kochenderfer, B. J., & Ladd, G. W. (1996). Peer victimization: Cause or consequence of school maladjustment? *Child Development, 67*, 1305–1317.

Kochenderfer, B. J., & Ladd, G. W. (1997). Victimized children's responses to peers' aggression: Behaviors associated with reduced versus continued victimization. *Development and Psychopathology, 9*, 59–73.

Ladd, G. W., Kochenderfer, B. J., & Coleman, C. (1996). Friendship quality as a predictor of young children's early school adjustment. *Child Development, 67*, 1103–1118.

Lambert, E. B. (1999). Do school playgrounds trigger playground bullying? *Canadian Children, 42*, 25–31.

Lickona, T. (2000). Sticks and stones may break my bones AND names WILL hurt me. Thirteen ways to prevent peer cruelty. *Our Children, 26*, 12–14.

Loeber, R., & Dishion, T. J. (1984). Boys who fight at home and school: Family conditions influencing cross-setting consistency. *Journal of Consulting and Clinical Psychology, 52*, 759–768.

Morris, V. G., Taylor, S. I., & Wilson, J. T. (2000). Using children's stories to promote peace in classrooms. *Early Childhood Education Journal, 28*, 41–50.

Noll, K., & Carter, J. (1997). *Taking the bully by the horns.* Reading, PA: Unicorn Press.

Olweus, D. (1991). Bully/victim problems among schoolchildren: Basic facts and effects of a school based intervention program. In D. J. Pepler & K. H. Rubin (Eds.), *The development and treatment of childhood aggression* (pp. 441–448). Hillsdale, NJ: Lawrence Erlbaum.

Olweus, D. (1993). Victimization by peers: Antecedents and long-term outcomes. In K. H. Rubin & J. B. Asendorf (Eds.), *Social withdrawal, inhibition, and shyness in childhood* (pp. 315–341). Hillsdale, NJ: Lawrence Erlbaum.

Olweus, D. (1997). Bully/victim problems in school: Facts and intervention. *European Journal of Psychology of Education, 12*, 495–510.

Roland, E. (1989). Bullying: The Scandinavian research tradition. In D. P. Tattum & D. A. Lane (Eds.), *Bullying in schools* (pp. 21–32). London: Trentham Books.

Saufler, C., & Gagne, C. (2000). *Maine project against bullying. Final report.* Augusta, ME: Maine State Department of Education. (ERIC Document Reproduction Service No. ED 447 911).

Schwartz, D., Dodge, K. A., & Coie, J. D. (1994). The emergence of chronic peer victimization in boys' play groups. *Child Development, 64*, 1755–1772.

Slee, P.T. (1995). Bullying in the playground: The impact of interpersonal violence on Australian children's perceptions of their play environment. *Children's Environments, 12*, 320–327.

Slee, P. T., & Rigby, K. (1994). Peer victimisation at school. *AECA Australian Journal of Early Education, 19*, 3–10.

Smith, P. K., & Sharp, S. (1994). The problem of school bullying. In P. K. Smith & S. Sharp (Eds.), *School bullying* (pp. 1–19). London: Routledge.

Vladimir, N., & Brubach, A. (2000). *Teasing among school-aged children.* (ERIC Document Reproduction Service No. 446 321).

Whitney, I., Rivers, I., Smith, P. K., & Sharp, S. (1994). The Sheffield project: Methodology and findings. In P. K. Smith & S. Sharp (Eds.), *School bullying* (pp. 20–56). London: Routledge.

Janis R. Bullock is Professor, Early Childhood Education, Department of Health and Human Development, Montana State University, Bozeman.

Creating School Climates That Prevent School Violence

REECE L. PETERSON and RUSSELL SKIBA

Many programs whose purpose is to prevent violence or inappropriate behavior are also programs that might prevent disaffection, dropping out of school, drug and alcohol abuse, and poor academic performance. In other words, many prevention-oriented interventions are interventions that are not specific to violence or behavior and that address universals that affect a variety of possible negative outcomes related to schooling. In this article, we will identify and discuss some of the intervention options that are intended to prevent violence and inappropriate behavior in school by directly or indirectly affecting the social climate of the school.

School climate might be defined as the feelings that students and staff have about the school environment over a period of time. These feelings may have to do with how comfortable each individual feels in the environment and whether the individual feels that the environment is supportive of learning (or teaching), is appropriately organized, and is safe. Climate may also address other positive or negative feelings regarding the school environment. We would hypothesize that comfortable and supportive feelings would support effective and efficient learning and teaching as well as positive student behavior and attitudes. Conversely, negative feelings such as concern, fear, frustration, and loneliness would negatively affect learning and behavior. Therefore, school climate is a reflection of the positive or negative feelings regarding the school environment, and it may directly or indirectly affect a variety of learning outcomes.

The typical measures of school climate are surveys of students, parents, staff, and sometimes community members regarding what they think about the school. They include judgments about issues such as teacher-student relationships, security and maintenance, administration, student academic orientation, and student behavioral values (Kelly et al., 1936). These surveys usually use some form of Likert-type rating items and attempt to identify both specific strengths and weaknesses regarding these issues. Recently, a variety of safety-oriented surveys have attempted to identify the degree to which conflict, vio-

lence, and other disruptions contribute to a negative school climate as well. Data from these surveys may be useful in assessing and intervening to positively affect school climate.

Many have identified three components to a comprehensive approach to violence prevention in schools. These include (a) prevention, (b) identification and intervention for students at risk for having difficulty, and (c) effective responses once inappropriate behavior has occurred. Although all three components must be implemented simultaneously and effectively in a truly comprehensive approach, the focus here is on the first of these components, basic prevention. Almost all programs that focus on basic prevention of violence, drug abuse, dropping out, or whatever also focus on creating a positive school climate. Whether at the school or the individual level, effective intervention requires a wide spectrum of options that move significantly beyond a narrow focus on punishment and exclusion, which themselves can contribute to a negative school climate.

Security measures, video cameras, locker searches, and metal detectors, which are clearly intended to reduce school crime and violence, may also affect school climate. In some cases, and for some students and staff, these measures may improve the safety element of school climate, but for others they may negatively affect climate by creating an atmosphere of fear or intimidation.

A vast array of ideas have been proposed regarding how schools can affect and improve their social climate. Many of these ideas and programs emphasize a similar set of ideas. Many emphasize creating "caring in schools" or "caring learning environments" (Noddings, 1992); others stress "building a sense of community" in schools (Sergiovanni, 1994; Whelage, Rutter, Smith, Lesko, & Fernandez, 1989); and many others emphasize the development of adult-child relationships (Feedman, 1993; Charney, 1998). Mentoring programs, peer- and cross-age tutoring programs, school-within-a-school programs, cooperative learning, home base/homeroom programs, looping (in which teachers advance grade levels each year to remain with students), programs emphasizing welcoming and belonging in schools: All could be considered programs emphasizing these principles and the idea of small, close-knit learning communities. Although these certainly focus on improving climate and all probably have a role in violence prevention as a result, they have not generally been viewed as violence-prevention programs. Perhaps they should be viewed that way.

Instead here we will focus on several prominent approaches for schools to improve school climate, in part to prevent violence or at least to improve student behavioral conflicts. These will include (a) parent and community involvement, (b) character education, (c) violence-prevention and conflict-resolution curricula, (d) peer mediation, and (e) bullying prevention.

Parent and Community Involvement

Parent involvement promotes a healthy and consistent learning environment by establishing mutual goals between parents and educators and by developing activities that cut across home and school (Christenson, 1995; Weiss & Edwards, 1992). Parent involvement programs actively engage parents through a variety of activities that enable them to participate more fully in their children's education both at home and at school. Although most of the emphasis is placed on parent involvement, increased involvement of a variety of community members and volunteers may also be important and may have similar benefits.

Family-school collaboration is a cooperative process of planning that brings together school staff, parents, children, and community members to maximize resources for child achievement and development. Although connections between parent involvement and school violence have rarely been studied, increased parent involvement can result in home environments that are more conducive to learning and that improve communication and consistency between home and school. These changes can lead to safer, more responsive schools.

Strategies for Creating Involvement

Traditionally, parent involvement roles have been limited to activities such as Parent-Teacher Organization meetings and parent-teacher conferences. Parent involvement experts have identified six ways that schools can promote parent involvement in learning (Epstein, 1992). The first three ways take place in the home setting. First, schools can help parents increase involvement by teaching them better child-rearing skills through parenting components. One New Jersey middle school taught parents to use home-school contracts to better manage their children's inappropriate behavior (Smith, 1994). Second, schools may also assist parents by stressing learning at home. In the Parents Assuring Student Success (PASS)

program, parents learn how to supplement schoolwork by instructing their children at home in academic tasks such as reading and time management (Ban, 1993). Third, all parent involvement programs include an element of increased communication. The Parents As Teachers of Children (PATCH) program, for example, provides numerous support contacts for both parents and staff and holds regular staff, training, and supervision meetings during which concerns can be addressed (Williamson, 1997).

Fourth, providing opportunities for volunteering can increase parental and community involvement. New Haven's School Development engages a Parent Program team to promote parent volunteers in social activities, as classroom aides, and as members of the school development committee (Haynes & Corner, 1996; Warner, 1991; Lloyd, 1996). Fifth, parents may develop a higher degree of ownership in programs that include a component of decision making. The Parent in Touch Program in the Indianapolis Public Schools, for example, involves parents in planning the academic curriculum (Warner, 1991). Sixth, and last, collaborating-with-community components use community resources to strengthen school programs. The Utah Center for Families in Education, a community center developed specifically to meet the needs of school-aged children and their families, is run jointly by state officials, school administrators, school families, and members of the community (Lloyd, 1996).

Some programs have been directed at parents of students with challenging behavior. For example, one elementary school in California required parents of students at risk for expulsion to attend regular meetings to develop a solution regarding their child's behavior. The collaborative team approach used in these meetings was rated highly successful by both parents and teachers (Morrison, Olivos, Dominguez, Gomez, & Lena, 1993). Parent management training, which teaches parents effective methods of behavior management to decrease their children's aggressive behavior, has also been used with families of students exhibiting aggressive or disruptive behavior.

Outcomes of Involvement

Parent involvement is positively associated with student success, higher attendance rates, and lower suspension rates. One Iowa high school increased attendance rates by improving communication with parents about stricter attendance rules and involving parents in the implementation process (Kube & Ratigan, 1991). Increased parent involvement has also been shown to lead to greater teacher satisfaction, improved parent understanding and parent-child communication, and more successful and effective school programs.

Parent involvement provides an important opportunity for schools to enrich current school programs by bringing parents and community members into the educational process. Increased parent involvement has been shown to result in increased student success, increased parent and teacher satisfaction, and improved school climate. Schools can encourage involvement in a number of areas including parenting, learning at home, communication, volunteering, decision making, and community collaboration. Effective parent and community involvement programs are built on a careful consideration of the unique needs of the community. To build trust, effective approaches to parent involvement rely on a strength-based approach emphasizing positive interactions. Though specifics may vary, all parent involvement programs share the goal of increasing parent-school collaboration to promote healthy child development and safe school communities.

Character Education

Many schools have looked for ways to provide proactive guidance for students to learn the positive behaviors and values that should be a part of the education of all people. Many experts have called for schools to be more active in teaching the moral and civic values that are an essential part of our social fabric and sense of community. These calls are not new, and they reach back to philosophers such as Kant and Buber and to educators such as Dewey, who published his book *Moral Principles in Education* in 1909 (Henley, Ramsey, & Algozzine, 1999). "A successful school, like a successful business, is a cohesive community of shared values, beliefs, rituals and ceremonies. The community celebrates its saga by telling the stories of heroes and heroines who embody the core values of the community" (Brendtro, Brokenleg, & Van Bockern, 1990, p. 31). These efforts at creating and teaching a core group of values could be called *character education*.

Character education is a broad term that is used to describe the general curriculum and organizational features of schools that promote the development of fundamental values in children at school. Although both family and religious institutions may have more primary roles in this process, few deny that the schools may also have a role here. Many have said that schools and classrooms exude values whether consciously or not (Henley, Ramsey, &, Algozzine, 1999). According to London (1987, p. 671), character education includes two primary components: (a) education in civic virtue and in the qualities that teach children the forms and rules of citizenship in a just society; and (b) education in personal adjustment, chiefly in the qualities that enable children to become productive and dependable citizens.

Implementing Character Education

Character education may include a variety of subcomponents that can be a part of a larger character education program or that can be self-standing components. These include social skills instruction and curriculum, moral development instruction and curriculum, values clarification instruction and curriculum, caring education and curriculum, school values statements, and perhaps others as well. In addition, other programs such as cooperative-learning strategies, participatory decision making for students, and service learning are sometimes also classified as components of character education. At the same time, character education itself is often viewed as simply one component of some larger school reform and improvement strategies. For example, the "Basic School" as proposed by Boyer, has four components: The School As Community, A Curriculum With Coherence, A Climate for Learning, and A Commitment to Character (Boyer, 1995).

In some schools value statements become almost part of the school logo and identity.

According to Lickona (1988, p. 420), the moral or character education of elementary students is designed to accomplish three goals:

1. To promote development away from egocentrism and excessive individualism and toward cooperative relationships and mutual respect;
2. To foster the growth of moral agency—the capacity to think, feel, and act morally; and
3. To develop in the classroom and in the school a moral community based on fairness, caring, and participation—such a community being a moral end in itself as well as a support system for the character development of each individual student.

To accomplish these goals, Lickona advocates four processes that he feels should be going on in the classroom: building self-esteem and sense of community, learning to cooperate and to help others, moral reflection, and participatory decision making.

Specific qualities sought in children are

1. Self-respect that derives feelings of worth not only from competence but also from positive behavior toward others;
2. Social perspective taking that asks how others think and feel;
3. Moral reasoning about the right thing to do;
4. Moral values such as kindness, courtesy, trustworthiness, and responsibility.

Examples

Two examples of different kinds of programs within the framework of character education might be "Character Counts!" and school value statements.

Character Counts. "Character Counts!" is an ethics and character-building curriculum program designed for students aged 4–19 (Character Counts, 2000). The program teaches and develops a consensus regarding a set of ethical values that transcend race, creed, politics, gender, and wealth. The Character Counts! curriculum and the coalition that supports it work to overcome the false but surprisingly powerful notion that no single value is intrinsically superior to another; that ethical values vary by race, class, gender, and politics; and that greed and fairness, cheating and honesty, all carry the same moral weight (Anderson, 1999). The "Six Pillars of Character" that form the core of ethical values for the program are

1. *Trustworthiness.* Be honest; don't deceive, cheat, or steal. Be reliable—do what you say you'll do. Have the courage to do the right thing. Build a good reputation. Be loyal—stand by your family, friends, and country.
2. *Respect.* Treat others with respect; follow the Golden Rule. Be tolerant of differences. Use good manners, not bad language. Be considerate of the feelings of others. Don't threaten, hit, or hurt anyone. Deal peacefully with anger, insults, and disagreements.
3. *Responsibility.* Do what you are supposed to do. Persevere: Keep on trying! Always do your best. Use self-control. Be self-disciplined. Think before you act. Consider the consequences. Be accountable for your choices.
4. *Fairness.* Play by the rules. Take turns and share. Be open-minded; listen to others. Don't take advantage of others. Don't blame others carelessly.
5. *Caring.* Be kind. Be compassionate and show you care. Express gratitude. Forgive others. Help people in need.
6. *Citizenship.* Do your share to make your school and community better. Cooperate. Stay informed. Vote. Be a good neighbor. Obey laws and rules. Respect authority. Protect the environment.

School Value Statements. Many schools, particularly elementary schools, have chosen to identify a set of school-wide value statements that are intended to provide a schoolwide base of expectations for student behavior. In some cases, these value statements are a part of a larger character-education program that includes citizenship education, social-skills instruction, and service learning (for example, the Character Counts! program), but in other cases the set of values may not be part of such a program and may be self-standing.

The value statements tend to be a list of positive characteristics that all faculty and students can accept as desirable goals for student behavior. The values are usually prominently displayed in key locations in the school and are sometimes included on stationery, newsletters to parents, and assembly programs. In some schools these value statements become almost part of the school logo and

identity, and they are referred to and used in a variety of situations.

These value statements are distinguished from school or classroom rules in that they identify positive traits and goals rather than specific appropriate or inappropriate behaviors. For example, these three simple values or goals: "Be safe; Be respectful; and, Be responsible" can be distinguished from the following three rules: "Be in position; Keep hands and feet to self; and, Start work on time," which are much more specific and focus on particular behaviors regardless of their motivation. As a result, schools often use the value statements as the justification for the creation and implementation of more specific rules for various situations or locations in school.

An example of one such value statement might be the seven virtues identified by Ernest L. Boyer, president of the Carnegie Foundation for the Advancement of Teaching (1995). These seven virtues are

1. Honesty
2. Respect
3. Responsibility
4. Compassion
5. Self-discipline
6. Perseverance
7. Giving

Although the exact wording may vary, there tends to be considerable overlap in the values content identified by various schools. This is not unexpected if the values identified truly represent a core of values to which the larger community ascribes.

To implement these value statements, many schools have established a "values committee" of students, parents, teachers, administrators, school board members, and clergy from various faiths to attempt to devise a list of values. Sometimes these are then discussed in school assemblies, homerooms, and in public hearings to obtain input and to develop a sense of community and school consensus around the values; such a discussion also permits parents not only to be informed but to support these values in their children. In an era when the boundaries between school and religious as well as family responsibilities for values may be controversial, most schools have attempted to develop and include only those values that all faiths and families are likely to be able to fully endorse.

In addition to simply being posted or distributed, most schools that implement these value statements also encourage all teachers to employ these values in working with students in their classes, and many suggest that class instruction be devoted to ensuring that students understand the values and related rules and also to building consensus on the importance of the values.

Most schools also attempt to recognize students whose behavior exemplifies one or more of these values.

This is often done by posting names prominently in the school hall near the office, recognizing these students in honors or awards ceremonies or assemblies, and providing recognition certificates, and also by providing special privileges such as lunch with the principal or a special parking spot, or by distributing tangible awards such as small prizes or other items donated by local businesses and citizens or certificates for free or discounted food items. Additionally, many schools code these values into their overall district "Codes of Conduct" and school discipline systems, by reinforcing behavior in accord with the values and by creating other consequences for violations of these values.

Outcomes of Character Education

Character-education programs, as with many practices in schools, have logical and common-sense value. If violence and inappropriate behavior in school are among the causes of deteriorating home and community values as well as poor moral judgment by the student perpetrators, then character-education programs directly address these causes. Although character-education programs are widely accepted and have been advocated by a wide array of prominent organizations and individuals, there is little or no research evidence for or against the effectiveness of these efforts to prevent violence or to reduce other kinds of behavior problems. Although local evaluations of some programs, such as Character Counts!, have been conducted, there have been no major national studies of these specific types of programs, let alone character education more generally. Part of the difficulty arises because character education is a general philosophy and does not prescribe specific practices. As a result it is not easy to evaluate the effectiveness of such approaches because they are difficult to define, and the outcomes are hard to pin on such a general program or philosophy. Even individual examples of such programs, such as Character Counts!, which identifies the character goals and provides some curriculum materials, do not provide specific practices regarding how the program is to be instilled throughout the school environment; thus they challenge evaluation.

There is virtually no empirical evidence about the measurable outcomes of having school value statements. Again, they have logical and common-sense value and may serve to supplant deteriorating home and community values. It is not clear that these school value statements can compensate for larger community value deficits, but such efforts by schools are viewed with a "can't hurt" attitude and with the belief that this is the right thing for schools to do. Although these value statements may not change the attitudes or behaviors of chronically disruptive students, they may positively affect many other students in a preventative way and provide meaning for their prosocial behavior.

Violence-Prevention and Conflict-Resolution Curricula

Violence-prevention and conflict-resolution curricula teach students to use alternatives to violence when resolving their interpersonal and personal problems. These programs rely on ongoing instruction and discussion to change the perceptions, attitudes, and skills of students. A number of violence-prevention curricula have become available since the mid-1980s. Such programs typically strive to provide knowledge about violence and conflict, to increase students' understanding of their own and others' feelings, and to teach students the personal and interpersonal skills necessary to avoid violence.

Curricula vary in their emphasis. Conflict-resolution curricula focus on understanding conflict and learning negotiation-based responses to conflict. Violence-prevention curricula emphasize increasing students' knowledge about violence and teaching students alternatives to fighting. Social problem-solving curricula tend to focus on understanding feelings and on teaching students problem-solving strategies for dealing with their personal and interpersonal problems.

Peer mediation can substantially change how students approach and settle conflicts.

Lessons cover a variety of topics, including the prevalence of violence or conflict, identifying and expressing feelings, managing anger, using conflict resolution, appreciating diversity, and coping with stress. Instructional formats include teacher lecture, class meeting, or discussion. Students are encouraged to explore their own reactions and responses, often through videotaped scenarios and self-reflection worksheets. Finally, most programs include a role-playing component to provide opportunities to practice alternative skills and behaviors.

Violence-prevention and conflict-resolution curricula are most often part of a broader program. Instruction in conflict resolution is typically presented in conjunction with a classroom or schoolwide peer-mediation program. Some programs provide guidelines for school discipline or classroom management that are consistent with the curricula. Others focus on building family relationships and parent involvement in the school community.

Outcomes for Violence-Prevention Curricula

The use of schoolwide violence-prevention or conflict-resolution curricula is very recent; there have been few evaluations to date. This does not mean that such programs are ineffective. Rather, it suggests that any school that commits to using a violence-prevention curriculum may wish to undertake its own evaluation of the effectiveness and usefulness of the approach.

A number of programs have documented positive changes in student attitude and behavior. Among the most successful has been the Resolving Conflict Creatively program. In a large-scale evaluation of the program, a majority of teachers reported less physical violence and increased student cooperation in their classrooms. Other documented benefits of such curricula include improvements in classroom climate and student self-esteem, reductions in fighting and other disciplinary violations, and lower rates of both suspension at the middle school level and dropping out at the high school level. Teachers in successful programs have reported that they find themselves listening more attentively to students.

Some curricula emphasize social cognition or social problem solving in attempting to change student thinking about social interactions. Students exposed to such programs often learn to identify a greater variety of prosocial responses to hypothetical conflict situations. It is important to note, however, that improved ability to describe solutions to hypothetical situations does not guarantee improved behavior.

The effectiveness of violence-prevention curricula may well depend on how extensively the program is implemented. Teachers in successful programs are highly committed to the program and teach it regularly. In one study, student gains were directly proportional to the number of lessons they had received. Comparisons of different approaches have found that a teacher-directed approach might be best for decreasing the isolation of at-risk students. A comparison of violence-prevention with conflict-resolution curricula found that both are effective but that conflict-resolution programs seemed more successful in reducing the most serious types of violence.

In the face of a culture of violence that seems to pervade our schools and society, curricula that teach students the attitudes and skills they need to avoid violence seem to provide one sound strategy for violence prevention. Although differing in their emphases, violence-prevention, conflict-resolution, and social problem-solving curricula all attempt to increase student knowledge, to improve their awareness of feelings, and to teach new skills that can provide an alternative to violence. Because the field is young, schools seeking to implement the program should carefully evaluate the curriculum and plan implementation. The most important challenge in adopting such a curriculum may be to find an approach that is appropriate and can be fully accepted by faculty to ensure a high level of commitment and consistency in implementation.

Peer Mediation

Peer mediation is a negotiation-based strategy that teaches student mediators strategies to help resolve conflict among their peers. The student mediators then use these strategies to help keep minor school conflicts from escalating over time into more serious incidents (Bodine & Crawford, 1998). More important, peer mediation teaches students (mediators and disputants) an alternative set of skills that they can apply in conflict situations. Over time, students in schools with effective peer-mediation programs learn that there are alternatives to violence for solving personal problems or resolving interpersonal conflict.

In mediation, an impartial third party attempts to help others in a dispute come to a "win-win" rather than a "win-lose" resolution of conflict (Fisher & Ury, 1991). In peer mediation, student mediators are taught an interest-based negotiation procedure, along with communication and problem-solving strategies, to help their peers settle disagreements without confrontation or violence. Interest-based negotiation attempts to identify the interests that lie beneath the surface positions in a dispute. In the process of training, mediators learn that conflict can be resolved constructively and that their role as mediators is not to judge or to force an agreement or solution. Rather, students come to mediation voluntarily and are guided by peer mediators to move from blaming each other to devising solutions acceptable to all parties.

Peer-mediation programs grew out of programs such as the Community Boards program in San Francisco or Resolving Conflict Creatively in the New York City Public Schools that were developed by attorneys and child advocates in the mid-1970s (Lantieri & Patti, 1996). Some programs teach all students in the school processes to mediate disputes (Lantieri & Patti, 1996). Others select and train a cadre of students who act as the school's conflict managers....

Peer mediation has been used in a variety of situations. Although in some peer-mediation programs students learn arbitration only in informal situations such as the playground, in other programs, students learn to bring peer mediation into the classroom for resolving disputes. Some more formal programs may even establish a mediation office in which all peer mediation occurs. Although it can be implemented as a stand-alone program, most conflict-resolution programs recommend that peer mediation be used as one piece of a broader curriculum of violence prevention and conflict resolution.

Outcomes of Peer-Mediation Programs

The spread of peer-mediation programs around the country has outpaced research on their effects; as a result, there is much we still need to know about the effectiveness of peer mediation. Yet a wide variety of studies conducted in different locations and situations have found that peer mediation appears to be a promising strategy for improving school climate. A well-conducted peer-mediation program can be successful in changing the way students approach conflict. Students appear to be able to learn the steps of peer mediation as well as to use and retain them over a period of months. The use of peer mediation can substantially change how students approach and settle conflicts. In one middle school, 83% of students trained in peer mediation reported "win-win" settlements whereas 86% of untrained controls reported that conflicts resulted in a "win-lose" outcome (Johnson & Johnson, 1996).

These changes in turn appear to lead to other positive outcomes. Student attitudes toward negotiation may become more positive, with students more willing to help friends avoid fights and solve problems and less likely to believe that certain individuals deserve to be "beaten up." Although some studies have found no overall differences in perceptions of school climate, a number of others have reported that both students and teachers believe that peer mediation significantly improved their school climate. There is also evidence that implementing peer-mediation programs can be associated with fewer fights, fewer referrals to the office, and a decreased rate of school suspension (Johnson & Johnson, 1996). Finally, for the student mediators themselves, learning the mediation process has been shown to increase self-esteem and even to improve academic achievement.

Thus, peer mediation can have positive effects on student-conflict resolution and school climate. Yet the incompleteness of our knowledge, combined with occasional failures in peer mediation, suggests that success is not automatic. Rather, the benefits of peer meditation may depend on how well the program is planned and carried out. To be most effective, peer mediation should be part of a whole school effort. Teachers, administrators, and other staff need to understand and support the goals and processes of such a program. Although peer mediation is often implemented independently of other components, integrating peer mediation into a broader program that includes life-skills or violence-prevention curriculum appears to increase the effectiveness of the program (Lantieri & Patti, 1996).

Without training in negotiation, students appear to resolve most conflicts by either withdrawing or forcing a solution. A well-conducted peer-mediation program can teach students alternative strategies to aggression and withdrawal for settling conflicts. In particular, student mediators learn communication and problem-solving strategies that can enable them to help their peers find mutually satisfying solutions to disputes. This can lead to improved school climate, and even decreased office referrals and suspensions. Yet peer mediation is complex; to be successful, a program must be adequately planned and the mediators well trained. A facilitator or a team must attend to logistical details, must ensure that peer mediators are trained in both the assumptions and processes of mediation, and must monitor the success of mediators. With adequate attention to these details, peer mediation appears to be a promising tool that, used as part of a broader

program, can help teach students methods to settle their conflicts without resorting to violence.

Bullying Prevention

In the last three years, incidents of violent retribution have led to an increased awareness of the problem of bullying. Although often overlooked in schools, a large number of students report having been bullied. Bullying has detrimental psychological effects on children, such as low self-esteem, depression, and suicide.

A student is being bullied or victimized when exposed, repeatedly over time, to intentional injury or discomfort inflicted by one or more other students. This may include using physical contact or verbal assault, making obscene gestures or facial expressions, and being intentionally excluded. Bullying implies an imbalance of power or strength in which others victimize one child.

Surprisingly, large proportions of students are bullied in schools. In the United States, approximately 20% of students are bullied (Whitney & Smith, 1993). Most bullying occurs in places with little adult supervision, such as playgrounds and hallways. Bullies are typically larger than their victims and have more positive attitudes toward the use of violence than other students. Victims are less popular and often without a single friend in class; they tend to be more anxious and insecure than other students and commonly react by crying, withdrawal, and avoidance when attacked. Such reactions may be reinforcing to bullies.

Bullying has serious consequences for the victims, the perpetrators, and the school. Victims report feeling vengefulness, anger, and self-pity after a bullying incident (Borg, 1998). Left untreated, such reactions can evolve into depression, physical illness, and even suicide. In addition, students who engage in aggressive and bullying behaviors during their school years may engage in criminal and aggressive behavior after adolescence. In classrooms exhibiting high numbers of bullying problems, students tend to feel less safe and are less satisfied with school life (Olweus & Limber, 1999).

Bullying is often tolerated and ignored. Some have estimated that teachers rarely detect this problem and only intervene in 4% of all incidents (Craig & Pepler, 1997). In addition, students tend to believe that bullied students are at least partly to blame for their victimization, that bullying makes the victims tougher, and that teasing is simply done in fun (Oliver, Hoover, & Hazler, 1994). Students who report such incidents believe that nothing will be done.

Bullying prevention programs are a whole school effort designed to send a message that bullying will not be accepted in school. Well-designed and well-implemented programs can create an overall climate of warmth and adult involvement and can educate students to recognize instances of bullying.

One program incorporating intervention decreased bullying by 50%.

Effective bullying prevention programs rely on a number of components to reduce and prevent bullying problems. Through improved supervision, classroom rules against bullying, positive and negative consequences for following and violating rules, and serious talks with the bullies and victims, prevention plans strive to develop a school environment characterized by warmth and positive adult involvement. Other programs include a school conference day to discuss bullying, meetings with parents of bullies and victims, and regular classroom meetings. At the elementary level, worksheets, role plays, and relevant literature may be incorporated into existing curriculum. Such measures give the message that "bullying is not accepted in our school, and we will see to it that it comes to an end."

Individual interventions (e.g., keeping a victim close to a teacher at all times) are somewhat effective but may not significantly reduce bullying behavior. Comprehensive prevention programs have been implemented and evaluated in many cultures with encouraging results (Olweus & Limber, 1999).

Outcomes of Bullying Prevention Programs

There is an extensive knowledge base showing that well-designed bullying prevention programs can reduce, eliminate, and prevent bully-victim problems as well as improve overall school climate significantly. One program incorporating school, classroom, and individual interventions decreased bullying by 50% and reduced the reported intensity of bullying incidents (Olweus, 1993). Prevention programs have been shown to reduce general antisocial behavior such as fighting, vandalism, and truancy while increasing student satisfaction with their school.

Effective programs have two key prerequisites: awareness and adult involvement. To create a school climate that discourages bullying, school staff and parents must become aware of the extent of bully-victim problems in their own school. In addition, effective prevention also requires a commitment on the part of all adults to reduce or eliminate bullying. All bullying prevention programs recommend a prevention committee at the school level and a coordinator of prevention activities and curricula. The committee typically assesses the extent of the problem by designing and administering an anonymous student questionnaire. Using these data, the committee can make recommendations about which components are to be implemented and what materials are needed.

Most bullying occurrences are undetected or ignored, leading to detrimental effects for victims, bullies, and school climate. A well-conducted prevention program teaches students that bullying is unacceptable behavior and will not be tolerated. Effective programs have significantly reduced the occurrence of bullying and have improved school climate.

Conclusion

There appear to be a variety of programs that could be categorized as approaches intended to positively affect school climate and that also may be promising strategies for violence reduction. In addition to the five programs discussed briefly in this article, there may be a variety of other curricula that are of positive value. Although the evidence for the impact of these programs is not yet as strong as would be desired, each has enough evidence to conclude that it is at least a promising approach. Clearly other factors could negatively affect climate, even where one or more of these programs were in place; however, the existence of these curricula would be likely to positively affect school climate and also to reduce the likelihood of school violence. In addition, the compound effect of having more than one of these programs in place simultaneously has not yet been studied, but such an effect could be promising and could strengthen further the positive outcomes.

References

Anderson, E. (1999, October 3). The beginnings of Character Counts, *The Lincoln Journal Star* B3.

Ban, J. R. (1993). *Parents assuring student success (PASS): Achievement made easy by learning together*. Bloomington, IN: National Educational Service.

Bodine, R. J., & Crawford, D. K. (1998). *The handbook of conflict resolution education: A guide to building quality programs in schools*. San Francisco: Jossey-Bass.

Borg, M. G. (1998). The emotional reactions of school bullies and their victims. *Educational Psychology*, 18, 433–444.

Boyer, W. (1995, September). Character in the basic school—Making a commitment to character. Article from *Principal Magazine*. Available: http://www.naesp.org/char.html

Brendtro, L., Brokenleg, M., & Van Bockern, S. (1990). *Reclaiming youth at risk: Our hope for the future*. Bloomington, IN: National Education Service.

Charney, R. S. (1998). *Teaching children to care: Management in the responsive classroom*. Greenfield, MA: Northeast Foundation for Children.

Christenson, S. L. (1995). Families and schools: What is the role of the school psychologist? *School Psychology Quarterly*, 10(2), 118–132.

Craig, W. M., & Pepler, D. J. (1997). Observations of bullying and victimization in the school yard. *Canadian Journal of School Psychology*, 13, 41–60.

Epstein, J. L. (1992). School and family partnerships: Leadership roles for school psychologists. In S. L. Christenson & J. C. Conoley (Eds.), *Home-school collaboration* (pp. 215–243). Silver Spring, MD: The National Association of School Psychologists.

Feedman, M. (1993). *The kindness of strangers; Adult mentors, urban youth, and the new voluntarism*. San Francisco: Jossey-Bass.

Fisher, R., & Ury, W. (1991). *Getting to yes* (2nd ed.). New York: Penguin Books.

Haynes, N. M., & Comer, J. P. (1996). Integrating schools, families, and communities through successful school reform: The school development program. *School Psychology Review*, 25(4), 501–506.

Henley, M., Ramsey, R., & Algozzine, R. (1999). *Teaching students with mild disabilities* (3rd ed.). Boston: Allyn & Bacon.

Johnson, D. W., & Johnson, R. T. (1996). Conflict resolution and peer-mediation programs in elementary and secondary schools: A review of the research. *Review of Educational Research*, 66, 459–506.

Kelley, E., Glover, J., Keefe, J., Halderson, C., Sorenson, C., & Speth, C. (1986). *School climate survey*. Comprehensive Assessment of School Environments. Reston, VA: National Association of Secondary School Principals.

Kube, B. A., & Ratigan, G. (1991). All present and accounted for: A no-nonsense policy on student attendance keeps kids showing up for class—and learning. *The American School Board Journal*, 22–23.

Lantieri, L., & Patti, J. (1996). *Waging peace in our schools*. Boston: Beacon Press.

Lickona, T. (1988, February). Four strategies for fostering character development in children. *Phi Delta Kappan*, 419–423.

Lloyd, G. M. (1996). Research and practical application for school, family, and community partnerships. In A. Booth & J. F. Dunn (Eds.) (pp. 255–264). *Family-school links. How do they affect educational outcomes?*

London, P. (1987, May). Character education and clinical intervention: A paradigm shift for US schools. *Phi Delta Kappan*, 667–673.

Morrison, J. A., Olivos, K., Dominguez, G., Gomez, D., & Lena, D. (1993). The application of family systems approaches to school behavior problems on a school-level discipline board: An outcome study. *Elementary School Guidance & Counseling*, 27, 258–272.

Noddings, N. (1992). *The challenge to care in schools: An alternative approach to education*. New York: Teachers College Press.

Oliver, R., Hoover, J. H., & Hazier, R. (1994). The perceived roles of bullying in small town midwestern schools. *Journal of Counseling and Development*, 72, 416–420.

Olweus, D. (1993). *Bullying at school: What we know and what we can do*. Malden, MA: Blackwell Publishers.

Olweus, D., & Limber, S. (1999). Bullying prevention program. In D. S. Elliot (Ed.), *Blueprints for violence prevention*. Denver, CO: C & M Press.

Sergiovanni, T. J. (1994). *Building community in schools*. San Francisco: Jossey-Bass.

Smith, S. E. (1994). Parent-initiated contracts: An intervention for school-related behaviors. *Elementary School Guidance & Counseling*, 28(3), 182–188.

Thompson, S. M. (1996). Peer mediation: A peaceful solution. *School Counselor*, 44, 151–154.

Warner, I. (1991). Parents in touch: District leadership for parent involvement. *Phi Delta Kappan*, 178, 372–375.

Weiss, H. M., & Edwards, M. B. (1992). The family-school collaboration project: Systemic interventions for school improvement. In S. L. Christenson, & J. C. Conoley (Eds.), *Home-school collaboration* (pp. 215–243). Silver Spring, MD: The National Association of School Psychologists.

Whelage, G., Rutter, R., Smith, G., Lesko, N., & Fernandez, R. (1989). *Reducing the risk: Schools as communities of support*. London: The Falmer Press.

Whitney, L., & Smith, P. (1993). A survey of the nature and extent of bully/victim problems in junior/middle and secondary schools. *Educational Research*, 35, 3–25.

Williamson, L. (1997). Parents as teachers of children program (PATCH). *Professional School Counseling*, 1, 2, 7–13.

Reece L. Peterson is an associate professor of special education and communication disorders at the University of Nebraska-Lincoln. Russell Skiba is an associate professor in the Department of Counseling and Educational Psychology, Indiana Policy Institute, Indiana University, Bloomington. This article originally appeared in Preventing School Failure, *Spring 2000, pgs. 122–129. Reprinted with permission of the Helen Dwight Reid Educational Foundation. Published by Heldref Publications, 1319 18th St. N.W, Washington, D.C. 20036-1802. Copyright 2000.*

From *The Clearing House*, January/February 2001, Vol. 74, No. 3, pp. 155-163. © 2001 by the Helen Dwight Reid Educational Foundation. Reprinted by permission.

Discipline and the Special Education Student

If special education students are subject to a different disciplinary standard, they are not fully participating in the mainstream curriculum. An effective disciplinary code that applies to all students can help create a more productive learning environment.

James A. Taylor and Richard A. Baker Jr.

John is a special education student who attends only one resource class each day. Otherwise, he participates in regular education classes. During English class, the teacher corrects him for disruptive behavior, but he continues to make inappropriate comments. The teacher asks him to step into the hallway so that she can address his behavior privately. As she begins speaking to him, he walks away, then turns to her and says, "Shut up, you bitch." The teacher submits a referral to the assistant principal, who consults the district handbook and recommends that John spend three days in the supervised suspension center.

Because of John's status as a special education student, however, personnel at the district level—without conducting a hearing or a meeting with John's individualized education program (IEP) team—allow John to spend the three days at home. The district's concern is with John's protections under the Individuals with Disabilities Education Act. But is the district's action in compliance with federal law?

The general belief among teachers and administrators is that the Individuals with Disabilities Education Act insulates special education students from experiencing consequences for their disciplinary infractions and sets them apart from the school's regular disciplinary pro-

cedures. Horror stories abound about students whose behavior, like John's, threatens the safety of staff and students, disrupting learning for themselves and other students.

The misperception that educators are supposed to tolerate such behavior is largely the result of the unclear administrative procedures outlined under the Education for All Handicapped Children Act of 1975 (Public Law 94-142) and the Supreme Court decision in *Honig v. Doe* (1988). Aware of these unclear procedures and educators' common misunderstanding of the law, the U.S. Congress took care, when reauthorizing the Education for All Handicapped Children Act as the Individuals with Disabilities Education Act in 1990 (Public Law 101-476) and 1997 (Public Law 105-17), to address the issue of appropriate disciplinary procedures for special education students. Educators need to know the provisions of the current law as they develop schoolwide discipline plans and the individualized education programs required for special education students.

The 1997 Individuals with Disabilities Education Act amendments clarify that the only disciplinary procedure that applies exclusively to special education students is the determination of a long-term change of placement—that is, a long-term suspension or removal to an alternative

school setting. If the disciplinary measure for behavior infractions lasts for 10 or fewer days, and 45 or fewer days for weapon or drug infractions, the special education student receives the same treatment that students without disabilities receive. If, however, the special education student's suspensions are recurrent and add up to more than 10 days in a school year or more than 45 days for a serious infraction, the local education agency must conduct an assessment of the student's behavior and implement an intervention plan to address the student's behavior problems.

After conducting classroom observations and closely examining the evaluation of the student's disability and the implementation of the student's individualized education program, a committee designated by the local education agency must decide whether or not the student's behavior is a manifestation of the student's disability. If the committee determines that it is, the student's IEP team must immediately rewrite the student's program to correct the behavior. If the committee determines that the behavior is not a manifestation of the disability, the child must be disciplined "in the same manner... applied to children without disabilities" (Individuals with Disabilities Education Act, 20 U.S.C. § 1415 [k][5]).

In the case of John, the district should have applied the same disciplinary measures that it applies to students without disabilities. If the district plans to treat John differently, or if the behavior is recurrent and disciplinary measures have exceeded 10 days, the district must hold a meeting with the IEP team to determine whether this behavior is a manifestation of John's disability. If the team decides that it is not a result of the disability, the district must assign the same disciplinary consequences to John that it assigns to students without disabilities.

A Discipline Policy for All Students

To meet the federal standard, schools need a humane and just administration of discipline that respects and protects all students' rights to a free and public education. Comprehensive discipline guidelines must cover the treatment of students with and without disabilities. Moreover, the discipline plan must do more than take corrective action for offenses; it must also prevent discipline problems and support positive behavior (Charles, 1999).

As administrators and IEP teams develop behavioral intervention plans for students with disabilities, they should keep in mind the overall goal of implementing a schoolwide discipline system that is more than merely corrective. Special education students must understand that they are subject to the same disciplinary measures as other students. Such practices as before-school and after-school detentions, weekend detentions, additional written work, or required community service, commonly found in school discipline plans, do not create a change in special education placement and may serve as corrective measures for disciplinary infractions that are not directly related to the safety of fellow students or disturbance of the learning environment. Integrating these alternatives into behavioral intervention plans for special education students reminds them of the consequences of their choices. The discipline plan for all students should also incorporate preventive and supportive discipline measures.

Preventive Discipline

Preventive discipline promotes behaviors that are beneficial to the learning environment. By affirming and practicing them and reflecting on their meaning, everyone can practice showing concern, modeling courtesy, and supporting one another. Translating classroom rules and procedures into affirmative "we" statements to which the students and teachers commit themselves helps to identify good behaviors and strengthens the sense of belonging that both learners and adults need.

For example, Mr. Boudreaux has taught 7th graders for several years and knows that they will enter the classroom in an energetic, boisterous manner. Without a preventive discipline plan, the students will take a long time to settle down and focus on the lesson. Mr. Boudreaux, however, meets the students at the door and requires them to enter according to a specific procedure. First, he says, we enter in silence, then go to the materials shelf, read the assignments on the board, and assemble our materials. Instruction begins within three minutes of classroom entry, with all students having materials in place. In this way, Mr. Boudreaux meets all students' need for structure, limits, and routine.

Learning experiences that are worthwhile and enjoyable provide the foundation of a quality preventive discipline plan. Three elements—fun, focus, and energy—are essential components of a preventive discipline plan (Taylor & Baker, 2001), particularly for students with disabilities, whose classes and activities are often unchallenging and devoid of opportunities for creative expression.

Supportive Discipline

Supportive discipline helps students channel their own behaviors productively. As a weight lifter needs a spotter to provide support during a challenging lift, students need positive intervention. The teacher and students need a set of common signals so that either can ask for or offer assistance without judgment or confrontation. Such agreed-upon techniques as "eye drive" (a deliberate look that signals affirmation or correction), physical proximity, silent signals, and head movement can communicate the need for a refocus to productive behavior.

The teacher's goal is not to control the students but rather to support students as they learn to control themselves. A supportive disciplinary action is an offer to help, not a judgment or imposition of will. To minimize the need for corrective discipline, educators need to explain the supportive elements of this approach to students with disabilities and to their parents.

Several supportive techniques have been developed by Mr. Boulanger, an 8th grade teacher. His signals remind students that they are responsible for controlling themselves. When he stands in front of the room and looks intently from student to student, they understand and respond to his signal by focusing on the task at hand. Through routine and consistent reinforcement, each student learns that the purpose of these signals is to help them achieve the level of excellence they desire.

Corrective Discipline

Even the best preventive and supportive approaches sometimes fail, at which point corrective action becomes necessary. Educators must administer corrective discipline expeditiously, invoking well-known guidelines about consequences for certain kinds of behavior. The purpose of corrective discipline is not to intimidate or punish but to provide natural consequences for disciplinary infractions that disrupt the learning environment.

The person in authority must never ignore disruptive behavior. One helpful technique for remaining calm is to administer corrective action in a matter-of-fact manner, adopting the demeanor of a state trooper. "May I see your driver's license, insurance card, and automobile registration? You were traveling 50 miles per hour in a 35 miles per hour zone."

Invoke the insubordination rule when necessary. Use a predetermined plan to command assistance if it is necessary to correct the situation. The behavior intervention plan that the Individuals with Disabilities Education Act regulations now require must include clear corrective procedures.

All students deserve well-disciplined learning environments that are fun, focused, and full of creative energy.

For example, Mrs. Thibodaux has developed a set of consequences for the most common infractions. Each student knows that being late to class will mean a period of after-school detention for a certain number of school days. Each knows that repeated failure to complete assignments will result in a telephone conference with a parent during work hours. Educators must work out these corrective measures ahead of time. Although the measures are not harsh or excessively punitive, they should be consistently inconvenient for the students and parents.

The U.S. Congress has now made it clear that schools should not allow children with disabilities to disrupt learning environments. All students need guidance to become respectful, responsible citizens who enjoy and effectively exercise their rights. If educators make excuses for special education students' behaviors, they deny them the benefits contained in the laws. All students deserve well-disciplined learning environments that are fun, focused, and full of creative energy. Developing discipline systems that combine preventive, supportive, and corrective measures for all students will move our schools toward that ideal.

References

Charles, C. M. (1999). *Building classroom discipline*. New York: Addison, Wesley, Longman.

Education for All Handicapped Children Act of 1975, Public Law 94-142 (1975).

Honig v. Doe, 484 U.S. 305 (1988).

Individuals with Disabilities Education Act, 20 U.S.C. § 1400 *et seq.* (1997).

Taylor, J. A., & Baker, R. A. (2001). High-stakes testing and the essential curriculum. *Basic Education, 45* (5), 11.

James A. Taylor (jtaylor@edleaders.com) is President and **Richard A. Baker Jr**. (rbaker@edleaders.com) is Vice President of Edleaders.com, 4925 Elysian Fields, New Orleans, LA 70122.

TREND **WATCH**

E-Mentality: Is e-learning affecting classroom behavior?

By Jennifer J. Salopek

Back in the dark ages of e-learning, savvy developers knew that the key to a quality learning experience was to include some of the winning aspects of a classroom session: information, hands-on exercises, ability to get feedback, and so forth. But now, the pendulum has swung back, and it seems that the elements particular to e-learning are being incorporated into the classroom. Why?

Perhaps it's because as learners become more exposed to and comfortable with e-learning, particularly its just-in-time nature, their expectations for any learning experience—including classroom sessions—are changing. And as those expectations change, so must classroom trainers adapt their techniques and approaches.

"We got into e-learning to attract people who never got into the classroom," says Leslie Darling, chief learning officer at Element K. "But now, it's definitely affecting classroom behavior. People wander in and out of conference sessions as never before. If they don't immediately see what they're looking for, they leave."

Further, Darling believes that e-learning, being more self-directed, has encouraged people to assert their right to choose. She notes that in the past, managers often chose what courses employees would take but didn't necessarily communicate the learning objectives. E-learning "forces participants into a needs analysis role," she says. "They're ex-

pected to bring something back, so they try to be more efficient with their time."

Others aren't so sure. "People have always voted with their feet," says Kit Horton of William Horton Consulting. "But I don't think people are so comfortable with e-learning yet that it's changing their behavior." Although Horton doesn't believe learners have expectations based on their computer use, she does think that "people who have grown up on television have shorter attention spans. They want to see something happen." To reach those learners, trainers create presentations with lots of live demonstrations and simulations—interactivity that has evolved as it has traveled from lab to e-learning and back to the classroom.

As learners become more **exposed** to and comfortable with e-learning, their expectations for any **learning experience**— including classroom sessions—are changing.

E-learning has also made training a part of everyone's job. When you can locate and pass along information quickly to help people do their work, you're performing a training function. "We're combining work and learning more efficiently," says Darling—and that, too, has

had an effect on people's classroom expectations. "It has really diminished our tolerance for long classes," she says.

What can training professionals do to accommodate those changing expectations? First, says Mike Groszko, manager of the DaimlerChrysler Quality Institute, make sure the medium fits your message. "The capabilities of each medium attract different kinds of content. Both are effective; the challenge is to do the right things to improve learning. That can happen in both venues if it's done well."

Many learning professionals find that they're using classroom time more judiciously. "You must use the classroom for what it's best for," says Darling. She cites problem solving, dynamic feedback, and collaboration as activities that are most effective in a classroom setting.

Take mundane tasks out of the classroom, suggests Susan Musselman, global director of training for Six Sigma at Starwood Hotels and Resorts. Send materials in advance, and post them on the Web. "That way, we're able to accomplish more in the classroom. We can do more in the same amount of time." Diane Valerioti, manager of learning and development at Donovan Data Systems, agrees. "E-learning will never replace the classroom entirely. There will always be a need for customized, face-to-face instruction." But to make the most of her customers' training time, she pushes them to the Web for documentation and help after a class.

Maximizing learners' time is a crucial part of keeping them from voting with their feet. Instructors don't always have a fair chance when people listen for only five minutes before ditching a session, says Sue Reber, Element K's instructional design lead. Still, it's an instructor's responsibility to grab learners' attention right away, she says. "We must keep learners at the top of our minds at all times, and immediately demonstrate what's in it for them. We must make them want to stay."

Although classroom abandonment would have been considered rude five years ago, "it's now set up as an expectation for our trainers," says Darling. "We understand that participants owe it to themselves to get what they need." She suggests sending out or posting information about what topics a session will cover, letting participants attend only the portion they need.

As an instructor, you must set expectations up front and maintain control of the classroom. If you spend the first 15 to 20 minutes explaining what you'll cover, "you'll cause participants to make a decision," says Darling. Then if any participants step out or come in late, "Let them know that you might not be able to catch them up at that time. Hold them responsible."

The buzz phrase *discovery learning* reflects how e-learning has changed learners' expectations. In a January article in *e-Learning*, Michael Allen writes: "Students do the selecting, organizing, and structuring of information in order to accomplish selected tasks. They see the functional value of what they are learning while they are learning. They benefit from working directly with the content."

Though Allen discusses discovery learning only in the e-learning environment, the same principles are being used effectively by classroom trainers to maximize learning. Once again, the pendulum swings.

"The best classroom sessions are instructor-facilitated rather than instructor-led," says Reber. She notes that learners get to choose their own focus through hands-on practice, a method Element K calls cognitive apprenticeship. "The instructor is much less tied to doing everything in the book in order." The result, she says, is classroom training that targets student needs and is more results oriented.

"In the past, we used classroom time to activate and demonstrate. Now we're able to move beyond those steps, to apply and integrate. We can focus more on job context, which increases the probability of learning transfer."

In that facilitative mode, a classroom trainer's role is changing. It's also a good way to keep the attention of the e-learning generation, says Darling. "The instructor gives a problem and reviews the available resources," she says, "then coaches learners through the case or activity. Learners may approach the problems in whatever order they choose."

Darling also thinks the evolving role is good for trainers: "The biggest and most exciting change is that this approach allows the classroom to be more dynamic, and allows the instructor to truly be a coach." She notes, however, that it won't be for everyone. "Coaching in that way is tougher and more intense than presenting material. There's none of the drama and showmanship that many trainers enjoy."

Clearly, what differentiates e-learning from classroom training most is the element of choice. As instructors incorporate new techniques and approaches to increase learners' choices, more training managers will be able to echo Groszko, who says, "We think our classroom training is good enough that people *do* get what they want."

Jennifer J. Salopek *is a contributing editor of* T+D; *jjsalopek@earthlink.net.*

UNIT 6

Cultural Diversity and Schooling

Unit Selections

Key Points to Consider

- What is multicultural education? To what does the national debate over multiculturalism in the schools relate? What are the issues regarding it?

- If you are a female, have you ever felt that you were discriminated against or, at the least, ignored? Describe your experiences.

- If you are a male, have you ever felt that you were being favored? Relate your experiences.

- How can schools more effectively address the issues of gender bias?

- How do children learn to be prejudiced? How can they learn tolerance and acceptance of diversity?

- How would you define the remaining equity issues in the field of education? How would you rank order them?

- What has been the impact of public voucher programs on minority students enrolled in them. In terms of academic benefits, do you think they have been positive, negative, or mixed? Explain.

- Are there social class issues that affect students' lives in schools? Explain them.

 **Links: www.dushkin.com/online/**
These sites are annotated in the World Wide Web pages.

American Scientist
http://www.amsci.org/amsci/amsci.html

American Studies Web
http://www.georgetown.edu/crossroads/asw/

Multicultural Publishing and Education Council
http://www.mpec.org/mpec.html

National Institute on the Education of At-Risk Students
http://www.ed.gov/offices/OERI/At-Risk/

Prospects: The Congressionally Mandated Study of Educational Growth and Opportunity
http://www.ed.gov/pubs/Prospects/index.html

The concept of "culture" encompasses all of the life ways, customs, traditions, and institutions that a people develop as they create and experience their history and identity as a people. In the United States of America, many very different cultures coexist within the civic framework of a shared constitutional tradition that guarantees equality before the law for all. So, as we all have been taught, out of many peoples we are also one nation united by our constitutional heritage.

The civil rights movement in America in the 1950s and 1960s was about the struggle of cultural minorities to achieve equity: social justice before the law under our federal Constitution. The articles in this unit attempt to address some of these equity issues.

There is an immense amount of unfinished business before us in the area of intercultural relations in the schools and in educating all Americans regarding how multicultural our national population demographics really are. We are becoming more and more multicultural with every passing decade. This further requires us to take steps to ensure that all of our educational opportunity structures remain open to all persons regardless of their cultural backgrounds or gender. There is much unfinished business as well with regard to improving educational opportunities for girls and young women; the remaining gender issues in American education are very real and directly related to the issue of equality of educational opportunity.

Issues of racial prejudice and bigotry still plague us in American education, despite massive efforts in many school systems to improve racial and intercultural relations in the schools. Many American adolescents are in crisis as their basic health and social needs are not adequately met and their educational development is affected by crises in their personal lives. The articles in this unit reflect all of the above concerns plus others related to efforts to provide equality of educational opportunity to all American youth and attempts to clarify what multicultural education is and what it is not.

The "equity agenda," or social justice agenda, in the field of education is a complex matrix of gender- and culture-related issues aggravated by incredibly wide gaps in the social and economic opportunity structures available to citizens. We are each situated by cultural, gender-based, and socioeconomic factors in society; this is true of all persons everywhere. We have witnessed a great and glorious struggle for human rights in our time and in our nation. The struggle continues to deal more effectively with educational opportunity issues related to cultural diversity and gender.

The "Western canon" is being challenged by advocates' multicultural perspectives in school curriculum development. Multicultural educational programming, which will reflect the rapidly changing cultural demographics of North American schooling, is being advocated by some and strongly opposed by others. This controversy centers around several different issues regarding what it means to provide equality of opportunities for culturally diverse students. The traditional Western cultural content of general and social studies and language arts curricula is being challenged as Eurocentric.

Helping teachers to broaden their cultural perspectives and to take a more global view of curriculum content is something that the advocates of culturally pluralistic approaches to curriculum development would like to see integrated into the entire elementary and secondary school curriculum structure. North America is as multicultural a region of the world as exists anywhere. Our enormous cultural diversity encompasses populations from many indigenous "First Americans" as well as peoples from every European culture, plus many peoples of Asian, African, and Latin American nations and the Central and South Pacific Island groups. There is spirited controversy over how to help all Americans to better understand our collective multicultural heritage. There are spirited defenders and opponents of the traditional Eurocentric curriculum.

The problem of inequality of educational opportunity is of great concern to American educators. One in four American children does not have all of basic needs met and lives under poverty conditions. Almost one in three lives in a single-parent home. More and more concern is expressed over how to help children of poverty. The equity agenda of our time has to do with many issues related to gender, race, and ethnicity. All forms of social deprivation and discrimination are aggravated by great disparities in income and accumulated wealth. How can students be helped to have an equal opportunity to succeed in school?

Some of us are still proud to say that we are a nation of immigrants. In addition to the traditional minority/majority group relationships that evolved in the United States, new waves of immigrants today are again enhancing the importance of concerns for achieving equality of opportunity in education. In light of these vast sociological and demographic changes, we must ensure that we will remain a multicultural democracy.

The social psychology of prejudice is something that psychiatrists, social psychologists, anthropologists, and sociologists have studied in great depth since the 1930s. Tolerance, acceptance, and a valuing of the unique worth of every person are teachable and learnable attitudes. A just society must be constantly challenged to find meaningful ways to raise human aspirations, to heal human hurt, and to help in the task of optimizing every citizen's potential. Education is a vital component to that end. Teachers can incorporate into their lessons an emphasis on acceptance of difference, toleration of and respect for the beliefs of others, and the skills of reasoned debate and dialogue.

The struggle for optimal representation of minority perspectives in the schools will be a matter of serious concern to educators for the foreseeable future. From the many court decisions upholding the rights of women and cultural minorities in the schools over the past years has emerged a national consensus that we must strive for the greatest degree of equality in education as may be possible. The triumph of constitutional law over prejudice and bigotry must continue.

Decisions That Have Shaped U.S. Education

Education in the United States would be very different without these landmark decisions by the Supreme Court.

Perry A. Zirkel

Of the thousands of published court decisions concerning elementary and secondary education in the United States, which ones have had the greatest impact on the practices of K–12 education and on subsequent court cases in education law? School-law experts, like movie critics or sports commentators, are bound to differ in their choices of the most significant cases. Examining Supreme Court decisions during the past six decades (Zirkel, 1998; Zirkel, Goldberg, & Richardson, 2001), however, reveals important rulings that deal with equality in education, freedom of expression, discipline and school safety, and the complex relationship between religion and government in U.S. education.

The Brown v. Board of Education ruling struck down, after more than 50 years, the "separate but equal" doctrine of Plessy v. Ferguson.

Equality in Education

Several significant cases that have reached the U.S. Supreme Court deal with providing children with equal education. The right to an education in the United States derives from state—not federal—law, but the Fourteenth Amendment to the U.S. Constitution guarantees all citizens equal protection under both state and federal law; this guarantee of equal protection includes prohib-

iting discrimination in U.S. public schools. The U.S. Congress has reinforced and implemented this guarantee with civil rights statutes.

Citing the equal protection clause of the Fourteenth Amendment to the U.S. Constitution, the Brown decision made clear that laws that upheld segregation were unconstitutional.

Desegregation

Brown v. Board of Education (1954)
In perhaps the best-known U.S. Supreme Court decision in the past century, the *Brown* Court struck down, after more than 50 years, the "separate but equal" doctrine of *Plessy v. Ferguson* (1896). Citing the equal protection clause of the Fourteenth Amendment to the U.S. Constitution, the decision made clear that laws that upheld segregation were unconstitutional and ruled that separate schools deprive minority children of equal educational opportunities, even if the physical facilities and other factors are equivalent. A long line of more than 30 subsequent Supreme Court decisions have dealt with the implications of the *Brown* ruling. Today, the clear unconstitutionality of segregation by law or policy reminds us of the significant impact of the *Brown* decision, but the

intractability of de facto segregation also reveals the Court's limited influence in bringing about social and school reform.

Per-Pupil Expenditure
San Antonio Independent School District v. Rodriguez (1973)

Many states finance public schools in significant part through local property taxes, a funding strategy that often results in a notable disparity in the per-pupil expenditures among school districts. The Supreme Court's *Rodriguez* decision allowed the states a more relaxed standard for justifying their funding policies and held that the Fourteenth Amendment's equal protection clause permits any kind of school finance system, as long as it provides a minimum education for every student. The result has been a testing of the issue of per-pupil expenditure in state courts, which often rule against the funding policies established by state legislatures.

Students with Limited English Proficiency
Lau v. Nichols (1974)

Ducking the Fourteenth Amendment equal protection clause, the *Lau* Court relied on the much narrower grounds of the regulations and guidelines issued under Title VI of the Civil Rights Act of 1964, which prohibits federally funded programs from discriminating on the basis of race or national origin. The *Lau* Court held that Title VI required school districts to take affirmative steps to rectify the language deficiency of students with limited English proficiency. Carefully avoiding dictating a particular methodology, the Court left the remedy to the local level, where teaching English as a second language is often favored over a bilingual curriculum.

Special Education
Board of Education v. Rowley (1982)

The parents of a student with a hearing disability, attending a regular elementary class in a public school, requested a sign language interpreter in all her academic classes. The *Rowley* Court ruled that the Individuals with Disabilities Education Act's statutory entitlement to a "free and appropriate public education" for all students, including those with disabilities, means that school authorities must comply with the act's procedural requirements, which include developing individualized education programs for students with disabilities. They must also ensure that these individualized education programs are reasonably designed to provide educational benefit. In this case, the Supreme Court concluded that the district had complied with the act's procedural requirements and that the student's individualized education program provided educational benefit, even

though the district did not provide a sign language interpreter.

Barnette held that public school officials may not force students to salute the flag.

Accommodating Disabilities
School Board v. Arline (1987)

The *Arline* case considered whether an employee with a serious contagious disease—in this case, tuberculosis—is covered by Section 504 of the Rehabilitation Act of 1973, which prohibits federally funded organizations, including school districts, from discriminating against any individual on the basis of a disability. The answer of the *Arline* Court essentially was "it depends"—requiring information about the disability and decisions about whether the employer could reasonably accommodate the employee. Subsequent court decisions made clear that this individualized approach applies to employees and students with AIDS and that, in most cases, accommodation rather than segregation or exclusion is the reasonable—and therefore required—approach. Accommodation on behalf of students and employees with disabilities is an important feature of U.S. schools today.

Freedom of Expression

Freedom of speech is guaranteed in the First Amendment to the U.S. Constitution, but the expression covered by that freedom takes different forms.

Courts continue to cite Tinker as meaning that school officials may not censure or censor student speech unless it creates a substantial disruption of school operations.

Saluting the Flag
West Virginia State Board of Education v. Barnette (1943)

The *Barnette* Court held that public school officials may not force students to salute the flag. The students in this case were Jehovah's Witnesses, but the Court invoked the freedom of expression guaranteed in the First Amendment, as suggested in the Court's famous dictum that "[i]f there be any fixed star in our constitutional constellation, it is that no official, high or petty, can prescribe what shall be orthodox in politics, nationalism, religion, or other matters of opinion" (at 639). Subsequent lower court decisions extended the boundaries of *Barnette* to include teachers.

Student Speech

Tinker v. Des Moines Independent Community School District (1969)

John Tinker, Christopher Eckhardt, and John's sister Mary Beth challenged the school suspensions that they had received for wearing armbands to school in protest of the Vietnam War. The court ruled that teachers and students do not "shed their constitutional rights... at the schoolhouse gate" but that such constitutional rights should be "applied in light of the special characteristics of the school environment" (at 506). Subsequent lower court rulings have cited these two parts of this complex decision, with opposite results. In the 1970s and 1980s, courts leaned toward protecting student speech; since the late 1980s, they have emphasized the need to ensure school order. Courts continue to cite *Tinker* as meaning that school officials may not censure or censor student speech unless it causes a substantial disruption of school operations. *Tinker* continues to play a significant role in student speech cases today. For example, three recent lower court cases concerning student Internet communications applied *Tinker's* test of substantial disruption to determine whether students could be disciplined for home-based Web sites or e-mail that used vulgarities or threats about school personnel.

Censorship

Hazelwood School District v. Kuhlmeier (1988)

Students in a high school journalism class had produced an issue of the school newspaper from which the principal, prior to publication, deleted two pages that included articles on divorced parents and teenage pregnancy. The *Hazelwood* Court decided in the principal's favor, ruling that, for school-sponsored activities involving student expression, public school officials may exercise content-based control as long as their actions are related to legitimate education purposes. In subsequent cases dealing with First Amendment protections of expression, from student dress to students' threats, lower courts have looked to the pole stars of *Tinker* and *Hazelwood* for guidance, with the distinct majority of the decisions favoring school authorities.

Teachers' Speech

Mt. Healthy City School District v. Doyle (1977)

A teacher with a record of tactless behavior claimed that the school district did not renew his contract because he had provided information for a disc jockey's public criticism of the principal's student dress code. The *Mt. Healthy* decision spelled out a three-step freedom of expression clause to public employees, including public school teachers. First, the employee must prove that the expression concerns a public, not intramural, issue and that the right to speak outweighs the employer's responsibility to provide effective public services. Second, the employee must show that the expression was a sub-

stantial factor in the adverse action being challenged. Third, the employer must prove that it would have taken the adverse action regardless of the employee's protected expression.

Subsequent lower court decisions have largely favored districts' actions. The message of *Mt. Healthy* is that public school employees have First Amendment freedom of expression but they should think thrice before engaging in such expression in the face of possible adverse action, such as nonrenewal or termination. Some teachers have sought more extensive protections of expressions through collective bargaining agreements or local policies.

School Libraries

Board of Education, Island Trees Union Free School District No. 26 v. Pico (1982)

A local school board had directed the high school and junior high school libraries to remove books that the school board characterized as "anti-American, anti-Christian, anti-Semitic, and just plain filthy" (at 857). The Supreme Court ruled that school boards may not remove books from school libraries simply because they dislike the books' ideas; their reasons must reflect rational grounds, such as educational suitability, rather than political orthodoxy. Recent lower court decisions have reinforced the boundary between the review policies of school libraries and the discretionary powers of school boards in choosing school curriculums.

Student Discipline and School Safety

At what point does concern for school safety interfere with students' and teachers' rights under the U.S. Constitution? The Supreme Court has tried to answer this question in several important cases.

Student Suspensions and Expulsions

Goss v. Lopez (1975)

The Supreme Court held that for suspensions of up to 10 school days, school officials must provide at least oral notice of the charges and, if the student protests, an explanation of the evidence and an opportunity for the student to tell his or her side of the story. Citing the Fourteenth Amendment's guarantee that every citizen receive the due process of law, the Court also warned that longer suspensions may require more formal procedures in terms of notice and a hearing. Twenty-five years of lower court case ruling have elaborated these procedural protections for a wide range of situations, from short-term suspensions in interscholastic athletics to lengthy expulsions from school. In recent years, rulings have favored public school officials, particularly in the wake of the student violence at Columbine High School in Littleton, Colorado, in 1999.

Corporal Punishment
Ingraham v. Wright (1977)

The *Ingraham* Court concluded that the Eighth Amendment's guarantee against cruel and unusual punishment applies to the prison, not school, context and that if the corporal punishment is excessive and violates the Fourteenth Amendment's guarantee of due process, a student can bring a civil suit or even criminal prosecution for assault and battery. Subsequent legal cases have shown that civil suits and criminal prosecutions for assault and battery are difficult to win and that administrative action in terms of teacher discipline—including discharge—and state statutes outlining strict guidelines for such student discipline provide effective remedies.

Searches of Students
New Jersey v. T.L.O. (1985)

When a vice principal searched a female student's pocketbook after a teacher reported that the student had been smoking in a school lavatory, the purse yielded not only a pack of cigarettes but also evidence of drug dealing. Although the *T.L.O.* decision established that students are protected by the Fourth Amendment's clause against unwarranted searches and seizure of property, the ruling also held that public school authorities need only have *reasonable suspicion* (rather than the higher standard of *probable cause*) to initiate such searches, depending on the objectives of the search, the age and gender of the student, and the nature of the infraction. Lower courts have applied the *T.L.O.* test to a variety of student searches, with mixed results for invasive strip searches and outcomes overwhelmingly in favor of school authorities for noninvasive searches.

Random Drug Tests
Vernonia School District 47J v. Acton (1995)

The *Vernonia* Court ruled that a school district policy that mandated random drug testing of students who participated in school athletic programs was constitutional. Weighing the students' interest in privacy against the school's interest in a safe environment, the Court concluded that urinalysis of public school student athletes meets the reasonableness requirement for student searches under the Fourth Amendment, noting the student athletes' reduced expectation of privacy because of preseason physicals, communal undress, and other rules for interscholastic athletics. More recently, citing *Vernonia*, lower court decisions have usually concluded that random or mass drug testing of students participating in extracurricular activities is unconstitutional.

Sexual Harassment
Franklin v. Gwinnett County Public Schools (1992)

In the *Franklin* case, a female student sued the school district, claiming that her teacher had sexually harassed her. The *Franklin* Court concluded that Title IX of the Education Amendments of 1972, which prohibits federally funded programs from discriminating on the basis of gender, implicitly authorizes a suit by the victim for money damages. Because gender discrimination includes sexual harassment, the Court allowed the student's suit for damages to proceed to trial, providing the foundation for *Gebser* and *Davis*.

Gebser v. Lago Vista Independent School District (1998)
Davis v. Monroe County Road of Education (1999)

In *Gebser*, the Court held that the district may be liable for employee-to-student sexual harassment only when an official has the authority to institute corrective measures, has notice of the harassment, and deliberately takes no action against the employee's misconduct. In *Davis*, the Court applied the same standard to peer sexual harassment that deprives the victim of access to the school's opportunities. *Gebser* and *Davis* have channeled rather than stemmed the tide of harassment litigation in the schools.

Disruptive Students in Special Education
Honig v. Doe (1988)

The question in *Honig* was whether the school could expel for more than 10 days two students who were classified as emotionally disturbed and who engaged in various safety-related offenses that were a manifestation of their disability. The U.S. Department of Education interprets an exclusion for more than 10 consecutive days as a change in the student's placement in special education, but according to the Individuals with Disabilities Education Act (IDEA), special education students can be removed from their placement only through an agreement between the school and the student's parents or by a preliminary injunction from a court that finds the student substantially likely to injure self or others. In the turbulent wake of *Honig*, the lower courts have been stingy in granting preliminary injunctions. Although the 1997 amendments to the IDEA clarified what constitutes removal and offered schools some other options for dealing with disruptive behavior, the hands-off approach to the offenses committed by special education students runs counter to the current climate of zero tolerance of rule infractions in U.S. public schools. The current controversy in Congress concerning the perceived double standard for the zero tolerance offenses of special education students illustrates that school officials need to keep close track of post-*Honig* developments.

The Role of Religion in U.S. Education

The First Amendment guarantees citizens the free exercise of religion and prohibits the government from establishing a religion. These two First Amendment clauses—the "free exercise" and "establishment" clauses—sometimes come into conflict in school settings.

Government Aid to Religious Schools
Lemon v. Kurtzman (1971)

The *Lemon* decision ruled that government salary supplements for teachers of secular subjects in parochial schools violate the First Amendment's establishment clause. More important, the *Lemon* Court explained a three-part test for determining whether a challenged policy or activity violates the First Amendment establishment clause. For the policy or activity to pass muster, its purpose must be secular, its primary effect must neither advance nor inhibit religion, and its implementation must not excessively entangle government with religion. Today, the uncertain status and unpredictable results of tests of the *Lemon* decision serve as a reminder of the Supreme Court's ambivalence about the role of religion in public schools.

> The Court held that clergy-led invocations and benedictions at public school graduations violate the First Amendment's clause prohibiting the establishment of religion.

Prayer at School Events
Lee v. Weisman (1992)

Following a practice of rotating among different religious faiths, a principal invited a rabbi to offer the invocation and benediction at a middle school graduation ceremony and gave the rabbi a generally well-regarded resource pamphlet containing guidelines for keeping such prayers nonsectarian. The Court concluded that the principal exercised undue control of religious practice by his choice of a member of the clergy and his provision of guidelines for the prayers and did so in a situation that was not voluntary, noting that although attendance at the graduation ceremony was nominally voluntary, it was effectively required. The Court held that clergy-led invocations and benedictions at public school graduations violate the First Amendment's clause prohibiting the establishment of religion. Subsequent lower court cases have focused on student-initiated and student-conducted prayer ceremonies at graduations and other school events. In its recent decision in *Santa Fe Independent School District v. Doe* (2000), the Court ruled that student-initiated and student-conducted prayers at football games also violate the First Amendment's establishment clause, but the ruling only partially resolved these ongoing controversies. School officials need to proceed with utmost caution in this murky area.

Issues for the New Century

Although the amount of education litigation has leveled off in the past 15 years, the hottest topics in the courts today include student expression, in light of *Tinker* and *Hazelwood*; issues related to the role of religion in schools, as illustrated by *Lemon* and *Lee*; sexual and other such harassment, as guided by *Gebser* and *Davis*; student safety cases, ranging widely from *Vernonia* to *Honig*; and—countering the trend toward favoring school officials—special education cases in the long wake of *Rowley*. The Supreme Court's decisions will continue to shape education in the new century.

References

Board of Education, Island Trees Union Free School District No. 26 v. Pico, 457 U.S. 853 (1982).
Board of Education v. Rowley, 458 U.S. 176 (1982).
Brown v. Board of Education, 347 U.S. 483 (1954).
Davis v. Monroe County Board of Education, 526 U.S. 629 (1999).
Franklin v. Gwinnett County Public Schools, 503 U.S. 60 (1992).
Gebser v. Lago Vista Independent School District, 524 U.S. 274 (1998).
Goss v. Lopez, 419 U.S. 565 (1975).
Hazelwood School District v. Kuhlmeier, 484 U.S. 260 (1988).
Honig v. Doe, 484 U.S. 305 (1988).
Ingraham v. Wright, 430 U.S. 651 (1977).
Lau v. Nichols, 414 U.S. 563 (1974).
Lee v. Weisman, 505 U.S. 577 (1992).
Lemon v. Kurtzman, 403 U.S. 602 (1971).
Mt. Healthy City School District v. Doyle, 429 U.S. 274 (1977).
New Jersey v. T.L.O., 469 U.S. 325 (1985).
Plessy v. Ferguson, 163 U.S. 537 (1896).
San Antonio Independent School District v. Rodriguez, 411 U.S. 1 (1973).
Santa Fe Independent School District v. Doe, 530 U.S. 290 (2000).
School Board v. Arline, 480 U.S. 273 (1987).
Tinker v. Des Moines Independent Community School District, 393 U.S. 503 (1969).
Vernonia School District 47J v. Acton, 515 U.S. 646 (1995).
West Virginia State Board of Education v. Barnette, 319 U.S. 624 (1943).
Zirkel, P. A. (1998). National trends in education litigation: Supreme Court decisions concerning students. *Journal of Law and Education, 27,* 235–245.
Zirkel, P. A., Goldberg S., & Richardson, S. (2001). *Supreme Court decisions affecting education.* Bloomington, IN: Phi Delta Kappa International.

Perry A. Zirkel is University Professor of Education and Law, Lehigh University, 111 Research Dr., Bethlehem, PA 18015.

Educating African American Children: Credibility at a Crossroads

by Brenda CampbellJones and Franklin CampbellJones, Ed.D.

If you make a man feel that he is inferior, you do not have to compel him to accept an inferior status, for he will seek it himself. If you make a man think he is justly an outcast, you do not have to order him to the back door. He will go without being told; and if there is no back door, his very nature will demand one.[1]

The overwhelming majority of teachers in America are White (Kailin 1999). However, school student populations are more diverse today than ever before. In schools today, questions of equity are challenging educators to re-evaluate an issue that has been simmering for decades: if we believe that all students can learn, then why are there disproportionate numbers of African American children having difficulty in school (Johnson 1996)? Teachers must be willing to learn continuously in order to respond to the needs of African American students. They must be cognizant of historical forces and respond effectively to issues of culture and diversity in order to facilitate student learning and enrich their ability to learn and teach. This approach promotes inclusiveness and institutionalizes processes for learning about differences that might exist between teachers and their students (Lindsey, Nuri-Robins, and Terrell 1999). This allows teachers an opportunity to establish operating norms that respond to the cultural capital of African American children, subsequently strengthening the bond between student and teacher.

A Crisis of Credibility

When promises made are not fulfilled, a rationality deficit develops, and the system in which such promises were made suffers a crisis of credibility. *Crisis* refers to a contradiction between what was promised and what was delivered. Habermas (1975) calls this credibility crisis a "legitimation deficit," which is basically an erosion of belief in the system. This erosion of legitimation creates among citizens to whom promises were made a feeling that things have not worked out as expected and that there are forces that place the system beyond their control (Habermas 1975).

For many African Americans, a rationality deficit fueled by broken promises, a feeling that matters are beyond their control, has existed for generations. One need only reference United States history to gain a sense of the depth of this deficit, which for African Americans calls the credibility of the system into question (Low and Clift 1981). The promises of the Thirteenth, Fourteenth, and Fifteenth Amendments—to abolish 250 years of slavery and affirm the constitutional rights of citizens regardless of race, color, or previous condition of servitude—are called into question. The promises of equal education for all of this nation's citizens, in light of the 1954 Supreme Court case of *Brown v. the Board of Education of Topeka*, abolishing separate but equal schools, are in dispute. The promises of the 1964 Civil Rights Act with its massive regulatory and administrative powers are at doubt (Loewen 1995). For the majority of African Americans there exists an inchoate feeling that certain forces put the operation of the system beyond their control (Jones 1993).

Espousing a belief in educating all children but practicing the art of educating only a few is contradictory.

These doubts exist about schools as well as about society at large. Although many educators chant the phrase "all children can learn," the question of whether African American children should or can be educated as well as their Euro-American counterparts is still discussed by some educator-scholars (Herrnstein and Murray 1994). Low expectations for African American children are pervasive in the school community (Berliner and Biddle 1995). "Low expectations" refers to the beliefs—those of teachers, administrators, parents, students, and policymakers—that African American students cannot achieve at levels equal to or better than their Euro-American peers. Espousing a belief in educating all children but practicing the art of educating only a few is contradictory.

It has the potential to deepen the legitimation crisis of public schools: their ability to provide quality education to African American children (Argyris 1993).

Although many educators believe they can provide quality schooling for Black children, covert acts of discrimination against African American children continue, often unbeknownst to those performing the actions (Berliner and Biddle 1995). Paley (2000) examined her attitudes and the behaviors she exhibited toward Black students in her classroom. She concluded that she responded to her students indifferently because they were Black and she was White. Only after deep self-reflection about her actions and the intentions associated with them was she able to change her attitudes and behaviors toward teaching African American children. After Black parents stated that their children were being singled out for disciplinary actions, Paley states:

> The next day… I begin to watch myself: Do I respond to each child in a similar way? What sort of behaviors draws my negative attention? The self-scrutiny proceeds with no formal plan but is rather a collection of random thoughts and fragments of conversations on scraps of paper.[2]

Claude Steele (1992), in his research on stereotype vulnerability, maintains that African American students face a constant, devaluating assault while they attend school. In school, more than any other place in society, African American children are socialized to believe that their cultural currency is low relative to their Euro-American counterparts. It is in school that they begin to accept this devaluation as the way things are and eventually begin to "disidentify" with school. Disidentification comes in the form of nonparticipation in school activities, academics, and eventually dropping out of school. In self-defense, they shield themselves from an institution they perceive as intentionally inflicting injury upon their psyches, and they are subsequently thrust into the cycle of underachievement.

What must be done to eliminate the deficit of rationality in our public schools and remove the crisis of legitimation in educating African American children? Habermas argues that the legitimation crisis can be solved "by transposing the integration of inner nature in toto to another mode of socialization, that is, by uncoupling it from norms that need justification."[3] In light of this claim, it would appear that schools would have to disengage from current unsuccessful means of educating African American children. These ways of operating are steeped in traditions—beliefs and rituals—that rest on a historical foundation of educational segregation and inequality. In short, teacher, counselor, administrator, and policymaker attitudes must change. This will not be an easy chore, for it requires constant metacognitive processing, akin to rewriting the script while participating in a play. To gain a greater perspective on the task at hand, attention will now be given to the efficacy of history and tradition and how they play a part in the orientation toward educating African American children.

Efficacy of History and Tradition

Gademer (1991) posits that history does not belong to us; we belong to it. In this perspective, tradition—the act of handing down—acquires power and shapes attitudes and behaviors from one generation to the next. Grounded in history, tradition sanctions the actions of the next generation based on the actions and attitudes of the previous. All education depends on this process. The role of each teacher, counselor, or administrator carries an inertia that overshadows individualism. A person who takes on the role of teacher is faced with assuming, aside from one's own individuality, all the societal characteristics, legal charges, and cultural attributes of the position.

Rosenholtz (1991), in her study of the teacher's workplace and the social organization of schools, would tend to corroborate Gademer's claim. Her findings reveal that teachers conform to the policies, structures, and traditions of the everyday world of work that exist around them. They quickly learn how to classify items properly, perform tasks, and express sentiments in line with the tradition of the organization.

As mentioned previously, the historical legacy of education in America is rooted in acts of separatism and inequality, and these attributes currently operate in the lexicon of the education profession. A quick examination of terminology displayed in Table 1 bears witness to this fact. In the left-hand column are culturally destructive terms used in schools today to describe students or families who are subjugated to oppression, while terms in the right-hand column describe students or families who benefit from entitlement (Lindsey et al. 1999).

In any public school in America today, one can find teachers, counselors, psychologists, administrators, and policymakers using these terms as they attempt to ensure student academic performance. However, using this terminology normatively in mediating the responsibility of educators to educate all children to high academic standards guarantees success for some and failure for others. Because subjugation and oppression are integral aspects of the African American legacy, the continued use of these terms to guide the work of educators will ensure the propagation of this tradition (Ladson-Billings 1994; Freire 1990; Lindsey et al. 1999).

This is how history and tradition influence the work of educators. If left unchecked, such policies will continue to devalue African American children despite educators' best intentions. This article will next examine ways in which teachers can uncouple from norms that perpetuate the legitimation crisis. How teachers use personal reflection to improve their teaching craft as well as their ability to see color will be highlighted.

Table 1

WORDS USED TO DESCRIBE OPPRESSED AND ENTITLED GROUPS

OPPRESSED	ENTITLED
Inferior	Superior
Culturally Deprived	Privileged
Culturally Disadvantaged	Advantaged
Deficient	Normal
Different	Similar
Diverse	Uniform
Third World	First World
Minority	Majority
Underclass	Upper Class
Poor	Middle Class
Unskilled Workers	Leaders

Self-reflection to Improve Teaching

An important step in the uncoupling process is engaging in self-reflection. Reflection is a recursive process that engages individuals to fold back on themselves to uncover blind spots that naturally occur in their field of vision. Some researchers suggest that this process of circularity enables us to discuss our blind spots and how it is that we have come to see (Maturana and Varela 1992). Lambert (1995) refers to reflection as an inner dialogue with oneself whereby a person calls forth his or her own experiences, beliefs, and perceptions about an idea.

> *A veiled curriculum may exist containing characteristics that contribute to the constant devaluation of African American students.*

As a part of her own transformation, Paley (2000) maintained a journal and reflected upon her behavior, feelings, and attitudes as she taught African American children. She refers to this as a way of getting to the "hidden" curriculum, those things that are taught to children through our interactions with them (Margolis and Romero 1998). It is within the hidden curriculum that values, beliefs, and assumptions about student achievement dwell. It is here that a veiled curriculum may exist con-

taining characteristics that contribute to the constant devaluation of African American students suggested earlier by Steele (1992). Teachers face the intense challenge of searching for these characteristics and raising them to the surface for critical examination. To examine one's assumptions and beliefs about educating children—in particular, given the history of our country, African American children—is crucial to becoming a successful teacher of Black children.

Some individuals engage in the process of self-reflection naturally. They frequently engage in a recursive analysis of their emotions, thoughts, and actions. For most, however, this process must be a conscious activity. The following is a protocol adapted from the work of Simon Hole and Grace McEntee (1999) that gives structure to the reflective process.

Step 1. Collect stories. Some educators find that keeping a set of index cards or a steno book close at hand provides a way to jot down stories as they occur. Others prefer to wait until the end of the day and write in a journal.

Step 2. What happened? Choose a story that strikes you as particularly interesting. Write it succinctly. Avoid judgmental terms and state only the facts as much as possible.

Step 3. Why did it happen? Fill in enough of the context to give the story meaning. Answer the question in a way that makes sense to you. Look for the underlying causes for what happened, such as deeply seated values, beliefs, structures, processes, etc.

Step 4. What might it mean? Developing understanding is integral for future actions. Recognizing that there is more than one answer is an important step. Explore possible meanings rather than determine the meaning.

Step 5. What are the implications for practice? Consider how your practice might change given any new understandings that have emerged from the earlier steps.

Over time, teachers will find the process of self-reflection revealing about reasons for their actions and improving their practice. The following is an unfinished list of strategies that can emerge as teachers engage in self-reflection to improve upon their practice and create a more credible system for African American students.[4]

- Videotape instruction for critical analysis of teacher interaction with African American students to analyze critical elements of instructions: e.g., wait time, expectation, opportunities for higher levels of engagement with the curriculum, etc.

- Visit the homes of African American students in an effort to establish relationships and become familiar with the knowledge, lives, and views of African American students so that the information can be used to develop curriculum and instruction.

- Use parents as resources to learn more about their children and use their expertise to provide a culturally relevant curriculum.
- Perform an audit of the classroom curriculum materials to ensure that students are honored with literature that both reflects positively upon African Americans and provides a sense of who they are.
- Facilitate learning by increasing variety, space, stimulus variability, and opportunity for social interaction and movement. African American students tend to focus on the social dimension of the teaching-learning process. Therefore, classroom activities should emphasize cooperation rather than competition.
- Build upon the students' use of the Black dialect in the classroom as a means of teaching language flexibility so that students can learn how to make good decisions about the kind of language to use in particular contexts.

One of the greatest blind spots that exists in American education is the myth of not seeing color.

See Color in African American Children

Despite America's historical disdain for blackness (Elliot 1995), a great sense of strength and dignity has emerged from the identity of color among African Americans. Through the descriptor of color, African Americans blossomed culturally, socially, and spiritually (Aptheker 1951). In many instances, African Americans define themselves through color. To fail to see their color is to fail to see them (Tatum 1997). However, one of the greatest blind spots that exists in American education is the myth of not seeing color.

Often teachers and other educators express their ability to ignore color in children (Lindsey et al. 1999; Delpit 1995). These professions of color-blindness, though possibly well intended, are problematic and present a huge blind spot in orientation when educating African American children (McIntosh 1989). West (1994) eloquently argues that race matters in America. To ignore the presence of race in the fabric of American culture places African American children at risk for what West terms nihilism. He describes nihilism as the lived experience of coping with a life of horrifying meaninglessness, hopelessness, and lovelessness.

Why would ignoring color in African American children channel them toward a state of dejection? Simply put, a critical definer of the African American experience has been color. For 350 years *Colored*, *Negro*, and *Black*

have all been used legally and colloquially, to describe African Americans, and each is a reference to color. As a result of forced socialization through the lens of color, a tradition of self-definition by this lens has been handed down to the current generation of African American children. Only within the past forty years have terms such as Afro-American and African American been accepted as legitimate descriptors in mainstream America. "Why do Black youths, in particular, think about themselves in terms of race?" asks Tatum (1997). Her response was simple: "Because that is how the rest of the world thinks of them."[5]

This point recognizes America's historical legacy and permits educators to embrace current reality as they educate African American children. Such an embrace affords teachers the freedom to see children as they see themselves and build upon their cultural attributes.

Research on successful teachers of African American children offers abundant insights into the attitude educators must take in pursuing the goal of successfully educating Black children. Successful teachers do not insist on the assimilation of African American children. They do not presume these children to be like White children who simply need a little extra help. They also understand the full impact of racism on the plight of children. Moreover, successful teachers of African American children view collective growth and achievement above and beyond individual success, regularly challenge curricular and social viewpoints that were erroneous and problematic, and view their teaching as relational and thus only as effective as their relationships with their students. As a result, these teachers engage in "culturally relevant teaching"—a pedagogy that seeks to empower their students intellectually, socially, emotionally, and politically by using cultural referents to impart knowledge, skills, and attitudes (Ladson-Billings 1994).

Teachers must become culturally responsive to African American children by relating academic content to their cultural backgrounds. Grounded in intrinsic motivational theory, a culturally responsive approach engages students in the academic content through the lens of the students' culture. A framework for culturally responsive teaching consists of four motivational components (Wlodkowski and Ginsberg 1995):

1. *Establishing inclusion:* creating a learning atmosphere in which students and teachers feel respected by and connected to one another.
2. *Developing attitude:* creating a favorable disposition toward the learning experience through personal relevance and choice.
3. *Enhancing meaning:* creating challenging, thoughtful learning experiences that include student perspective and values.
4. *Engendering competence:* creating an understanding that students are effective in learning something they value.

This framework establishes core conditions for culturally responsive teaching; it is crucial to developing intrinsic student motivation. A holistic endeavor, this approach affords teachers the opportunity to plan lessons, refine pedagogy, and develop assessments that capture the innate eagerness of children to learn.

"Can African American children be educated in a system that delegitimizes their cultural capital?" is a question that looms large in America.

Conclusion

Returning to our original premise, the majority of teachers in America are White and the student population is more diverse than ever before. "Can African American children be educated in a system that delegitimizes their cultural capital?" is a question that looms large in America. If educators fail to consider ways that African American children are devalued in the current school culture, if teachers do not consider the efficacy of history and tradition in the daily rituals of teaching, and if educators fail to use critical self-reflection to surface deep-seated assumptions about race and culture, then the answer is a resounding "No, schools can not adequately educate African American students." The educational system is at a unique nexus that goes far beyond its original design by embracing the culture of all the children it serves and thereby advancing the cultural capital of society. If schools fail to meet this challenge, African American children will continue to achieve below their Euro-American counterparts. In that case, the legitimation gap will continue its existence behind the shroud of the espoused value "all children *can* learn," when indeed "all children *do* learn."

Notes

1. C. H. Woodson, *The Mis-education of the Negro* (Washington, D.C.: Associated Publishers, 1933), 84.
2. Vivian Paley, *White Teacher* (Cambridge: Harvard University Press, 2000), xiv.
3. Jurgen Habermas, *Legitimation Crisis*, trans. by Thomas McCathry (Boston: Beacon Press, 1975), 93.
4. Elizabeth Bondy and Ross, Dorene Doerre. "Confronting Myths about Teaching Black Children: A Challenge for Teacher Educators." *Teacher Education and Special Education* v. 21.
5. Beverly Tatum, *Why Are All the Black Kids Sitting Together in the Cafeteria? And Other Conversations about Race* (New York: Basic Books, 1997), 53.

Bibliography

Aptheker, Herbert. *A Documentary History of the Negro People in the United States*. New York: Carol Publishing Group, 1951.

Argyris, Chris. *Knowledge for Action: A Guide to Overcoming Barriers to Organizational Change*. San Francisco: Jossey-Bass, 1993.

Berliner, D., and Biddle, B. *The Manufactured Crisis: Myths, Fraud, and the Attack on America's Public Schools*. Cambridge, Mass.: Perseus Books, 1995.

Bondy, Elizabeth, and Ross, Dorene Doerre, "Confronting Myths about Teaching Black Children: A Challenge for Teacher Educators." *Teacher Education and Special Education* v. 21, Fall 1998, 241–254.

Boyd-Franklin, N., and Franklin, A. *Boys into Men: Raising Our African American Teenage Sons*. New York: Penguin Group, 2000.

Campbell Jones, Franklin. "Educational Leadership in a Diverse Society: Toward a Tradition of Empowerment and Emancipation." *Educational Leadership and Administration*, Fall 2000, 175–182.

Dalton, Harlan. *Confronting Fear between Blacks and Whites*. New York: Doubleday, 1995.

Delpit, Lisa. *Other People's Children*. New York: The New Press, 1995.

Demott, Benjamin. *The Trouble with Friendship: Why Americans Can't Think Straight about Race*. New York: Atlanta Monthly Press, 1995.

Derman-Sparks, Louise, and Phillips, Carol. *Teaching/Learning Anti-racism: A Developmental Approach*. New York: Teachers College Press, 1997.

Elliot, Jane. *Blue Eyed*. 93 minutes. California News Reel/San Francisco, 1995. Videocassette.

Feagin, Joe R., and Vera, Hernan. *White Racism: The Basics*. New York-London: Routledge, 1995.

Freire, Paulo. "Cultural Action for Freedom." *Harvard Education Review*, 68, no. 4, Winter 1998, 471–521.

Fullan, Michael. *Leading in a Culture of Change*. San Francisco: Jossey-Bass, 2001.

Gademer, Hans-Georg. *Truth and Method*. New York: Crossroad Publishing Corporation, 1991.

Habermas, Jurgen. *Legitimation Crisis*. Translated by Thomas McCathry. Boston: Beacon Press, 1975.

_____. *Moral Consciousness and Communicative Action*. Cambridge, Mass.: MIT Press, 1990.

Herrnstein, R., and Murray, C. *The Bell Curve*. New York: The Free Press, 1994.

Hole, S., and McEntee, G. "Reflection Is at the Heart of Practice." *Educational Leadership*, 34–37, 1999.

Howard, Gary. *We Can't Teach What We Don't Know: White Teachers, Multiracial Schools*. New York: Teachers College Press, 1999.

Johnson, Ruth. *Setting Our Sights: Measuring Equity in School Change*. Los Angeles: The Achievement Council. 1996.

Jones, Franklin. "Project Pipeline: A Hermeneutic Approach for Recruiting Underrepresented American Mathematics and Science Teachers into the Public School Workforce." Ed.D. diss., University of San Francisco, 1993.

Jones, Franklin, and Noli, Pam. *Creating a Diversity Sensitive Environment for Powerful Student Learning*. Hayward, Calif.: California School Leadership Academy, 1996.

Kailin, J. "How White Teachers Perceive the Problem of Racism in Their Schools: A Case Study in 'Liberal' Lakeview," *Teachers College Record*, 100, (4), 1999, 724–750.

Katz, Judith K. *White Awareness*. Norman and London: University of Oklahoma Press, 1978.

Ladson-Billings, Gloria. *The Dreamkeepers*. San Francisco: Jossey-Bass, 1994.

Lambert, Linda. *The Constructivist Leader*. New York: Teachers College Press, 1995.

Lindsey, Randall B., Nuri-Robins, Kikanza, and Terrell, Raymond D. *Cultural Proficiency: A Manual for School Leaders*. Thousand Oaks, Calif.: Corwin Press, 1999.

Low, A., and Clift, V. *Encyclopedia of Black America*. New York: McGraw-Hill, 1981.

Loewen, J. *Lies My Teacher Told Me*. New York: The New Press, 1995.

McIntosh, P. "White Privilege: Unpacking the Invisible Knapsack." *Peace and Freedom*, 49, (4), 1989, 10–12.

Maher, F. A. "Learning in the Dark: How Assumptions of Whiteness Shape Classroom Knowledge." *Harvard Educational Review*, 67, 1997, 321–349.

Margolis, E., and Romero, M. "The Department Is Very Male, Very White, Very Old, and Very Conservative: The Functioning of the Hidden Curriculum in Graduate Sociology Departments." *Harvard Educational Review*, 68, 1998, 1–32.

Maturana, H., and Varela, F. *The Tree of Knowledge: The Biological Roots of Human Understanding*. Boston: Shambhala Publications, 1992.

Paley, Vivian G. *White Teacher*. Cambridge: Harvard University Press, 2000.

Rosenholtz, Susan. *Teachers' Workplace: The Social Organization of Schools*. New York: Teachers College Press, 1991.

Sergiovanni, Thomas. *Moral Leadership: Getting to the Heart of School Improvement*. New York: Jossey-Bass, 1992.

_____. *Building Community in Schools*. San Francisco: Jossey-Bass, 1994.

Steele, Claude. "Race and the Schooling of Black Americans." *The Atlantic Monthly*, April 1992, 68–78.

Tatum, Beverly. *Why Are All the Black Kids Sitting Together in the Cafeteria? And Other Conversations about Race*. New York: Basic Books, 1997.

West, Cornel. *Race Matters*. New York: Vintage Books, 1994.

Wlodkowski, Raymond, and Ginsberg, Margery. "A Framework for Culturally Responsive Teaching." *Educational Leadership*, 53, September 1995, 17–21.

Woodson, C. H. *The Mis-education of the Negro*. Washington, D.C.: Associated Publishers, 1933.

Brenda CampbellJones is an associate professor at Azusa Pacific University, Temecula Valley Regional Center, in Menifee, California.

Franklin CampbellJones, Ed.D., is an assistant professor in the Charter College of Education at California State University, Los Angeles.

**From the
Trenches**

The Evils of Public Schools

Edward G. Rozycki

He who passively accepts evil [is] as much involved in it as he who helps to perpetuate it. He who accepts evil without protesting against it is really cooperating with it.

—Martin Luther King

Introduction

My fifth-grade experience in Longfellow public school was a joy: a really educational experience.[1] Sixth grade was another story.

My sixth-grade teacher, Mrs. P., was much taken by my "artistic ability." One fine day she told me, "You're going to enter the Gimbel's Department Store Art contest on Healthy Living and win a prize!" I was somewhat flattered and excited at the thought that I would be permitted to while away several weeks of afternoons painting at a poster rather than following along the prescribed curriculum.

I began planning a poster on Healthy Living. What might I do? "Never you mind about that," said Mrs. P. "I have an old poster here you can just copy! Look! Isn't it wonderful?"

I was speechless. I was being told to do something that, even then, I recognized as deep-down dishonest. But the importunity was not coming, as it usually did, from classmates who were already seeing to my loss of innocence by teaching me—with full details—an obscenity a day. No, the temptation was coming from a member of that moral aristocracy, Teachers, who—my parents had drilled into me—were Ones Who Must Be Obeyed, Ones Who Knew Best What Was Good for Me.

I summoned up the courage to say that I didn't want to just copy someone else's work. Mrs. P. responded, "I'm

very disappointed in you. It's either paint this poster, or do arithmetic drills." So I painted.

With disgust and loathing I finished the poster. It was better than the original. Everyone admired it, especially She Who Had to Be Obeyed, Who Knew Best What Was Good for Me. The poster was hung in the front of the room for general approbation while awaiting shipment to the exhibition.

I don't know what came over me. A day after finishing that vile poster, right after lunch, I walked up to it and took a dish of black paint and spattered it onto the painting. I trembled, confused with the righteousness of my disobedience.

I hurried back outside believing no one had seen me. I was wrong. Carolyn N. was a witness. She ran to tattle to Mrs. P., who berated me as soon as I returned to class. She put me on a diet of four-place addition drills with no recess for two weeks. Strangely, she didn't call my parents and inform them of my "misbehavior." Dear, sweet Carolyn, at Mrs. P's behest, cleaned up the poster. It was submitted in my name. It won a prize. When my parents and Mrs. P. accompanied me to the awards ceremonies, they remarked on how indifferent I seemed to the honor.

No Special Fault

The Devil gets up into the belfry by the Vicar's skirts.

—T. Fuller, 1732

Clearly, such incidents are not restricted to public schools. I know, for example, of two private schools—one, of the ancient elite—where the headmasters sold drugs to the students. Only one of the headmasters was caught. In general, private education takes a quite different view of wrongdoing than the view that is promulgated in public schools.[2] Private education is thus, by its own definitions, not susceptible to the faults attributable to public education.

Even though parochial school kids no longer come home bearing tales of nuns wielding yardsticks in the classroom like Crusaders slaying heathen, students in those schools have recently told me that their teachers have used extended periods of class time to make them write letters supporting political agendas. The students were told to sign their parents' names without asking permission, even though the parents might well have opposed or taken no position on the political issue.

Corruption of educational mission is not unique to public education. But public schools do provide unique opportunities for corruption, for five interrelated reasons:

a. they are schools of last resort in a compulsory system;
b. this makes them susceptible to constraint by under-informed courts to institute procedures often contrary to good educational practice;
c. special, often emphemeral, interest groups can gain control over school practices by combing vociferousness with legal ingenuity;
d. not only naive idealists, but the weak-minded and pathologically sentimental, are seduced into assuming teaching positions that they—often with good reason—abandon at the rate of 10 percent per year nationally; consequently
e. the remaining educators do not possess sufficient sense of profession to risk opposing those whose efforts in the long run distort and demand the educational mission—for which no practical consensus exists—of the public school.

Educating(?) Peter

Hate Is Love. War Is Peace.
—George Orwell, *1984*

My memories of my sixth-grade artistic award were provoked by my recent reviewing—perhaps the tenth—of the video *Educating Peter* in a class of graduate students in education.[3] (I watch this video about twice a year.) The plot: An undersocialized, physically abusive white male child suffering Down syndrome is placed in a third-grade class with a teacher whose sole preparation seems to be rationalizing why onions are like peaches, if only you taste them the right way. The teacher, unable to handle Peter even with the help of what appears to be an extra adult, compels her students—with the complicity of school staff—to "take ownership of the situation." A few sessions of psychobabblic indoctrination help the third-graders to comprehend the causal complexities of Peter's behavior and their role in provoking it. This means that now it is expected that Peter's behavioral outbursts—

even the violent ones—will be interdicted by the students rather than by the teacher.

In an interview, the teacher explains how it is important, in this all-white school in Virginia, that her students learn to live with people different from themselves. She tells how by "raising her expectations"—one imagines her commanding her synapses to fire in unison, her dendrites to do drills—Peter is brought to make academic progress.

We see students reacting with shock and dismay to Peter's behavior. The adults in the video (and the narrator) assure us that these students are "learning to accept differences." There is no evidence for this remote probability. From the looks of things they could just as well be learning resignation in the face of power—both Peter's power and that of the adults who condone what to them as "normal kids" is forbidden.

The students, choked, kicked, pushed by Peter, are encouraged to rationalize, to declare that Peter has become their best friend, that Peter has taught them more than he himself has learned, that this has been just the peachy-keenest of classes. The students blush as they are interviewed, not being able—unlike the adults who provide them example—to suppress the natural embarrassment the innocent feel about deliberately mouthing what they believe to be false.

The film purports to take no sides in the controversy about inclusion but merely "tell a story." It is cleverly edited to produce a certain effect. I remember an earlier version I saw some years ago. It was different from the version I purchased from Ambrose Video Publishing. A crucial scene has been edited out.

In the early version, the boys are sitting outside in a field, Peter, unprovoked, kicks a boy—call him Johnny—square in the middle of the face. Here the cut occurs. Johnny, outraged, jumps on Peter. The teacher intervenes, and remonstrates with Johnny, who is moved off to the side. Splice here. Johnny cries to himself, unconsoled by an adult.

At the end of the year, we find Peter "accepted" into the group, having "fewer outbursts, mostly toward the end of the day."

In the present version, one sees the kick and then Johnny crying, alone and unconsoled. That he should not be consoled is inexplicable, assuming there are adults present. But knowing he has just been rebuked—which has been spliced out of the film—explains the lack of consolation. Johnny's isolation is part of his "punishment" for "fighting" back.

EDUCATING PETER: AS GRADUATE STUDENTS SEE IT

Party	Benefit Received	Kind of Benefit	Cost Suffered	Kind of Cost
Peter	Interaction with normal children	Immediate Substantial Intrinsic	Not treated as a moral being, a full person	Symbolic Immediate Intrinsic
Peter's Parents	Happier child at home Easier to live with	Immediate Substantial Intrinsic	Dependency on external support systems	Substantial Immediate Extrinsic
Student Featured in Video	Teacher approval	Immediate Substantial Intrinsic	Loss of academic learning	Substantial Immediate Extrinsic
	Learn tolerance	Remote Symbolic	Moral corrosion	Symbolic Immediate Intrinsic
Featured Student's Parent	Pride in school Approbation	Immediate Substantial Intrinsic	Child's loss of academic learning	Substantial Immediate Extrinsic
			Moral corrosion	Symbolic Immediate Intrinsic
Student Not Featured in Video	Learn tolerance	Remote Symbolic	Loss of academic learning	Substantial Immediate Extrinsic
			Moral corrosion	Symbolic Immediate Intrinsic
Non-Featured Student's Parent			Child's loss of learning	Substantial Immediate Extrinsic
			Moral corrosion	Symbolic Immediate Intrinsic
Teacher (Featured in Video)	Recognition	Immediate Substantial	Adjustment	Substantial Immediate
Principal (Featured in Video)	Recognition	Immediate Substantial		

At the end of the year, we find Peter "accepted" into the group, having—in the words of his teacher—"fewer outbursts, mostly toward the end of the day."

One of my students remarked that what the third-graders had accomplished was akin to changing a dangerous animal into a pet. Peter was exempted from normal discipline, clearly treated as possessing diminished responsibility, and given almost bizarrely effusive encouragement and reward for trivial accomplishments. He was "managed."

Immediate Costs and Remote, Improbable Benefits

My fame will be your consolation.

—Richard Wagner (to his betrayed wife)

The students who watched *Educating Peter* with me were asked to pay attention to four questions: What are the benefits of including Peter in the third-grade classroom? Who receives what kind of benefit? What are the costs of including Peter in the third-grade classroom? Who pays what kind of cost? The table on the previous page summarizes several years of responses from my graduate students.

What Cost "Charity"? What Cost "Justice"?

Everyone loves justice in the affairs of another.

—Italian proverb

It is not clear when we examine the chart whether or not it gives support to inclusion. Many costs and benefits go unperceived, so they do not come to be factored into political decisions to support or resist inclusion. But even allowing for a full disclosure of the costs and benefits assigned to each constituency of the school community, the lack of an *implementable* consensus on what the school is

about obscures a clear choice. Yet those with power, the principal and the teacher, clearly tend to maximize their benefits and minimize their costs.

Supporters of public education—among whom I count myself—worry about the persistent and growing interest in vouchers and schooling arrangements that threaten the very existence of public schools. They need only watch *Educating Peter,* though, to understand where some of that impetus comes from.

Peter's education could be seen as a form of charity bestowed on the less fortunate. It is a debauched form of "charity," however, that comes through a compulsory system. Our courts have decided that the practice of inclusion is an improvement on justice. But the lopsided redistribution of scarce schooling resources—where the needs of some take precedence over the needs of many—may just bring about every child's educational starvation.

Notes

1. See Edward G. Rozycki, "Educational Assessment: Confusing Status with Achievement." *Educational Horizons,* Fall 1993, 7–10.
2. See Peter Cookson, Jr., and Caroline Hodges Persell, *Preparing for Power: America's Elite Boarding Schools* (New York: Basic Books, 1985).
3. *Educating Peter.* Home Box Office. VHS Tape. 20 minutes. (New York: Ambrose Video Publishing, 1993).

Edward G. Rozycki is a twenty-five-year veteran of the school district of Philadelphia. He is an associate professor of education at Widener University, Widener, Pennsylvania.

From *Educational Horizons,* Winter 2002, pp. 57-60. © 2002 by Educational Horizons. Reprinted with permission of the author.

**The
Cutting Edge**

Can Every Child Learn?

Gary K. Clabaugh

"The key element in teaching success isn't technical skill, more resources, or smaller classes; the key to success is higher expectations. Teachers will get more if they expect more. The mantra to chant daily is 'Every child can learn.'"

That's the tune that a lot of people are dancing to these days. George W. Bush and a remarkably diverse assortment of governors, national and state legislators, educational entrepreneurs, school superintendents, and ordinary, right-thinking Americans all assert, "Every child can learn." In fact, this overworked and underconsidered motto is as ubiquitous as dog doo on the public green.

Despite definitive research that points to nonschool factors as keys to school success, those embracing this motto implicitly dismiss the idea that "schooling failures" are really symptoms of social failures. They seem to believe that positive thinking can cancel out the educational consequences of the 20 percent poverty rate among U.S. children. They must believe that positive thinking can defeat our inner city infant mortality rate, which outstrips that of the Third World. They must imagine that positive thinking can help hundreds of thousands of U.S. youngsters who literally have no home where they can do their homework. (On an average night in D.C., for instance, homeless shelters contain 1,300 youngsters.[1]) They must suppose that positive thinking can cancel out the educational impact of long-term separation or divorce, experienced by 40 percent of all children born to post-1966 marriages—not to mention disruption in the stepfamily, the fate of one-third of those same kids.[2]

To hear the Pollyannas tell it, nothing can stand up to a strong conviction that "Every child can learn." When teachers believe this to the marrow of their being, all will be well.

Anyone, upon a little reflection, can see that this is humbug. Yes, most (but not all) children can learn to stay away from Mom when she's high or to keep out of the way of Mom's boyfriend when he's looking for someone to abuse. Sure, most (but not all) children can learn to wait until Mom is just high enough to say "yes" before asking her for food money. But few children can learn to do algebra, appreciate Shakespeare, or balance chemical equations if they are abused, scared, sick, hungry, or bereft of love and security. Under those circumstances, one can't even learn to read. They're too busy trying to survive.

Frankly, it's foolish to expect quality schoolwork from children in such situations. Even the most skillful teaching, up-to-date texts, clean and safe schools, and enlightened educational practices are relatively impotent in the face of these and similar difficulties. So let's forget about conquering all with wishful thinking and face the fact that social injustice and ferocious unfairness erode school effectiveness all across America.

For that matter, we can even question the literal truth of the claim that "Every child can learn." An exercise on the following page helps us think this through.

My skilled and experienced university colleagues specializing in special education assure me that there is only one thing listed that "every child" *might* be able to learn. That's to salivate on cue. They say only comatose children would probably be unable to learn to do this. They assure me, however, that many children can't learn to do *any* of these other things.

We see that the slogan is literally false. Then what can we make of its persistent use? Is the key to successful teaching, at least in some general sense, still higher expectations? Will teachers get more if they expect more? The answer plainly is *"No."*

So why is the motto ubiquitous? It's popular because claiming that "Every child can learn" shifts responsibility to educators and conceals the causes of school failure in ways useful to those in power. Can every child learn? Not in any sense that's meaningful to educators.

"EVERY CHILD CAN LEARN"

Testing the Slogan's Limits

Please respond to the following phrase completions, checking the box best reflecting your view. (Some examples share the same wording. Remember, though, *learning how* to govern one's impulses, for instance, is not the same thing as *learning to* govern one's impulses.)

Every child can LEARN THAT...	Strongly Disagree	Disagree	Undecided	Agree	Strongly Agree
I have a name					
2 follows 1					
Shoes can have shoelaces					
Thomas Jefferson was the third President of the U.S.					
I shouldn't act on impulse					
Chopin composed nocturnes for piano					
Every child can LEARN HOW TO...	Strongly Disagree	Disagree	Undecided	Agree	Strongly Agree
Recognize my name					
Imitate					
Spell my name					
Do long division					
Govern my impulses					
Perform Chopin nocturnes					
Every child can LEARN TO...	Strongly Disagree	Disagree	Undecided	Agree	Strongly Agree
Salivate on cue					
Play					
Tie my shoes					
Use long division as a tool					
Govern my impulses					
Be delighted by Chopin nocturnes					

Notes

1. "Bright Futures and Broken Dreams," The Children's Defense Fund, quoted by William Rasberry, column, *The Philadelphia Inquirer*, September 28, 1991, 8.

2. Gary Clabaugh and Edward Rozycki, *Understanding Schools: The Foundations of Education* (New York: Harper-Collins, 1990), 169.

Gary K. Clabaugh is a professor of education at La Salle University in Philadelphia, Pennsylvania. He directs La Salle's Graduate Program in Education and coordinates arts and sciences graduate programs.

From *Educational Horizons*, Winter 2002, pp. 61-62. © 2002 by Educational Horizons. Reprinted with permission of the author.

School Vouchers Showdown

THE ISSUES:

BY KENNETH JOST

Christine Suma has lived in Cleveland all her life. But no one in her family has ever attended a Cleveland public school—neither she, her husband nor any of their 12 children.

"The public schools don't have the best record in Cleveland," Suma explains. "I don't want my children where they may get an education and they may not. I don't want them where they might be safe or not. I don't want to take a risk with my children. I want a sure bet."

Like their parents, the Suma children have all gone to parochial schools in Cleveland. Up until 1996, the Sumas had to pay the tuition out of their own pockets. Today, however, the family receives about $1,500 in taxpayer funds for each of the children under a controversial school voucher program now facing a constitutional showdown before the Supreme Court.

Suma, who intervened in the case to urge the high court to uphold the program, says the vouchers provide the kind of school choices for her children already enjoyed by higher-income families. "I want my education tax dollars put where I want them to go," Suma Says. "This voucher system is giving us opportunities."

Doris Simmons-Harris—A single mother of three children who have gone to Cleveland's public schools—has her complaints about the system too. But she believes vouchers can only exacerbate the Cleveland schools' major problem: lack of money.

"Our quality went down since I went to school," Simmons-Harris says. "They cut out art classes and after-school activities because of money. My child's in a class in which every child doesn't have a book."

Two of Simmons-Harris' children have graduated from Cleveland schools; her younger son—who has a behavioral disability—is in high school now. She lent her name to the pending legal challenge against the voucher program in part because she believes the plan would ignore special-needs students like her son.

"He could never go to a private school because of his handicap," Simmons-Harris says. "The public schools take children with a handicap, but a private school would not."

The school vouchers debate has raged for more than a decade over an array of educational policy issues.[1] Advocates of "school choice"—largely, but not exclusively, political conservatives—say families deserve the chance to use public funds at whatever school, public or private, best serves their children's needs. And a voucher system, they say, will create competition that will force stultified public school systems to take needed steps to improve.

Opponents—including teachers' unions and school administrators as well as civil liberties and civil rights groups—argue that vouchers will benefit at most only a few students while diverting resources from the public schools that will continue to educate the vast majority of American youngsters.[*] In addition, they say neither of the two major public voucher programs operating today —in Cleveland and Milwaukee—has actually produced significant academic gains for the students using the vouchers to attend private schools. A third program, in Florida, has only 44 voucher students.

So far, the Cleveland and Milwaukee programs both are also attracting fewer students than the number of vouchers that could be awarded. The Wisconsin legislature capped Milwaukee's program at 15 percent of the system's current enrollment; that would allow slightly more than 15,000 students, but only 10,882 are currently receiving vouchers. In Cleveland the number of voucher students is theoretically limited by the size of the state appropriation for the program. But over the past three years the program has not spent some 37 percent of the $33.8 million allocated.

The issue has split racial and ethnic minorities, who constitute the major populations served by the big-city systems most often depicted by critics as "failing schools." School choice advocates have gained allies among African-Americans and Latinos by touting vouchers as an immediate option for minority youngsters to escape low-performing schools.

"For right now, vouchers are the only means to provide parents with the opportunity to select a school environment from a menu of schools that's best for their children," says Kaleem Caire, president of the two-year-old Black Alliance for Educational Options (BAEO).

Traditional civil rights groups, however, insist that vouchers will end up hurting most minority youngsters. "Vouchers might be good for the few poor kids who can take advantage of them," says Theodore Shaw, associate director of the NAACP Legal Defense and Educational Fund. "But systemically, they are going to further undercut public education, where the vast majority of African-American, Latino and poor children are going to remain."

Despite the broad-ranging debate, the issue facing the Supreme Court when it hears arguments Feb. 20 on the constitutionality of the Cleveland voucher program is a narrow one. The justices will be asked to decide whether the program—now in its sixth year—aids religious schools in violation of the Establishment Clause, the Bill of Rights provision that bars any law "respecting the establishment of religion."

Opponents—who filed a federal court challenge to the plan after the Ohio Supreme Court gave its blessing to the program—emphasize that virtually all of the 4,456 students currently receiving vouchers are attending religious schools.

"This is nothing but a direct subsidy of the educational mission of religious denominations," says Barry Lynn, executive director of Americans United for Separation of Church and State. "And in the same way that one should not expect taxpayers to support churches, they should not be expected to support church-related educational facilities either."

Supporters counter that both the Cleveland and Milwaukee systems leave it up to parents to decide where to use the tax-paid stipends.

"The scholarship program is neutral on its face," says Clint Bolick, litigation director of the Institute for Justice, the Washington-based libertarian law firm that has spearheaded the voucher movement. "Funds are directed to religious schools only through the true private choices of individual parents, therefore, satisfying Establishment Clause requirements."

The case—formally called *Zelman v. Simmons-Harris*, after Ohio's superintendent of public instruction, Susan Tave Zelman—reaches the Supreme Court after a series of recent decisions that somewhat loosen the restrictions on government programs that benefit religious schools. In the most recent of those decisions, the court in *Mitchell v. Helms* in 2000 approved a federally funded program for lending computers and other equipment to parochial schools.[2]

The court is expected to decide the Cleveland case before the justices take their summer recess at the end of June. Whatever the outcome, though, supporters and opponents of vouchers vow to continue their fight in state legislatures around the country.

Voucher proponents say they have the momentum on the issue. "The movement is progressing extremely well," says Bolick, "and I think it will continue to produce educational opportunities for children regardless of what happens in the Supreme Court."

But opponents point out that legislatures in only three states—Wisconsin, Ohio, and, most recently, Florida—have approved voucher plans, while voters have rejected voucher or tuition tax-credit ballot proposals in five states since 1990. (*See chart*, "Vouchers in Cleveland.")

"It's very hard to believe that they have momentum, since every single ballot initiative has been defeated," says Robert Chanin, general counsel of the National Education Association (NEA), the country's largest teachers' union. "Everybody keeps proposing [voucher statutes], and nobody passes them."

Pollsters get somewhat different results on school vouchers depending on the phrasing of the question, but the most recent polls indicate that a majority of Americans oppose the idea, and that support has declined since the late 1990s. In the most favorable result for voucher advocates, 44 percent of respondents said last year that they would favor a proposal that would allow parents to send their children to any school of their choice with the government paying all or part of private school tuition; 54 percent of the respondents said they would oppose such a proposal.[3]

As the voucher debate continues, here are some of the major questions that divide supporters and opponents:

Do school voucher plans improve students' educational performance?

Six years into the Cleveland voucher program, student test scores have risen enough to encourage supporters, but not enough to impress or win over opponents. The results in other programs are similarly murky, though researchers generally appear to agree that African-American students in privately funded voucher schemes are making distinctive gains.

Researchers at Indiana University's Indiana Center for Evaluation have officially evaluated Cleveland's program each year since its inception.[4] They found no significant differences in academic progress between voucher students and comparable public school students after the first year. In the next two evaluations, they measured distinctive gains in language and science, but not in reading, mathematics or social studies.

In the most recent of the Indiana evaluations—published in September 2001—researchers found that students who entered the voucher program as kindergartners had higher test scores as first-graders than other students, but by the end of third grade the gap had narrowed.

"Vouchers make at least a small but statistically significant difference," says Kim Metcalf, the center's director and an associate professor in the department of curriculum and instruction at the university's School of Education.

In Milwaukee's voucher program, scant information exists about students' academic performance, partly because test scores have not been collected since the 1994–95 school year, when the program was limited to secular schools and had few participants. The legislature dropped testing and evaluation requirements when it expanded the program. The official evaluator—John Witte, director of the University of Wisconsin's La Follette School of Public Affairs in Madison—reported no significant academic gains for voucher students compared to others, though research teams from Harvard and Princeton did find some distinctive gains for voucher students in some areas.[5]

Voucher supporters acknowledge that the evidence of academic gains is spotty at best. "The findings range from mildly positive to strongly positive," Bolick says. But, he adds, "I am unaware of any study that does not find at least mildly positive results from school choice in terms of academic performance. I expect those findings will grow stronger when later studies are done in terms of graduation rates."

"The impacts are not detectable for any groups other than African-Americans," says Paul E. Peterson, a prominent voucher advocate and director of the Program on Education Policy and Governance at Harvard's Kennedy School of Government in Cambridge, Mass.

Voucher opponents say studies show the programs do not produce the academic gains supporters predict. "There is almost nothing in the research literature that suggests vouchers succeed as an academic intervention," says Alex Molnar, a confirmed voucher opponent who taught at the University of Wisconsin in Milwaukee before moving to Arizona State University at Tempe last August. "There is no clear benefit one way or another with respect to the academic performance of students."

"When you get behind the hired guns or the committed proponents and look at the more objective [studies]—those written by researchers retained by a specific state—at best it's a wash," says Chanin, the NEA lawyer.

The evidence of gains among African-American students comes from three privately funded scholarship programs in Dayton, Ohio; New York City and Washington, D.C. A study by Peterson's group at Harvard released in September 2000 found that African-American students scored 6 percentiles higher in overall test performance than control-group students. But no statistically significant effects, positive or negative, were found among other ethnic groups.[6]

Peterson calls the gains for black students "fairly sizable"—comparable, he says, to the gains found in a recent class-size reduction experiment in Tennessee. "If you got that kind of impact in subsequent years, you could talk about reducing the test-score gap between blacks and whites," he says.

Indiana University's Metcalf acknowledges the gains but questions whether they can be attributed to vouchers. "We don't know how that effect was produced," he says. "One possible reason is that [scholarship students] have been put in classrooms with higher-achieving classmates whose families are more supportive of education. It may be a peer effect, not related to the productivity of the school itself."

Overall, two disinterested research organizations—the U.S. General Accounting Office and the Rand Corporation, the respected private research organization—find that the evidence of academic gains among voucher students is inconclusive so far. "Long-term effects on academic skills and attainment are as yet unexamined," Rand researchers write in a book-length study published last summer.[7] The GAO says "little or no" evidence of academic gains has been found in official evaluations in Milwaukee and Cleveland.[8]

For his part, Metcalf agrees that the evidence is inconclusive, but he sees a trend in favor of vouchers. "It isn't clear yet whether it's a good thing or a bad thing, but the data have not been negative about vouchers," Metcalf concludes.

Do voucher plans hurt public schools?

With no recent test scores, Milwaukee's voucher program offers no good opportunity to examine its effect on students receiving the stipends. But one prominent researcher says the decade-long experiment does provide useful—and encouraging—information about the effects on the overall performance of the city's public schools.

To test the hypothesis that vouchers will encourage public schools to change because of increased competition, Harvard economics Professor Caroline Hoxby studied academic performance in Milwaukee public schools since the start of the experiment. She found above-average gains in many of the schools—and particularly high gains in schools in low-income neighborhoods that she said faced the greatest "competition" from vouchers.

"Overall,... public schools made a strong push to improve achievement in the face of competition from vouchers," Hoxby writes in an aca-

The Nation's Three Public Voucher Programs

Milwaukee's Parental Choice Program is the oldest and largest of the nation's three publicly funded voucher programs. Florida's "A-Plus" program is the newest, and the only statewide program. The Supreme Court will rule this month on whether the Cleveland program violates the U.S. Constitution.

Program (Date Established)	Number of students receiving vouchers	Amount of voucher	Eligibility Requirements	Percentage of voucher students attending religious schools
Milwaukee Parental Choice Program (1990)	10,882	$5,553 (max.) (based on tuition)	Parents' income 175% of poverty level ($30,000 for household of four); child attended public school (any grade) or private schools (K-3), enrolled in Choice program prior years.	70% (est.)
Cleveland Pilot Scholarship and Tutoring Program (1995)	4,456	$2,250 (max.; varies with income) (Parent pays min. 10% of tuition)	Parents' income up to 200% of federal poverty level ($35,000) for maximum amount; others receive $1,875; schools limited to $2,500 tuition.	96-99%*
Florida "A-Plus" Accountability and School Choice Program (1999)	44	$3,700 (max.)	Child attended Florida public school graded "F" in 2 out of 4 previous years (two schools so far); no income eligibility.	90.9%

* Lower figure for 1999-2000 school year, from Ohio Dept. of Education; higher figure for 2001-2002 school year from the education newsletter Catalyst-Cleveland.

Sources: Wisconsin Dept. of Public Instructions; Ohio Dept. of Education; Florida Dept. of Education

demic paper on her study.[9] In an interview, she is more direct: "They improved a lot for three years in a row at an absolutely unprecedented rate. As an educational researcher, I've never seen improvement like that."

Rand researcher Brian Gill finds Hoxby's study provocative. "I don't think that's a definitive result, but it's certainly very promising," he says. But two other experts familiar with the Milwaukee program—with opposite viewpoints on vouchers—dismiss the report.

"I don't think there's any evidence" for Hoxby's conclusion, says Witte, who supports vouchers targeted at low-income students and is the official evaluator of the Wisconsin project. "Test scores did go up, but they've now flattened out. I think they went up because there was an

enormous push to get them up"—not because of the voucher program.

Voucher opponent Molnar also finds Hoxby's study unpersuasive. He says the test scores she used are "incomplete" and "not comparable" between different schools. More broadly, he says, Hoxby's conclusion requires "a series of [unrealistic] assumptions" about the reasons for the changes in reported test scores. "It's silly," Molnar says. "Schools and schooling are complex. [Hoxby's conclusion] flies in the face of all the things that we know about human beings and human nature."

A similar debate is raging over the effects of Florida's "A-Plus Accountability and School Choice Program," which provides vouchers to students attending public schools that fail to improve performance one year after receiving an "F" grade in a state

evaluation. Jay P. Greene, a research associate at Harvard's Program on Education Policy and Governance, found evidence that schools that received a failing grade in 1999—and thus faced the threat of vouchers—achieved test-score gains more than twice those recorded at other schools in Florida. But Gregory Camilli, a professor of education at Rutgers Graduate School of Education, concludes that Greene "vastly overestimated" the test score gains and contends that other aspects of Florida's program besides the threat of vouchers may be responsible for any improvement.[10]

Critics of vouchers say that far from helping, the stipends will actually hurt public schools—first, by providing incentives for better students to leave the public education system, and, second, by diverting money and other resources from already struggling public schools.

The evidence on the so-called cream-skimming issue is sketchy and inconclusive. Official evaluators Witte in Milwaukee and Metcalf in Cleveland say students entering the two voucher programs had achievement levels and demographic characteristics similar to other low-income public school students. On the other hand, the parents of voucher students—predominantly, single mothers—had slightly higher education levels and appeared more strongly motivated than parents of other students.

As for the fiscal impact, critics say the methods of funding both the Cleveland and Milwaukee programs take money from the public school systems. Supporters counter that both school systems continue to receive more per capita state aid than the cost of the vouchers, and that in any event the schools save money by having fewer students to educate.

Most broadly, voucher opponents contend that vouchers divert energy and attention, as well as money, from more productive education reforms.

"You've got powerful long-term studies that demonstrate the impact of early childhood education on the later educational success of children who participate in those programs," Molnar says. "Would I choose vouchers over that? No."

"What about reducing classroom size? The evidence suggests that that is a powerful intervention. What about providing high-quality educational opportunities for poor children over the summer? Research suggests that poor kids 'fall behind' because of what happens over the summer. Would I choose vouchers over any of those? No."

But Bolick of the Institute for Justice insists that the Cleveland and Milwaukee programs—as well as the newer, more limited program in Florida—have pressured the school systems to change because of the fear of losing voucher students to private schools.

"The Cleveland system was one of the absolute worst in the country," Bolick says. "Two years ago, it failed every one of 28 of the state's criteria. This year, it passed three. These were the first stirrings of signs of life in an extremely troubled system."

Competition, Bolick says, is the key: "The rules of economics are not suspended at the schoolhouse door."

Do school voucher plans unconstitutionally subsidize religious schools?

When Milwaukee began its voucher program in 1990, the rules effectively limited participation to a handful of secular private schools established to serve low-income, minority students. Five years later, after lobbying by the Roman Catholic archdiocese and the business community, the Republican-controlled legislature expanded the program to include parochial schools.

"Catholic schools were the moving force on the 1995 legislation," Witte says. "The archdiocese was heavily involved."

The change—signed into law by then-Gov. Tommy Thompson, now President Bush's secretary of Health and Human Services—was immediately challenged in court as an unconstitutional subsidy for religious schools. But the Wisconsin Supreme Court rejected the challenge in 1998—allowing the program to more than triple its enrollment at the beginning of the 1998–1999 school year.

Parochial-school advocates have battled over public-funding issues since the mid-1800s. In a series of decisions since 1948, the U.S. Supreme Court has approved some programs that provided aid to parochial-school students but barred more direct subsidies. The court's most recent decisions have loosened, but not eliminated, restrictions on the use of public funds at church-affiliated schools.

Church-state separationists argue that the use of vouchers at parochial schools violates the Constitution's prohibition against government establishment of religion. "The one central message [in the First Amendment] is that government is not intended to directly support religion—not one particular religion or religion in general," says Lynn of American United for Separation of Church and State.

But parochial-school advocates argue that both the Cleveland and Milwaukee programs meet the Supreme Court's guidelines on aid to religious schools. Scholarships are constitutional, says Mark Chopko, general counsel of the U.S. Conference of Catholic Bishops, if they are awarded "based on neutral, non-religious criteria that do not create incentives for choosing to attend religious schools."

Chopko acknowledges the financial problems facing parochial schools. "They're running at the line or below the line constantly," he says. But he forcefully denies that either of the programs in Cleveland or Milwaukee is a "bailout" for the parochial systems. "Absolutely not," he says.

Instead, Chopko views the programs as supporting Catholic schools' updated mission of providing education for mostly non-Catholic, mostly minority students in inner cities. "The participation of religious schools in these programs has been to qualify as providers of the assistance," Chopko continues. "The beneficiaries are really the children in these school districts."

Lynn, however, says Catholic schools—as well as schools operated by Christians, Jews, Muslims or other faiths—serve primarily religious purposes.

"Religious schools exist to promote faith," says Lynn, a United Church of Christ minister. "It doesn't just happen in a religion class. Religion imbues the curriculum in a Catholic school or a Muslim school from the time the bell rings in the morning until the children are dismissed in the afternoon."

Opponents of the Cleveland program are basing their legal challenge on the undisputed evidence that the

Vouchers in Cleveland

March 3, 1995 *Federal judge, ruling in school desegregation case, orders state takeover of Cleveland public school system.*

June 28, 1995 *Ohio General Assembly approves Pilot Scholarship Program aimed at providing vouchers for low-income families in Cleveland; signed by Gov. George Voinovich on June 30.*

January 1996 *Challenge to voucher program filed in state court.*

July 31, 1996 *State court judge rules program constitutional.*

September 1996 *Program takes effect for 1996–97 school year.*

May 27, 1999 *Ohio Supreme Court rules program unconstitutional but says program does not improperly aid religious schools.*

June 29, 1999 *Gov. Bob Taft signs bill re-enacting program.*

July 20, 1999 *New challenge filed in federal court.*

Aug. 24, 1999 *Federal Judge Solomon Oliver issues preliminary injunction against program.*

Nov. 5, 1999 *Supreme Court, by 5–4 vote, stays injunction, allowing program to continue, pending further proceedings.*

Dec. 20, 1999 *Judge Oliver rules program unconstitutional.*

Dec. 11, 2000 *Federal appeals court in Cincinnati affirms lower court decision, 2–1.*

Sept. 25, 2001 *Supreme Court agrees to hear appeal by state, private schools and pro-voucher parents.*

Feb. 20, 2002 *U.S. Supreme Court to hear arguments; decision expected by July.*

vast majority of the schools participated in the program are church-affiliated and enroll all but a very small number of the voucher students. Of the 50 schools currently participating, only four are secular; the others include 37 Catholic schools, seven affiliated with other Christian denominations and two Islamic academies.

The opponents contend that the program inevitably operates to channel students to parochial schools because of the relatively low limit on tuition—$2,500—that participating schools can charge. Catholic schools—subsidized by church funds—typically have significantly lower tuition than secular private schools.

"When the government sets up a program and says you can spend this money only in the limited universe of schools—the vast majority of which are religious—that's not a free and independent choice by the parents," says the NEA's Chanin. "It's a choice dictated by the government."

Bolick says he expects more non-religious schools to participate in the programs over time. In any event, he says, the predominant role of parochial schools in the programs today is no grounds for throwing them out.

"The question is whether the fact that only a few non-religious schools elected to throw an educational life preserver should mean that the while voucher program should be invalidated," Bolick says. "In my view, to ask the question is to answer it."

Legal advocates and experts have differing views about how the court is likely to rule on the constitutional issues. Apart from that, however, Rand researcher Gill sees "no good reason" to exclude Catholic schools from voucher programs.

"There is some research indicating that they may have unique benefits" for at-risk students, especially African-Americans, Gill says. Another reason "is the common-sense notion that to exclude the largest

number of private schools seems counterproductive."

---

*An estimated 47.2 million youngsters attended public schools and 5.9 million were in private schools in fall 2001, according to the National Center on Education Statistics. Catholic schools enroll close to 50 percent of private school students, other religious schools about 35 percent and nonsectarian schools about 15 percent.

Notes

1. For background, see Kathy Koc, "School Vouchers," *The CQ Researcher*, April 9, 1999, pp. 281–304; David Masci, "School Choice Debate," *The CQ Researcher*, July 18, 1997, pp. 625–648.
2. See Kenneth Jost, *Supreme Court Yearbook, 1999–2000* (2000), pp. 61–66. For background, see Patrick Marshall, "Religion in Schools," *The CQ Researcher*, Jan. 12, 2001, pp. 1–24.
3. "The 33rd Annual Phi Delta Kappa/Gallup Poll of the Public's Attitudes Toward the Public Schools," Phi Delta Kappan (September 2001), pp. 44–45, http://www.pdkintl.org/kappan/kimages/kpoll83.pdf. The telephone

sample of 1,108 adults was conducted May 23–June 6, 2001.

4. The annual evaluations are at www. indiana.edu/~iuice.

5. See John F. Witte, *The Market Approach to Education: An Analysis of America's First Voucher Program* (2000), pp. 119–143; Jay P. Greene, Paul E. Peterson, and Jiangtao Du, "Effectiveness of School Choice: The Milwaukee Experiment," Program in Education Policy and Governance, John F. Kennedy School of Government, Harvard University (March 1997), www.ksg. harvard.edu/pepg; Cecilia Elena Rouse, "Schools and Student Achievement: More Evidence from the Milwaukee Parental Choice Program," Princeton University (December 1996), www.irs. princeton.edu/ pubs.

6. William G. Howell, Patrick J. Wolf, Paul E. Peterson and David E. Campbell, "Test-Score Effects of School Vouchers in Dayton, Ohio, New York City, and Washington, D.C.: Evidence from Randomized Field Trials," Program on Education Policy and Governance, John F. Kennedy School of Government, Harvard University (August 2000), http:// data.fas.harvard.edu/pepg.

7. Brian P. Gill *et al.*, *Rhetoric Versus Reality: What We Know and What We Need to Know About Vouchers and Charter Schools* (2001), p. xvi.

8. General Accounting Office, "School Vouchers: Publicly Funded Programs in Cleveland and Milwaukee" (August 2001), pp. 27–31.

9. Caroline M. Hoxby, "How School Choice Affects the Achievement of Public School Students," paper presented at Hoover Institution, Stanford, Calif., Sept. 20–21, 2001 (http://post.economics. harvard.edu/faculty/hoxby/papers.html).

10. See Jay P. Greene, "An Evaluation of the Florida A-Plus Accountability and School Choice Program," Manhattan Institute (2001), www.manhattan-institute. org; Gregory Camilli and Katrina Bulkley, "Critique of 'An Evaluation of the Florida A-Plus Accountability and School Choice Program,'" Education Policy Analysis Archives (March 4, 2001), www.epaa.asu.edu.

Kenneth Jost has covered legal affairs as a reporter editor and columnist since 1970, and has been a CA Researcher staff writer since 1993. He is a graduate of Harvard College and Georgetown University Law Center, where he is an adjunct professor. He is author of the annual Supreme Court Yearbook (CQ Press) and contributes to the American Bar Association Journal and other publications. His recent reports include "Rethinking the Death Penalty" and "Affirmative Action."

Meeting the challenge of the URBAN High School

If it takes a village to raise a child, it may also take the equivalent—teachers, parents, elected officials, business leaders and anyone else who cares about kids—to create a successful high school.

by JOYCE BALDWIN

"Hi, teach!"

This snappy, disrespectful first line in *Up the Down Staircase* effectively sets the tone of Bel Kaufman's portrayal of her experiences as a teacher in New York City high schools. Kaufman draws a deft portrait of a situation that is at once funny and sad, a story of how teachers and students try to cope with a system that simply doesn't work for them. The book, which was a great success when published in 1964, sold more than six million copies and was made into a hit movie staring Sandy Dennis.

In a forward to a paperback edition issued in 1991, thirty years after she wrote the classic, Kaufman described her story as one of plunging "Sylvia Barrett, the young, inexperienced, idealistic teacher, into the maelstrom of an average city high school, where, inundated with trivia in triplicate, she had to cope with all that is frustrating and demeaning in the school system, while dealing with larger human issues."

At the beginning of the new millennium, many educators and students view their own school situations as similar to that experienced by Sylvia Barrett. In a comment about the current urban school crisis, Kaufman notes that "Everything described in my fiction is today reality. Only computers and condoms are new." Her story now, she says, "seems more timely than ever, and more urgent."

The Scope of the Problem

Since Ms. Kaufman wrote that observation, the crisis in the nation's schools has deepened, especially in large, impersonal urban schools. While there are high schools that do an excellent job of effectively educating students, in many cases schools are not really meeting the needs of today's young people. Symptoms of this problem include students who are too often absent from school and too often drop out altogether. According to the National Education Association, in 1998 nearly 12 percent of 16-to-24-year-olds were without a high school credential; this included 29.5 percent of Hispanic youth; 13.8 percent of black, non-Hispanic youth; 7.7 percent of white, non-Hispanic youth; and 4.1 percent of Asian/Pacific Islander youth.

One reason for these troubling statistics is that the traditional high school has served as a sorting device, sending graduates off to college or to pursue a vocation or service work and sending students who did not graduate to unskilled jobs. Even though the changing workplace now requires many more people to think creatively rather than perform only manual labor or service work, too many high school students do not graduate, and many who do still do not meet the entrance requirements of colleges and universities. This is particularly true in urban areas where the high school graduation rate is much lower than the national rate.

The problem is compounded by the fact that few, if any, high schools teach reading even though many ninth grade students do not have the basic skills to pass required courses and advance to the next grade. In large urban schools, which have never graduated more than half of their students or prepared more than two-in-five students for postsecondary education, there is a significant schism between students who achieve at a high academic level and those who do not.

A "shopping mall" approach to secondary education allows students to take only the courses they want and does not place too many demands on students except those in a high-pressure, high-achievement group. This relaxed approach to education coupled with the fact that high schools often do not demonstrate how education and the world of work are connected prompts too few students to take challenging courses. Although some students tackle rigorous academic work, they represent only a small minority of high school students, and there is an appalling lack of scientific literacy or interest in mathematics, according to Charles J. Sykes who cites a "legacy of dumbness" in his book *Dumbing Down Our Kids* (St. Martin's Press, 1995).

TURNAROUND HIGH SCHOOL
Urban Academy *As a Student Views it*

Stephanie Perez is a senior at Urban Academy, one of the high schools that is part of the Julia Richman Education Complex in New York City. Before Stephanie arrived at Urban Academy—or simply "Urban" as the students refer to it—Julia Richman had been transformed into a group of small schools remodeled from a large, impersonal school that was seriously being considered for closure, a school described in the press as "known… more for its shoplifting than for its scholars."

Today, Stephanie can't say enough positive things about her experience at Urban. And she should know. Before coming to this school, Stephanie attended a "traditional" high school where she felt she was "wasting my time, just memorizing things, taking a test and not really retaining anything." Then Stephanie attended a small alternative school that she describes as "not challenging." She says, "I just would sit in class and talk with friends, and no one noticed."

At Urban, People Notice.

"The most critically important factor [about Urban] is its size—it's small and personal, and I get the attention I need from teachers," says Stephanie. "Since the school is small, the curriculum is both personalized and challenging. Before I came to Urban, I attended a large traditional high school. The work I do here is more rigorous, demanding, and definitely more interesting."

Stephanie also cites the multicultural aspects of Urban as important to her learning. "I have the opportunity to get to know other students from different backgrounds very well," she explains. "This gives students the chance to see different issues from different perspectives." She says learning in a culturally diverse atmosphere "helps you with social interaction, it teaches you how to deal with people that you've never dealt with before and it helps with the class discussions, too."

At Urban, classes are about an hour long, allowing sufficient time for students to read an assignment and then discuss it or, in science classes, to get involved in laboratory work. On Wednesdays, students are in class only half the day and spend the rest of the day in field work. The school's success is reflected in the fact that, in 2000, 100 percent of Urban's graduates were accepted to college.

"One of the things Urban taught me was how to use the city as a resource for my research," says Stephanie. "I've learned how to use city libraries, museums and other cultural institutions more to my advantage. While most of my assignments and projects are started at school, a lot of my work and research are done outside of the traditional classroom setting and my education feels more hands on."

Students who attended Julia Richman before it was revamped probably wouldn't recognize their school as the one Stephanie describes. But for Stephanie and other students like her, the school is the best.

Even kids making every effort to get the most they can out of their school day face situations that their best intentions cannot resolve, such as violence. U.S. Department of Education data show that, in 1996, more than one-quarter million students, ages 12 through 18, were also victims of nonfatal serious violent crime at school and that in a four-year period more then 1.5 million teachers were victims of crimes. Drug and alcohol abuse are problems for teens, too, and contribute to low achievement rates in school.

A Disconnected Society

The urgency of the situation in our schools must be viewed in the context of larger changes that have taken place in our society. In *Bowling Alone* (Simon & Schuster, 2000), Robert D. Putnam cites data attesting to the fact that people tend to live more and more in isolation, not reaching out to connect with others. At home, families too often do not interact, spending less and less time vacationing together, attending religious services together, or just talking together. These features of modern life affect parents and children alike; everyone has a busy schedule and many families even find it difficult to gather for a meal on a regular basis. One study showed that, since 1980, the one-time family ritual of eating dinner together declined by a third, dropping from the 50 percent range to 34 percent. Teenagers may also spend many hours watching television or surfing the Internet, unsupervised and not in close association with another adult.

Students who attend large urban schools report feelings of anonymity, of being just one person among thousands of other youth without an adult in their lives to help negotiate problems and provide support. Many students do not have a relationship in their schools with even one caring adult who knows them personally and participates significantly in their development. Yet in many ways, young people do signal how important it is to them to have strong social and civic connections: across the country, they are becoming involved in volunteer and community service activities in unprecedented numbers.

Our new knowledge-based economy with its emphasis on problem-solving and the ability to cope with change makes it imperative that high school graduates attend college. Yet too many students are unable to meet college entrance requirements and those who do often find postsecondary education to be highly challenging. Many students have difficulty transitioning to college not only because of educational deficits but because their high schools have not provided opportunities for them to interact socially in ways that will help prepare them to live and study in a college or university environment.

---

*The traditional high school has served as a **sorting** device, sending graduates off to college or to pursue a **vocation** or service work and sending students who did not graduate to unskilled jobs.*

Looking Back

How have we reached this crossroads? The history of the American high school began in 1821 when the English Classical School of Boston (later renamed English High School), was established as the first public high school in the country. In the 1880s Calvin M. Woodward and other educational leaders sparked an interest in vocational training with the first manual training high school opening in Baltimore in 1884. Other such schools soon followed with the purpose of training youngsters to become employable plumbers, bricklayers or other manual workers.

Early in the 20th century, John Dewey sparked an interest in educating the whole child so that youngsters would be able to take on the mature responsibilities of participation in a democracy and enjoy meaningful work and economic success. Educators today find themes in Dewey's concepts that are relevant to current school redesign efforts.

In the middle of the last century, the launch of the Soviet Union's Sputnik, the world's first satellite, caused the United States to rethink its school system, and in a 1959 Carnegie Corporation-sponsored report, James Conant urged that mathematics, science and foreign language curricula be strengthened.

Other changes in the latter part of the century stemmed from the Vietnam War and its accompanying student protests, which resulted in the addition of electives that students sought as relevant to their lives.

Toward the close of the 20th century, the Internet and other changes in global technology further exacerbated the need for redesign of obsolete urban schools.

Learning from High School Redesign Efforts

Educators have made progress in revamping failing middle schools, and there are examples of dramatic changes in urban high school redesign, situations in which schools on the brink of being closed have been rescued at the last minute, transformed in a way that captures the mind as well as the heart. Whole new schools have also been created, based on new approaches to teaching and learning. These isolated efforts provide information about what works and what does not.

One tenet of urban high school change is the creation of smaller schools, learning communities where teenagers are known as individuals by one, and hopefully more than one, adult. Small schools provide settings where the hopes and dreams of youth can be nurtured, where teenagers can be nudged and prompted to learn, and where a teacher can help rescue a student before he or she slides behind or passively lets the studying pile up until it is unmanageable.

Some educators hope to break the cycle of failure in part by addressing the need to help students successfully negotiate the transition from the middle school to the high school. The Talent Development High School Model, which was created by educators and researchers at Johns Hopkins University features a Ninth Grade Success Academy, a self-contained school-within-a-school that includes programs designed to help all students meet with success in college preparatory algebra and language arts courses. To bolster social and study skills, a Talent Development High School includes a freshman seminar tailored to help students develop computer and study skills as well as understand the connection between their high school studies and college and career.

This model also provides block scheduling that includes increased time for learning, a core requirement of college preparatory courses for all students, Career Academies for grades 10, 11 and 12, and strategic reading, transition to advanced mathematics and freshman seminar courses as well as alternative after-hours programs for those students with serious attendance problems.

These and other schools, including those in the Annenburg Rural Challenge program, help students make the link between what they learn in school and work by providing field internships. For example, pupils in Rural Challenge schools study the history of their towns, publish newspapers, work at a local library or a nearby museum and find other opportunities to complement their studies.

Although small schools can provide the leverage needed for change, experts say that creating a "small" setting in which students and teachers can interact merely provides the foundation for helping students achieve and that schools must work on many issues including the need to have high standards for all students.

---

*"We have good teachers in America; they are **committed,** and they work very hard. But they are in a system that no longer functions very well when we have to raise **standards** significantly with the rising workplace requirement."*

GENE BOTTOM —Director of High Schools That Work and Senior Vice President of the Southern Regional Education Board.

"Comprehensive high schools are trying to be everything to all students and are probably little to most," says Judy B. Codding, a co-author of *The New American High School* (Corwin Press, 1998).

Codding, who was principal of Pasadena High School for five years beginning in 1988, says academic rigor is the bedrock of school redesign. "The purpose of a high school is to prepare all students for college without the need for remediation," she explains. "That doesn't mean that all kids need to go to a four-year college, but they do need to have the knowledge and skills

TURNAROUND HIGH SCHOOL

Bel Air High School *As a Teacher Views it*

It was like a dark tunnel, with no end, no results," says Genny Galindo describing how she felt a few years back about her teaching job. "You would like to see results at the end of a hard days' work, to see your students be successful."

But at Bel Air High School in El Paso, Texas, the students were simply not interested. "They just kept doing the same old thing over and over and coming up with the same results, and it was [thought to be] all the students' fault."

The school, which is in a low socioeconomic-level community, was on the brink of being closed. Only about five percent of students even thought about applying to college.

But then six years ago, things changed radically. A new principal, Vernon Butler, took over; one of the first things Butler asked was that all staff members write a letter to reapply for their jobs.

"We wrote about what we believed in as educators, what we had done for the school, for our students, about our teaching methods and strategies, our contributions to the community," says Galindo. "He wanted to know what we would be willing to do for Bel Air and were we going to take the challenge."

Galindo says she found the new approach appealed to her integrity as a teacher.

"Hey! We're not here just to collect a check," she says softly. "Are we helping our country with the training of minds? Are we doing our part?"

Only 57 of the 132 teachers remained at Bel Air. The teachers who stayed took up Butler's challenge and transformed the school. "I started looking at new [teaching] strategies," she says. "We learned new ways to convey the information to our students; we also became very high-tech with computers. I found a new me."

Galindo says Butler provided the "vision that we needed." The school now has high academic expectations for all students and, she explains, Butler models compassion and supportive behavior with teachers that transfers to the students.

"He believed that this group could do it, that the parents and the students of the community could rise to the challenge regardless of their background," Galindo says. Now she proudly reports that some of her students from this border town in Texas have gone on to be successful at leading colleges including Georgetown, Notre Dame and Yale.

Bel Air High School still has room for improvement, as indicated in part by its overall low SAT scores. In a letter to parents and the community, Butler said, "We still have much to do to help our students accomplish their goals." But in May 2000 Bel Air was named a National Blue Ribbon School of Excellence by the U.S. Department of Education. That recognition was Galindo's biggest reward.

"We were crying, we were laughing, we were hugging; we wanted to tell the whole world," she says. "The community deserved it. All the changes and all the hard work had paid off."

---

to live productive lives. If teens don't have that, they will be assigned to a life of poverty."

The reality, however, is that expectations for students do vary. "Our (Philadelphia) data and other data nationally show that in the large urban schools we simply are not offering students the courses, the rigorous learning that they need," says Rochelle Nichols-Solomon, senior program director of the Philadelphia Education Fund. "We generally have a different set of expectations for students of color and poor students enrolled in the comprehensive (or non-magnet) high schools, even though we have the rhetoric of high standards for all students."

Expectations for Faculty and Students

The kinds of skills, knowledge, support and expertise that teachers need are

an important aspect of school redesign. "My attention is focused on the teachers, and the expectations for them and support for them that will then in turn help them be more effective with the students," Nichols-Solomon says.

Her sentiments are echoed by Steve Leonard, principal of Jeremiah E. Burke High School in Dorchester, Massachusetts. Leonard has been instrumental in turning the school from a failing institution where few of the more than 1,000 students (most either African American or of African descent) even considered higher educaton into one where almost 100 percent of seniors are applying to college. "The key to improving students' academic performance," he says, "is to improve teachers' instructional performance. One cannot happen without the other."

Faculty commitment is key to the success of High Schools That Work (HSTW), a large-scale effort of the Southern Regional Education Board (SREB) that

aims "to improve the way all high school students are prepared for work and further education."

"You must engage the faculty in a dialogue. You must do that," says Gene Bottoms, director of High Schools That Work and senior vice president of SREB. "We have good teachers in America; they are committed, and they work very hard. But they are in a system that no longer functions very well when we have to raise standards significantly with the rising workplace requirement."

"Unlocking from that system is the biggest challenge we have," Bottoms says. "That system is built on the ability model that says some students can learn complicated material but most students can't, so you dumb down the curriculum for the rest of the students. What we say is that you can teach the rest what you've been teaching to the best, but you will have to teach it differently. To get faculty to really begin to believe and shift

Whole-District School Reform

In June 2000, Carnegie Corporation awarded 15-month planning grants to ten urban school district-community partnerships nationwide. These grants are the first phase of the Schools for a New Society initiative launched by the Corporation in an effort to provide long-term support for the revamping of large comprehensive urban schools.

"Every student in America is entitled to attend a good high school in order to be prepared for the world of the 21st century," says Vartan Gregorian, president of Carnegie Corporation of New York. "They are owed a high-performance education where much is offered and much is expected. We don't expect instant success in turning around every low-achieving high school in each of the ten cities, but we are determined to help build the will that believes no student can be written off. To do less would be to abdicate the Corporation's role as a leader in education reform."

Although the participating districts have been actively seeking to redesign their schools, revamping efforts have been more successful in the elementary and middle schools. The challenge at the high school level is much greater, requiring new leadership strategies and a new and dynamic vision of the high school. A key component of this initiative is the partnership teams composed of school officials, teachers, parents and students as well as community stakeholders who are crucial to the success of a high school reform effort. These stakeholders include unions, college personnel, elected officials, business leaders, and leaders of community-based and youth development organizations.

"With this initiative, Carnegie Corporation will encourage and support the development of high schools for all students where there is effective teaching and learning, where students are invested in their own education and support their peers to achieve, and where there are clear pathways to higher education, careers and community participation," says Michele Cahill, a nationally recognized youth development expert and educator who created the initiative and who will lead the Corporation's long-term effort.

The ten district-community partnerships that received Carnegie Corporation planning grants are: Boston Plan for Excellence in the Public Schools Foundation, The Chattanooga-Hamilton County Public Education Fund, Houston Annenberg Challenge, Indianapolis Public Schools Education Foundation, Inc., New Futures for Youth Inc. (Little Rock), Portland Public Schools Foundation (Oregon), Health and Education Leadership for Providence, Linking Education and Economic Development in Sacramento, San Diego Foundation, and Clark University (Worcester).

Upon completion of blueprints for effective secondary schools, five of the ten partnerships will be invited into the second phase of the initiative that will fund implementation of the plans. Beginning in the fall of 2001, when the second phase is launched, Carnegie Corporation anticipates committing $40 million over five years in direct grants, which will require a one-to-one match from public or private funds.

In December 2000, Carnegie Corporation, along with Open Society Institute (OSI) and the Bill and Melinda Gates Foundation, announced another initiative—this one a partnership with New York City's public schools—aimed at redesigning some of the city's large comprehensive high schools that serve approximately 76,000 students across the city. The three foundations will make a five-year, $30 million investment in the initiative, known as the New Century High Schools Consortium for New York City, which aspires to help create effective high schools for all students and the implementation of small-school designs.

The consortium is targeting the lowest performing academic comprehensive high schools that serve students from low income neighborhoods and will back plans for both large-school redesign and development of small schools. The consortium expects to choose approximately ten large-scale high school redesigns and sponsor the creation of a number of new secondary schools serving grades 7 through 12.

"Small-school designs have a proven track record of helping all students achieve," says Patty Stonesifer, president and co-chair of the Bill and Melinda Gates Foundation. "A number of New York City high schools have successfully implemented small-school models and this partnership will help bring these innovations to scale by supporting both new small high schools and the redesign of large high schools." Adds Gara LaMarche, director of U.S. Programs for OSI, "Far too many failing high schools crush the aspirations of poor students of color, and serve as conveyor belts for the criminal justice system, not for the opportunity that is their birthright. The good news is that we know how to do better, and in this New York City partnership, we will."

from the old ability model to an effort-based model you have to change your language, mindset and teaching techniques."

The HSTW program bolsters learning in part by advocating a solid academic core curriculum and by enrolling grade nine youth who lag behind in an 18-week program geared to help them catch up so they will be as prepared as their peers to take the more rigorous algebra and language arts classes. Results so far have been promising. Some examples: At Loganville High in Georgia, where the HSTW principles have been implemented, 86 percent of students pursue education after graduation (up from 62 percent before HSTW); chronic absences are down and the dropout rate has gone from nine percent to less than four percent. In 1998, in Oklahoma schools participating in the program, students averaged above 50 percent in math, science and reading for the first time.

Engaging Parents and Youth

Parental involvement is another element that can affect a student's success. Schools can reach out to involve parents by keeping them informed and by organizing volunteer activities and providing parent education programs.

"There's no way we're going to raise the achievement level of students unless we engage parents on behalf of their kids," says Codding. When Codding saw that only a small fraction of parents attended a back-to-school program at Pasedena High School, she set up a structure that reached out to parents with telephone calls and mailings to inform them about their teenagers' school programs including the names of students' advisors, advocates and head teachers. "The line of communication became clear to parents," Codding explained.

Youth, too, must be heard. Students clearly, often plaintively, describe their world, providing information central to successfully redesign urban high schools. "We know the way to effect change is to have that change be based in reality, to be data-based," says Michele Cahill, senior program officer in the Education Division of Carnegie Corporation. "Quantitative data are becoming more available, but there are also incredibly important qualitative data—narratives that convey the experiences of young people in school. This youth voice has been missing in the past, yet a key part of changing the high schools is seeing young people as assets and seeing them as active learners. We recognize the need to hear the youth voice because we get new information from that about what needs to be changed and what might work that we can't get from any other source."

A Clarion Call

Overarching themes echoed by urban educators are the need to personalize education and to tailor rigorous education to reach all high school students, not just some of the students. This requires a revamping of the system, not just a minor alteration, and a commitment from all members of the school community as well as members of the larger community. High school redesign is one of the greatest challenges facing our nation at the start of this new millennium: the challenge to create a vision of the American urban high school that will provide the best education possible for each and every student.

"It's not too late," says Nichols-Solomon. "Older students can be engaged. I've seen ninth grade students running to beat the clock to get into school. They can get energized."

As a high school biology teacher, Joyce Baldwin had an up-close view of a classroom; now she writes about education from a wider perspective. She also enjoys writing about health and medicine and is the author of DNA Pioneer: James Watson and the Double Helix (*Walker Publishing Company, 1994*).

From *Carnegie Reporter,* Spring 2001, pp. 22-29. Reprinted with permission of the Carnegie Corporation of New York, 437 Madison Avenue, New York, NY 10022.

UNIT 7

Serving Special Needs and Concerns

Unit Selections

Key Points to Consider

• What are the strengths and weaknesses of home schooling programs?

• Describe life in an American suburban high school. What concerns do you have about student experience of this setting? If possible, use your own experiences as a guide.

• What are the advantages of a small class size? the disadvantages? Explain your own position in this discussion.

 **Links: www.dushkin.com/online/**
These sites are annotated in the World Wide Web pages.

Consortium on Inclusive Schooling Practices
http://www.asri.edu/cfsp/brochure/abtcons.htm

Constructivism: From Philosophy to Practice
http://www.stemnet.nf.ca/~elmurphy/emurphy/cle.html

Kenny Anthony's Gifted and Talented and General Educational Resources
http://www2.tsixroads.com/~kva/

National Association for Gifted Children
http://www.nagc.org/home00.htm

National Information Center for Children and Youth With Disabilities (NICHCY)
http://www.nichcy.org/index.html

People who educate serve many special needs and concerns of their students. This effort requires a special commitment to students on the part of their teachers. We celebrate this effort, and each year we seek to address special types of general concern.

People learn under many different sets of circumstances, which involve a variety of educational concerns both within schools and in alternative learning contexts. Each year we include in this section of this volume articles on a variety of special topics that we believe our readers will find interesting and relevant.

The journal literature thematically varies from year to year. Issues on which several good articles may have been published in one year may not be covered well in other years in the professional and trade publications. Likewise, some issues are covered in depth every year, such as articles on social class or education and school choice.

This year the special concerns we address are related to several critical topics. We begin with a very interesting discussion of the nature of teaching and the pursuit of truth. "Education without candor is no education at all," according to Gary K. Clabaugh. Next there is a very informative synthesis of the merits and problems with home schooling. This comparison of positives and negatives regarding home schooling is fair, but the rationales of proponents and opponents of home schooling remain basically unexamined. Yet this discussion of home schooling does raise the concerns and hopes that are regularly expressed about this movement.

Other topics of importance are addressed. The many psychological and legal problems of gay and lesbian couples who adopt children are discussed. The interests and concerns of both parents and children are examined. This is followed by a very pertinent article on life and teaching and learning in suburban high schools. What the author describes in her interviews with faculty and students of two East Coast high schools should be read by everyone. This is followed by a discussion as to how one can use various forms of jazz music in improving overall literacy education. Finally, the unit concludes with a very important report on research on reducing class sizes. This is a thorough summary report on these findings. The authors discuss the results of research following efforts to reduce class sizes in several states. They examine the problematics of the research designs as well as what we can learn from the experiments themselves.

Since first issued in 1973, this ongoing anthology has sought to provide discussion of special social or curriculum issues affecting the teaching/learning conditions in schools. Fundamental

forces at work in our culture during the past several years have greatly affected millions of students. The social, cultural, and economic pressures on families have produced several special problems of great concern to teachers. Serving special needs and concerns requires greater degrees of individualization of instruction and greater attention paid to the development and maintenance of healthier self-concepts by students.

The Cutting Edge

Teaching and the Truth

Gary K. Clabaugh

Joseph Ellis, a Pulitzer Prize-winning author and history professor at Mount Holyoke College, wove his war experiences in Vietnam into his history lectures. Apparently that helped popularize his courses. Trouble is, Ellis never served in Vietnam. From 1969 until 1972 he was on active duty as a commissioned officer in the Army, but as a history teacher at West Point.

A journalist from the *Boston Globe* found out about Ellis's fabrications and wrote an exposé. Following an internal investigation, Mt. Holyoke's president announced that Ellis will be suspended for a year without pay and must also give up his endowed chair. "The year away should give him and the college time for reflection and repair," the president said.

Evidently it's anathema for a history professor to lie to his students about the past—even his own past. Would Mt. Holyoke have reacted differently had Ellis been a math or business professor and the stories not been integral to the subject matter? We can only guess. In any case, Ellis isn't hair-splitting. Following notice of his punishment, he issued a statement declaring, "I am solely responsible and wish to express my personal regret to all students, faculty and administrators who have been affected."[1]

Professors are expected to tell the truth, at least as they understand it. That's their business. But do expectations for teacher honesty change when we move from college to secondary school? Imagine a high school biology teacher, for example, who is asked about evolution by a youngster from a religiously conservative family. The student might say something like this: My church teaches, and my family believes, that the earth is just 6,000 years old. But the text claims that the earth is nearly 800,000 times older. Which is correct?"

The claim that the earth is a mere 6,000 years old lacks scientific credibility, and our biology teacher knows it. How, then, should she respond to the student's question? Here are some possibilities. You decide how our teacher might best respond and still honor her profession.

1. "The claim that the earth is 6,000 years old is not supported by present scientific evidence."

2. "The Biblical account might be understood as an allegory."
3. "Which account do *you* think is more credible?"
4. "That's a question for your parents."
5. "If you believe that the earth is 6,000 years old, it is for you."
6. "Your parents are right—the earth really is only 6,000 years old."

Answer 1 is the unvarnished truth, 2 offers an alternative, and 3 begs the question. Regarding 4, the student knows what his parents think; he wants an answer from the teacher. Answer 5 is evasive, though it's possibly wise. Response 6 is a lie, pure and simple. Which of these responses can our high school instructor choose and still properly call herself a teacher?

Given teachers' uncompetitive pay and shoddy treatment, it might be naïve to expect them to take risks for honesty's sake. But you're not asked to decide what is prudent here. You're only deciding what this teacher must do to remain true to the essential nature of teaching.

Let's take this inquiry to first grade. Six-year-olds frequently ask their teacher if Santa Claus is real. Here are some possible responses.

1. "No, Santa Claus is not real."
2. "Santa Claus is the spirit of giving."
3. "Do you think Santa is real?"
4. "That's a question for your parents."
5. "If you believe in him, he's real for you."
6. "Certainly he's real—I've seen him myself."

Number 1 is the truth, the whole truth and nothing but the truth. Answer 2 is probably over the children's heads. Answer 3 serves the teacher, not the children. Six-year-olds want an answer. Regarding answer 4, maybe it should be up to parents whether their kids are lied to about Santa Claus. But our question is, should the teacher support the lie? Answer 5 is logically true but not an honest answer, and 6 is a lie. Which of these answers can our teacher give without betraying his calling?

The preceding examples involved student-initiated issues. The teacher was required only to react. But what about teacher-initiated truth telling? What, for instance, should a social studies teacher teach about our slave-owning founding fathers, about European settlers' ethnic cleansing of Native Americans, about the lynching of black Americans, about U.S. war crimes in Vietnam, or about J. Edgar Hoover's contemptible and illegal conduct as director of the FBI? Can any self-respecting social studies teacher dodge these and similar issues and still be a teacher rather than a propagandist for the status quo?

Perhaps you're thinking that elementary teachers get off relatively easy when it comes to telling the truth. But elementary education is routinely sanitized to the point of sterility. Only occasionally do elementary educators deal truthfully with issues that matter. Here is one conspicuous exception. Notice how starkly different it is. At Carbon Canyon Christian School in California, parochial school students as young as five raised a 1,000-pound steer ("T-bone" by name) that then was slaughtered in front of them. The lesson was intended to teach them where meat comes from.

About half the children in the 170-student school, all of whom had parental permission to watch, saw a butcher use a stun gun to kill the steer and then butcher it. The youngsters then were shown the heart and other internal organs. Only a few got queasy, said Dave Kincer, pastor and principal. The rest reportedly were fascinated.

True to form, there were protests. In fact, students from other schools formed a human chain outside the campus to block the slaughter, and animal rights groups charged that the children were being desensitized to violence against animals.[2] But the children certainly learned that meat doesn't mysteriously appear in Styrofoam packages somewhere in the nether reaches of the supermarket. They are better able to make an informed choice about eating it too.

A wide range of vital topics are shunned or rendered harmless by educators in order to avoid becoming the target of no-nothing parents, civic "activists," opportunistic politicians, or self-appointed guardians of public morality. What inevitably suffers are truth and relevance. This is how schooling becomes devitalized, immaterial, and boring. This also is how teachers become irrelevant, neutered apologists for the status quo. Admittedly, one person's truth is another's foolishness—truth depends on the authority one is obedient to. But education without candor is no education at all. Moreover, a teacher's character and inner spirit is the curriculum that counts, because that's what people remember about school after they've forgotten everything else.

Notes

1. College Suspends Ellis for War Lies."*Philadelphia Inquirer*, August 18, 2001, p. 4.
2. "California Children See How a Steer Is Slaughtered." *Philadelphia Inquirer*, May 5, 2001, p. 6.

Gary K. Clabaugh is a professor of education at La Salle University in Philadelphia, Pennsylvania. He directs La Salle's Graduate Program in Education and coordinates arts and sciences graduate programs.

From *Educational Horizons,* Fall 2001, pp. 10-11. © 2001 by Educational Horizons. Reprinted with permission of the author.

Common Arguments about the Strengths and Limitations of Home Schooling

MICHAEL H. ROMANOWSKI

Today in American culture, few people are unfamiliar with home schooling. Most either know someone who home schools their children or have heard of a family that has selected this increasingly popular alternative to public and private school education. By all accounts, the movement has been growing steadily over the past few years. The U.S. Department of Education estimated that approximately fifteen thousand students were home schooled in 1984, with that number increasing to between two hundred thousand and three hundred thousand students in 1988. Currently, it is estimated that between 1.2 and 1.7 million students in grades K–12 are home schooled in the United States (Lines 1998; Ray 1999). This spectacular growth not only testifies to the demand by parents for alternative and less-institutionalized options for their children's education, but also has established home schooling as a significant and legitimate force in the American educational landscape.

One of the more fascinating aspects of this educational movement is that today's home schooling families represent a diverse sampling of the American population. Once reserved primarily for fundamentalist Christians with religious motivations for educating their children at home, home schooling now embraces such a wide range of families that it has surfaced as a mainstream alternative form of education. The recent upsurge in home schooling's popularity has drawn people from all ethnic groups and social classes, and a rapidly increasing number of minority families home school their children (Knowles 1988; Nazareno 1999; Ray 1999; Wahisi 1995). Ideologically, home schoolers represent a broad cross-section of American society; one can find families holding to conservative and liberal, religious and secular values, beliefs, and political viewpoints (Mayberry 1987; Van Galen 1988). Home

schooling's rapid growth, coupled with the diversity of its practitioners, all but discredits the long-accepted view that public schools serve children from diverse backgrounds equally well. But as with all forms of education, there are both pros and cons to home schooling. In this article, I address why families choose home schooling, and I summarize the most common arguments put forth by advocates and critics of home schooling regarding the perceived strengths and limitations of this unique form of education.

Why Families Choose Home Schooling

Although there are numerous reasons families choose to home school their children, Van Galen (1988) appropriately places home schoolers into two distinct categories: ideologues and pedagogues. The ideologues argue that they home school their children for two reasons: "they object to what they believe is being taught in public and private schools and they seek to strengthen their relationships with their children" (Van Galen 1988, 55). These parents have specific beliefs, values, and skills that they want their children to learn and embrace. Because they are convinced that these things are not being adequately taught in public school, they opt for home schooling.

The ideologues' argument is essentially religiously based. Often "these parents view the public schools as grounded in secular humanist philosophy that does not include strong Christian values" (Marchant and MacDonald 1994, 66). They move beyond issues such as school prayer and argue that public schools fail to take religion seriously throughout the curriculum. This becomes problematic for these families because "their religious beliefs and the education of their children were inextricably intertwined"

(Marchant and MacDonald 1994, 77). These parents have a deep concern for their children's moral, ethical, and spiritual development, and they feel that public schools do not provide appropriate moral or ethical instruction, much less religious values. Therefore, they home school their children in an attempt to avoid public school's perceived attempt to strangle religion's influence.

Pedagogues, on the other hand, teach their children at home primarily for pedagogical reasons. They are not so concerned with the content of public education, but rather they believe that whatever public schools teach, they teach ineptly. These parents "share a respect for their children's intellect and creativity and a belief that children learn best when pedagogy taps into the child's innate desire to learn" (Van Galen 1988, 55). Pedagogues home school primarily because of what they believe will be the educational benefit to their children. These parents have usually observed children who suffered both emotionally and academically because of the schools' shortcomings, and they recognize "that the schools are often unwilling or unable to serve children with unique learning styles or scholarly needs" (Van Galen 1988, 57). They challenge the power of public schools to sort, select, and label their children based on what they see as a limited measure of their child's ability, and they believe "that breaking from the traditional formal model of teaching will lead to improved understanding and learning in their children" (Marchant and MacDonald 1994, 66).

The Strengths of Home Schooling

First, research indicates that when parental involvement in children's education is high, students are more likely to become academically successful and reach their potential (Simmons 1994). That is the essence of home schooling. Parents are intimately involved not only in their child's education but in the details of their child's life. More important, that involvement takes place in a sustained and continuous relationship rather than serving simply a supplemental role.

Many parents who home school seek to strengthen the quality of their relationships with their children. Advocates argue that home schooling enables families to build tight bonds amid a society where the family institution is falling apart. The time that parents spend home schooling their children "produces more meaningful communication, emotional intimacy, and a closer family life" (Ballman 1987, 82). In homes where there are several siblings being home schooled, that unique bond extends to the sibling relationships. No other factor in life will have more of an effect on a child's life than the family, and home schooling enables the family to play its important role more actively.

Second, critics of home schooling argue that unless children are exposed to the social life that is found in public schools, they will be misfits incapable of socializing properly. For many critics, that lack of socialization is cited as the major drawback of home schooling. However, home schoolers present a different perspective. They argue against traditional understandings of the socialization process and maintain that there are both positive and negative forms of socialization. Ballman (1987) defines the positive and negatives aspects of socialization in the following manner:

> Positive socialization helps a child to grow and develop to his full potential in life. When a child's personality develops in a warm atmosphere of love and acceptance, he will usually socialize well with all age groups, including his own. Negative socialization, on the other hand, separates a child from his parents and restricts a child's socializing primarily to his age-mates. This can have detrimental and long-term effects on a child's potential sociability among a wide age dispersement. (71)

Because home school children spend most of their time around their parents in an accepting atmosphere, they, unlike their public school counterparts, are able to engage socially in multiage situations with a high level of confidence. Beyond the classroom walls, how often do people limit their interaction to individuals of their own age? That type of peer socialization inadequately prepares students for normal life situations, where they must interact with people of all ages.

Home schoolers also argue that other institutions, groups, and activities outside the home can provide students with important socialization skills. On average, home schooled students are involved in 5.2 activities outside the home, with 98 percent engaged in two or more (Ray 1997). Their involvement in such activities as scouting, dance classes, group sports, 4H, and volunteer work demonstrates that home schoolers are not isolated from the outside world. Rather, "home schooled children are more frequently exposed to a wider variety of people and situations than could be expected in a traditional classroom environment where their exposure is limited to 25-35 people of similar age and socioeconomic background" (Nelsen 1998, 35). Also, home school students are more likely "to develop a sense of self-worth and a stable value system—which is the basic ingredient for positive sociability" (Moore 1982).

It is important to understand that a child's self-concept and the socialization process are closely related. Ray (1989) discusses several studies that indicate that home school students' social development is comparable to or more advanced than that of public school students. One particular study used the Piers-Harris Children's Self-Concept Scale to measure the central core of personality with home school children in grades 4-12 (Taylor 1986). Home school students scored significantly higher than public school students, indicating that they had a more positive self-concept. Insofar as self-concept is a basic factor of positive sociability, we can conclude that home schoolers are not socially deprived nor inferior in socialization (Taylor 1986).

Third, education is not exclusively about a child's intellect; it also includes character. Many home school advocates argue that their view of morality and their deeply held beliefs and values are not being adequately taught in public schools, if at all. Therefore, they opt for home schooling to assure that their children are provided numerous opportunities to learn and embrace the morals and values that they deem appropriate. For example, parents can teach their children the importance of prayer and faith and instruct them in religious precepts with direct reference to the Bible or other Scriptures. Home schooling allows families to integrate their personal beliefs and values, whatever they may be, into all areas of the curriculum.

Fourth, every child's emotional and educational needs are complex, and any attempt to conform the needs of a child to the school or classroom is impossible and possibly detrimental to the student. This is standard practice in public schools, where students must adhere to a rigid curriculum that doesn't always address their academic needs or interests. In the public school classroom, the instruction is designed for twenty-five to thirty students, and that forces each student to accommodate the instruction instead of the instruction's accommodating the students' needs and learning styles. Successful students make the adjustment while others, although intelligent and full of potential, become discouraged, fail, and are labeled and left behind to struggle in the lower academic tracks.

Home schooling, on the other hand, easily allows teachers to adjust the curriculum and instruction to fit the individual needs of students because home schoolers generally use a one-on-one tutoring style of teaching. Other factors are the following:

- Home educators do not have to contend with large classes, so the teacher can easily tailor the curriculum and instruction to meet the needs and interests of the student, and she can pace learning according to the student's level of understanding. In addition, the one-on-one teaching style provides the individual student with undivided attention, allows for quicker diagnosis of problems, offers more opportunities to ask questions, and lets student develop a deeper understanding of subject matter.
- Home school teachers enjoy a benefit that many public school teachers would cherish: flexibility. The home school teacher can make spontaneous decisions as needed without all the red tape and administrative constraints.
- Home school teachers can easily seize teachable moments because everyday experiences provide the foundation for learning. For example, a math lesson on measurement might start with a textbook or a worksheet and end with mixing and baking a cake.
- Traditional time constraints are removed within home schools. Instruction is not pitted against the clock and children are not forced to stop what they are doing, pack away their project, change gears, and think

about a new subject. If a child is interested in reading a story, the home school educator can adjust the schedule to allow the student to continue. Also, teachers can easily develop units of study using an integrated approach and making the student's interests the basis of unit studies. As we know, learning occurs when interest is high.

Finally, in thirteen years of public schooling, students endure many negative learning experiences. Most learn to cope, but the consequences can be serious. However, home schooling provides the supportive environment of a concerned family, where wounds suffered from bad learning experiences can heal and students can recover and slowly regain their confidence. That confidence building is more likely to be found in homes than schools.

Additionally, home schools enhance the confidence of students by minimizing the importance of grades and encouraging students to learn for the sake of gaining knowledge. Unlike the public school classroom, which fosters extrinsically motivated learners, home schooling cultivates learners who are intrinsically motivated and seek after knowledge. Many home schooled students still have the joy of learning, while their counterparts in public school slowly lose this joy as they progress through their education.

The Limitations of Home Schooling

The main criticism of home schooling centers on the issue of socialization. Critics charge that home schooled children are isolated from the outside world and are socially handicapped. By being sheltered from the real world, children are seldom presented with the opportunities to learn sorely needed social interaction skills. More important, "it is not only socially desirable but also an important part of education for children to interact with their own age group" (Simmons 1994, 48). Unless these children are exposed on a daily basis to the social life found in public schools, they will lack the skills needed to successfully adapt to real-life situations when they are older.

Second, although home schoolers rightly argue that their children can obtain basic socialization skills from a wide variety of experiences independent of school, there are important limitations to this interaction. For example, home schooled children seldom are exposed to the diversity of beliefs and backgrounds that they would encounter in most public school classrooms. Even though they are involved in various activities outside of their homes, such as field trips and other activities with fellow home schoolers, the participants usually are a very select group of students who for the most part share similar values, background, and social class. This type of interaction simply provides the children with a controlled social group unlike those they will face when they enter college or the work force. Even when home schooled students engage in community activities such as sports teams, the few hours spent in practice and playing games do little to expose students to differing viewpoints and lifestyles.

Academically, the lack of peer interaction in the classroom is detrimental to a home school student's education. To receive a complete education, students need to engage in discussions, share ideas, compete, and work with other students. This interaction helps determine how students confront problems, shapes the manner in which they see the world, and influences students' goals and aspirations (Simmons 1994). More important, the interaction provides students with a means to compare and contrast themselves against their peers in a variety of areas that move beyond standardized test scores. According to Simmons, "the home school might stand as a lonesome contrast to the active, bustling, energy-filled classroom where students are constantly exchanging ideas and enjoying each other's company" (1994, 48).

Third, another limitation of home schooling is that the instructor may lack the resources or facilities to deliver a well-rounded curriculum. Although there are countless "sequenced and integrated curriculum materials now available for home schooling, a home simply cannot provide the numerous and diverse enrichment activities such as band, orchestra, choral activities, forensics, and many sports without some cooperation from some established educational institution" (Simmons 1994, 47). Most home schoolers would agree that such extracurricular activities are a vital part of one's education and that local home school groups adequately provide those opportunities. However, they may not be of the same quality and depth as those of other educational institutions.

Regarding resources, funding, and facilities, it is important to understand that home schools are no different than public schools. Just as our current public school budget is inequitable, so are personal incomes. The majority of families (82 percent) who have the ability to choose home schooling earn yearly incomes in the range of $25,000 to $75,000 and above (Ray 1999). Does family income affect educational outcomes? Home school advocates argue that income has no effect on standardized test performance (Ray 1999, 1991). However, simply using standardized test scores as the sole basis for determining the relationship of income to education overlooks other important aspects of schooling. Income indeed affects the overall educational experience for the 18 percent of home school families whose finances fall below the $25,000 level. Limited resources affect their ability to provide adequate educational opportunities and equipment, such as computers; field trips and other experiences that cost money such as entrance fees to museums; science materials such as microscopes and other laboratory facilities; access to tutors to teach courses such as Spanish or to other needed specialized professional assistance; and simple everyday school materials. All of these can prove to be a financial burden for poorer home school families. Even though home school support groups provide some assistance, this is limited. As in the public school system, where wealthier schools have the resources to provide more opportunities to their students, wealthier families can often provide a better overall home school education.

Fourth, critics of home schooling argue that parents may have too much freedom under current legislation. Only ten states require that parents have a high school diploma or general equivalency diploma to home school. "Perhaps the biggest and most legitimate concern about home schooling is making certain that children are being taught by a 'qualified adult'...the term qualified is not referring to teacher licensure but rather the ability to 'present instruction to children in a coherent and skillful manner'" (Simmons 1994, 47). Certainly most parents who home school are well meaning and highly motivated, but they may lack the ability and professional preparation that they need to provide effective instruction. Not everyone can teach.

Regarding instruction, several other issues are relevant and worth addressing. One concern is that few individuals have the self-discipline to push aside interruptions during the typical day. The baby crying, the phone ringing, or the siblings fighting can all cause an academic program to suffer. Certainly it can be argued "that learning never stops and that the interruptions themselves can provide learning opportunities, but the fact remains that certain clearly defined learning tasks demand intense concentration and unbroken periods of study" (Simmons 1994, 47–48).

Another concern is the scope and depth of knowledge required in some content areas as home school children move into the secondary level. Are parents able to teach students higher levels of math, complex biological terms, or an in-depth analysis of American history? Although resources such as tapes and books can aid instruction (again, finances may play a role), most students need a teacher who has expertise in the subject to provide the appropriate level of instruction or to deal with the complexities of particular academic areas. It is difficult to accurately assess, diagnose, and determine the curriculum and instruction that would most appropriately meet the needs of a particular child—even when it is the teacher's own child.

Finally, many of the skills that are important for successful students, employees, and professionals are not fully developed at home. For example, the home school curriculum does not always emphasize organizational skills, time management, intense study habits, or the ability to work with others. For instance, the same flexibility that enables home schools to provide extra time for students to fully develop and write a report can prove problematic if students neglect to develop skills needed to manage time and meet deadlines.

Conclusion

Currently, home schooling's popularity is rapidly increasing, and the movement is beginning to play a significant role in the education of America's children. This alternative form of education has gained legitimacy because of its proven effectiveness and success in both academic and social areas. However, there are no simple yes-or-no answers to the many complex questions that home schooling generates. Advocates and critics view education and related issues from very different perspectives, and each perspective sheds new light and insight on these issues.

Nevertheless, most of us can agree that all forms of education contain various strengths and weaknesses. The bottom line is that the education of children in the United States should primarily be the responsibility of the parents. Parents have the right to determine what form of schooling best meets the needs of their children. More important, the expectation that public education should adequately serve the needs of children from broad and diverse backgrounds should be dismissed. Public schools do not, cannot, and probably should not be expected to meet the needs of every child in the community. Instead, parents, schools, and the community need to work together to educate all children, no matter what form of education parents choose. Instead of constantly comparing and contrasting public and home schools, we need to learn from one another and then use this information to improve the learning experiences of all children.

Key words: home schooling, strengths, limitations, families, education

REFERENCES

Ballman, R. E. 1987. *The how and why of home schooling.* Westchester, IL: Crossway Books.
Knowles, J. G. 1988. Introduction: The context of home schooling in the United States. *Education and Urban Society* 21(1): 5–15.
Lines, P. M. 1998. *Homeschoolers: Estimating numbers and growth.* Washington, DC: U.S. Department of Education, Office of Educational Research and Improvement, National Institute on Student Achievement, Curriculum, and Assessment.
Marchant, G., and S. MacDonald. 1994. Home schooling parents: An analysis of choices. *People and Education* 2 (1): 65–82.
Mayberry, M. 1987. The 1987–1988 Oregon Home School Survey: An overview of findings. *Home School Researcher* 4 (1): 1–9.
Moore, R. S. 1982. Research and common sense: Therapies for our home and schools. *Teachers College Record* 84 (2): 355–77.
Nazareno, A. 1999. Home schools effective, group says after study. *Miami Herald*, 24 March.
Nelsen, M. B. 1998. Beyond the stereotypes: Home schooling as a legitimate educational alternative. *The High School Magazine* 6 (2): 32–37.
Ray, B. 1989. Home schools: A synthesis of research on characteristics and learner outcomes, *Education and Urban Society* 21 (1): 16–31.
——. 1991. *Home education in North Dakota: Family characteristics and student achievement.* Salem, OR: National Home Education Research Institute.
——. 1997. Home education across the United States. *Home School Court Project* 13 (3).
——. 1999. *Home schooling on the threshold: A survey of research at the dawn of the new millennium.* Salem, OR: National Home Education Research Institute.
Simmons, B. J. 1994. Classroom at home. *American School Board Journal* 181 (2): 47–49.
Taylor, J. W. 1986. Self-concept in home-schooling children. Ph.D. diss., Andrews University, Berrien Springs, MI.
Van Galen, J. A. 1988. Ideology, curriculum and pedagogy in home education. *Education and Urban Society* 21(1): 52–68.
Wahisi, T. T. 1995. Making the grade: Black families see the benefits in home schooling. *Crisis* 102 (7): 14–15.

Michael H. Romanowski is an associate professor in the Center for Teacher Education at Ohio Northern University in Ada, Ohio.

From *The Clearing House,* November/December 2001, pp. 79-83. Reprinted with permission of the Helen Dwight Reid Educational Foundation. Published by Heldref Publications, 1319 Eighteenth St., NW, Washington, DC 20037-1802. © 2001.

The Other Marriage War

There's one group that is pursuing legal union—and its kids need the stability.

BY E. J. GRAFF

IMAGINE WAKING UP ONE MORNING TO THE NEWS THAT because of a recent court decision, you may no longer be your child's legal parent. Forget all those times you've read *Goodnight Moon*, those long nights you spent in a steam-filled bathroom trying to keep your sick child breathing. In the eyes of the law, you may suddenly be just a kind stranger. No emergency room, insurance plan, schoolteacher, tax man, or judge will count you as essential to your child.

Sound like one of Kafka's nightmares? It's what happened to thousands of California parents last October, when a San Diego court struck down the procedure by which, for 15 years, lesbian co-mothers—parents who helped to imagine, create, feed, clothe, and raise a child, but who didn't give birth—had legally adopted their children. Many California lawyers' phones rang nonstop until the decision was erased from the books while it went up on appeal.

Welcome to the world of lesbian and gay parents, where you can be a parent one day and not the next; in one state but not another; when you're straight but not when you're gay. At any moment, your heterosexual ex might find a judge willing to yank the kids after you come out. Or you might hear your parental fitness debated by strangers—on radio, on TV, and in newspapers—using language that makes your children wake up at night from dreams that the government has taken you away.

Yes, the climate for lesbian and gay parents has improved dramatically in the past 20 years. There can't be an American left who hasn't heard about Heather and her two mommies. And though the children's book by that name kicked off an antigay uproar in the early 1990s, by the end of the decade the mainstream media were covering Melissa Etheridge and Julie Cypher's two babies without a blink (except, perhaps, at the unfortunate David Crosby connection). The lesbian baby boom began in Boston and San Francisco in the mid-1980s. In both cities, after mainstream doctors refused to offer donor insemination (DI) services to unmarried women, lesbians started their own sperm banks and DI clinics. Since then,

two-mom families have popped up everywhere from Maine to Utah, from Alaska to Florida. In smaller numbers, gay dads have followed, taking in foster children, hiring surrogates, or adopting (as individuals, if necessary) whenever they could find birth moms, local authorities, or judges who'd help. And that's only the latest incarnation of gay and lesbian parenting. Lesbians and gay men have long become parents the conventional way: through heterosexual marriage.

But law is lagging badly behind this social transformation. Although many *Prospect* readers may know two-mom or two-dad families, they probably do not know about the daily legal insecurity, the extra level of anxiety and effort, and the occasional shocking injustices those families face. Society is still profoundly ambivalent about lesbians and gay men—and about the unfamiliar, sometimes queasy-making idea of queers raising kids. As a result, unpredictable legal decisions about lesbian and gay parents too often leave their children in limbo.

THE KIDS ARE ALL RIGHT

Is there any reason to worry about how these kids are raised? No. More than 20 studies have been done on about 300 children of lesbians and gay men. Some compare children of divorced lesbian moms or gay dads with children of divorced heterosexual moms or dads; others compare two-mom families with mom-and-pop families that used the same DI clinic. The results are quite clear: Children of lesbian or gay parents turn out just fine on every conceivable measure of emotional and social development: attachment, self-esteem, moral judgment, behavior, intelligence, likability, popularity, gender identity, family warmth, and all sorts of obscure psychological concepts. Whatever the scale, children with lesbian or gay parents and children with heterosexual parents turn out equally well—and grow up to be heterosexual in the same overwhelming proportions.

Not surprisingly, antigay pundits challenge this conclusion. Brigham Young University law professor Lynn Wardle and his followers argue that the population samples in these studies have been exceedingly small, haven't been "randomly" chosen, and don't accurately represent lesbian and gay parents as a whole. All these charges are accurate, as far as they go. But the conclusion drawn by Wardle and company—that the results are therefore meaningless—is not. Here's the problem: No one can ever get a "random" sample of lesbians or gay men, much less of lesbian or gay parents, so long as there's any stigma to being gay—and any realistic fear that the children might be taken away. For the most part, researchers have had to make do with samples of lesbian or gay parents who will consent to being studied and match them with groups of heterosexual parents. Does that limitation invalidate these studies? Maybe it would if results varied dramatically, but because they are remarkably consistent, the vast majority of social scientists and physicians accept them. Social science deals with people, not elements on the periodic table. Like doctors, they must always make informed decisions based on the best and latest evidence.

That's why organizations such as the American Psychological Association, the National Association of Social Workers, the American Academy of Child and Adolescent Psychiatry, and the American Counseling Association have released statements in support of lesbian and gay parents. This February, for instance, the American Academy of Pediatrics came out with a report that had been vetted by an unprecedented number of committees and had taken four years to wend its way toward the academy's full approval. Its conclusion: "No data have pointed to any risk to children as a result of growing up in a family with one or more gay parents." Nor, the AAP found, is parents' sexual orientation an important variable in how kids turn out.

So what is? If basics like food, shelter, clothing, and health care are covered, what matters to kids is the happiness and satisfaction of the parents. Are the parents happily mated and content with the way household responsibilities are shared? Or are they miserable and sniping at each other, whether together or separated? You can guess which type of household will produce happier and more confident kids. Harmony helps children; conflict and disruption hurt. Despite the yammering of the conservative marriage movement, *how* households are run matters more than *who* (read: which sex or sexual orientation) runs them.

There's another right-wing line of challenge to these studies: shouting about statistical blips. Occasionally, intriguing differences do show up between the children of lesbian moms and those of heterosexual moms. Here, conservatives want it both ways: They want to throw out the common findings because of methodological suspicions while making a big deal about onetime results. But in every case, these variations are differences, not deficits. For instance, in one study of kids with divorced moms, the lesbians' daughters were more comfortable than the heterosexual women's daughters in "rough-and-tumble" play, more likely to play with trucks and guns—although

the sons were no more likely to play with tea sets or Barbies. More controversially, a British study found that more of the divorced lesbians' children said that they had imagined or tried a same-sex romance; but as adults, they still called themselves straight or gay in the same proportions as the straight moms' kids. Is it good, bad, or neutral that lesbians might raise their children to feel free to try out all sides of themselves in gender and sexuality? Or are these results too small to be generalized? The answers depend on your political point of view. And in a pluralist society, that must be taken as an argument for freedom of choice in child-rearing.

JUDGE NOT

So what do these children need from society? The same thing all children need: clear and enforceable ties to their parents. Child psychologist Anna Freud once wrote that children "can handle almost anything better than instability." Not coincidentally, trying to shore up a family's stability is the goal of much marriage-and-family law.

Except if your parents are gay. Think about that shocking red-and-blue presidential-election map we saw in November 2000. If a map were to be drawn of the legal situation for lesbian and gay parents, it would look kaleidoscopic by comparison, with the colors constantly shifting. The answers to some questions may be predictable by geography. On others, even in the supposedly liberal states, how well you're treated depends on your judge.

For instance, did you think that divorced lesbians or gay men, if reasonably stable, could count on seeing their kids? Think again. Says Kate Kendell, executive director of the National Center for Lesbian Rights, "The good news is that more than half the states have good decisional case law that sexual orientation in and of itself is not a bar to custody." The bad news is that a lot of states don't. This February, Alabama's supreme court decided 9-0 that children are better off with a violent father than with a kind and reliable lesbian mom. As chief justice, Roy Moore (the judge who posted the Decalogue in his courtroom) wrote the opinion that overruled a lower court that had sent the kids to their mom. Here's an excerpt from his opinion:

> The common law designates homosexuality as an inherent evil, and if a person openly engages in such a practice, that fact alone would render him or her an unfit parent. Homosexual conduct is, and has been, considered abhorrent, immoral, detestable, a crime against nature, and a violation of the laws of nature and of nature's God.

Even when a state's antisodomy laws are not so explicitly invoked, judicial recoil can be obvious. A judge in Mississippi decided that a 19-year-old who left her violent husband and came out as a lesbian can see her infant only once a week, between 8:00 A.M. and 9:00 A.M. on Sundays at the local McDonald's, supervised by the ex.

Things are even iffier for two-mom families than for divorced parents who come out. Most judges just don't know what to do with these families. Adoption laws, written by state legislatures in the late nineteenth century, cover two situations: a couple adopting an orphan or a remarried parent who wants legally to link the child to the stepparent. A mother can add a father; a father can add a mother. But can a mother add *another* mother? Most judges say no, with attitudes ranging from uncertainty to outright antagonism; one Illinois judge, Susan McDunn, went so far as to appoint the Family Research Council as *guardian ad litem* for the children. Judges in up to half the states have allowed what's called "second-parent adoption," but in only seven states and the District of Columbia is this a statewide policy. Elsewhere, you're playing roulette: In Michigan, for instance, an Ann Arbor judge might grant one, while a Grand Rapids judge might say no. And advocates try not to appeal—because of the risk that the appeals court might flatly rule out second-parent adoptions, as has happened in the Wisconsin supreme court and in five other states' appellate courts (with cases in California, Nebraska, and Pennsylvania now on appeal to their top courts).

No biggie, some people think: Just write a will and some health care proxies, appoint a guardian, and you're all set. It's not that simple. The biomom better be the breadwinner, because the co-mom won't be able to list the child on her taxes or health insurance; nor can she pass on her Social Security benefits or pension. If the biomom dies, the biological grandparents can challenge the co-mom's guardianship and legally kidnap the child. And if the moms break up, cross your fingers for that child.

Many—one hopes most—divorcing couples put aside their anger to do what's best for their children. Not everyone does. We all know how hideous people can be when fighting over custody: They play dirty, cheat, lie, even kidnap, always persuading themselves that they're doing it for the kids. When lesbian couples have such no-holds-barred breakups, a spiteful biomom can pull legal rank. If the facts won't let her eviscerate her ex's right to custody or visitation, she may insist that the co-mom was never a parent at all, but just a babysitter, a visitor, a pretender, a stalker. (Because gay men don't give birth, they more often start out on an equal legal footing and can't use this trick.) A biomom and her attorney may exploit a judge's discomfort with homosexuality or cite the state's Defense of Marriage Act to blowtorch any legal link between the co-mom and the child. And if the biomom wins, it leaves tortuous and cruel case law on the state's books that can hurt other lesbian and gay families for decades.

These cases can be heartbreaking. There's the video of the moms' wedding, there's the co-mom's last name as the child's middle name, there's the Olan Mills picture of the three together—and there's the biomom in court saying, "Keep that dyke away from my child." How gratuitously nasty—and legally dangerous—can it be? After

getting a legal second-parent adoption in Illinois, one couple moved to Florida to take care of the biomom's dying mother. There the pair broke up. Florida has the dubious distinction of hosting the nation's most draconian ban on adoptions by lesbians and gay men. And so in court, the biomom is now arguing that Florida should refuse to recognize her ex's "foreign" adoption of the child. If this biomom wins, every other two-mom or two-dad family will have to think thrice about visiting Key West or Disney World: What if a Florida emergency room or police station refused to recognize their adoption?

Similar cases are percolating in Nebraska and North Carolina. If these biomoms win, the map of the United States could become a checkerboard of states where two-mom and two-dad families don't dare travel. Can you imagine having your parenthood dissolve when you hit the interstate? You might never leave home again.

"This is a level of damage," says Kendell of the National Center for Lesbian Rights, "that Jerry Falwell and Pat Robertson and Lou Sheldon and all their ilk can only dream of."

COHERENT LAWS AND PUBLIC POLICIES ARE DESPERATELY needed to help gay and lesbian parents order their families' lives. Fortunately, history's heading in the right direction. More and more state courts are coming up with guidelines that refuse to let a biomom shut out her ex, or a co-mom skip out on child support, if the pair together planned for and reared their child. The public and the media are sympathetic. Most policy makers are open to persuasion, understanding that even if they wouldn't want to be gay themselves, kids whose parents are gay deserve the most security possible.

Unfortunately, lesbian-gay-bisexual-transgender advocacy organizations can't change the legal landscape alone. Both in the courts and in public opinion, gay folks are too often cast as biased, the mirror image of the radical right. As a result, liberals and progressives—especially heterosexuals—can make an enormous difference in the lives of these families.

"Children who are born to or adopted by one member of a same-sex couple deserve the security of two legally recognized parents," reads the February report from the American Academy of Pediatrics. Originally written to be an amicus brief for co-moms or co-dads trying to sway a judge into waving the parent-making wand, the AAP report did much more: It gave editorial writers and talk shows across the country an excuse to agree. And aside from *The Washington Times* and press-release attacks from the usual suspects, agree they did, in an astonishing array of news outlets ranging from local radio shows to *USA Today* to *The Columbus Dispatch*.

So what, besides social tolerance, should the forces of good be working for? Policies and laws that tie these kids firmly to their real, daily parents. These children need strong statutes that let co-moms and co-dads adopt—

preferably without the intrusive home study, the thousands of dollars in legal fees, and the reference letters from colleagues and friends that are now required. They need decisive guidelines saying that an adoption in one state is an adoption in every state. And they need marriage rights for their parents. Much of marriage law is designed to help spouses rear families, letting them make a single shelter from their combined incomes, assets, benefits, pensions, habits, strengths, weaknesses, and knowledge. Today, when a heterosexual married couple uses DI, the man is automatically the legal father (as long as he has consented in writing) without having to adopt; if any marriage (or even some lesser system of recognition, like civil unions or registered partnership) were possible, the same could and should be true for lesbians.

By taking up this banner, liberals and progressives can prove that they have a practical commitment to real families and real children. As an Ontario judge wrote in 1995: "When one reflects on the seemingly limitless parade of neglected, abandoned and abused children who appear before our courts in protection cases daily, all of whom have been in the care of heterosexual parents in a 'traditional' family structure, the suggestion that it might not *ever* be in the best interests of these children to be raised by loving, caring, and committed parents who might happen to be lesbian or gay, is nothing short of ludicrous."

E.J. GRAFF, *the author of* What Is Marriage For? The Strange Social History of Our Most Intimate Institution, *is a visiting researcher at Brandeis University's Women's Studies Research Center and a contributing editor at the* Prospect.

Tales of Suburban High

Kay S. Hymowitz

WHEN AMERICANS think about public education, they tend to see a stark divide. On the one hand, there are the failed school systems of our big cities, blackboard jungles where drugs abound, gangs rule the hallways, and dropouts outnumber the barely literate graduates. On the other hand, there are the shining, achievement-oriented public schools of the suburbs, the institutions that have led so many middle-class parents to flee New York City for Westchester or Chicago for Highland Park. In these greener pastures, public education seems to be working fine: students do not have to pass through metal detectors each morning, most of them go on to college, and their parents (according to opinion surveys) are basically content.

The problem with this picture, as we have learned in recent decades, is that, despite their obvious advantages, all is far from well in suburban schools. In 1983, the National Commission on Excellence in Education cautioned that, across the country, SAT scores were flat, and students were falling behind their peers in other nations. College professors began to gripe about incoming students who, even with sterling records in high school, had never heard of the Re-

naissance, or thought Winston Churchill was a Civil War general.

Compounding these pedagogic worries have been concerns about the often poisonous social and moral environment of the high schools in more prosperous communities. After two teenagers turned Columbine High School in Colorado into a killing field in 1999, just about every suburban district in the country began fretting about potential violence. Many launched curriculums to combat sexual harassment, to root out homophobia, to discourage cattiness among girls, and, of course, to stop bullying among boys, the supposed root cause of the massacre at Columbine. More recently, cheating has become an issue, especially with the temptations posed by the Internet. In one much-publicized scandal, a biology teacher at a high school in suburban Kansas City discovered that 28 of her students had downloaded whole sections of their term papers. But when the teacher tried to fail the offenders, the superintendent and parents refused to back her up, apparently seeing nothing remarkable in the transgression. As one student told the chastened teacher, "We won."

That matters are as bad as these instances suggest is amply confirmed by two new books that take us inside the

classrooms of today's suburban high school: Elinor Burkett's *Another Planet: A Year in the Life of a Suburban High School** and Denise Clark Pope's *Doing School: How We Are Creating a Generation of Stressed-Out, Materialistic, and Miseducated Students.†* Burkett, an astute journalist with many previous books to her name, introduces us to Prior Lake High School outside Minneapolis, an overwhelmingly white, middle-class school that sends its better graduates to state universities. The pseudonymous Faircrest High School described by Pope, a lecturer at Stanford's School of Education, is located in a "wealthy California suburb," and is a more diverse institution. Though a third of its students are lower-income Hispanics, Filipinos, or blacks, it also boasts more National Merit scholars than Prior Lake, and more Ivy League aspirants.

For all their differences, both institutions are considered "good" schools. They feature plenty of Advanced Placement (AP) courses, college-hungry kids, and attentive teachers, and their facilities are so fine that one parent in Burkett's account, observing plans for a new school complete with archery and golf ranges, quipped that it looked more like a sports-entertainment complex. The question is: what exactly are these "good" schools good *at*?

AN INSTRUCTIVE place to start is with the teachers. In dress, demeanor, and interests, many of the pedagogues at Prior Lake High School can hardly be distinguished from the hormonal crew they are supposed to be educating. There is the math teacher who brags to his students that he has read only two books in his life, one about highschool football and the other about Elvis Presley. There is the English teacher, with bleached hair and a "Tommy" shirt (because "kids love brand names"), who performs card tricks for his students and regales them with stories about his lost career as a basketball player. And there is the memorable Sandra Sterge, an English teacher—I think—who makes constant sexual innuendos in class, calling attractive male students "hotties" and joking about spending the weekend with them at the Day's Inn.

I say I *think* Sandra Sterge is an English teacher, but it is hard to tell. She sees her role as making sure students "are happy and feel like they belong," which seems to boil down to keeping them entertained. We do not see this former beauty queen instructing students in grammar, essay-writing, or literature—the subjects traditionally associated with her profession. Instead Burkett shows her to us teaching public speaking with a "lip-sync unit," an exercise in which students rap songs with lyrics such as "I like big butts and I cannot lie" and "I'm long and I'm strong and I'm down to get the friction on."

Nor is Sterge alone at Prior Lake in using popular culture as a tool for... well, it is unclear for what. During study hall, students watch the melodramatic psychobabble of *The Maury Show*. The English department insists that students study *The Scarlet Letter*—the movie, not the book. Other teachers show educational fare like the cross-dressing Dustin Hoffman in *Tootsie*.

Keeping students properly diverted is also a key part of the program at Faircrest High in California. Especially striking is Pope's depiction of American-history classes. In one of them, the teacher as-

signs only two projects for the entire semester, so that the students can, in her words, focus "in-depth" and become "experts." As a practical matter, this means that aside from watching a few videos about World War II, they spend most of their time listening to each other's "brief, disconnected reports on... topics as varied as the history of the automobile or the life of Lucille Ball." Another history teacher begins a unit on the 1960's by dressing in a tie-dyed shirt and lighting incense.

As for Faircrest's elite AP course in American history, its chief distinction seems to be higher production values. Eve Lin (as Pope calls one of the school's star students) worked for 250 hours on her part of an "intensive" group research project. Pope describes the culmination of this effort, a presentation in which the members of the group, wearing NASA name tags and T-shirts, escort their classmates into a darkened room decorated with twinkling stars. Through several scene and costume changes, they take the class on makeshift rockets, show film clips about space travel, and, using cardboard cones and Styrofoam cups, demonstrate how the Apollo 13 crew managed to fix their damaged spacecraft—all of this while the music from *Star Wars* blasts in the background. The teacher pronounces the show "magnificent" and gives the group an A+.

Not all the teachers at Prior Lake and Faircrest confuse education with entertainment. Some are serious and demanding, and they attract the most motivated students. But almost all of these exceptional teachers seem to be tired soldiers from a different era, readying themselves for retirement. One math teacher at Prior Lake, a veteran of 27 years, drives her calculus students so hard that they get perfect scores on the AP test at twice the national rate. While most students at the school do a total of two or three hours of homework a week, hers do more than that for her class alone.

But with no school-wide policies on matters like tardiness, plagiarism, and grading, even the most conscientious teachers find themselves without support, and sorely tempted to compromise their standards. Sick of excuses for unfinished homework, they hand out work-

sheets to be completed in class and hold special study groups before each test, resigned to the fact that their students will cram the past month's assignments into a single all-nighter. The hard-driving calculus teacher at Prior Lake compares her school to East Berlin before the wall fell, a place where "nobody did much work because rewards bore little relationship to merit."

WHAT MAY be the saddest part of these accounts is that the students at Prior Lake and Faircrest are not the least bit engaged by the "edutainment" that increasingly dominates their curriculum. To the contrary, they are often contemptuous of their chummy, "with-it" teachers. Eve Lin walks away from the NASA demonstration knowing that her A+ does not add up to much. "All that work for a one-hour performance.... I think people really underestimate what students can do." Others are disgusted by the condescension they constantly experience in the classroom. "She thinks she redefines cool," says one student of Sandra Sterge, the lip-sync queen. "I'm embarrassed for her. Can't she behave like an adult?"

Still, unlike their inner-city peers, the vast majority of these middle-class kids accept their tiresome four years as fate, a necessary prelude to college, which is itself a necessary prelude to a good paycheck. They do not play hooky, threaten teachers, or get into knife fights. Rather, they size up the situation and treat high school like a game, knowing what it takes to win. As one girl tells Burkett, "You can get all A's without learning anything."

This is what Pope means by "doing school," and it takes many forms. Students sign up for courses that include a lot of group projects and then befriend smarter, more conscientious classmates who will perform most of the work. They try to be "interactive," as they sometimes put it, asking a question every few minutes to impress the teacher even as they sit at their desks doing homework for the next class. They whine that a test was too hard, even—or especially—if they know it was not. They try to win over teachers by asking how their training for the marathon is going or whether they enjoyed a weekend date. "I have no interest in the personal lives of the teachers," one girl says of the young man who teaches her government course, "but it's a game, and Mr. Carr is losing."

Whenever possible, they also pick teachers who are reputed to be easy graders or who assign journals or "creative writing" instead of research papers or tests. One of the five "ideal students" whom Pope follows in her book chooses to write her English report on Cesar Chavez—not for reasons of political commitment but because she has saved an A paper about him that she wrote in middle school. They use Cliffs Notes and log onto sparknotes.com to get summaries of the books they are supposed to read, and if such resources do not provide enough help, they cheat.

In all of this, moreover, the students are actively aided and abetted by their parents. In an interview with the *Atlantic Monthly*, Burkett said that nothing shocked her more about Prior Lake than the attitude of the parents, who see themselves not as the allies of the teachers and administrators but as their children's agents. If a teacher is too academically demanding, they lobby to get their child transferred to another class. If junior's grades flag, they demand extra-credit work to let him bring them up. And they gripe: "Why isn't my child getting a higher grade?" "My son never got a B before." As Burkett writes of Prior Lake, "I didn't meet one teacher there demoralized by the low pay. But I met dozens of teachers demoralized by abusive parents who were not willing to let them do their jobs by holding kids to higher standards or by making them work."

Their authority undermined at every turn—not least by their own behavior—teachers find that order in their classrooms is pretty much dependent on adolescent whim. After being called to task for runaway talking, one girl at Prior Lake protests, "It's not my fault, I have ADHD [Attention Deficit Hyperactivity Disorder]." A special-ed student whose disability gives him the right to copies of a teacher's lecture notes feels free to sleep during class. At Faircrest, when several students pull down their pants and moon their classmates, a teacher can do nothing more than tell them to "cut it out."

One of Pope's subjects, a talented but underchallenged student named Michelle, finds herself paired for a project with a class slacker who failed the last test and had not done the reading since the fall, when she lost her textbook. Just as Michelle begins their joint presentation, her partner saunters out of the classroom to go to the bathroom. Michelle presents the material as her classmates take notes. "Slow down!" they yell. "Shit, you weren't supposed to write a book!" The teacher pleads, "Be nice" and "No swearing," but no one listens.

IN HER inability to make sense of these chaotic scenes, Denise Clark Pope unwittingly illustrates how little our self-styled education experts have to tell us about the problems of suburban schools. She views Faircrest through the prism of ed-school cliché. Such schools, she argues, are too focused on achievement and competition, and give short shrift to cooperative learning—even as her examples demonstrate that the latter approach simply leaves the better students to carry the weaker ones. She also suggests, contradictorily, that they do not provide enough opportunities for individualized learning—even as Faircrest students choose paper or research topics that let them get away with as little original work as possible.

Pope is right to object to the cynicism of the game the schools ask their students to play, but she offers no vision of what an educated person should look like. Her chief concern is that young people become "passionately committed" to learning; *what* they learn seems to be a matter of indifference. As she sees it, a Faircrest student who adores her Mexican dance class and another who is deeply involved in his community-service project are models of educational excellence.

Elinor Burkett, who comes to her subject with fewer preconceptions and more curiosity, provides a fresher picture of the suburban high school. But she is no more able than Pope to explain what she has so astutely observed. Indeed, as their two accounts make clear, *none* of the usual suspects takes us very far in assigning blame for the stubborn mediocrity of schools like Prior Lake and Faircrest.

Multiculturalism certainly does not play much of a role; Burkett notes that most of the assigned books are by white males. Nor are the educators at these schools sophisticated enough to have been corrupted by postmodernism—most have not heard of Faulkner, much less Foucault. Burkett makes a strong case for the woeful influence of the religion of self-esteem, but this too seems insufficient. Indulgent as they may be at times, teachers and parents alike do set real goals for the students. At both schools, caffeine-driven, sleep-deprived teenagers have date books crammed with lab-report assignments, church activities, tennis practice, theater and band rehearsals, student-council meetings, and part-time jobs. Finally, the schools impose a measure of order and discipline. Administrators search students' cars, test them for drugs, send them home for wearing T-shirts with provocative messages, and even take them to task for hanging out with the wrong people.

Why, then, do so many middle-class Americans now act as if education is nothing more than a "game"? The ultimate culprits no doubt lie deep in our national character, and most of all in our relentless pragmatism, which here expresses itself in the inability of a single adult in this educational universe to offer a broader view. Along with any serious commitment to subjects like English and history, the idea of education as a way to sharpen mental discipline, to cultivate higher cultural interests, or to teach civic principles has simply disappeared. The course offerings at Prior Lake include journalism, theater, stress management, and "death education" (which includes field trips to a cemetery and an undertaker), and educators now refer to activities like student council and football as "co-curricular" rather than "extra-curricular."

WHEN EVERYONE accepts that education is simply a means to acquire a McMansion and an SUV, the distinction between reading a classic novel and producing an entertaining video dissolves, especially if both efforts are rewarded with a coveted A. When students see teachers standing in front of them lighting incense or nodding approvingly during student presentations about *I Love Lucy*, it is perfectly understandable if they conclude that these adults have nothing serious to offer them, and are undeserving of their respect.

In a discussion of Thomas Jefferson during an honors class at Prior Lake, students demand, "How is this relevant to my life?" When the subject is the Electoral College, they complain, "Why do we have to learn this?" To some extent, this is just typical adolescent provocation. But the truth is, their teacher, an amiable but vapid young man whose literary taste has never evolved beyond John Grisham, does not have the slightest idea how to answer them—how to explain, that is, the importance of some-

thing like citizenship, which does not impinge directly on their immediate wants and needs.

But teenagers are not simply looking to be amused and flattered. At the end of her book, Burkett is surprised to run into one class goof-off who, after graduation, had enlisted in the Marines. He finished basic training with a perfect score on his final exam. "In boot camp," he tells her, "they kick your butt if you don't try your hardest."

Most graduates of our suburban high schools must wait until after graduation—if then—to experience satisfaction of this sort. The education they receive during the decisive years of adolescence not only fails to spark their intellectual and moral imaginations, it hardly even

tries. Instead it aims to produce students like Eric, a top academic achiever at Prior Lake, highly regarded by his teachers. "My belief is that every part of life is a game," he tells Burkett. "The question is: what can I get away with before it's a problem."

---

* HarperCollins, 336 pp., $26.00.

†Yale University Press, 240 pp., $24.95.

KAY S. HYMOWITZ *is a contributing editor of* City Journal *and the author of* Ready or Not: What Happens When We Treat Children as Small Adults.

Learning with Jazz

The rich rhythms and stories in music ignite kids to read, write, sing, and soar!

By Lucille Renwick

Walk through the halls of Washington Rose Elementary School in Long Island, New York, and you find yourself enveloped by the sights and sounds of jazz. Pictures of famous jazz artists and time lines chronicling the evolution of jazz adorn the walls. The strains of jazz flow from Faye Nelson's second-grade classroom, where it's played from the moment the students walk in the door until they leave at the end of the day.

Teachers at Washington Rose, along with others in two Pemberville, Ohio, elementary schools, and in a Harrisburg, Pennsylvania-area elementary school, are proving that teaching jazz music and its history is no longer limited to the music curriculum. Standards-based lessons in language arts, social studies, and even science can spring from this unique American music form.

The use of jazz in each of the three schools began with a similar two-part goal: to enrich standard curricula and to raise students' understanding and appreciation of a music form widely recognized for its rich cultural heritage rooted in the African-American experience. Each found success in various ways: student confidence soared; student interest increased; and, in some cases, student achievement improved. Many of the teachers noted an added benefit—their students came to appreciate the influence of jazz on the music they listen to, such as pop, rock, and hip-hop.

In each school, teachers presented lessons focusing on different jazz artists and/or different types of jazz music—blues, bebop, swing, Dixieland, New Orleans jazz. They matched a book about a jazz musician with that artist's music to give their students a multisensory experience with the artist and his work. The teachers usually followed these lessons with activities such as theatrical performances and art projects.

"The children are challenged in so many different ways... but they're not intimidated by the work because they're so excited," said Paulette Taylor, a first grade teacher at Washington Rose.

Geographical Jazz

Students at Washington Rose Elementary have been studying jazz and its origins for the past three years as part of a pilot program called "Jazz Sampler." The "Jazz Sampler" project is a joint venture between Washington Rose Elementary and a Long Island-based non-profit organization called "Friends of the Arts." The program was developed to provide teachers with art- and literacy-based activities that meet New York State standards, and which they could incorporate into their lessons as they saw fit. It was also an effort to expose the predominantly African-American student body to another part of black history.

Each year of the project has focused on a different type of jazz; this year it is Latin Jazz. The project stresses literacy, but has also focused on social studies, geography, and science. For example, during a recent social studies lesson, Nelson's second graders learned how, during slavery, African drums were brought from Africa to many Caribbean and Latin American countries. Slaves played the drums to send messages. The drums remained an important part of the culture after slavery ended and, over time, influenced the music of the region. Today, drums are widely used throughout much of Latin music, including Latin jazz music. (Just try to imagine Desi Arnaz without his famous conga drums!)

Nelson builds on what students have learned by using the story of the drums in a geography lesson. On a world map, she has students trace the trail of the drums from Africa to the various Caribbean and Latin American countries. Then, covering the names of the countries on the map, Nelson hands each student a photocopy of the outlines of the countries and asks them to name as many as they can. Students craft stories about the country they would go to if they were a drum, and draw pictures of what their drums might look like.

"These lessons have helped them explore history in a way that really excites them and hooks them in," says Nelson. "Sometimes they even do more than I ask them because they're so intrigued with what they're learning."

Jazzed-Up Reading

Kathleen Hahn, a Title One reading teacher of first through fourth graders in Pemberville, Ohio, incorporated her own love of jazz into an annual reading week at two elementary schools.

"I thought it would be a lot of fun to listen to jazz, to read about jazz, and [to] learn about Mardi Gras," says Hahn. "I thought the children would love it."

To prepare for the week, Hahn scoured the jazz sections of bookstores, finding dozens of helpful children's and informational books. (See book list next page.) She wrote a letter asking parents to sign a list of tasks children promised to complete, such as reading a certain book or finishing a research project. Kids received a strand of Mardi Gras beads for completing assignments.

For several mornings before the reading week, Hahn and her colleagues played 15 minutes of jazz over the school's loudspeaker so students could develop an ear for it. During the week, teachers read picture books about a particular artist and played his or her music. Then, teachers showed snippets from videos on the artist and followed with a writing or comprehension lesson.

A highlight of the week was a musical students performed on the history of jazz, dressing as such notable figures as Billie Holliday, Bessie Smith, Charlie Parker, and Duke Ellington. After the perfor-

Jazz Activities

1. Read this...

Duke Ellington: The Piano Prince and His Orchestra By Andrea Davis Pinkney

2. Listen to this...

CD of Duke Ellington's Greatest Hits

3. Then try these activities...

• Duke Ellington was a composer. Discuss with your students the definition of a *composition* and what a composer does. Compare and contrast how Ellington might compose a piece of music to how students compose an essay.

• Duke Ellington earned his childhood nickname "Duke" because he always acted like a gentleman. Other words used to describe him include: *handsome, charming, refined, self-confident, graceful, polished, royal, sophisticated.* Ask students to define these words and the list other words that describe a gentleman.

• Read excerpts of *Duke Ellington* to find similes and metaphors. Some examples: "Duke's Creole Love Call was spicier than a pot of jambalaya." Encourage students to write their own similes and metaphors based on Ellington's music.

mance, each student wrote a story about the musician they portrayed.

At the end of the week, "a lot of kids had a real interest in jazz that they never had before," said Hahn. "I think they learned to appreciate a different kind of music, and that jazz really is American music. This was a perfect subject to get them enthused about reading and culture and music."

Picture-Book Jazz

Penn State University professors Rachel Grant and Dick Ammon, inspired by their love of jazz music and knowledge of the abundance of children's literature on jazz, developed a five-week-long program for sixth graders near Harrisburg, Pennsylvania. Their focus was on jazz history and how musical rhythms can be found in much of literature, especially in some of the picture books on jazz.

The professors primarily used picture books, which gave the students a quick biography of an artist. Like Hahn, they followed up with the artist's music. Then they discussed the music's structure and its characteristics, and worked with the students on how words and phrases often mimic the sounds of the music.

To introduce be-bop, for example, Grant read aloud *Charlie Parker Played Be Bop*, by Chris Raschka (Orchard Books, 1992), first slowly, showing them each illustration, and then a second time more quickly, reading the words with a beat. Ammon then played Dizzy Gillespie's "A Night in Tunisia" and pointed out how at the end of each measure one could say the words "Be bop," which is how this genre of jazz got its name.

The professors then introduced big band jazz by reading *Duke Ellington*, by Andrea Davis Pinkney (Hyperion, 1998), while they played Ellington's "C Jam Blues" and "Take the A Train." Grant reread the book, this time asking students to write down any words they heard that had a rhythmic quality.

Said Grant: "The children were connected in so many different ways—by the art in the books, the writing style, [and] the music. I think we were able to open their eyes to something they hadn't thought of before... "

Creating Jazz Lessons

You don't have to be an expert in music or a musician to incorporate jazz music into your curriculum. It's as easy as reading a book, listening to related music, and creating a meaningful activity. Over time, your students will gain a deeper understanding of jazz music's role in the culture and history of our country. And they may even come to appreciate the music itself. Like poetry, jazz can weave its way into the heart and mind, influencing the rhythms of our speech and the cadences of our thoughts.

"I never realized how lessons on music could draw students into learning so much," said Nelson of Washington Rose Elementary. "This has helped so many [students] realize so much about different parts of the world, different peoples. They've really grown in so many ways— academically, socially, culturally. It's wonderful to see."

LITERATURE RESOURCES

- *The Jazz of Our Street*, by Fatima Shaik (Dial Books for Young Readers, 1998).
- *If I Only Had a Horn: Young Louis Armstrong*, by Roxane Orgill (Houghton Mifflin, 1997).
- *Mysterious Thelonious*, by Chris Raschka (Orchard Books, 1997).
- *Hip Cat*, by Jonathan London (Chronicle Books, 1996).
- *What a Wonderful World*, by George David Weiss & Bob Thiele (Simon & Schuster, 1995).
- *Mama Don't Allow*, by Thacher Hurd (HarperCollins, 1985).
- *I'm Going to Sing: Black American Spirituals*, by Ashley Bryan (Macmillan, 1982).

HELPFUL WEB SITES

- Thelonious Monk Institute of Jazz **www.jazzinamerica.org**
- PBS Jazz Series Web site **www.pbs.org/jazz/**
- The Smithsonian Institute **www.si.edu/ajazzh/programs.htm**

Lucille Renwick is the Executive Editor of *Instructor*.

From *Instructor*, January/February 2002, pp. 30-31, 79. © 2002 by Scholastic Inc. Reprinted by permission of Scholastic Inc.

Small Class Size
and Its Effects

What does the evidence say about the effects of reducing class size?

Bruce J. Biddle and David C. Berliner

Studies of the impact of class size on student achievement may be more plentiful than for any other issue in education. Although one might expect this huge research effort to yield clear answers about the effects of class size, sharp disagreements about these studies' findings have persisted.

Advocacy groups take opposite stances. The American Federation of Teachers, for example, asserts that

> taken together, these studies… provide compelling evidence that reducing class size, particularly for younger children, will have a positive effect on student achievement. (Murphy & Rosenberg, 1998, p. 3)

The Heritage Foundation, by contrast, claims that "there's no evidence that smaller class sizes alone lead to higher student achievement" (Rees & Johnson, 2000).

Reviewers of class size studies also disagree. One study contends that "large reductions in school class size promise learning benefits of a magnitude commonly believed not within the power of educators to achieve" (Glass, Cahen, Smith, & Filby, 1982, p. 50), whereas another claims that "the… evidence does not offer much reason to expect a systematic effect from overall class size reduction policies" (Hanushek, 1999, p. 158).

That the American Federation of Teachers and the Heritage Foundation sponsor conflicting judgments is easy to understand. But why have reviewers come to such divergent views about the research on class size, and what does the evidence really say?

Early Small Field Experiments

To answer these questions, we must look at several research traditions, beginning with early experiments on class size. Experiments have always been a popular research technique because investigators can assign their subjects randomly to different conditions and then compare the results of those conditions—and this human intervention can appear to provide information about causes and effects. Experiments on class size, however, are nearly always done in field settings—schools—where uncontrolled events can undermine the research and affect results.

In Pursuit of Better Schools: What Research Says

Educational Leadership is pleased to publish the first in a series of research reports. This article is condensed from "Small Classes and Their Effects," a major research synthesis that appears as part of a series supported by the Rockefeller Foundation— *In Pursuit of Better Schools: What Research Says.* The Rockefeller Foundation supports research on major issues facing education today.

Further information about the series and a longer, downloadable version of this research synthesis may be found at http://edpolicyreports.org in early February. Look for more of this series in upcoming issues of *Educational Leadership.*

Small experimental studies on the effects of class size began to appear in the 1920s, and scores of them emerged subsequently. In the 1960s, informal reviews of these efforts generally concluded that differences in class size generated little to no effect. By the late 1970s, however, a more sophisticated research method, meta-analysis, had been invented, which facilitated the statistical assembly of results from small-but-similar studies to estimate effects for the studies' populations. Reviewers quickly applied meta-analysis to results from early experiments in class size (Glass & Smith, 1979; Educational Research Service, 1980; Glass et all, 1982; Hedges & Stock, 1983) and eventually emerged with a consensus that short-term exposure to small classes generates—usually minor—gains in student achievement and that those gains are greater in the early grades, in classrooms with fewer than 20 students, and for students from groups that are traditionally disadvantaged in education.

Most of these early class size experiments, however, had involved small samples, short-term exposures to small classes, only one measure of student success, and a single education context (such as one school or school district). Poor designs had also made results of some studies questionable. Researchers needed to use different strategies to ascertain the effects of long-term exposure to small classes and to assess whether the advantages of early exposure to small classes would generalize to other successes and be sustainable.

Surveys

Survey research has provided evidence on the effects of class size by analyzing naturally occurring differences in schools and classrooms and by asking whether these differences are associated with student outcomes.

Well-designed surveys can offer evidence about the impact of variables that experiments cannot manipulate—such as gender, minority status, and childhood poverty—but survey research cannot easily establish relationships between causes and effects. For example, if a survey examines a sample of schools where average class size varies and discovers that those schools with smaller classes also have higher levels of student achievement, has the survey ascertained that class size generated achievement? Hardly. Those schools with smaller classes might also have had more qualified teachers, better equipment, more up-to-date curriculums, newer school buildings, more students from affluent homes, or a more supportive community environment—factors that may also have helped generate higher levels of achievement. To use survey data to make the case for a causal relation between class size and student outcomes, then, researchers must use statistical processes that control for the competing effects of other variables.

Serious surveys of education achievement in the United States began in the 1960s with the famous Coleman report (Coleman et al., 1966). Written by authors with impressive reputations and released with great fanfare, this massive, federally funded study involved a national sample and took on many issues then facing education. Today, most people remember the report for its startling claim that student achievement is almost totally influenced by the students' families and peers and not by the characteristics of their schools. This claim was widely accepted—indeed, was greeted with dismay by educators and endorsed with enthusiasm by fiscal conservatives—despite flaws in the report's methods that were noted by thoughtful critics.

Since then, researchers have conducted surveys to establish whether differences in school funding or in the reforms that funds can buy—such as small class sizes—are associated with desired education outcomes. Most of these surveys, usually designed by economists, have involved questionable design features and small samples that did not represent the wide range of U.S. schools, classrooms, or students.

In the 1980s, economist Eric Hanushek began to review these flawed studies and to discuss their supposed impli-

cations. Hanushek, committed to the notion that public schools are ineffective and should be replaced by a marketplace of competing private schools, concluded that differences in public school funding are not associated with education outcomes (see Hanushek, 1986, and various publications since).

Other analysts have challenged Hanushek's methods and conclusions on several grounds. Larry Hedges and Rob Greenwald, for example, have pointed out that Hanushek merely counts the number of effects that he believes are statistically significant, but because most of the studies that he reviewed had small samples, he has, of course, found few statistically significant effects. When researchers combine those effects in meta-analyses, however, they find that differences in school funding and the benefits that funds can buy—such as small classes—do, indeed, have an impact (see Hedges, Laine, & Greenwald, 1994, and other publications since).

Other commentators have noted that Hanushek's reviews include many studies that used inappropriate samples or did not employ controls for other school characteristics whose effects might be confused with those of class size. In addition, most of the studies did not examine class size directly but looked instead at student-teacher ratio—that is, the number of students divided by the number of "teachers" reported for a school or school district. Such an approach ignores the actual allocation of students and teachers to classrooms and includes as "teachers" such persons as administrators, nurses, counselors, coaches, specialty teachers, and other professionals who rarely appear in classrooms. Such a ratio does not tell us the number of students actually taught by teachers in classrooms.

Hanushek has not responded well to such criticisms; rather, he has found reasons to quarrel with the details and to continue publishing reviews claiming that small classes have few to no effects. These efforts have allied Hanushek with political conservatives who have extolled his conclusions, complimented his efforts, and asked him to testify in various forms where class size issues are debated. Because of these responses and activities, it is no longer possible to give credence to Hanushek's judgments about class size.

Fortunately, a few well-designed, large-scale surveys have investigated class size directly (see, for example, Elliott, 1998; Ferguson, 1991; Ferguson & Ladd, 1996; Wenglinsky, 1997). These studies concluded that long-term exposure to small classes in the early grades can be associated with student achievement; that the extra gains that such exposure generates may be substantial; and that such gains may not appear with exposure to small classes in the upper grades or at the secondary school levels.

Trial Programs and Large Field Experiments

Other types of small class research have addressed some of the shortcomings of early experiments and surveys. In

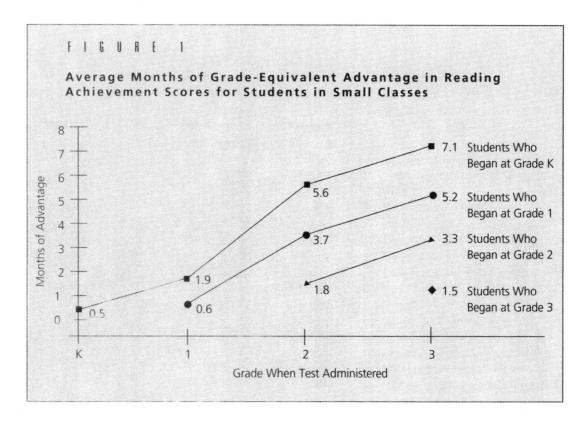

FIGURE 1

Average Months of Grade-Equivalent Advantage in Reading Achievement Scores for Students in Small Classes

the 1980s, state legislatures in the United States began political debates about the effects of small class size, and some states began trial programs or large-scale field experiments.

Indiana's Project Prime Time

In 1981, the Indiana legislature allocated $300,000 for a two-year study on the effects of reducing class size for the early grades in 24 randomly selected public schools. But initial results were so impressive that the state allocated funds to reduce class sizes in the 1st grade for all Indianan schools in 1984–85 and for K–3 by 1987–88, with an average of 18 students for each teacher.

Because of the statewide design of the initiative, it was impossible to compare results for small classes with a comparable group of larger classes. Some schools in the state had small classes before Project Prime Time began, however, so researchers compared samples of 2nd grade achievement records from six school districts that had reduced class size with three that had not. They found substantially larger gains in reading and mathematics achievement for students in small classes (McCivern, Gilman, & Tillitski, 1989).

These results seemed promising, but critics soon pounced on the design of the Project Prime Time study, decrying the fact that students had not been assigned to experimental and control groups on a random basis; pointing out that other changes in state school policy had also been adopted during the project; and suggesting that the state's teachers were motivated to make certain that small classes achieved better results because they knew

how the trial program's results were supposed to come out. Indiana students probably did benefit from the project, but a persuasive case for small classes had not yet been made. A better experiment was needed.

Tennessee's Project STAR

Such an experiment shortly appeared in Tennessee's Project STAR (Student/Teacher Achievement Ratio) arguably the largest and best-designed field experiment ever undertaken in education (Finn & Achilles, 1990; Finn, Gerber, Achilles, & Boyd-Zaharias, 2001; Folger, 1989; Grissmer, 1999; Krueger, 1999, 2000; Krueger & Whitmore, 2001; Mosteller, 1995; Nye, Hedges, & Konstantopoulos, 1999).

In the mid-1980s, the Tennessee legislature funded a four-year study to compare the achievement of early-grade students assigned randomly to one of three conditions: *standard classes* (with one certified teacher and more than 20 students); *supplemented classes* (with one teacher and a full-time, noncertified teacher's aide); and *small classes* (with one teacher and about 15 students). The study began with students entering kindergarten in 1985 and called for each student to attend the same type of class for four years. To control variables, the study asked each participating school to sponsor all three types of classes and to assign students and teachers randomly to each type. Participating teachers received no prior training for the type of class they were to teach.

The project invited all the state's primary schools to be in the study, but each participating school had to agree to remain in the program for four years; to have the class

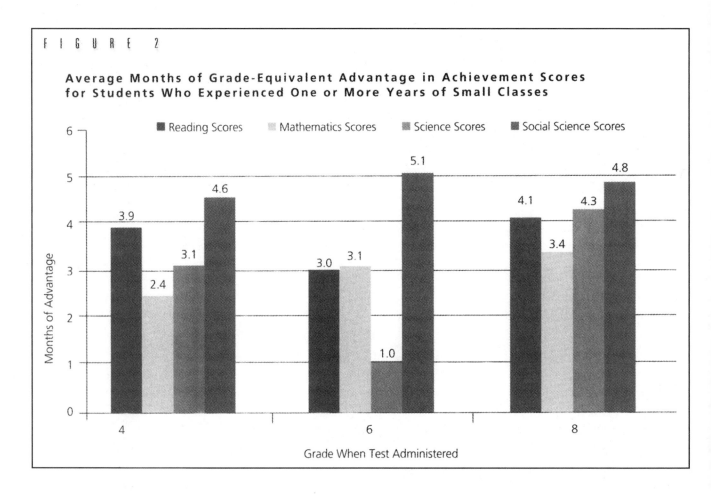

FIGURE 2

Average Months of Grade-Equivalent Advantage in Achievement Scores for Students Who Experienced One or More Years of Small Classes

■ Reading Scores   ▦ Mathematics Scores   ▦ Science Scores   ■ Social Science Scores

Months of Advantage

Grade When Test Administered

rooms needed for the project; and to have at least 57 kindergarten students so that all three types of classes could be set up. Participating schools received no additional support other than funds to hire additional teachers and aides. These constraints meant that troubled schools and those that disapproved of the study—and schools that were too small, crowded, or underfunded—would not participate in the STAR program, so the sample for the first year involved "only" 79 schools, 328 classrooms, and about 6,300 students. Those schools came from all corners of the state, however, and represented urban, inner-city, suburban, and rural school districts. The sample population included majority students, a sizable number of African American students, and students receiving free school lunches.

At the beginning of each year of the study, the sample population changed somewhat. Some participating students had moved away, been required to repeat kindergarten, or left the study because of poor health. Other families moved into the districts served by STAR schools, however, and their children filled the vacant seats. Also, because attending kindergarten was not then mandatory in Tennessee, some new students entered the STAR program in the 1st grade.

In addition, some parents tried to move their children from one type of STAR class to another, but administrators allowed only a few students to move from a standard class to a supplemented class or vice versa. By the end of the study, then, some students had been exposed to a

STAR class for four years, but others had spent a shorter time in such classes. These shifts might have biased STAR results, but Alan Krueger's careful analysis (1999) concluded that such bias was minimal.

Near the end of the each year, STAR students took the Stanford Achievement Test battery and received separate scores for reading, word-study skills, and mathematics. Results from these tests were similar for students who were in the standard and supplemented classes, indicating that the presence of untrained aids in the supplemented classes did *not* contribute to improving student achievement. Results for small classes were sharply different, however, however, with long-term exposure to small classes generating substantially higher levels of achievement and with gains becoming greater the longer that students were in small classes.

Figure 1 displays these two effects in reading achievement for average students. STAR investigators found that the students in small classes were 0.5 months ahead of the other students by the end of kindergarten, 1.9 months ahead at the end of 1st grade, 5.6 months ahead in 2nd grade, and 7.1 months ahead by the end of 3rd grade. The achievement advantages were smaller, although still impressive, for students who were only exposed to one, two, or three years of small classes. STAR investigators found similar (although not identical) results for word-study skills and mathematics.

Small-class advantages appeared for all types of students participating in the study. The gains were similar for boys and girls, but they were greater for impoverished students, African American students, and students from inner-city schools—groups that are traditionally disadvantaged in education.

These initial STAR findings were impressive, but would students who had been exposed to small classes in the early grades retain their extra gains when they entered standard size classes in 4th grade? To answer this question, the Tennessee legislature authorized a second study to examine STAR student outcomes during subsequent years of schooling.

At the end of each year, until they were in the 12th grade in 1997–1998, these students took the Comprehensive Tests of Basic Skills and received scores in reading, mathematics, science, and social science. The results showed that average students who had attended small classes were months ahead of those from standard classes for each topic assessed at each grade level. Figure 2 displays results from some of these tests, showing, for example, that when typical students who had attended small classes in the early grades reached grade 8, they were 4.1 months ahead in reading, 3.4 months ahead in mathematics, 4.3 months ahead in science, and 4.8 months ahead in social science.

Students who had attended small classes also enjoyed other advantages in the upper grades. They earned better grades on average, and fewer dropped out or had to repeat a year. And when they reached high school, more small class students opted to learn foreign languages, study advanced-level courses, and take the ACT and SAT college entrance examinations. More graduated from high school and were in the top 25 percent of their classes. Moreover, initial published results suggest that these upper-grade effects were again larger for students who are traditionally disadvantaged in education.

Figure 3 illustrates the percentages of students who opted to take the ACT or SAT exams as high school seniors. Roughly 44 percent of those from small classes took one or both of these tests, whereas only 40 percent of those from standard classes did so. The difference, however, was far greater for African American students. Instruction in small classes during the early grades had eliminated more than half of the traditional disadvantages that African American students have displayed in participation rates in the ACT and SAT testing programs.

Taken together, findings from the STAR project have been impressive, but they are not necessarily definitive. The STAR student sample did not quite match the U.S. population, for example, because very few Hispanic, Native American, and immigrant (non-English-speaking) families were living in Tennessee in the middle-1980s. Also, news about the greater achievement gains of small classes leaked out early during the STAR project, and one wonders how this may have affected participating teachers and why parents whose children were in other types of classes did not then demand that their children be reassigned to small classes. Finally, the STAR schools had volunteered to participate, suggesting that the teachers and principals in those schools may have had strong interests in trying innovative ideas. Questions such as these should not cause us to reject the findings from the STAR project, but we should keep in mind that this was a single study and that, as always, other evidence is needed to increase certainty about class size effects.

Wisconsin's SAGE Program

Findings from Project STAR have prompted class size reduction efforts in other states. One type of effort focuses on increasing the number of small, early-grade classes in schools in disadvantaged neighborhoods. STAR investigators supervised such a program in Tennessee in 1989, reducing K–3 class sizes in 17 school districts where the average family income was low. The results of this and similar projects in North Carolina, Michigan, Nevada, and New York have confirmed that students from small classes generate higher achievement scores when compared with their previous performance and with those of students in other schools. Most of these projects, however, have been small in scope.

A much larger project focused on the needs of disadvantaged students is Wisconsin's Student Achievement Guarantee in Education (SAGE) Program (Molnar et al., 1999, 2000; Zahorik, 1999). Led by Alex Molnar, this program began as a five-year pilot project for K–3 classes in school districts where at least 50 percent of students were living below the poverty level. The program invited all schools in these districts to apply for the program, but it was able to fund only a few of these schools, and no additional schools were to be added during the pilot project. Schools received an additional $2,000 for each low-income student enrolled in SAGE classrooms. All school districts that applied were allowed to enter the program, and 30 schools in 21 districts began the program at the K–1 grade levels in 1996, with 2nd grade added in 1997 and 3rd grade in 1998.

The SAGE program's major intervention was to reduce the average K–3 class size to 15 students for each teacher. To assess outcomes of the program, researchers compared results from small class SAGE schools with results from standard class size schools in the same districts having similar K–3 enrollments, racial compositions, average family incomes, and prior records of achievement in reading. Findings so far have indicated larger gains for students from small classes—in achievement scores for language arts, reading, and mathematics—that are roughly comparable to those from Project STAR. In addition, as with Project STAR, African American students have made relatively larger gains.

Like project STAR, the SAGE program studied schools that had volunteered for the program and provided them with sufficient funds to hire additional teachers. The SAGE program, however, involved more Hispanic, Asian, and Native American students than had the STAR project.

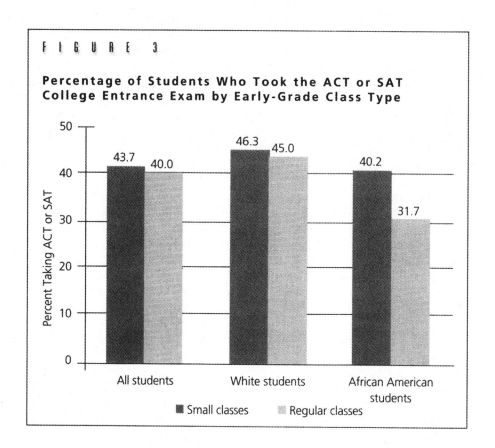

FIGURE 3

Percentage of Students Who Took the ACT or SAT College Entrance Exam by Early-Grade Class Type

All students — Small classes 43.7, Regular classes 40.0
White students — Small classes 46.3, Regular classes 45.0
African American students — Small classes 40.2, Regular classes 31.7

Y-axis: Percent Taking ACT or SAT (0, 10, 20, 30, 40, 50)

■ Small classes   ▨ Regular classes

After the announcement of findings from the initial effort, the Wisconsin legislature extended the SAGE program to other primary schools in the state. Therefore, what began as a small trial project has now blossomed into a statewide program that makes small classes in the early grades available for schools serving needy students.

The California Class Size Reduction Program

In 1996, California began a class size reduction program that has been far more controversial than such programs elsewhere. In earlier years, California had experienced many social problems, and major measures of achievement ranked California schools last in the United States. That year, however, a fiscal windfall became available, and then-governor Pete Wilson announced that primary schools would receive $650 annually for each student (an amount later increased to $800) if they would agree to reduce class sizes in the early grades from the statewide average of more than 28 students to not more than 20 students in each class (Hymon, 1997; Korostoff, 1998; Stecher, Bohrnstedt, Kirst, McRobbie, & Williams, 2001).

Several problems quickly surfaced. First, the California definition of a small class was larger than the size recommended in other studies. In fact, the size of small classes in California matched the size of standard classes in some other states. On the other hand, some California schools had been coping with 30–40 students in each classroom in the early grades, so a reduction to 20 students constituted an improvement.

The second problem was that the program's per-student funding was inadequate. Contrast the SAGE program's additional $2,000 for each student with the $650 or $800 offered by California. Nevertheless, the lure of additional funding proved seductive, and most California school districts applied to participate. This inadequate funding imposed serious consequences on poorer school districts, which had to abolish other needed activities to afford hiring teachers for smaller classes. In effect, then, the program created rather than solved problems for underfunded school districts.

In addition, when the California program began, many of its primary schools were overcrowded, and the state was suffering from a shortage of well-trained, certificated teachers. To cope with the lack of space, some schools created spaces for smaller classes by cannibalizing other needed facilities such as special education quarters, child care centers, music and art rooms, computer laboratories, libraries, gymnasiums, or teachers' lounges. Other schools had to tap into their operating budgets to buy portable classrooms, resulting in delays in paying for badly needed curricular materials or repairs for deteriorating school buildings. And to staff their smaller classes, many schools had to hire teachers without certification or prior training.

So far, results from the California program have been only modest. Informal evidence suggests that most students, parents, and teachers are pleased with their schools' smaller classes. And comparisons between the measured achievements of 3rd grade students from districts that did and did not participate in the early phases of the program have indicated minor advantages for California's smaller classes. These effects, however, have been smaller than those reported for the STAR and SAGE programs.

Extra gains from small classes in the early grades are larger when the class has fewer than 20 students.

In many ways, the California initiative has provided a near-textbook case of how a state should *not* reduce class size. After failing to conduct a trial program, California adopted an inadequate definition of class size, committed insufficient funds to the initiative, and ignored serious problems of overcrowding and teacher shortages. This example should remind us that small classes are not a panacea for education. To be effective, programs for reducing class size need careful planning and consideration of the needs and strengths of existing school systems.

What We Now Know About Small Classes

What should we conclude about the effects of small classes? Although the results of individual studies are always questionable, a host of different studies suggest several conclusions.

- When planned thoughtfully and funded adequately, small classes in the early grades generate substantial gains for students, and those extra gains are greater the longer students are exposed to those classes.
- Extra gains from small classes in the early grades are larger when the class has fewer than 20 students.
- Extra gains from small classes in the early grades occur in a variety of academic disciplines and for both traditional measures of student achievement and other indicators of student success.
- Students whose classes are small in the early grades retain their gains in standard size classrooms and in the upper grades, middle school, and high school.
- All types of students gain from small classes in the early grades, but gains are greater for students who have traditionally been disadvantaged in education.
- Initial results indicate that students who have traditionally been disadvantaged in education carry greater small-class, early-grade gains forward into the upper grades and beyond.
- The extra gains associated with small classes in the early grades seem to apply equally to boys and girls.

- Evidence for the possible advantages of small classes in the upper grades and high school is inconclusive.

Tentative Theories

Why should reducing class size have such impressive effects in the early grades? Theories about this phenomenon have fallen largely into two camps.

Most theorists focus on the teacher, reasoning that small classes work their magic because the small class context improves interactions between the teacher and individual students. In the early grades, students first learn the rules of standard classroom culture and form ideas about whether they can cope with education. Many students have difficulty with these tasks, and interactions with a teacher on a one-to-one basis—a process more likely to take place when the class is small—help the students cope. In addition, teachers in small classes have higher morale, which enables them to provide a more supportive environment for initial student learning. Learning how to cope well with school is crucial to success in education, and those students who solve this task when young will thereafter carry broad advantages—more effective habits and positive self-concepts—that serve them well in later years of education and work.

The need to master this task confronts all students, but doing so is often a more daunting challenge for students who come from impoverished homes, ethnic groups that have suffered from discrimination or are unfamiliar with U.S. classroom culture, or urban communities where home and community problems interfere with education. Thus, students from such background have traditionally had more difficulty coping with classroom education, and they are more likely to be helped by a reduction in class size.

Students whose classes are small in the early grades retain their gains in standard size classrooms and in the upper grades, middle school, and high school.

This theory also helps explain why reductions in class size in the upper grades may not generate significant advantages. Older students normally have learned to cope with standard classrooms and have developed either effective or ineffective attitudes concerning academic subjects—and these attitudes are not likely to change just because of a reduction in class size.

The theory also suggests a caution. Students are likely to learn more and develop better attitudes toward education if they are exposed to well-trained and enthusiastic teachers, appropriate and challenging curriculums, and physical environments in their classrooms and schools that support learning. If conditions such as these are not also present, then reducing class size in the early grades will presumably have little impact. Thus, when planning programs for reducing class size, we should also think about the professional development of the teachers who will participate in them and the educational and physical contexts in which those programs will be placed.

A second group of theories designed to account for class size effects focuses on the classroom environment and student conduct rather than on the teacher. We know that discipline and classroom management problems interfere with subject-matter instruction. Theories in this group argue that these problems are less evident in small classes and that students in small classes are more likely to be engaged in learning. Moreover, teacher stress is reduced in small classes, so teachers in the small class context can provide more support for student learning. Studies have also found that small instructional groups can provide an environment for learning that is quite different from that of the large classroom. Small instructional groups can create supportive contexts where learning is less competitive and students are encouraged to form supportive relationships with one another.

Theories such as these suggest that the small class environment is structurally different from that of the large class. Less time is spent on management and more time is spent on instruction, students participate at higher levels, teachers are able to provide more support for learning, and students have more positive relationships. Such processes should lead both to greater subject-matter learning and to more positive attitudes about education among students, with more substantial effects in the early grades and for those groups that are traditionally disadvantaged in education.

Gains from small classes in the early grades benefit all types of students, but gains are greater for students who have traditionally been disadvantaged in education.

These two theories are not mutually exclusive. On the contrary, both may provide partial insights into what happens in small classes and why small class environments help so many students. Collecting other types of evidence to assess such theories directly would be useful, particularly observational studies that compare the details of interaction in early-grade classes of various sizes and surveys of the attitudes and self-concepts of students who have been exposed to classes of different sizes. Unfortunately, good studies of these effects have been hard to find.

Policy Implications and Actions
Given the strength of findings from research on small classes, why haven't those findings provoked more reform efforts? Although many state legislatures have debated or begun reform initiatives related to class size, most primary schools in the United States today do not

operate under policies that mandate small classes for early grades. Why not?

This lack of attention has several causes, among them ignorance about the issue, confusion about the results of class size research and ineffective dissemination of those results, prejudices against poor and minority students, the politicizing of debates about class size effects and their implications, and practical problems associated with adopting small classes.

Recent debates about class size have become quite partisan in the United States, with Democrats generally favoring class size reductions and Republicans remaining hostile to them. Responding to President Bill Clinton's 1998 State of the Union address, the U.S. Congress set up a modest program, aimed at urban school districts with high concentrations of poverty, which provided funds for hiring additional teachers during the 1999 and 2000 fiscal years. This program enabled some districts to reduce class sizes in the early grades, and informal results from those cities indicated gains in student achievement.

Republicans have been lukewarm about extending this program—some apparently believing that it is ineffective or is merely a scheme to enhance the coffers of teachers' unions—and have welcomed President George W. Bush's call for an alternative federal program focused on high-stakes achievement tests and using results from those tests to apply sanctions to schools if they do not perform adequately.

The major problems standing in the way of reducing class sizes, however, are often practical ones. In many cases, cutting class sizes means hiring more teachers. With the looming shortage of qualified teachers, recruiting more teachers may be even more difficult than finding the funds to pay their salaries. Further, many schools would have to find or create extra rooms to house the additional classes created by small class programs, which would require either modifying school buildings or acquiring temporary classroom structures.

In many cases, meeting such needs would mean increasing the size of public school budgets, a step abhorred by fiscal conservatives and those who are critical of public education. The latter have argued that other reforms would cost less and be more effective than reducing class sizes. In response to such claims, various studies have estimated the costs of class size reduction programs or compared their estimated costs with those of other proposed reforms. Unfortunately, studies of this type must make questionable assumptions, so the results of their efforts have not been persuasive.

Nevertheless, reducing the size of classes for students in the early grades often requires additional funds. All students would reap sizable education benefits and long-lasting advantages, however, and students from educationally disadvantaged groups would benefit even more. Indeed, if we are to judge by available evidence, no other education reform has yet been studied that would provide such striking benefits. Debates about reducing class sizes, then, are disputes about values. If citizens are truly committed to providing a quality public education and a level playing field for all students regardless of background, they will find the funds needed to reduce the class size.

References

Coleman, J. S., Campbell, E. Q., Hobson, C. J., McPartland, J., Mood, A. M., Weinfeld, F. D., & York, R. L. (1966). *Equality of educational opportunity*. Washington, DC: U.S. Government Printing Office.

Educational Research Service. (1980, December). Class size research: A critique of recent meta-analyses. *Phi Delta Kappan, 70*, 239–241.

Elliott, M. (1998). School finance and opportunities to learn: Does money well spent enhance students' achievement? *Sociology of Education, 71*, 223–245.

Ferguson, R. F. (1991). Paying for public education: New evidence on how and why money matters. *Harvard Journal on Legislation, 28*, 465–498.

Ferguson, R. F., & Ladd, H. F. (1996). How and why money matters: An analysis of Alabama schools. In H. F. Ladd (Ed.), *Holding schools accountable: Performance-based reform in education* (pp. 256–298). Washington, DC: Brookings Institution.

Finn, J. D., & Achilles, C. M. (1990). Answers and questions about class size: A statewide experiment. *American Educational Research Journal, 27*(3), 557–577.

Finn, J. D., Gerber, S. B., Achilles, C. M., & Boyd-Zaharias, J. (2001). The enduring effects of small classes. *Teachers College Record, 103*(10), 145–183.

Folger, J. (Ed.). (1998). Project STAR and class size policy. *Peabody Journal of Education* (Special Issue), 67(1).

Glass, G. V., Cahen, L. S., Smith, M. L., & Filby, N. N. (1982). *School class size: Research and policy*. Beverly Hills, CA: Sage.

Glass, G. V., & Smith, M. L. (1979). Meta-analysis of research on class size and achievement. *Educational Evaluation and Policy Analysis,1*, 2-16.

Grissmer, D. (Ed.). (1999). Class size: Issues and new findings. *Educational Evaluation and Policy Analysis* (Special Issue), 21 (2).

Hanushek, E. A. (1986). The economics of schooling: Production and efficiency in public schools. *Journal of Economic Literature, 24*, 1141–1177.

Hanushek, E. A. (1999). Some findings from an independent investigation of the Tennessee STAR experiment and from other investigations of class size effects. *Education Evaluation & Policy Analysis, 21*(2), 143–163.

Hedges, L. V., Laine, R. D., & Greenwald, R. (1994). Does money matter? A meta-analysis of studies of the effects of differential school inputs on student outcomes. *Educational Researcher, 23*(3), 5–14.

Hedges, L. W., & Stock, W. (1983). The effects of class size: An examination of rival hypotheses. *American Educational Research Journal, 20*, 63–85.

Hymon, S. (1997, July 7). A lesson in classroom size reduction: Administrators nationwide can learn from California's classroom size reduction plan and how districts implemented it. *School Planning & Management, 36*(7), 18–23, 26.

Korostoff, M. (1998). Tackling California's class size reduction policy initiative: An up close and personal account of how teachers and learners responded. *International Journal of Educational Research, 29*, 797–807.

Krueger, A. B. (1999). Experimental estimates of education production functions. *The Quarterly Journal of Economics, 114* (2), 497–532.

Krueger, A. B. (2000). Economic considerations and class size. Princeton University, Industrial Relations Section, Working Paper #447.

Krueger, A. B., & Whitmore, D. M. (2001). The effect of attending a small class in the early grades on college-test taking and middle school test results: Evidence from Project STAR. *Economic Journal, 111*, 1–28.

McGivern, J., Gilman, D., & Tillitski, C. (1989). A meta-analysis of the relation between class size and achievement. *The Elementary School Journal, 90*(1), 47–56.

Molnar, A., Smith, P., Zahorik, J., Palmer, A., Halbach, A., & Ehrle, K. (1999). Evaluating the SAGE program: A pilot program in targeted pupil-teacher reduction in Wisconsin. *Educational Evaluation and Policy Analysis, 21*, 165–177.

Molnar, A., Smith, P., Zahorik, J., Palmer, A., Halbach, A., & Ehrle, K. (2000). Wisconsin's student achievement guarantee in education (SAGE) class size reduction program: Achievement effects, teaching, and classroom implications. In M. C. Wang & J. D. Finn (Eds.), *How small classes help teachers do their best* (pp. 227–277). Philadelphia: Temple University, Center for Research in Human Development and Education.

Mosteller, F. (1995). The Tennessee study of class size in the early school grades. *The Future of Children, 5*(2), 113–127.

Murphy, D., & Rosenberg, B. (1998, June). Recent research shows major benefits of small class size. *Educational Issues Policy Brief, 3*. Washington, DC: American Federation of Teachers.

Nye, B., Hedges, L. V., & Konstantopoulos, S. (1999). The long-term effects of small classes: A five-year follow-up of the Tennessee Class Size Experiment. *Educational Evaluation and Policy Analysis, 21*, 127–142.

Rees, N. S., & Johnson, K. (2000, May 30). A lesson in smaller class sizes. *Heritage Views 2000* [Online]. Available: www.heritage.org/views/2000/ed053000.html

Stecher, B., Bohrnstedt, G., Kirst, M., McRobbie, J., & Williams, T. (2001). Class-size reduction in California: A story of hope, promise, and unintended consequences. *Phi Delta Kappan, 82*, 670–674.

Wenglinsky, H. (1997). How money matters: The effect of school district spending on academic achievement. *Sociology of Education, 70*, 221–237.

Zahorik, J. (1999). Reducing class size leads to individualized instruction. *Educational Leadership, 57*(1), 50–53.

Author's note: Data in Figures 1 and 3 originally appeared in Finn et al. (2001). Jeremy Finn helped prepare the figures. Data in Figure 2 originally appeared in Krueger and Whitmore (2001). Alan Krueger helped prepare the figure.

Bruce J. Biddle is Professor Emeritus of Psychology and of Sociology at the University of Missouri, Columbia, MD 65211; BiddleB@missouri.edu.
David C. Berliner is Regents' Professor of Psychology in Education, College of Education, Arizona State University, Tempe, AZ 85287; Berliner@asu.edu.

UNIT 8

The Profession of Teaching Today

Unit Selections

Key Points to Consider

- What is "expertise" in teaching? Be specific; use examples.

- What are some ways in which teacher/student classroom interaction can be studied?

- What do you think of efforts to "reinvent" schools? What are your own visions of what is possible in schooling?

- Why has the knowledge base of teaching expanded so dramatically in recent years?

- List by order of importance what you think are the five most vital issues confronting the teaching profession today. What criteria did you use in ranking these issues? What is your position on each of them?

- What are the most defensible standards to assess the quality of a teaching performance? Explain the concept of accountability in schooling.

- What political pressures do teachers in the United States face today?

 **Links: www.dushkin.com/online/**
These sites are annotated in the World Wide Web pages.

Canada's SchoolNet Staff Room
http://www.schoolnet.ca/home/e/

Teachers Helping Teachers
http://www.pacificnet.net/~mandel/

The Teachers' Network
http://www.teachers.net

Teaching with Electronic Technology
http://www.wam.umd.edu/~mlhall/teaching.html

The task of helping teachers to grow in their levels of expertise in the classroom falls heavily on those educators who provide professional staff development training in the schools. Meaningful staff development training is extremely important. Several professional concerns are very real in the early career development of teachers. Level of job security or tenure is still an issue, as are the concerns of first-year teachers and teacher educators. How teachers interact with students is a concern to all conscientious, thoughtful teachers.

We continue the dialogue over what makes a teacher "good." There are numerous external pressures on the teaching profession today from a variety of public interest groups. The profession continues to develop its knowledge base on effective teaching through ethnographic and empirical inquiry about classroom practice and teachers' behavior in elementary and secondary classrooms across the nation. Concern continues about how best to teach to enhance insightful, reflective student interaction with the content of instruction. We continue to consider alternative visions of literacy and the roles of teachers in fostering a desire for learning within their students.

All of us who live the life of a teacher are aware of those features that we associate with the concept of a good teacher. In addition, we do well to remember that the teacher/student relationship is both a tacit and an explicit one—one in which teachers' attitude and emotional outreach are as important as students' response to our instructional effort. The teacher/student bond in the teaching/learning process cannot be overemphasized. We must maintain an emotional link in the teacher/student relationship that will compel students to want to accept instruction and attain optimal learning. What, then, constitutes those most defensible standards for assessing good teaching?

The past decade has yielded much in-depth research on the various levels of expertise in the practice of teaching. We know much more now about specific teaching competencies and how they are acquired. Expert teachers do differ from novices and experienced teachers in terms of their capacity to exhibit accurate, integrated, and holistic perceptions and analyses of what goes on when students try to learn in classroom settings. We can now pinpoint some of these qualitative differences.

As the knowledge base of our professional practice continues to expand, we will be able to certify with greater precision what constitutes acceptable ranges of teacher performance based on more clearly defined procedures of practice, as we have, for example, in medicine and dentistry. Medicine is, after all, a practical art as well as a science—and so is teaching. The analogy in terms of setting standards of professional practice is a strong one. Yet the emotional pressure on teachers that theirs is also a performing art, and that clear standards of practice can be applied to that art, is a bitter pill to swallow for many. Hence, the intense reaction of many teachers against external competency testing and any rigorous classroom observation standards. The writing, however, is on the wall–the profession cannot hide behind the tradition that teaching is a special art, unlike all others, which cannot be subjected to objective observational standards, aesthetic critique, or to a standard knowledge base. The public demands the same levels of demonstrable professional standards of practice as are demanded of those in the medical arts.

Likewise, we have identified certain approaches to working with students in the classroom that have been effective. Classroom practices such as cooperative learning strategies have won widespread support for inclusion in the knowledge base on teaching. The knowledge base of the social psychology of life in classrooms has been significantly expanded by collaborative research between classroom teachers and various specialists in psychology and teacher education. This has been accomplished by using anthropological field research techniques to ground theory of classroom practice into demonstrable phenomenological perspectives. Many issues have been raised—and answers found—by basic ethnographic field observations, interviews, and anecdotal record-keeping techniques to understand more precisely how teachers and students interact in the classroom. A rich dialectic is developing among teachers regarding the description of ideal classroom environments. The methodological insight from this research into the day-to-day realities of life in schools is transforming what we know about teaching as a professional activity and how to best advance our knowledge of effective teaching strategies.

Creative, insightful persons who become teachers will usually find ways to network their interests and concerns with other teachers and will make their own opportunities for creative teaching in spite of external assessment procedures. They acknowledge that the science of teaching involves the observation and measurement of teaching behaviors but that the art of teaching involves the humanistic dimensions of instructional activities, an alertness to the details of what is taught, and equal alertness to how students receive it. Creative, insightful teachers guide class processes and formulate questions according to their perceptions of how students are responding to the material.

To build their aspirations, as well as their self-confidence, teachers must be motivated to an even greater effort for professional growth in the midst of these fundamental revisions. Teachers need support, appreciation, and respect. Simply criticizing them while refusing to alter social and economic conditions that affect the quality of their work will not solve their problems, nor will it lead to excellence in education. Not only must teachers work to improve their public image and the public's confidence in them, but the public must confront its own misunderstandings of the level of commitment required to achieve teacher excellence. Teachers need to know that the public cares about and respects them enough to fund their professional improvement in a primary recognition that they are an all-important force in the life of this nation. The articles in this unit consider the quality of education and the status of the teaching profession today.

Reinventing the Middle School

Profiles in Caring: Teachers Who Create Learning Communities in Their Classrooms

If we want all students to experience high levels of learning, we must recruit teachers who care passionately about their students and their work, support these teachers in developing hands-on/minds-on lessons, and assist them in reaching out to parents and community.

By David Strahan, Tracy W. Smith, Mike McElrath, & Cecilia M. Toole

One of the fundamental principles of the middle school concept is that young adolescents learn best in small settings. The first recommendation of *Turning Points: Preparing American Youth for the 21st Century* (Carnegie Council on Adolescent Development, 1989) was to "create small communities for learning where stable, close, mutually respectful relationships with adults and peers are considered fundamental for intellectual development and personal growth" (p. 9). In *Turning Points 2000,* Jackson and Davis (2000) concluded: "In the ten years since the release of *Turning Points,* an enormous amount has been learned from schools across the nation about how these kinds of middle grades learning communities can be created" (p. 123). Our review of research supports this assertion and documents ways that teachers nurture "learning communities." This term, learning community, captures the essence of school success: students and teachers "learn" best as members of "communities."

A Growing Commitment to Community

In recent investigations, researchers have explored the nature of successful learning communities. Based on their comparisons of schools in the Child Development Project with matched non-project schools, Lewis, Schaps, and

Watson (1996) identified five principles of practice that create what they call "the caring classroom's academic edge":

- Warm, supportive, stable relationships
- Constructive learning
- Important, challenging curricula
- Intrinsic motivation
- Attention to social and ethical dimensions of learning.

Their data highlighted the "synergy of academic and social goals" and illustrated specific ways that "caring" classrooms can also be highly academic classrooms.

Summarizing a number of studies related to school culture and leadership, Peterson and Deal (1998) identified five recurring characteristics that describe schools that have become learning communities:

- Staff have a shared sense of purpose; they pour their hearts into teaching
- Norms of collegiality, improvement, and hard work underlie relationships
- Rituals and traditions celebrate student accomplishments, teacher innovation, and parental commitment

- Informal networks of storytellers, heroes, and heroines provide a social web of information, support, and history
- Success, joy, and humor abound. (p. 29)

While these reports provide convincing evidence that community enhances learning, they offer less insight into the ways that teachers go about creating learning communities on a day-to-day basis. In this article, we describe how some of the teachers we have studied have accomplished this task. Over the past three years, we have had opportunities to spend time in the classrooms of more than 40 middle-level teachers. Collectively, we have observed over 100 lessons and conducted over 200 interviews with teachers and their students. In these studies, we found that the essential dynamic was the creation of learning communities.

To illustrate this dynamic, we present three cases that have taught us a great deal. Each of these cases takes place in a very different setting. Betty Roberts teaches in a small K–8 school setting in the mountains. Jay Burns teaches in a prosperous suburban community. Darlene Wilson and Ashley Cooper teach in an urban middle school. Each of these teachers responds to the needs of students in a unique way and uses carefully crafted procedures to create a sense of community.

Betty Roberts creates community in a rural setting

Betty Roberts teaches in a small school that serves students in Pre-Kindergarten through 8th grade. During the 1998–99 school year, Betty had 30 students in her class, and taught all academic subjects to her students. At the time this data was collected, she was at the end of her fourteenth year of teaching.

A visit to Betty Roberts' classroom

Thirty students, two goldfish, one worm snake, one ringneck snake, five toads, one frog, a five-lined skink, a salamander, a preying mantis, 30 quail eggs, a teacher assistant, and Betty Roberts were the inhabitants of the classroom on the day we arrived. At the time of our observation, Betty's students were working on an assignment they had started the day before. At the beginning of the lesson, Betty spent less than seven minutes reviewing the purpose of the assignment before the class moved to work in groups at clusters of desks and spaces on the floor. Each group of six to eight students worked to write ballads about one of four different pirates. Betty and her teacher assistant circulated from group to group, monitoring students' progress and answering questions. Betty reviewed the characteristics of a ballad with one group. With a second group, she crouched on the floor to read aloud to them and provide additional directions and encouragement. At one point, she stood and patted her knees to demonstrate rhythm for a ballad. Betty moved

quickly from group to group, leaning into each group to read their drafts to make comments. During the group work, students were chatty but seemed productive. Each group seemed to have a "leader" although leaders were not assigned. All students seemed to be involved in the group's activities.

Students went in groups to the front of the room to "perform" their ballads. One student who had been isolated from his group "performed" the ballad he had written while the teacher assistant read it aloud. The teacher led the class in applause after each performance. Betty did a brief assessment of the group work by having students raise their hands if they thought working with the group was fun or easy, or if they learned something new. At the end of the lesson, Betty summarized the information about the pirates, asking students questions to review.

Betty reflects on her teaching

Betty spoke with conviction about her classroom community. She articulated without hesitation one of her primary goals: "My goal is social interaction as much as anything else and especially with all the stuff we're hearing is happening, children killing children. We're taking a real serious look at how children react with one another and interact" (Smith, 1999, p. 84). She understood that her students must feel "safe and free to take risks" (p. 79).

To build a successful community, Betty had established a number of classroom procedures. One of the most important was her emphasis on teamwork. Betty believes that people are more likely to stay involved in community work if they have opportunities to collaborate. She explained, "Unless they are actively grouped and working together, most of them are not engaged. This engages more [people] when they work in teams. So I try to do more teamwork, any kind of interactive planning together" (p. 87).

Betty spoke passionately about her students. She believes that the key to building a strong community, comprised of strong individuals, is to help each person find a niche in the community, a role he or she can play. Her personal goal is to convince her students "that they are valued and that they have a gift within them that is valuable and that they need to find it, find out what it is and they need to make the most of it… and I try to let them see what their beauty is and they are good folks and there is something to be joyful in every day" (p. 87). She views her classroom as an interdependent community of learners. She emphasized teamwork, collaboration, and responsibility, values that Jay Burns also encourages in his middle school classroom.

Jay Burns creates community in a suburban school

Jay Burns teaches in an affluent middle school that serves students in grades six, seven, and eight. Jay teaches language arts to about 100 students during the school day. At the time of this observation, Jay was at the end of his twenty-eighth year of teaching. During his career, he has taught language arts and social studies to students in grades seven, eight, and nine. He has also taught English to students in grades eight through twelve. He has been teaching 8th grade language arts for the past 17 years.

A visit to Jay Burns' classroom

Jay Burns' third period students sauntered into class, loaded down with Eastbay book bags on their shoulders, Tommy Hilfiger sweatshirts on their backs, and Nike tennis shoes on their feet. Twenty-eight of their growing bodies barely fit into this 8th grade classroom. Jay was writing on the board as they entered. A nod of his head was direction for one student to distribute a set of illustrated file folders to her classmates. Without further direction, students began to copy the problematic sentences into their notebooks:

> *in northern minnesota I did a number of things writed letters laying inthe sun and read.*
>
> *Yes dan the phone ringed at three oclock in the morning it were a wrongnumber.*

When they had finished copying and correcting, Jay began a discussion of the daily oral language activity. Jay asked questions about which changes were made and then commented on those changes with such questions and observations as the following, "And why was that? So you made a new sentence? You could do that. If it were a specific place, yes." During the discussion, there was some confusion about the conjugation of the verb "to lie," meaning "to recline." Jay indicated that he would look up the conjugation and explain it to the class later. Jay provided encouragement to students with comments such as, "There you go. Pat yourself on the back. Okay, you can, that would work. You are right! How did you know?" (Smith, 1999, p. 76)

Jay's priority is developmental appropriateness, and he considers students' social, physical, intellectual, and cognitive development as he plans instruction.

Following the daily oral language exercise, Jay reviewed the objectives for the day's class session. Next, he took the "status of the class" by calling the names of the students and recording what they said they would be working on during the class time. After the status of the class was taken, some students moved to the computer stations and a few moved to designated areas to do peer conferences. The rest of the students worked at their desks.

Jay moved around the room returning papers to students who were seated at their desks. To discuss these papers with students, he crouched to their seated height. He answered student questions and used hand gestures to communicate. Jay made comments to students regarding issues such as theme, tone, and realism; and he praised students with comments such as, "This is good. Very supportive, very thorough. Good." (p. 76).

Just before the class session ended, Jay reminded students of their homework—to complete their portfolios. He suggested that some students may need to come by later in the day to pick up edited papers.

Jay reflects on his teaching

Jay's curriculum and instruction are responsive to the needs of individuals and groups in his classroom. Jay's priority is developmental appropriateness, and he considers students' social, physical, intellectual, and cognitive development as he plans and implements instruction. The writing workshop structure Jay uses in his classroom allows him to monitor the progress of each writer individually. He described his students as "a sociable group." He explains that "they laugh and fool around while they're working… they just have fun with it" (Smith, 1999, p. 92). Jay tries to strike a balance between a directive leadership style and student input: "There are procedures and expectations that I have, but also they have a lot of input" (p. 92). He understands that students will produce better quality work if they believe they have ownership in the product. His classroom is often noisy with the sound of keyboards, computer printers, and voices. Writers are busy moving about, getting the tools and information they need to complete their assignments. Jay is also busy and moving. He spends most of his day talking to students, providing feedback on drafts they have submitted to him. Rather than imposing his idea of correctness on the pieces, Jay wants to discuss student works, using them as opportunities to help the individual writers grow.

In his interviews, Jay has offered suggestions for other teachers who wish to have effective relationships with their students:

1. Combine a high sense of structure and guidance with a high sense of choice and control.
2. Separate content from correction.
3. Model early, withhold judgment during the process; correct thoroughly when they are done, and let them correct/revise what you have pointed out.
4. Focus on process." (p. 95).

Jay's advice captures some of the ways he has learned to create learning communities in his classroom. His students demonstrate a sense of connection with their classmates, with the tasks of writing, and with their teacher.

Students on the STAR team at Washington Middle school also show a sense of connectedness. Their teachers, Darlene and Ashley, encourage a sense of community in a different fashion.

The STAR Team Creates Community in an Urban School

Washington Middle School is located in an urban setting with 675 students and 60 staff members. Over the past decade, a number of the working class families in this attendance zone have moved to more suburban settings, causing a shift in the school and community population.

The STAR (Strive To Attain Respect) team is a two-teacher team at this school. Darlene Wilson teaches math and science while Ashley Cooper teaches language arts and social studies. Darlene Wilson is the team leader. A veteran of nine years in teaching, she has gained a unique awareness of the needs of her students through her experiences as both teacher and parent. She is admittedly the mothering type, the one students feel they can go to with problems and concerns without disregarding her authority. Ashley Cooper is a second-year teacher with an undergraduate degree in Middle Grades Education from the local university. With this middle grades background, she has become a positive addition to the staff and a contributing member of the STAR team. Ashley feels fortunate to be teamed with Darlene, who not only understands the setting, but also is willing to learn from and not squelch Ashley's progressive ideas about teaching middle school children. Ashley has a solid command of her subject areas as is evidenced by the improved reading and writing scores of her students. She has also aligned herself with Darlene in taking a leadership role on the school improvement team.

A Visit with the STAR Team

On the day of this observation, all 46 students gathered in one classroom. The activity was an auction, and the front tables in the room were filled with well over a hundred different prizes. This was the Big Bucks Auction, and Ms. Wilson served as the auctioneer. Students had received Big Bucks as incentives for good behavior throughout the semester. Today's activity is the culminating event. Students could choose to bid on items of interest such as volleyballs, hair gel, WWF T-shirts, or chocolate bars. Ashley and Darlene had been orchestrating this event for months, seeking donations from a number of local stores and a wide variety of community sources, carefully selecting an odd montage of items that young adolescents crave. Observers watched as the students slowly entered the room and quietly took their places, anxiously anticipating their opening bid on the item they hoped no one else would want. The students were cooperative, sharing prizes with one another, lending money to those in need, and cheering with excitement as the bidding wars escalated. Observers noted that there were almost 50 students in this room, and these two teachers had the control and attention of every one of them.

The STAR team has initiated a number of community service projects allowing students to demonstrate citizenship and build character. Some of these projects were undertaken during school hours while others occurred after school through the SAVE (Students Against Violence) club. Interestingly enough, even after long and often tiresome days, these teachers' rooms were almost always open after school for tutorial sessions, small group discussions, or club meetings, a true indication of their commitment to the students. Darlene explained:

> We try to get the kids involved in different projects. You know, some kids are not so good at schoolwork. Maybe they can't draw, maybe they can't do some of these other things, but they can bring in some canned goods and they can go with us to deliver the stuff or they can go out here and weed the flowers around the school. (McElrath, 2000, p. 129)

Through their own energy and example, Darlene and Ashley often showed students how to put caring into motion.

Darlene and Ashley reflect on their teaching

When asked to talk about those aspects that have allowed them to become a more successful team, Ashley began with the following:

> We know each other well enough to know how the other is going to react in certain situations. We can play off that and read off that. The kids also see that we work together and there is nothing one of us does without the other one knowing about it. They see this and don't try to pull anything over on us. I really think that is the one thing that helps our team behave and respond, for the most part, to what we do. (McElrath, 2000, p. 125)

Both teachers emphasize consistency and high expectations as the keys to being successful with their students. The intimacy of a two-teacher team, guided by some unique strategies, allows this to occur more naturally.

Darlene and Ashley know that they need to rely on parents as much as possible in order to develop the sense of community and common cause that will allow their students to excel both academically and socially. Darlene reminded us of just how difficult a challenge this can be at times:

> With the diverse population in our community, we have to deal with a lot of problems, everything from racial feelings of injustice to an inability to communicate because of language barriers. Sometimes we have to go through liaisons, and sometimes the children are the only liaison we have. That can be hard. We have a few kids this year whose parents have not been involved because there is no liaison and this seventh grade child is the only one who speaks English in the family. That can make things difficult. (p. 129)

Darlene and Ashley believe that involving parents and communicating on a regular basis can solve a great deal of problems. Initial phone calls, positive messages, and informal social gatherings invite parents to participate in their child's education and model team beliefs to parents and students alike. The STAR team teachers have found that these efforts can help diffuse traditional barriers associated with home and school relationships while enhancing community views of team and school.

Creating Communities for Learning

Educational researchers and policy makers have agreed that one of the most powerful factors in promoting accomplishment is the extent to which the classroom is a learning community. The authors of *Turning Points* (Carnegie Council on Adolescent Development, 1989) articulated the essence of the concept of learning community as "a place where close, trusting relationships with adults and peers create a climate for personal growth and intellectual development" (p. 37). Recent studies have documented that constructivist learning, challenging curricula, and intrinsic motivation contribute to the success of learning communities. Most important, these studies have identified caring relationships as the heart of these communities. The four teachers profiled here have illustrated ways that individual teachers work with their students to bring to life the concept of community. While their situations are unique, their cases offer two powerful insights into the dynamics of learning communities.

First, the classroom communities they create grow from their own personal commitment to their students. While the concept of community seems to indicate the importance of group, the participants in this study were equally focused on the individuals in their classrooms. The participants in this study demonstrated their interest in the student/teacher relationship in a number of ways. First, they showed a vast knowledge of individual students. They spoke to the emotional, physical, cognitive, intellectual, and family needs and circum-

stances of students in their classes. These teachers learned a great deal about their students by working side-by-side with them. As Betty moved from group to group, she got down on her knees to work directly with students. During his lessons, Jay was moving about the room, conferencing with students. He worked closely with them, kneeling, bending, learning, or crouching to their seated height. When they visited a nursing home, Darlene and Ashley showed their students how to interact with the patients by taking the lead and modeling ways to initiate conversation.

Learning with their students, side by side, elbow to elbow, face to face, may have been the most powerful way that these teachers demonstrated their own personal commitment.

The second powerful insight into the dynamics of learning communities that these teachers have offered us is that they put their commitment to students in motion through procedures that fuse academic and social accomplishment. Students in their classes experienced very little tension between "what we learn" and "how we learn" or between "my success" and "our success." Their students achieved a great deal. They also learned to collaborate. These four teachers have developed working procedures that foster connectedness.

One procedure they share is the development of assignments that link inquiry and collaboration. While children were working in groups, Betty got the students' attention several times to have them assess their group dynamic. She also debriefed the students at the end of the lesson to monitor the effectiveness of the group work and to have the students consider their contributions to their groups. Jay incorporated collaboration into his writing workshop structure. Students provided oral and written responses to each other's writing, always working toward improving writing produced in the workshop. Darlene and Ashley linked academic and social learning in a flexible fashion.

Another procedure employed by all four teachers is involving students in classroom decisions on a continuous basis. In response to the question "What do you think makes a successful writing teacher?" Jay wrote, "Kids largely have control over topics and content, while aiming at a rubric or criterion for the end result" (Smith, 1999, p. 110). Jay seemed not only to indicate that he is willing to share control of the curriculum with his students but also that his success is derived from sharing ownership and control. His advice to writing teachers is to "combine a high sense of *structure* and *guidance* with a high sense of *choice* and control by *students*" (p. 100). The STAR Team also encouraged active participation through regular team meetings.

Finally, each of these teachers extends the community beyond the walls of the classroom. Betty Roberts believes that the most effective way to involve parents is a teacher-by-teacher approach. Although she supports school-wide open house meetings, she believes she has to take additional steps to involve parents. Some of her after-hours events have included Night Walks, a Star Party, and Weekend Stream Walk, a Computer Night, and a Candlelight Christmas. Jay Burns suggests that communication with parents is vital to a student's success in his classroom. He prepares a letter and syllabus describing the year's activities and expectations and sends it home for parents to review with their students. In addition, Jay makes frequent calls to parents, mostly when students are doing well. He suggests that parents are more supportive and students more attentive and motivated as a result of these calls. In the past couple of years, Jay has added student-led parent writing portfolio conferences to his efforts to involve parents. The STAR team encourages continuous communication with parents but also emphasizes service to the school community. Whether by bringing in canned goods, working on the school grounds, or visiting nursing homes, students learn to link their work in school with their membership in community.

When we walked away from the classrooms of Betty, Jay, Darlene, and Ashley, we realized that we had witnessed something powerful: teachers who transformed their classrooms from the ordinary to the engaging, students who accomplished challenging tasks in ways that seemed natural to them, and learning that inspired us as outsiders. If we want all students to experience this level of learning, there is little mystery about what we must do: recruit teachers who care passionately about their students and their work; support

these teachers in developing hands-on/minds-on lessons; and assist them in reaching out to parents and community.

References

Carnegie Council on Adolescent Development. (1989) *Turning points: Preparing American youth for the 21st century.* New York: Author.

Jackson, A., & Davis, G. (2000). *Turning points 2000: Educating adolescents in the 21st century.* New York: Teachers College Press.

Lewis, C., Schaps, E., & Watson, M. (1996). The caring classroom's academic edge. *Educational Leadership, 54*(3), 16–21.

McElrath, M. (2000). *Cause and affect: Examining the dynamics of high functioning middle school teams and the perceived impact of these teams on the well being of students.* Unpublished doctoral dissertation, University of North Carolina, Greensboro.

Peterson, K. D., & Deal, T. E. (1998). How leaders influence the culture of schools. *Educational Leadership, 56*(3), 58–30.

Smith, T. W. (1999). *Toward a prototype of expertise in teaching: A descriptive case study.* Unpublished doctoral dissertation, University of North Carolina, Greensboro.

David Strahan is a professor of curriculum and instruction at the University of North Carolina at Greensboro. E-mail: dbstrahan@yahoo.com

Tracy W. Smith is an assistant professor of curriculum and instruction at Appalachian State University, Boone, North Carolina.

Cecilia M. Toole is an adjunct professor at the University of North Carolina, Charlotte.

Mike McElrath is the coordinator of guidance for the Jamestown, New York, City Schools.

From *Middle School Journal,* September 2001, pp. 41-47. © 2001 by the National Middle School Association. Reprinted by permission.

Accountability: What's Worth Measuring?

We can't beat the accountability movement, so we had better join it and try to shape it, Ms. Raywid advises. Here are her suggestions for how to go about that task.

BY MARY ANNE RAYWID

I WISH the accountability movement that is now so strong had been launched for different reasons. It emerged, of course, from a growing mistrust of public schools and just how well they are serving us. Because that sentiment continues strong and is likely to be with us for some time to come, the press for accountability is likely to remain with us as well.

We can't beat the accountability movement, so we had better join it and try to shape it. Actually, there are things we can do that could turn it into a very positive force. After all, at root, accountability demands on openness on the part of the education system that we've not always seen and are all entitled to expect: information on just how well or how poorly each public school is doing. And what accountability then demands is that something be done about those schools that are failing.

I am very sympathetic to both these demands. Regarding the first, surely the public is entitled to know how the schools it pays for are faring. If they are *public* schools, surely information about them should be accessible to all. And regarding the second, there are schools in some places that have been failing for years, with little or nothing being done about it. In what was a new and very different kind of move in 1983, the chancellor of New York City's schools simply closed down a high school that was failing. Its numbers had been steadily worsening each year until finally it was failing, expelling, or otherwise pushing out 93% of its students. Only 7% of those enrolled were graduating. It is unforgivable to let things deteriorate to such a point.

Thus I am receptive to the idea of holding schools accountable and of forcing the failing ones to change. To my mind, accountability is a good thing. But the word is often used interchangeably with standards-based education, and they are not quite the same thing. For reasons that I hope will become clear, I think we ought to talk in terms of—and insist on—*accountability* rather than *standards-based education*. Doing so is by no means an abandonment of standards, but rather a broadening of concern.

The hard questions begin with "Accountable for what?" It seems reasonable to expect schools to do what they set out to do and thus to hold them accountable for fulfilling their own goals. This means that some school-to-school differences in accountability make sense, given the differences among us as to the goals to be sought in our schools. But there is also a great deal of commonality as to what we want schools to accomplish with our children. It is this that concerns me here: the goals and expectations for schools that I believe we share.

I've put the matter in the form of the question "What's worth measuring?" Of course, what's worth measuring depends on what's worth learning and acquiring and, hence, what's worth teaching and cultivating. What's worth measuring also depends on our expectations about the conditions and circumstances under which this teaching and cultivating ought to occur.

OUR GOALS FOR CHILDREN

There are really an awful lot of things we want our children to learn and our schools to teach them. We also have a number of different *kinds* of goals that we want to see fulfilled with and for our children, and we have some surrounding expectations that we want to see met. I'm going to present six rather different kinds of things that are worth learning—and thus worth measuring. I don't agree with the psychologist who launched the measurement movement in education by declaring that "whatever exists, exists in some amount and can be measured." He thought everything could be quantified, and I don't. But we can assess without quantifying, and, for me, if we have goals for children and expectations for schools, it's reasonable to try to find out whether they are being met. The short answer to my own question, then, is that whatever we're committed to accomplishing is worth measuring.

First, of course, are the things we call "basic skills"—the ability to read and report accurately on what one has read, to write, and to do elementary calculations. So important are these fundamental skills that they fill a lot of the time for the first three grades of a child's schooling. Much of the teaching that takes place in schools after the first three years calls for the application of these skills, so they really are essential groundwork. Thus it is important that we measure how well a child has learned them.

Second, there are all those pieces of information we want students to pick up: number facts, spelling facts, grammar facts, history facts, biology facts, geography facts, cultural facts, etc. There are lists and lists of these facts, without which you can't be an educated person. You can't even function very well in our society without many of them—like the number facts necessary to determine whether you are being given the right change. Teaching these facts is a perfectly reasonable expectation for schools, it seems to me, even though in some respects facts are really the lowest level of what we want youngsters to learn. They are necessary. But they are only a beginning.

Third, we want learners to be able to do something with all the facts they've learned. There's not much point in having learned the rules of grammar if you can't put together a grammatical sentence. Other applications are even more involved. We want learners to be able to select and retrieve from the information stored in their heads those facts relevant to a given situation, to be able to assemble them, and then to apply them so as to appropriately respond to a challenge or solve a problem.

Fourth, something else that's well worth measuring because it's so very much worth learning is the set of skills involved in using one's mind. We're not born knowing how to do that. And ironically, schools tend to give the most exercise—and hence developmental assistance—along these lines to the ablest students. The youngsters who need the most help in developing such intellectual skills and inclinations as weighing evidence, judging sources, making legitimate inferences, and distinguishing observations from assumptions are the very ones we tend not to bother with such matters. Instead, we focus on getting them to concentrate on those things that can be acquired by rote and drill—the fact-type learnings. But unless all youngsters are helped to acquire the habits of mind involved in sound judgment and good decision-making, they can never be

aware of themselves as creatures of intellect, as beings with the ability to take control of their lives and to alter their circumstances if need be. They can thus never be the citizens we want them to be, with the power to realize their own goals while helping to shape society.

Then there's a whole different kind of learning, the fifth type I find to be important, that we want very much for children to acquire. One principal summed it up recently: "Schools are about all those things that make individuals good and bad." We want our children to grow up as caring, empathetic, compassionate human beings with a sense of stewardship for the land and for one another. We also want them to grow up with integrity, initiative, a sense of responsibility, and a sense of humor. Schools really are in the person-shaping business: they can operate in ways that encourage and reinforce the traits and dispositions just mentioned, or they can operate so as to discourage and squelch them. Since these are the attitudes and inclinations that distinguish a good citizen and a good neighbor from a parasite or an assassin, we certainly want schools to instill them and children to acquire them. So this is yet another sort of goal, and we ought to measure progress toward it.

The sixth goal covers a lot of territory: we expect a school to contribute to a child's individual development. It means, for instance, that we want to see school make a difference in a child's cognitive development. Learning those facts and learning what to do with them are important, but we want school to do more than that. We want school to stimulate young minds to grow and expand their capacity. A school that doesn't lead to such growth isn't fulfilling reasonable expectations, and we need a way to find out whether this is the case. In other words, a school loaded with high achievers has got to make them still better learners. If not, there's been no value added, and that's what individual development is about. It's also about helping youngsters to develop whatever may be their particular talents. Whether it's music or writing or leading others or gymnastics, school ought to be a place that helps young people develop their talents.

These, then, are six different goals for learners that I think most of us can agree are important for schools to work toward: learning basic skills, learning facts, learning how to use information, acquiring desirable habits of mind, developing character and other desirable traits, and developing individuals talents. But this isn't all. In addition to these goals and expectations for learners, we have certain expectations that apply specifically to schools.

REASONABLE EXPECTATIONS OF SCHOOLS

First, given that children are required to attend them, it seems reasonable to expect schools to be *effective* in teaching our children. This means we expect them to be successful with their students. We wouldn't accept a doctor's diagnosis of "incurable" without going elsewhere for another opinion, and we shouldn't settle for the diagnosis "uneducable" from a school. In other words, we don't expect schools to say, "Well, if you've got success in mind, you really should be sending us a different batch of kids."

On the contrary, we expect schools to be welcoming, user-friendly places, where all six of those different kinds of goals I named are pursued with all youngsters, where all are treated with respect and compassion, and where all can meet with some degree of success. This is a tall order.

But, as if this weren't enough, we also expect schools to carry out their functions in particular ways. For instance, we don't want any of those goals of ours to be pursued lackadaisically or perfunctorily. It's not enough merely to take a class to a concert; the teacher must demonstrate genuine engagement with the music. If instead, the teachers are grading papers or chatting together while the music plays, that's not modeling much by way of music appreciation.

Similarly in a classroom, if the teacher isn't fully engaged in listening and attending when children speak but is demonstrating what it is to half listen to another person, then it's anybody's guess whether children can take from these experiences the lessons we want them to learn. So just going through the motions in classrooms isn't enough. Activities must be conducted with a quality—an emotional tone—that can be as important as the content. Just how serious are teachers about what they are doing? We don't want them to appear to be in dead earnest all the time—in fact, that would be awful—but we do want them to be focused and trying all the time. This is certainly a central enough dimension of what we want school to be that it is worth measuring.

Another thing we expect from schools is that they teach in such a way that youngsters acquire positive attitudes toward what they are learning. If a teacher manages to convey the essentials of reading but strips all pleasure and delight from doing so, it's a questionable success. If a youngster manages to stumble his way through geometry but acquires a hatred for math in the process, that is also a questionable success. As a famous educational thinker put it many years ago, "It's not that children should do what they want, but it's important that they want what they do." And being able to generate this kind of positive receptivity with respect to learning is a legitimate expectation of schools and teachers. If learning new things is drudgery to be undergone only under duress, we haven't done much toward creating a lifelong learner. And since this is so widely voiced a concern, we surely ought to be making regular checks on how well teachers and schools are dealing with it.

These last several lessons are a part of the school's culture and hence of its "hidden curriculum." This curriculum consists of the messages typically delivered otherwise than directly in words and usually only as an accompaniment to announced purposes and content. Sometimes it is conveyed in the arrangements. For instance, one famous principal insists that sending children to schools that are too large for teachers and administrators to learn their names teaches students that who they are as individuals, what they are experiencing, and how they feel about it are things that

don't matter. Sending them to schools where the toilets are broken or the doors to the stalls have been removed also conveys a message about what doesn't matter. In this case, their need for privacy has no importance. It seems reasonable to expect schools to treat both the children required to attend them and the teachers who teach in them with respect. And since this expectation is as reasonable as it is important, it's worth measuring.

So to our six goals we've added five expectations of schools: that they be successful, that they be welcoming and user-friendly places, that teachers be fully engaged in their teaching, that schools cultivate a receptivity to learning, and that the school's unspoken messages—its hidden curriculum—be positive and desirable ones.

SOME NOTES ABOUT MEASURING

Just how do we measure success with these goals and expectations? That is a matter that must be left to another time. But I can underscore some things to be kept in mind in seeking an answer to the question. Several things need to be said about the six goals for learners and five expectations of schools stated here. First, all appear reasonable, widely shared, and well worth seeking. This means that all are worth measuring in order to determine whether students and schools are living up to what we want from them.

It is also worth noting that holding schools accountable for meeting our list of school expectations directly implicates a number of people beyond teachers: principals, in particular, and their office staffs, but also librarians and counselors and coaches and cafeteria workers and security guards and custodians. Moreover, another thing our two lists make clear is that the answer to how well students and schools are faring is not going to be accessible simply through a single observation of a school; it takes a lot more than that. This is why ongoing evaluation is absolutely necessary to school accountability. The public can't determine whether its goals and expectations are being met without real evaluation—which must rely not only on what is directly observable but also on a great deal of indirect observation.

Another thing that merits emphasis is that, of our 11 goals and expectations, the standards-based education that many states have embarked on addresses only the first two goals for learners that we identified as widely shared (basic skills and information). The best tests perhaps address a bit of the third goal (ability to use information). That's why I think we ought to talk about "accountability" in preference to "standards-based education." Many people talk as if the standards we've set are sufficient to render the schools accountable, but they certainly won't render them accountable for all our goals and expectations. It's going to take a lot more than a series of tests to do that.

It seems clear that paper-and-pencil tests aren't going to suffice. For half of our goals for students (the fourth through the sixth), we'll need some other measure, just as we will for all five of the expectations for schools. I have several suggestions in this regard. At the outset, we must recognize that there's not going to be any single test for any one of them. We can't afford the bad judgments that reductionist measures are sure to support. Many of us find it absurd to think you can determine how much a youngster knows from a single test score, and the same is true for each of these other goals and expectations. We'll need to have a lot of other data to consider, and we'll have to construct an answer to how well students and schools are faring from weighing a variety of evidence that must first be gathered and then assembled. So don't look for a single measure that will reveal all, and don't settle for any measure that purports to do so. There aren't any. But here are several things you might put together.

First, you might look to what are called "unobtrusive measures" for evidence that can be revealing about both goals and expectations. Such measures don't involve any special test or assignment or activity, but rather the devising of telling questions that can be answered from observations. Actually, a lot of the data we need to gather with respect to our school expectations will provide unobtrusive measures for everybody but the data collector. These measures make no demands on class time. They include such data as the attendance rates in schools and classrooms, the school dropout rate, the number of suspensions and expulsions, retention rates, the extent of teacher turnover. Each of these offers powerful testimony on whether schools are meeting our expectations.

But these are not what school evaluators usually have in mind when they speak of "unobtrusive measures." Here are a couple of the sorts of things they might be more likely to cite. John Goodlad used to say that one measure of how user-friendly first-grade classrooms are is the number of children who vomit before leaving home on school days. Another measure might be how quickly, and with what sorts of facial expressions, children *and* teachers leave school at the end of the day. Or we might look at the incidence of graffiti in and around the building. You can put together a set of such observations that should yield partial answers on some of the school expectations.

Student performance and behavior are other unobtrusive evaluation measures. Our fifth goal for learners, for instance—the development of character and other personal traits—could be measured by how youngsters carry out service-learning activities: how responsible they are, how sincere their efforts are, the degree of integrity and commitment and stewardship they display. The sixth goal for learners—individual development—may best be displayed through exhibitions in which the community is invited at intervals to observe students' artwork, dancing, singing, storytelling, or debating. In judging such performances, we need a set of carefully devised criteria for judging that are to be applied by a review panel consisting of parents and community members, some relevant experts, some teachers, and some fellow students.

Figuring out the measurements and doing the measuring will not be a simple task. But it is one that real accountability requires. If you agree that the goals and expectations I've stated here are both important and desirable, then we must try, despite the difficulty, to arrive at reliable and credible ways to check how well schools are succeeding at them. In this era of extreme accountability, it just might be our only way to keep test scores from deciding everything.

MARY ANNE RAYWID is professor emerita of educational administration and policy studies, Hofstra University, Hempstead, N.Y., and a member of the affiliate graduate faculty at the University of Hawaii, Manoa. This article is adapted from a speech to a conference on assessment, sponsored by the Hawaii Charter School Resource Center, May 2001.

Early Childhood Education

DISTANCE LEARNING FOR TEACHERS ADDS A NEW DIMENSION

New ways for teachers to learn may add up to better education for young children.

by MICHAEL deCOURCY HINDS

Once upon a time, children had to be six years old before they started school. Younger children had to pass their time in "child-care centers" with "caregivers." Back then, people thought the centers were just for baby-sitting and didn't need much money. But that meant nice caregivers were always leaving for better-paid jobs. It also meant that most centers didn't have enough fun stuff like paper and paint, books, games and computers. Imagine what it was like for children, especially poor children who didn't have much fun stuff at home, either. Then, all of a sudden, things began to change. Grown-ups discovered that ba-
bies are eager to learn language and toddlers think reading, math and science are really neat. Around that time, child-care centers became "care-and-education centers" that encouraged all children to learn amazing things while they play. That was also when people discovered that caregivers were really teachers who needed to be trained like teachers and paid like teachers so they can stay with the children. Everyone, especially children from poor families, lived more happily ever after.

Apart from the fairy-tale ending, this is the unfolding story of America's revolution in early education
and its nascent preschool reform movement. As a nation, we are still in the olden days. Only since the 1990s have Americans begun to appreciate young children's phenomenal, and largely uptapped, capacity to learn. In fact, it is still news to most Americans that infants and toddlers are budding linguists, scientists and mathematicians. The research is both exciting and unsettling as it starkly reveals the vast gulf between the kind of early care and education that promotes love of learning and success in school and life—and the way America ware-

houses most children in mediocre centers.

Growing awareness of the research, though, has begun to build momentum for preschool reform. The term refers to substantial improvements in the care and education of millions of preschoolers as well as the expansion of quality programs to millions of other poor and underserved children. Universal preschool, say some, is as inevitable as its timing is uncertain. Today, the greatest part of the educational challenge is bringing caregivers into the teaching profession.

Never mind the costs for now, the logistics alone are daunting: Three million caregivers and preschool teachers need training in child development and the latest research-based methods for nurturing young children's intellectual growth. But few community colleges or university-based schools of education are sufficiently up to speed on the recent research to have incorporated it in their courses. Short workshops and conferences that are typically used for professional development cannot do justice to the material. And, because the research is so new and preschool budgets are so small, educational publishers have not rushed to develop comprehensive curricula that would give preschool teachers a step-by-step guide.

A Pioneering Effort Suggests the Scope of the Challenge

The revolution in early education presents quite a challenge for Head Start, the federal preschool program that has a staff of 180,000 in 18,200 centers for approximately 860,000 children around the country. But Head Start has long been a leader in teacher training, largely because of its policy of recruiting one-in-three staff members from its own community of parents with low-incomes and limited education. The program consistently allocates two percent of its budget for teacher training and technical assistance; that works out

to be $130 million of the $6.2 billion budget for 2001.

As a result of its policies and tuition assistance programs over the years, 90 percent of its staff have degrees in early childhood education or have obtained a Child Development Associate credential or a state certificate to teach in a preschool classroom; 41 percent of its head teachers have an associate's or bachelor's degree in early childhood development or a related field. In 1998, Congress recognized the need for better educated preschool teachers and mandated that at least 50 percent of Head Start teachers must have a two- or four-year degree by 2003. All Head Start teachers also need training in the new research-based teaching methods, but most will have to wait for schools of education to catch up, says Tom Schultz, director of Head Start's Program Support Division. "We are in the middle of a sea change in the early education field," he says. "As the new research is absorbed in colleges and universities, Head Start programs can take advantage of it."

To accelerate this process, the National Head Start Association, an independent organization that works to improve Head Start, came up with a high-tech plan—one that might serve as a model for providing professional development training not only for preschool teachers but for those teaching K–12 grades, as well.

The plan: Have scholars share their research and new teaching techniques directly with the nation's caregivers and preschool teachers using satellite television, the Internet and locally trained facilitators. In other words, provide pre-K teachers with a distance-learning curriculum. The program starts with a 44-hour course on new research on literacy and teaching strategies to develop children's language and pre-literacy skills. In subsequent years, the distance-learning program—called the *HeadsUp! Network*—can offer similar courses in teaching preschool math, science and other topics such as nurturing preschoolers' social and emo-

tional development and teaching young children with disabilities.

"We set up the network to provide unified training to a national audience so that everybody would get the same information," says Sarah M. Greene, the association's president and chief executive officer. Support for the distance-learning project has come from a growing number of states and foundations, including The Heinz Endowments, The Knowledge Works Foundation, AT&T and Carnegie Corporation of New York. Foundations are particularly interested in the *HeadsUp! Network* as a promising model for strengthening professional development programs for all teachers, from pre-K through 12th grade, says Michael H. Levine, executive director of the I Am Your Child Foundation and, until earlier this year, deputy chair and senior program officer in the Corporation's Education Division. "The potential reach and cost effectiveness of this type of program is very significant," he says.

Distance learning has been around in one form or another since the late 1800s when students at the University of Wisconsin were allowed to take history courses by corresponding with a professor. Today, more than 1,600 institutions offer more than 54,000 courses that rely, wholly or in part, on the Internet, according to the United States Distance Learning Association, a trade group in an industry that is estimated to reach $12 billion in annual sales by 2003. Corporations have made the most use of distance learning, with companies like Anderson, an international consulting firm, using "e-learning" for the periodic training of its 77,000 employees in 83 countries.

Distance learning has also made major inroads in the K–12 grades, both for teachers' professional development and for use in their classrooms. Since 1991, the Annenberg/CPB Channel has been offering professional development workshops in most academic subjects; some of the support materials are now available on its web site (www.learner.org).

Designed to improve K–12 teaching, the distance education project grew out of a college-level distance learning television program that was started in 1981 by the philanthropist Walter H. Annenberg and the Corporation for Public Broadcasting. In 1988, the U.S. Department of Education began supporting distance learning programs for K–12 students in rural schools. The program, called Star Schools, now provides instructional programming in dozens of subjects, ranging from algebra to Swahili, and it reaches 1.6 million students a year in all 50 states.

Research indicates that student achievement is essentially the same in both distance learning courses and traditional classroom courses. The one significant difference is that more students drop out of distance learning programs than traditional courses. Those who complete the courses tend to like the high-tech format, but those who quit cite feelings of isolation and complain about the faster pace of online courses and, of course, technical difficulties. A 1999 study at an Illinois community college illustrates the attrition problem. It found that 64 percent of the students completed distance education courses compared with 83 percent who completed traditional classroom courses.

When the *HeadsUp! Network* began offering its professional development program in literacy last year, it became one of the country's largest distance learning programs. It reached up to 6,000 caregivers and teachers at 2,000 centers. In addition, more than 70 colleges offer the program for credit towards an associate's or bachelor's degree in early childhood development or education. Any organization—be it a child-care center or children's library—can receive the distance learning program and share it with teachers, librarians, parents and anyone else interested in children's education. Participating organizations must pay a monthly subscription fee of $75, install a $250 satellite dish to receive the televised program and

have access to the Internet to follow the course on line.

Four states—Ohio, Pennsylvania, California and Nebraska—initially signed on as network sponsors and two others—Illinois and Missouri—joined this year; more are expected to join. By this fall, there could be up to 3,000 participating organizations. "At that point, we would have enough subscribers to be financially viable," says Libby Doggett, a *HeadsUp! Reading* project manager. She says the program should reach 12,000 child-care workers in 2001–2002, and 20,000 in 2002–2003.

Every Wednesday night during school year 2000–2001, a satellite orbiting more than 22,000 miles above the Equator sent the network's first professional development course, called *HeadsUp Reading,* to child-care workers in public and private child-care centers and in colleges around the country. The two-hour program, which will be refined and offered again this year, has a breezy talk-show format with literacy experts presenting the latest research and showing video clips from classrooms to illustrate strategies for applying the research. And unlike many distance-learning programs, which involve individual students sitting in front of their home computers, the *HeadsUp! Network* sends its live broadcasts to groups of child-care workers and students gathered at child-care centers and in college classrooms. Viewers can call in questions during part of the program and a trained facilitator, usually a local college professor, leads discussions at each site before and after the program and during several breaks.

Formal evaluations are underway, but a preliminary snapshot of the program's impact, conducted by the Center for the Improvement of Early Reading Achievement, reported that the program produced significant knowledge and performance gains among teachers in early literacy education. Even before those results were announced, in southern Ohio, in the foothills of the Appalachian Mountains, *HeadsUp! Reading*

was already a big hit according to the reviews of many Head Start teachers and the program's local facilitator, Barbara Trube. An educator with much experience in Head Start programs and elementary schools, Trube is an assistant professor in the Department of Education at Shawnee State University in Portsmouth. "The teachers are so excited about what they are doing in *HeadsUp! Reading,* especially when they see that the children are learning more," says Trube, who also incorporates the program into her education courses.

A few minutes before 7 p.m. on a Wednesday last spring, Trube began ushering a dozen veteran preschool teachers and a few college students into two conference rooms—one for "talkers" who like to share ideas during the telecast and one for "writers" who like to take notes and follow the TV program in silence. "We try to accommodate everyone's learning style," explains Trube, who popped back and forth between the rooms, discussing homework assignments and technical problems (handouts for that night's program weren't available because the *HeadsUp! Reading* web site, www.huronline.org, had been down all day).

Then it was showtime, as "Class 19: Third Session on Reading," came alive on a large, wall-mounted television set. "Hello everyone and welcome to *HeadsUp! Reading,*" said Mike Rutherford, the program's host. He introduced that night's two faculty members: Jerlean E. Daniel, associate professor in the School of Education at the University of Pittsburgh and a past president of the National Association for the Education of Young Children, and Toni S. Walters, professor in reading and language arts at the School of Education at Oakland University in Michigan and the author of several books on teaching reading.

Because of the wide differences in the educational backgrounds of child-care workers and preschool teachers, *HeadsUp! Reading* avoids educational lingo and presents information in a simple, but sophisticated manner that takes very little knowledge for granted. "Jeri and Toni, why is it important for teachers to think about books themselves, the actual items, rather than just teaching reading?" Rutherford asked, early in the program. "Well, you know Mike, all books are not created equal—there is some real trash out there and there are some high-quality books," replied Daniel. "And so, as teachers, we have to be highly intentional and careful about the selections. Toni, I know you've got some ideas on this as well." "Yes," Walters chimed in, "there is so much children can get from books, beginning from birth throughout life. It's important that they have a good selection that reflects what the world is like, the people in the world, the kinds of things that happen in the world where we live."

Picking up speed as it moved along, Class 19 focused on strategies for selecting high-quality, developmentally and culturally appropriate books. Translating theory into practice, the program featured several charming video clips of preschoolers taking a class trip to a public library in Cincinnati, Ohio.

On this particular night in Portsmouth, Ohio, the television program was followed by presentations of posters, maps and books that the preschool teachers had done as homework. There was no formal discussion of that night's television program, but several teachers said they had picked up some good ideas and others said they planned to take a taped copy of the program home for a second viewing.

The library program had a big impact on Terri Will, one of many Head Start teachers who took the course for credit toward an associate's degree. Like many of her colleagues, Will is a high-school graduate whose first contact with Head Start was as a low-income parent with three of her four children in the Portsmouth program. That was a dozen years ago, and her initial volunteer work evolved into a paid job as a bus driver and as an assistant teacher, after she obtained a one-year certificate in early childhood development. Now 45, she continues to do both jobs, earning about $12 an hour.

"I'm almost ashamed to admit it," she said in an interview several weeks after the class on reading, books and libraries. "I used to take all 20 of my kids to the library, sit them on the floor and expect them all to pay attention to my reading four or five small books. But they couldn't see the print or appreciate the pictures! Naturally they wiggled and misbehaved and wondered what everyone else was doing. Looking back on that now, it seems to primitive! It didn't work at all, but that was the way it was done. I feel like I had blinders on because I was mostly concerned that they sat quietly and behaved—their behavior was more of a concern than the actual books. I didn't realize how impressive the library could be to them, how books could be so important at this time in their lives. I see that differently now."

Will now uses the library more creatively. "I take the children through the stacks and ask about their favorite things that they want to read about. The library has books on all their interests from airplanes to bumblebees to books on divorce and dying. Now, I also choose really large, colorful books, some with pop-up illustrations and flaps, to read out loud. I read to only three or four children at a time and I ask questions about the story and the pictures. I find that the children automatically behave when they are interested in the books and when I'm interested in the books. The whole quality of my reading has gone up 150 percent!"

Will said that the 22-week *Heads-Up! Reading* course had made her a better teacher and made her feel more professional. It strengthened her confidence, she said, by validating some of her own teaching methods. The course made her realize the importance of structured language and literacy lessons, and how they could be seamlessly woven into every part of the children's day.

Very Young and Eager to Learn

Terri Will and her Head Start colleagues are pioneers on the new frontier of education. Brain research, which has been widely publicized (and oversimplified) since the early 1990s, opened the nation's eyes to the intellectually fertile preschool years. Studies on child development and education, including some that had sat on shelves for years, suddenly gained wider readership and influence.

Researchers tell us that children start thinking in complex ways just weeks after birth, not when they enter kindergarten or first grade, as previously assumed. The human species, it seems, has an innate ability for learning language, math and science—a proclivity that can be nourished or starved, with predictable results. Four-month-old babies rapidly learn to distinguish between similar sounds like "ba" and "pa," and they suck and wiggle with excitement and attentiveness when learning new sounds. Infants can also tell when one pile of objects is larger than another, and they recognize the difference between adding objects and subtracting them from the piles. When toddlers play on their own with specially weighted blocks, they develop hypotheses about the blocks' center of gravity and solutions for balancing them. As they walk up and down a ramp, preschoolers tend to think like physicists, making observations and predictions about motion. Not only are toddlers eager to learn about dinosaurs, they enjoy sorting toy ones into categories that include diet, habitat and behavior.

The research clearly demonstrates the need for responsive teachers and enriched learning environments, where fun and games are designed to lead children through a structured learning process. Responding in kind to babies' coos and clucks, and encouraging them to mouth sounds in front of a mirror turn out to be very valuable lessons: One study indicates that the earlier babies babble fluently, the earlier that they reach every other milestone in acquiring language.

In just the last four years, ideas about applying this new understanding of children's early development to classroom practices have begun flowing out of consensus-building conferences, commissions and expert panels. "We've recognized that children need to be challenged with ideas, with learning—and that is very, very new, believe it or not," says Susan B. Neuman, an expert in children's literacy who recently joined the Bush Administration as Assistant Secretary of Education for Elementary and Secondary Education. "We need to prepare children to think conceptually," she adds, "not just teach them numbers and shapes, but teach them about measurement and size so they can build a connection between the abstract symbols and what they see in the world."

The terms daycare and preschool once distinguished between full-day custodial care and half-day programs that had more of an academic focus. Now, as education is expected in all programs, the terms are used interchangeably.

Currently, research is being applied to lesson plans, learning units and teaching strategies with impressive results. But as yet there are no comprehensive curricula to guide preschool teachers. What is needed, according to a 2001 report called *Eager to Learn: Educating our Preschoolers*, done for the National Research Council, is "curricula that encourages children to reflect, predict, question, and hypothesize, setting them on course for effective, engaged learning."

In describing the magnitude of the preschool reform opportunity—and its challenge—Anne Mitchell, president of Early Childhood Policy Research, says: "We need to make the same kind of investment in early education that we do in higher education. We all know that going to college makes a huge difference. The same is true with early childhood education."

Child-care Centers Today: Mostly Parking Lots for Kids

As research keeps raising the bar on what children need to thrive in preschool, the nation's child-care programs look worse and worse. Only one-in-eight child-care centers was considered good-to-excellent in a recent study. Most were ranked as mediocre-to-poor, and some even provided less than the minimal care necessary to safeguard children's health, safety and development. Infants and toddlers tend to be the most neglected, with 40 percent of their programs providing less than minimal services in a four-state survey in 1995. More than one-third of family-based child-care services put the children's well-being in jeopardy, and only one-in-eleven of these programs was considered good, researchers said in 1994. Unfortunately, the children who are most in need of an enriching mix of care and education—those from low-income families—tend to be enrolled in lower-quality programs from birth.

Most programs operate on shoestring budgets, in part, because many states have not raised their reimbursement rates for years and, in part, because families can't pay the higher fees that are needed to sustain high-quality private programs. A 1998 survey of urban child-care costs by the Children's Defense Fund found that the average costs for four-year-olds in child-care centers exceeded $3,000, rising to more than $5,000 per child in 17 states. In 15 states, child-care costs were more than the annual tuition at a public college. The Census Bureau reports that one-out-of-three families with young children earns less than $25,000 a year; if both parents work full time at the minimum wage, their income is about $21,400 a year.

Not only does inadequate public funding contribute to the poor quality of child-care programs, inadequate state standards for caregivers and preschool teachers encourages mediocrity. To put the situation in perspective, hairdressers in more than 40 states are required to have between 1,000 and 2,100 hours of training at an accredited school to obtain a license, yet most states only require that professional child-caregivers and teachers be high school graduates. A 2000 study done at Wheelock College reports that most states do not require any pre-service training in child development for caregivers and teachers. State requirements for annual in-service professional development training for staff are also minimal—ranging from zero hours in Michigan to 24 hours in Maine.

Because caregivers are teachers, they should have a bachelor's degree in early childhood education, according to the National Research Association, an operating arm of the National Academy of Sciences. Research has closely linked program quality to teaching quality—and that is directly related to the level of the teachers' own education.

College graduates, however, have little economic incentive to work in preschool. According to the U.S. Department of Labor, Bureau of Labor Statistics, child-care workers earn an average of $7.42 an hour, or about the same as parking lot attendants; preschool teachers earn an average of $9.43 an hour, or about $3 an hour less than the average animal trainer. Kindergarten teachers, by comparison, earn an average of $24.51 an hour.

Not surprisingly, child-care centers throughout the country report staggering turnover rates that range between 30 and 40 percent a year, according to the Center for the Child Care Workforce, an advocacy organization in Washington, D.C. In a recent study, done with the Institute of Industrial Relations at the University of California at Berkeley and funded by the David and Lucile Packard

Foundation, the center analyzed turnover rates in 75 child-care centers in California. The average turnover rate of the centers was 30 percent, but that masked much higher rates in individual centers. In one year, six centers reported losing all of their assistant teachers and nine centers reported losing all of their master teachers. Turnover among child-care staff is a particular problem for young children, as research indicates that their ability to learn is diminished when they lack strong and stable attachments to their teachers.

"The question of who will teach our children is as pressing at the preschool level, if not more so, as for higher grades," says Marcy Whitebook, the study's director and a senior researcher at the Institute of Industrial Relations. "Without a skilled and stable workforce, efforts to provide growth-enhancing experiences for children are severely constrained. Compensation for those who care for your children must be increased dramatically and quickly."

Preschool Reform: Moving Beyond Lip Service

Even before the latest research, of course, the benefits of enriching preschool programs like Head Start for children of poor families were widely known—and almost as widely ignored. In general, the nation has been long on lip service to children's needs and short on cash for their programs. The Congressional Budget Office reports, for example, that federal spending on all programs for children in the mid-1990s was about one-fifth of the spending on programs for people 65 and older—even though poverty affected twice as many children as older Americans.

At the moment, preschool reform has grabbed the political spotlight, if not the public budget. During the presidential campaign last year, George W. Bush repeatedly promised to "leave no child behind," borrowing a trademarked slogan from the mission statement of the Children's Defense Fund (CDF).

Yet after President Bush introduced his first budget, Marian Wright Edelman, CDF's founder and president, criticized the budget for leaving many children behind. She noted, among other things, that the Bush budget cut $220 million from programs that provide care and education for young children and that the budget also abandoned the goal of enrolling one million children in Head Start preschool programs by 2002. Currently, Head Start serves 860,000 3-to-5-year-old children from families living below the federal poverty level, or only 43 percent of the children eligible for the program; and because of long waiting lists in many areas, most children are only allowed to enroll in one or two nine-month, part-day sessions. "We must not let the words 'leave no child behind' become a fig leaf for unjust political and policy choices that, in fact, will leave millions of children and the poor behind," Edelman says.

For now, the most persuasive reason to consider preschool reform as a real possibility is the simple fact that the public—and the economy—increasingly demand it now that most mothers of young children are in the workforce. Most families—and more politically important, three-out-of-four middle-class families—have come to rely on programs that care and educate their preschoolers.

The most recent government statistics show that, in 1995, 13 million children under age 6, or nearly 60 percent of this age group, were receiving some form of non-parental care, including that delivered by child-care centers, family child-care providers, in-home caregivers and relatives. Children whose mothers work outside the home spent an average of 35 hours a week in daycare and children whose mothers do not have outside jobs average 20 hours a week in daycare.

Since 1990, when the percentage of America's children in daycare passed the halfway mark, the cultural debate about daycare versus maternal care became moot. "Child-care research has moved from asking whether child-care is detrimental to attempting to understand how variations in quality affect children's development," notes a study done at Mathematica Policy Research in 1996.

For children from low-income families, in particular, the long-term benefits of attending preschool programs are significant, according to W. S. Barnett's review of 36 studies done prior to 1995. The research review concluded that children who attended good preschools were less likely to be held back a grade, less likely to be placed in special education classes and more likely to succeed in school and to graduate than their peers who did not attend preschool.

Now, preschool reform is widely seen as the only way the nation can meet its number one educational goal, set at the 1989 Education Summit in Charlottesville, that "all children start school ready to learn." As it is, one-in-three children—and possibly up to two-in-three children in poor urban areas—arrive in kindergarten or first grade ill-prepared to learn. Academically, they lack the most basic knowledge about numbers and letters and are unfamiliar with scores of skills (print reads left to right) and concepts (numbers represent quantity) that are prerequisites to learning to read and do math. A disproportionate number of children from disadvantaged families fall behind in kindergarten, and many never catch up. About 40 percent of children, for example, do not learn to read with fluency and comprehension, a deficit that undermines their ability to learn anything in school.

Preschool reform, which includes open access to preschool programs, promises to narrow this intransigent achievement gap between affluent and poor children—a gap that is widening along with the influx of poor, non-English-speaking immigrants. Census reports indicate that one-in-five Americans speak a language other than English at home; in the federal Head Start preschool program, 22 percent of the children speak Spanish at home and four percent speak a total of 139 other languages.

Experts say that preschools' popularity, track record and promising educational advances have reached a critical mass, giving preschool reform a life of its own. In its forecast, this year's report from the National Research Council concludes: "Looking to the future, there can be little doubt that the United States is on its way to universal, voluntary, pre-

school attendance, not as the result of government mandate or expert recommendation, but as a consequence of parental demand and a myriad of private, state and federal initiatives that are continuing to extend early education throughout the country."

It remains to be seen whether or not the United States will ultimately follow every other modern industrial nation in supporting a universal preschool program, but many experts say that the pressure for major preschool reforms can only increase as a new revolution in early child-

hood education rolls around the country. So, nearly 20 years into the K–12 school reform movement, the end is not in sight, but the beginning has suddenly snapped into focus: It's preschool reform.

Michael deCourcy Hinds is the Corporation's chief writer. Previously, he was a national correspondent for The New York Times *and he also wrote citizens' guides to social issues at Public Agenda, a nonprofit, nonpartisan public policy research organization.*

The Winding Path: Understanding the Career Cycle of Teachers

SUSAN K. LYNN

Teachers are a primary component for educational excellence, and the need to attract and retain highly capable individuals to the teaching profession is clear (Holmes Group 1986, Carnegie Forum 1986, National Governors Association 1986). In response to that need, numerous reform efforts, including programs, plans, and recommendations, have emerged in an attempt to professionalize teaching and make the career more rewarding. Many of those reforms are predicated on the assumption that teachers develop through different career stages and undergo continual change.

The model proposes that a supportive, nurturing environment can assist a teacher in the pursuit of a positive career progression.

Within the adult development and career development literature are theories and studies that acknowledge that teachers have different attitudes, knowledge, skills, and behaviors at various points during their career. Early models viewed teachers' careers as progressing through three or four sequential stages (Burden 1982; Newman, Burden, and Applegate 1980). Later models have attempted to incorporate the career stages and principles of adult growth and development (Fessler 1985, Leithwood 1990, Super 1994). The literature suggests that the characteristics of teachers that appear to change are their concerns, instructional behaviors, understanding of children,

awareness and understanding of the school and teaching environment, and perceptions of themselves, their work, and their professions. The literature describes the variability that occurs in the areas of personal awareness, cognitive development, interpersonal development, and theoretical knowledge. Implied is the idea that as teachers' characteristics change, their needs with regard to professional activities, relationships, and interests will change accordingly.

The teacher career cycle model incorporates both the literature on career stages and the literature on adult growth and development (Fessler 1992) (see figure 1). The model is an attempt to describe the teacher career cycle within the context of a dynamic and flexible social system. The career cycle itself progresses through stages, not in a lock-step, linear fashion, but in a dynamic manner reflecting responses to personal and organizational environmental factors.

Among the variables from the personal environment that affect the career cycle are family support structures, positive critical incidents, life crises, individual dispositions, and avocational outlets. The organizational environment of schools and school systems compose a second major category of influence on the career cycle; among the influential variables are school regulations, management style of administrators and supervisors, atmosphere of public trust in the community, expectations of the community for its educational system, activities of professional organizations and associations, and union atmosphere.

FIGURE 1. Model of the Teacher Career Cycle and Environmental Influences

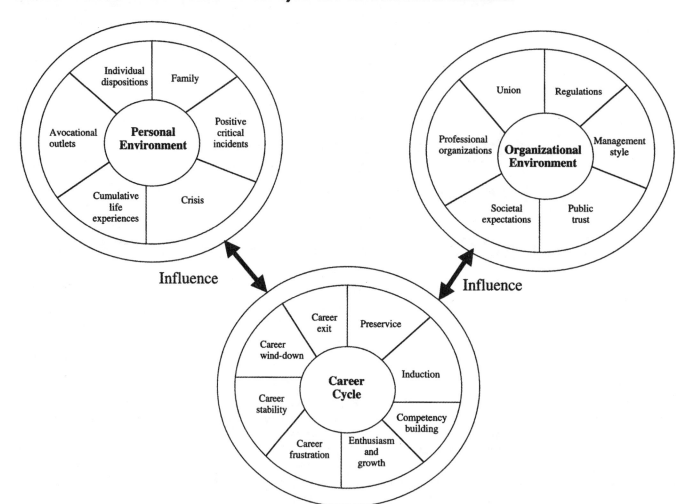

During the induction period new teachers strive for acceptance by students, peers, and supervisors and attempt to achieve comfort and security in dealing with everyday problems and issues.

The model proposes that a supportive, nurturing environment can assist a teacher in the pursuit of a positive career progression. Alternatively, an environmental atmosphere that includes negative pressures and conflicts can have an adverse effect on a teacher's career path. Fessler's (1992) career cycle model, based on self-reported characteristics of teachers on the variables of enthusiasm, interactive teaching skills, attitudes toward students and teaching, and attitudes toward the teaching profession, consists of eight stages: preservice, induction, competency building, enthusiasm and growth, career frustration, career stability, career wind-down, and career exit.

Preservice

The preservice stage is the beginning period of preparation for a specific professional role. This includes initial study in a college or university or retraining for a new role or assignment, either by attending a higher education institution or participating in staff development within the work setting. Typically a teacher who changes positions within the profession, as from teaching high school algebra to teaching fourth grade, or who changes professions completely, as from teaching third grade to owning a business, will find herself back in the preservice career phase.

Induction

The induction stage is generally defined as the first few years of teaching, when the teacher is socialized into the professional and social fabric of the school and community. For example, as a first-year teacher Sarah is implementing a discipline strategy recommended by several of her colleagues who are veteran teachers. Although she recognizes the inappropriateness of the strategy from the perspective of her preservice preparation program, Sarah uses the strategy with her students merely to placate her colleagues. They are socializing her to be in sync with their more traditional teaching practices.

During the induction period new teachers strive for acceptance by students, peers, and supervisors and attempt to achieve comfort and security in dealing with everyday problems and issues. Although induction is usually viewed as the time when teachers go from preservice preparation to full-time classroom instruction, as Sarah did, teachers may also experience the induction stage when shifting to another grade level or subject, another building, or another job.

Competency Building

During this stage of the career cycle, the teacher strives to improve teaching skills and abilities by seeking out new materials, methods, and strategies. Teachers at this stage are receptive to new ideas, attend workshops and conferences willingly, and enroll in graduate programs through their own initiative. They see their job as challenging and they are eager to improve their repertoire of skills. For example, to help his students concept-map short stories, Frank, a fifth-year middle school English teacher, implements a new computer program he learned about while attending a computer education conference during the summer. Frank and other competency-building teachers are attempting to develop a feeling of confidence and comfort in their teacher knowledge and skills.

Fessler (1992) considers this a critical period in the career cycle. He suggests that those teachers who are successful in building confidence in and skill with their teaching competencies will likely move forward to an enthusiastic and growing stage, whereas those who do not may experience a level of frustration that can even result in early career exit.

Enthusiasm and Growth

At the enthusiasm and growth stage, teachers have reached a high level of competence in their jobs but continue to progress as professionals. Teachers in this stage love their jobs, look forward to going to school and to interacting with their students, and are constantly seeking new ways to enrich their teaching. Hollie, a secondary physical education teacher, can be identified as being in an enthusiastic and growing phase of her career cycle. She is a master teacher who is competent and self-confident; she is also active in her state physical education organization, attends the yearly conference, and serves on numerous committees. Her students describe her as en-

thusiastic and as someone who appears to love her job. Within the school district Hollie lends a helping hand to other teachers and organizes workshops for the districts' secondary physical education teachers. Enthusiastic and growing teachers like Hollie not only experience high levels of job satisfaction, but also tend to have a positive impact on the climate of the school community.

Career Frustration

Unlike the enthusiasm and growth phase, the career frustration stage reflects a lack of job satisfaction, and the teacher may even question his or her choice of entering the profession. Frustration and disillusionment with teaching characterize this career stage, and teacher burnout is common. Erika, a fifth-grade educator in her seventh year of teaching, has entered the career frustration stage. She has mixed emotions about her tenure as a teacher in a large inner-city school. Although Erika appreciates the relationships she has established with her colleagues, she harbors deep frustration with the factors that make the job so difficult: large classes, state testing of students, limited resources for classroom materials, mountains of paperwork, and a low salary. She feels powerless in the face of an immovable bureaucracy. Historically this frustration occurs during career midpoints; however, such feelings are on the rise among teachers in the relatively early years of their careers, particularly among teachers who face the continual threat of job loss due to budget cuts or those who face environmental problems too severe to overcome.

Career Stability

This stage marks the point when teachers may move into patterns of maintenance, stagnation, or renewed growth. Environmental factors play a huge role in determining which direction a teacher will go. For some it is a period when they have lost their enthusiasm for teaching and are simply going through the motions. For others, stability may reflect a period of maintaining a competent and steady commitment to teaching. Chad, a sixteen-year veteran of high school social studies teaching, is in the stability phase of his career. Chad still enjoys teaching but has settled into simply meeting the letter of his contract. He works hard during the school day but refuses to take work home. He takes on no extra activities. Teaching has become just another job. The stability stage of the career cycle can take place at any time for a variety of reasons. The needs of teachers at this stage vary greatly, as should professional development opportunities.

Career Wind-Down

Teachers preparing to leave the profession enter the career wind-down stage. For some, it may be a pleasant period during which they reflect on the many positive experiences they have had and look forward to a career change or retirement. For example, after twenty-nine years as an elementary school teacher and principal, Betsy is approaching her final year with a deep sense of satisfaction. She reflects on her career feeling good about the children whose lives she has influenced and grateful for having had the opportunity to make a difference. In contrast, for ten years Harry has loved his job as a sixth-grade teacher/coordinator of the gifted program. However, he learns that he has been reassigned to a traditional fourth-grade classroom for the following year. For teachers like Harry career wind-down may be a period of mixed emotions, such as resentment for a forced job termination or reassignment or yearning to get out of an unrewarding job. The teacher remains excited by the profession but definitely feels that it is time to move on.

…teachers must be motivated to seek continued growth through professional development that advocates personalized and individualized support systems.

A person may spend weeks, months, or even several years in this stage. Although the career wind-down stage is generally viewed as a precursor to leaving the profession, for some teachers, like Harry, it may lead to a preservice or induction phase for a new position or role within a school or a new career outside of education.

Career Exit

The exit stage of a teacher's career represents the period of time after the teacher leaves the job, either through retirement after many years of service, involuntary dismissal, an elected career change, or temporary career exit for child care or other necessity. This may also be a time of alternative career exploration or of moving to a non-teaching position in education such as administration. For example, Brenda entered the career-exit stage after ten years as an art teacher when she accepted a position as an assistant principal, whereas Bill, a high school history and economics teacher, entered the career-exit stage to fulfill a lifelong dream of seeking elected office. Most career exits stimulate professional growth and offer gratification. When a teacher's leaving is involuntary, however, the exit can result in personal crisis.

Summary

Movement in and between these eight stages is dynamic and flexible rather than static and linear. Teachers do not necessarily circulate through all the stages. At first glance it does appear that the model (Fessler 1992) represents a linear process, with an individual's entering at the preservice phase and progressing through each phase to the career exit. However, the significance of the teacher career cycle model lies in the implication that teachers move in and out of career stages in response to personal and organizational environmental conditions.

Consider the following scenario as a demonstration of the dynamic nature of the career cycle. A teacher in the career wind-down stage is about to leave the profession. Unexpectedly, his wife dies. The dramatic change in his personal life may result in a reassessment of his career wind-down decision. Depending on the nature of additional personal and organizational environmental conditions, the teacher may renew a commitment to teaching and enter an enthusiastic and growing phase, or he may remain in the profession, being stable but stagnant.

Conclusion

Educational leaders should view a teacher's professional development and provide inservice and professional growth opportunities in light of his or her career cycle phase. Teacher development theory is predicated on the assumption that the needs of the beginning or novice teacher in the induction phase differ from that of an experienced teacher who has reached the enthusiasm and growth stage or has entered the stable phase. As a result, teachers must be motivated to seek continual growth through professional development that advocates personalized and individualized support systems.

To that end, induction-year teachers should be provided an individualized program that integrates the beginning teacher into the professional social fabric of the school. Such attention helps the beginner to recognize and manage the debilitating effects of isolation, self-doubt, stress, and anxiety often associated with the first year of teaching. The program should foster skills and habits that allow the beginning teacher to reduce or eliminate management problems known to trouble many beginning teachers. On the other hand, support systems for the enthusiastic and growing teacher might include opportunities for advanced study, collaboration and leadership, presenting at professional meetings, and increased autonomy.

For all teachers across the career cycle, the concept of staff development and professional growth should be broadened to include concern for the personal needs and problems of teachers, such as financial loss, divorce, illness of a loved one, and chemical abuse by a family member. Support systems should assist teachers in dealing with personal environmental factors that may likely affect their career path. Organizational policies on liberal sabbaticals, modification of job assignments, job sharing, and leaves of absence should be examined to provide support for teachers at various phases of the career cycle. Teachers at all career stages need support and assistance to realize their professional potential.

Key words: career cycle, job satisfaction, professional development, support systems

REFERENCES

Burden, P. 1982. Implications of teacher career development: New roles for teachers, administrators and professors. *Action in Teacher Education* 4(4): 21–25.

Carnegie Forum on Education and the Economy. 1986. *A nation prepared: Teachers for the 21st century.* Washington, DC: Carnegie Forum on Education and the Economy.

Fessler, R. 1985. A model for teacher professional growth and development. In *Career-long teacher education*, ed. P. J. Burke and R. C. Heideman. Springfield, IL: Charles C. Thomas.

-----. 1992. The teacher career cycle. In *The teacher career cycle: Understanding and guiding the professional development of teachers*, ed. R. Fessler and J. Christensen. Boston: Allyn and Bacon.

Holmes Group. 1986. *Tomorrow's teachers.* East Lansing, MI: Author.

Leithwood, K. 1990. The principal's role in teacher development. In *Changing school culture through staff development*, ed. B. Joyce. Alexandria, VA: Association for Supervision and Curriculum.

National Governors Association. 1986. *Time for results: The governors' 1991 report on education.* Washington, DC: National Governors Association.

Newman, K., P. Burden, and J. Applegate. 1980. *Helping teachers examine their long-range development.* Paper presented at the annual conference of the Association of Teacher Educators, Washington, D.C.

Super, D. 1994. A life-span, life-space perspective on convergence. In *Convergence in career development theories: Implications for science and practice*, ed. M. Savikas and R. Lent. Palo Alto, CA: CPP Books.

Susan K. Lynn is an associate professor of physical education at Florida State University, in Tallahassee.

From *The Clearing House,* March/April 2002, pp. 179-182. Reprinted with permission of the Helen Dwight Reid Educational Foundation. Published by Heldref Publications, 1319 Eighteenth St., NW, Washington, DC 20037-1802. © 2002.

UNIT 9

A Look to the Future

Unit Selections

Key Points to Consider

- What might be the shape of school curricula by the year 2020?

- What changes in society are most likely to affect educational change?

- What will be the effects of teenage drinking and the "children's revolution" among working couples on the future of American school demographics?

- How can schools prepare students to live and work in an uncertain future? What knowledge bases are most important? What skills are most important?

- What is made possible in the classroom by the new learning and communications technologies that have been developed?

- What should be the philosophical ideals for American schools in the twenty-first century?

 **Links: www.dushkin.com/online/**
These sites are annotated in the World Wide Web pages.

Goals 2000: A Progress Report
http://www.ed.gov/pubs/goals/progrpt/index.html
Mighty Media
http://www.mightymedia.com
Online Internet Institute
http://www.oii.org

We see the possibility of great change in how students learn in schools, which is being brought about by the revolution in computer-generated learning resources. The World Wide Web is here, and the electronic availability of massive knowledge bases is multiplying the possibilities of what teachers can do with their students. Making adequate computing equipment and educational software available to all teachers is one of the economic challenges that school systems face.

Which education philosophy is most appropriate for our schools? This is a complex question, and we will, as a free people, come up with alternative visions of what it will be. Let us explore what might be possible as more students go on the Internet and the wonder of the cyberspace revolution opens to teachers and students. What challenges can we expect in using the technology of the cyberspace revolution in our schools? What blessings can we hope for? What sorts of changes need to occur in how people go to schools as well as in what they do when they get there?

The breakthroughs that are developing in new learning and communications technologies are really quite impressive. They will definitely affect how human beings learn in the very near-term future. While we look forward with considerable optimism and confidence to these educational developments, there are still many controversial issues to be debated in the early years of the twenty-first century. The "school choice" issue is one. Some very interesting new proposals for new forms of schooling, both in public schools and private schools, are under development. We can expect to see at least a few of these proposals actually tried.

Some of the demographic changes and challenges involving young people in the United States are staggering. Ten percent of all American teenage girls will become pregnant each year, the highest rate in the developed world. At least 100,000 American elementary school children get drunk once a week. Incidence of venereal disease has tripled among adolescents in the United States since 1995. The actual school dropout rate in the United States stands at 30 percent.

The student populations of North America reflect vital social and cultural forces at work to destroy our progress. In the United States, a massive secondary school dropout problem has been developing steadily through the past decade. The next decade will reveal how public school systems will address this and other unresolved problems brought about by dramatic upheavals in demographics. In the immediate future, we will be able to see if emergency or alternative certification measures adopted by states affect achievement of the objectives of our reforms.

At any given moment in a people's history, several alternative future directions are open to them. North American educational systems have been subjected to one wave after another of recommendations for programmatic change. Is it any wonder that change is a sensitive watchword for persons in teacher educa-

tion on this continent? What specific directions it will take in the immediate future depend on which recommendations of the reform agenda are implemented, which agencies of government (local, state/provincial, and federal) will pay for the very high costs of reform, and which shifts in perceived national educational priorities by the public will occur that will affect fundamental realignments of our educational goals.

Basic changes in society's career patterns should also be considered. It is estimated that in the United States the average nonagricultural worker now makes a major job change about five times in his or her career. The schools will surely be affected, indirectly or directly, by this major social phenomenon. Changes in the social structure due to divorce, unemployment, and job retraining efforts will also have an impact. Educational systems are integral parts of the broader social systems that created them; if the larger social system experiences fundamental change, this is reflected in the educational system.

In the area of information science and computer technologies applicable for use in educational systems, the development of new products is so rapid that we cannot predict what technological capacities may be available to schools 20 years from now. We are in a period of human history when knowledgeable people can control far greater information (and have immediate access to it) than at any previous time. As new information-command systems evolve, this phenomenon will become more and more meaningful to all of us.

The future of education will be determined by the current debate concerning what constitutes a just, national response to human needs in a period of technological change. The history of technological change in all human societies since the beginning of industrial development clearly demonstrates that major advances in technology and breakthroughs in the basic sciences lead to more rapid rates of social change. Society is on the verge of discoveries that will lead to the creation of entirely new technologies in the dawning years of the twenty-first century. All of the social, economic, and educational institutions globally will be affected by these scientific breakthroughs. The basic issue is not whether schools can remain aloof from the needs of industry or the economic demands of society but how they can emphasize the noblest ideals of free persons in the face of inevitable technological and economic changes. Another concern is how to let go of predetermined visions of the future that limit our possibilities as free people. The schools, of course, will be called upon to face these issues. We need the most enlightened, insightful, and compassionate teachers ever educated by North American universities to prepare the youth of the future in a manner that will humanize the high-tech world in which they live.

All of the essays in this unit can be related to discussions on the goals of education, the future of education, or curriculum development.

The Kind of Schools We Need

Our schools, as they are now designed, often tacitly encourage the re-creation of a yellow-school-bus model of education. Yet we know there is a better way, Mr. Eisner says. That better way ought to be a part of the agenda the community discusses with teachers and school administrators, as we strive together to create the kind of schools we need.

BY ELLIOT W. EISNER

As EVERYONE knows, there is both great interest in and great concern about the quality of education in American schools. Solutions to our perceived educational ills are often not very deep. They include mandating uniforms for students to improve their behavior; using vouchers to create a competitive climate to motivate educators to try harder; testing students each year for purposes of accountability; retaining students whose test scores have not reached specific levels; paying teachers and school administrators bonuses in relation to the measured performance of their students; and defining standards for aims, for content, for evaluation practices, and, most important, for student and teacher performance.

Ironically, what seldom gets addressed in our efforts to reform schools is the vision of education that serves as the ideal for both the practice of schooling and its outcomes. We are not clear about what we are after. Aside from literacy and numeracy, what do we want to achieve? What are our aims? What is important? What kind of educational culture do we want our children to experience? In short, what kind of schools do we need?

What we do seem to care a great deal about are standards and monitoring procedures. We want a collection of so-called best methods that will guarantee success. We want a testing program that will display the results of our efforts, often in rank-ordered league standings. We want an assessment program that allows little space for personal judgment, at least when it comes to evaluation. Personal judgment is equated with subjectivity, and we want none of that. We want to boil down teaching and evaluation practices to a scientifically grounded technology.

Whether we can ever have a scientific technology of teaching practice, given the diversity of the students we teach, is problematic. Artistry and professional judgment will, in my opinion, always be required to teach well, to make intelligent education policy, to establish personal relationships with our students, and to appraise their growth. Those of us who work in the field of education are neither bank tellers who have little discretion nor assembly line workers whose actions are largely repetitive. Each child we teach is wonderfully unique, and each requires us to use in our work that most exquisite of human capacities, the ability to make judgments in the absence of rules. Although good teaching uses routines, it is seldom routine. Good teaching depends on sensibility and imagination. It courts surprise. It profits from caring. In short, good teaching is an artistic affair.

But even artistry can profit from a vision of the kind of education we want to provide. The reason I believe it is important to have a vision of education is because without one we have no compass, no way of knowing which way we are headed. As a result, we succumb to the pet ideas that capture the attention of policy makers and those with pseudo-solutions to supposed problems. Is it really the case that more testing will improve teaching and learning or that uniforms will improve student behavior and build character? I have my doubts. We need a conception of what good schools provide and what students and teachers do in them.

So let me share with you one man's vision of the kind of schools we need.

The kind of schools we need would provide time during the school day at least once a week for teachers to meet to discuss and share their work, their hopes, and their problems with their colleagues. It is the school, not the university, that is the real center of teacher education.

The idea that the school is the center of teacher education is built on the realization that whatever teachers become professionally, the process is not finished when they complete their teacher education program at age 21. Learning to teach well is a lifetime endeavor. The growth of understanding and skill in teaching terminates only when we do.

This fact means that we need to rethink whom the school serves. The school serves the teachers who work there as well as the students who learn there. The school needs to be designed in a way that affords opportunities to teachers to learn from one another. Such learning is so important that it should not be an addendum, relegated to an after-school time slot. Teachers, like others who do arduous work, are tired at the end of the day. Learning from our colleagues certainly deserves space and attention, and, even more important, it requires a reconceptualization of the sources of teacher development. One thing we can be sure of is that the school will be no better for the students who attend than it is for the teachers who teach there. What we do typically to improve teaching is to send teachers somewhere else to be "inserviced"—every 6,000 miles or so—usually by someone who has never seen them teach. The expectation is that what teachers are exposed to will somehow translate more or less automatically into their classrooms. Again, I have my doubts.

Teaching from a cognitive perspective requires a change in paradigm, what Thomas Kuhn once described as a "paradigm shift." Such shifts are changes in conception. From a behavioral perspective, change requires the development of those sensibilities and pedagogical techniques that make it possible to realize the conceptions and values that one defines for oneself educationally. Of course, the cognitive and the behavioral cannot truly be separated; I make the distinction here for purposes of clarity. What one conceptualizes as appropriate gives direction and guidance to what one does. And what one is able to do culminates in what one achieves. Schools ought to be places in which teachers have access to other teachers so that they have an opportunity to create the kind of

supportive and educative community that culminates in higher-quality education than is currently provided.

The kind of schools we need would make teaching a professionally public process. By "professionally public" I mean that teachers would have opportunities to observe other teachers and provide feedback. No longer would isolated teachers be left to themselves to figure out what went on when they were teaching; secondary ignorance is too prevalent and too consequential to depend on one's personal reflection alone. I used the term "secondary ignorance," and I used it intentionally. I like to make a distinction between what I refer to as *primary* ignorance and *secondary* ignorance.

Primary ignorance refers to a condition in which an individual recognizes that he does not know something but also recognizes that, if he wanted to know it, he could find out. He could inquire of others, he could use the library, he could go to school. Primary ignorance is a condition that in some sense is correctable and often easily correctable.

Secondary ignorance, however, is another matter. When an individual suffers from secondary ignorance, not only does she not know something, but she does not know that she does not know. In such a situation, correcting the problem may not be possible. Secondary ignorance is as consequential for the process of parenting and for the sustenance of friendships as it is for the conduct of teaching. The way in which one remedies secondary ignorance is not through self-reflection, but through the assistance of others. Really good friends can help you understand aspects of your behavior that you might not have noticed. These observations need not be negative. It is as important to appreciate one's virtues as to become cognizant of one's weaknesses.

For this process to occur professionally, teachers need access to other teachers' classrooms. Teaching needs to be made a professionally public endeavor. The image of the teacher isolated in a classroom from 8 a.m. to 3 p.m. for five days a week, 44 weeks per year, is not the model of professional teaching practice that we need. If even world-class artists and athletes profit from feedback on their performance from those who know, so too do the rest of us. We need a conception of schooling that makes possible teachers' access to one another in helpful and constructive ways. This will require redefining what the job of teaching entails.

For most individuals who select teaching as a career, the expectation is that they will be with children exclusively, virtually all day long. But teachers also need to interact with other adults so that the secondary ignorance that I described can be ameliorated.

The model of professional life that I am suggesting will not be easy to attain. We are often quite sensitive about what we do in our own classrooms, and many of us value our privacy. Yet privacy ought not to be our highest priority. We ought to hold as our highest priority our students' well-being. And their well-being, in turn, depends on the quality of our pedagogical work. This work, I am arguing, can be enhanced with the assistance of other caring adults.

The kind of schools we need would provide opportunities for members of subject-matter departments to meet to share their work. It would recognize that different fields have different needs and that sharing within fields is a way to promote coherence for students.

Departmentalization in our schools has been a long-standing way of life. It usually begins at the middle school level and proceeds through secondary school. Teachers of mathematics have a field and a body of content that they want to help students understand; so too do teachers of the arts. These commonalities within subject-matter fields can promote a wonderful sense of esprit, a sense built on a common language to describe shared work. The strength of the educational programs in these fields can be promoted when teachers in departmentalized systems have opportunities to meet and share their work, to describe the problems they have encountered, and to discuss the achievements they have made. In short, different fields often have different needs, and these different needs can be met within the school through the colleagueship that teachers within a discipline share. The department in the middle school and in the high school provides a substantial structure for promoting the sense of community I have described.

The kind of schools we need would have principals who spend about a third of their time in classrooms, so that they know firsthand what is going on. We often conceive of the role of the school principal not only as that of a skilled administrator but also as that of an educational leader. At least one of the meanings of educational leadership is to work with a staff in a way that will make leadership unnecessary. The aim of leadership in an educational institution is to work itself out of a job.

What this approach requires, at a minimum, is an understanding of the conditions of the school and the characteristics of the classrooms in which teachers work. To understand the school and the classroom requires that school administrators leave their offices and spend at least a third of their time in teachers' classrooms. In the business community this is called "supervision by walking around."

The term supervision is a bit too supervisory for my taste. I am not sure that school administrators have "super" vision. But they should have a grasp of what happens in their schools—substantively, as well as administratively. Administrators can be in a position to recognize different kinds of talents among faculty members; they can help initiate activities and support the initiatives of teachers. They can develop an intimacy that will enable them to promote and develop the leadership potential of teachers. Thus, paradoxically, the principal as leader is most successful when he or she no longer leads but promotes the initiative and leadership of others.

The kind of schools we need would use videotaped teaching episodes to refine teachers' ability to take the practice of teaching apart—not in the negative sense, but as a way of enlarging our understanding of a complex and subtle process. No one denies that teaching is a subtle and complex art. At least it is an art when it is done well. To teach really well, it is necessary to reflect on the processes of one's own teaching and on the teaching practices of others. Our ability to perform is related, as I suggested above, to our understanding of the relationship between teaching and learning. This relationship can be illuminated through the analysis of videotaped episodes of teaching practices. Just what is a teacher up to when he or she teaches? What are the consequences? What are the compromises and trade-offs that exist in virtually any context? What institutional or organizational pressures in a school must teachers contend with? How does a teacher insert herself into her teaching? What does his body language express?

Questions such as these can be profitably addressed through the analysis of videotapes. Indeed, the collaborative analysis of a teaching episode can provide a very rich resource that can illuminate differences in perspective, in educational values, and in the meanings being conveyed. This is all to the good. Teaching is not reducible to a single frame. From my perspective, the use of such tapes not only can make our understanding of teaching more appropriately complex, but it can also refine our ability to see and interpret the process of teaching. And the more subtle perspective on teaching that such analysis creates can only enhance the quality of what we have to say to one another about the kind of work we do.

The kind of schools we need would be staffed by teachers who are as interested in the questions students ask after a unit of study as they are in the answers students give. On the whole, schools are highly answer-oriented. Teachers have the questions, and students are to have the answers. Even with a problem-solving approach, the focus of attention is on the student's ability to solve a problem that someone else has posed. Yet the most intellectually demanding tasks lie not so much in solving problems as in posing questions. The framing of what we might oxymoronically call the "telling question" is what we ought to care much more about.

Once students come to deal with real situations in life, they will find that few of them provide defined problems. On the contrary, the primary task is often to define a problem so that one can get on with its solution. And to define a problem, one needs to be able to raise a question.

What would it mean to students if they were asked to raise questions coming out of a unit of study? What kinds of questions would they raise? How incisive and imaginative would these questions be? Would the students who do well in formulating questions be the same ones who do well when asked to converge upon a correct answer?

What I am getting at is the importance of developing an intellectual context designed to promote student growth. That context must surely give students an opportunity to pose questions and to entertain alternative perspectives on what they study. The last thing we want in an intellectually liberating environment is a closed set of attitudes and fealty to a single set of correct answers.

The kind of schools we need would not hold as an ideal that all students get to the same destinations at the same time. They would embrace the idea that good schools increase the variance in student performance and at the same time escalate the mean.

To talk about the idea that schools should increase individual differences rather than reduce them may at first seem counterintuitive and perhaps even antidemocratic. Don't we want all students to do the same? If we have a set of goals, don't we want all students to achieve them? To both of those questions I would give a qualified yes and no.

Individuals come into the world with different aptitudes, and, over the course of their lives, they develop different interests and proclivities. In an ideal approach to educational practice—say, one in which teaching practices were ideally designed to suit each youngster—each youngster would learn at an ideal rate. Students whose aptitudes were in math would travel farther and faster in that subject than students who had neither interest nor aptitude in math but who, for example, might have greater aptitude in language or in the visual arts. In those two fields, students would travel faster and farther than those with math aptitudes but with low interests or proclivities in language or the arts. Over time, the cumulative gap between students would grow. Students would travel at their own optimal rates, and some would go faster than others in different areas of work.

What one would have at the end of the school year is wide differences in students' performance. At the same time, since each program is ideally suited to each youngster, the mean for all students in all of the areas in which they worked would be higher than it would be in a more typical program of instruction.

Such a conception of the aims of education would actually be instrumental to the creation of a rich culture. It is through our realized aptitudes that we can contribute to the lives of others and realize our own potential. It is in the symbiotic relationships among us that we come to nurture one another, to provide for others what they cannot provide—at least, not as well—for themselves, and to secure from others the gifts they have to offer that we cannot create—at least, not as well—for ourselves.

The idea that getting everyone to the same place is a virtue really represents a limitation on our aspirations. It does not serve democratic purposes to treat everybody identically or to expect everyone to arrive at the same destination at the same time. Some students need to go farther in one direction and others need to go farther in a different direction because that's where their aptitudes lie, that's where their interests are, and that's where their proclivities lead them.

The British philosopher and humanist Sir Herbert Read once said that there were two principles to guide education.[1] One was to help children become who they are not; the other was to help children become who they are. The former dominates in fascist countries, he believed, where the image defined by the state becomes the model to which children must adapt. The fascist view is to help children become who they are not. Read believed that education was a process of self-actualization and that in a truly educational environment children would come to realize their latent potentials. In this age of high technology and highly monitored systems and standards, I believe that Read's views bear reflection.

The kind of schools we need would take seriously the idea that a child's personal signature, his or her distinctive way of learning and creating, is something to be preserved and developed. We are not in the shoe manufacturing business. By saying that we are not in the shoe manufacturing business, I mean that we are not in the business of producing identical products. On an assembly line, one seeks predictability, even certainty, in the outcomes. What one wants on both assembly lines and airline flights are uneventful events. No surprises.

In education, surprise ought to be seen not as a limitation but as the mark of creative work. Surprise breeds freshness and discovery. We ought to be creating conditions in school that enable students to pursue what is distinctive about themselves; we ought to want them to retain their personal signatures, their particular ways of seeing things.

Of course, their ways of seeing things need to be enhanced and enriched, and the task of teaching is, in part, to transmit the culture while simultaneously cultivating those forms of seeing, thinking, and feeling that make it possible for personal idiosyncrasies to be developed. In the process, we will discover both who children are and what their capabilities are.

The kind of schools we need would recognize that different forms of representation develop different forms of thinking, convey different kinds of meaning, and make possible different qualities of life. Literacy should not be restricted to decoding text and number.

Normally the term literacy refers to the ability to read, and numeracy, the ability to compute. However, I want to recast the meaning of literacy so that it refers to the process of encoding or decoding meaning in whatever forms are used in the culture to express or convey meaning. With this conception in mind and with the realization that humans throughout history have employed a variety of forms to express meaning, literacy becomes a process through which meanings are made. Meanings, of course, are made in the visual arts, in music, in dance, in poetry, in literature, as well as in physics, in mathematics, and in history. The best way to ensure that we will graduate semiliterate students from our schools is to make sure that they have few (or ineffective) opportunities to acquire the multiple forms of literacy that make multiple forms of meaning possible.

That meanings vary with the forms in which they are cast is apparent in the fact that, when we bury and when we marry, we appeal to poetry and music to express what we often cannot express literally. Humans have invented an array of means through which meaning is construed. I use the word *construe* because meaning making is a construal, both with respect to the perception of forms made by others and with respect to the forms that we make ourselves.

We tend to think that the act of reading a story or reading a poem is a process of decoding. The individual reading a story must *make* sense of the story; he or she must produce meanings from the marks on the page. The mind must be constructive, it must be active, and the task of teaching is to facilitate effective mental action so that the work encountered becomes meaningful.

The kind of schools we need would recognize that the most important forms of learning are those that students know how to use outside of school, not just inside school. And the teachers in such schools would consistently try to help students see the connections between the two. The transfer of learning cannot be assumed; it needs to be taught.

The idea that transfer needs to be taught is not a new one. I reiterate an old idea here because it is absolutely fundamental to effective education. If all that students get out of what they learn in history or math or science are ideas they rapidly forget and cannot employ outside of the context of a classroom, then education is a casualty. The point of learning anything in school is not primarily to enable one to do well in school—although most parents and students believe this to be the case—it is to enable one to do well in life. The point of learning something in school is to enrich life outside of school and to acquire the skills and ideas that will enable one to produce the questions and perform the activities that one's outside life will require.

In the field of education, we have yet to begin to conceive of educational evaluation in these terms. But these are precisely the terms that we need to employ if what we do in school is to be more than mere jumping through hoops.

The kind of schools we need would take seriously the idea that, with regard to learning, the joy is in the journey. Intrinsic motivation counts the most because what students do when they can do what they want to do is what really matters. It is here that the educational process most closely exemplifies the lived experience found in the arts. We ought to stop reinforcing our students' lust for "point accumulation."

Point accumulation is *not* an educational aim. Educational aims have to do with matters of enlightenment, matters of developing abilities, matters of aesthetic experience. What we ought to be focusing our attention on is the creation of conditions in our classrooms and in our schools that make the process of education a process that students wish to pursue. The joy must be in the journey. It is the quality of the chase that matters most.

Alfred North Whitehead once commented that most people believe that a scientist inquires in order to know. Just the opposite is true, he said. Scientists know in order to inquire. What Whitehead was getting at was the idea that the vitality, challenge, and engagement that scientists find in their work is what matters most to them. At its best, this kind of satisfaction is an aesthetic experience.

We don't talk much about the aesthetic satisfactions of teaching and learning, but those of us who have taught for more than a few years know full well the feeling we experience when things go really well in our teaching. When things go really well for students, they experience similar feelings.

We ought not to marginalize the aesthetic in our understanding of what learning is about because, in the end, it is the only form of satisfaction that is likely to predict the uses of the knowledge, skills, and perspectives that students acquire in school. There is a huge difference between what a child *can* do and what a child *will* do. A child who learns to read but has no appetite for reading is not really succeeding in school. We want to promote that appetite for learning, and it ought to be built on the satisfactions that students receive in our classrooms. It is the aesthetic that represents the highest forms of intellectual achievement, and it is the aesthetic that provides the natural high and contributes the energy we need to want to pursue an activity again and again and again.

The kind of schools we need would encourage deep conversation in classrooms. They would help students learn how to participate in that complex and subtle art, an art that requires learning how to listen as well as how to speak. Good conversation is an activity for which our voyeuristic interest in talk shows offers no substitute.

It may seem odd recommending that deep conversation be promoted in our classrooms. Conversation has a kind of shallow ring, as if it were something you do when you don't have anything really important to do. Yet conversation, when it goes well, when the participants really listen to each other, is like an acquired taste, an acquired skill. It does not take much in the way of resources, but, ironically, it is among the rarest features of classroom life. It is also, I believe, among the rare features of our personal life, and that is why we often tune in to Oprah Winfrey, Larry King, and other talk show hosts to participate vicariously in conversation. Even when the conversations are not all that deep, they remain interesting.

How do we help students learn to become listeners? How do we enable them to understand that comments and questions need to flow from what preceded and not simply express whatever happens to be on one's mind at the time? How do we enable students to become more like the members of a jazz quartet, whose interplay good conversation sometimes seems to emulate? Conversation is akin to deliberation, a process that searches for possible answers and explores blind alleys as well as open freeways. How do we create in our classrooms a practice that, when done well, can be a model of intellectual activity?

Of course, all of us need to learn to engage in deep conversation. In many ways, we need to model what we expect our students to learn. But I am convinced that conversation about ideas that matter to students and teachers and that occupy a central place in our curriculum can be a powerful means of converting the academic institutions we call schools into intellectual institutions. Such a transformation would represent a paradigmatic shift in the culture of schooling.

The kind of schools we need would help students gradually assume increased responsibility for framing their own goals and learning how to achieve them. We want students eventually to become the architects of their own education. The long-term aim of teaching is to make itself unnecessary.

Saying that the long-term aim of teaching is to render itself unnecessary is simply to make explicit what I hope readers have gleaned from my arguments here. Helping students learn how to formulate their own goals is a way to enable them to secure their freedom. Helping them learn how to plan and execute their lives in relation to those goals is a way of developing their autonomy. Plato once defined a slave as someone who executes the purposes of another. Over the grade levels, we have conceived of teaching as setting problems that students solve. Only rarely have we created the conditions through which students set the problems that they wish to pursue. Yet this is precisely what they will need to be able to do once they leave the protected sphere of the school.

It is interesting to me that, in discourse about school reform and the relation of goals and standards of curriculum reform, the teacher is given the freedom to formulate means but not to decide upon ends. The prevailing view is that professional judgment pertains to matters of technique, rather than to matters of goals.

I believe this conception of school reform is shortsighted. If our students were simply inert entities, something like copper or plastic, it would be possible in principle to formulate methods of acting on them that would yield uniform responses. A thousand pounds of pressure by a punch press on a steel plate has a given effect. But our students are not uniform, they are not steel, and they do not respond in the same way to pressures of various kinds. Thus teachers will always need the discretionary space to determine not only matters of means but also matters of ends. And we want students, gradually to be sure, to have the opportunity to formulate ends as well. Withholding such opportunities is a form of de-skilling for both teachers and students.

The kind of schools we need would make it possible for students who have particular interests to pursue those interests in depth and, at the same time, to work on public service projects that contribute to something larger than their own immediate interests. This twofold aim—the ability to serve the self through intensive study and the desire and ability to provide a public service—is like the head and tail of a coin. Both elements need to be a part of our educational agenda.

The long-term aim of education may be said to be to learn how to engage in personally satisfying activities that are at the same time socially constructive. Students need to learn that there are people who need services and that they, the students themselves, can contribute to meeting these people's needs. Service learning is a move in the right direction. It affords adolescents an opportunity to do something whose scope is beyond themselves. The result, at least potentially, is the development of an attitude that schools would do well to foster. That, too, should be a part of our curricular agenda.

The kind of schools we need would treat the idea of "public education" as meaning not only the education of the public inside schools, but also the education of the public outside schools. The school's faculty will find it difficult to proceed farther or faster than the community will allow. Our task, in part, is to nurture public conversation in order to create a collective vision of education.

Realistically speaking, our responsibilities as educators extend beyond the confines of our classrooms and even beyond the walls of our schools. We also have responsibilities to our communities. We need desperately to create educational forums for members of the community in which the purposes and processes of education can be discussed, debated, and deliberated and from which consensus can be arrived at with regard to our broad mission as an educational institution. Parents need to know why, for example, inquiry-oriented methods matter, why rote learning may not be in the best long-term interest of their children, why problem-centered activities are important, and why the ability to frame telling questions is crucial.

Most parents and even many teachers have a yellow-school-bus image when it comes to conceiving what teaching, learning, and schooling should look like. The yellow school bus is a metaphor for the model of education that they encountered and that, all too often, they wish to replicate in the 21st century. Our schools, as they are now designed, often tacitly encourage the re-creation of such a model. Yet we know there is a better way. That better way ought to be a part of the agenda the community discusses with teachers and school administrators. Principals and school superintendents ought to perform a leadership role in deepening that community conversation. Without having such a conversation, it will be very difficult to create the kind of schools we need.

I acknowledge that the features of schooling that I have described will not be easy to attain, but they are important. We get so caught up in debating whether or not we should extend the school year that we seem to forget to consider what should go into that year. We seem to forget about our vision of education and the kind of educational practices that will move the school in the direction we value. Too often we find ourselves implementing policies that we do not value. Those of us in education need to take a stand and to serve as public advocates for our students. Who speaks for our students? We need to.

Some of the features I have described—perhaps all of them—may not be ones that you yourself cherish. Fine. That makes conversation possible. And so I invite you to begin that conversation in your school, so that out of the collective wisdom of each of our communities can come a vision of education that our children deserve and, through that vision, the creation of the kind of schools that our children need.

Note

1. Herbert Read, *Education Through Art* (New York: Pantheon Books, 1944).

ELLIOT W. EISNER is Lee Jacks Professor of Education and Art, Stanford University, Stanford, Calif. His book, The Arts and the Creation of Mind, *was published in 2002 by Yale University Press. © 2002, Elliot W. Eisner.*

PERSONAL FUTURES

The World Is Your Classroom: Lessons In Self-Renewal

An innovative society is made up of individuals who continuously renew their thinking throughout their lives, the late John W. Gardner argued eloquently in his classic book *Self-Renewal*.

By John W. Gardner

"Keep on growing," the commencement speakers say. "Don't go to seed. Let this be a beginning, not an ending."

It is a good theme. Yet a high proportion of the young people who hear the speeches pay no heed, and by the time they are middle-aged they are absolutely mummified. Even some of the people who make the speeches are mummified. Why?

Unfortunately the commencement speakers never tell us why their advice to keep on learning is so hard to follow. The people interested in adult education have struggled heroically to increase the opportunities for self-development, and they have succeeded marvelously. Now they had better turn to the thing that is really blocking self-development—the indi-

vidual's own intricately designed, self-constructed prison, or to put it another way, the individual's incapacity for self-renewal.

A prison is not quite the appropriate image because the individual does not stop learning in all aspects of his life simultaneously. Many young people have stopped learning in the religious or spiritual dimensions of their lives long before they graduate from college. Some settle into rigid and unchanging political and economic views by the time they are 25 or 30. By their mid-30s most will have stopped acquiring new skills or new attitudes in any central aspect of their lives.

As we mature, we progressively narrow the scope and variety of our lives. Of all the interests we might

pursue, we settle on a few. Of all the people with whom we might associate, we select a small number. We become caught in a web of fixed relationships. We develop set ways of doing things.

As the years go by, we view our familiar surroundings with less and less freshness of perception. We no longer look with a wakeful, perceiving eye at the faces of people we see every day, nor at any other features of our everyday world.

That is why travel is a vivid experience for most of us. At home we have lost the capacity to see what is before us. Travel shakes us out of our apathy, and we regain an attentiveness that heightens every experience. The exhilaration of travel has many sources, but surely one of

John W. Gardner

John W. Gardner, longtime member of the World Future Society's Board and more recently a member of its Council, died of cancer February 16 at his home in Palo Alto, California. He was 89 years old.

Gardner was a social philosopher who worked actively for the causes he believed in, one of which was the World Future Society.

One of his lifelong interests was renewal—the renewal of both organizations and individuals—and his book, *Self-Renewal*, is now a classic. As a tribute to Gardner, THE FUTURIST reprints a section of that book which reflects his belief that people must keep learning all their lives and rediscover and repackage themselves as they move on to new challenges.

Gardner first came to public attention as president of the Carnegie Corporation, where he helped to shape the future of American education. He served as Secretary of Health, Education, and Welfare during the administration of President Lyndon B. Johnson. (Gardner was the only Republican in the cabinet.)

In 1970, he founded Common Cause, a lobby aimed at making government more responsive to citizen needs and less to special interests. In 1978, he chaired the organizing committee that formed the Independent Sector, a coalition of nonprofit organizations, foundations, and corporate philanthropy programs. His life and work were the subject of a recent PBS documentary.

World Future Society President Edward Cornish offered this tribute: "Possibly the greatest job satisfaction I have had in being president of the World Future Society is having an opportunity to meet some of the wisest and noblest people to walk this earth. John Gardner was such a person. For me, as I am sure for many others, he will be remembered as a hero in his thinking and a saint in his doing."

them is that we recapture in some measure the unspoiled awareness of children.

It is not unusual to find that the major changes in life—marriage, a move to a new city, a change of jobs, or a national emergency—break the patterns of our lives and reveal to us quite suddenly how much we had been imprisoned by the comfortable web we had woven around ourselves. Unlike the jailbird, we don't know that we've been imprisoned until after we've broken out.

It was a characteristic experience during the Second World War that men and women who had been forced to break the pattern of their lives often discovered within themselves resources and abilities they had not known to exist. How ironic that it should take war and disaster to bring about self-renewal on a large scale! It is an expensive way to accomplish it.

When we have learned to achieve such self-renewal without wars and other disasters, we shall have discovered one of the most important secrets a society can learn, a secret that will unlock new resources of vitality throughout a society. And we shall have done something to avert the hardening of the arteries that attacks

so many societies. People who have lost their adaptiveness naturally resist change. The most stubborn protectors of their own vested interest are those who have lost the capacity for self-renewal.

Self-Development

No one knows why some individuals seem capable of self-renewal while others do not. But we have some important clues as to what the self-renewing person is like, and what we might do to foster renewal.

For self-renewing men and women the development of their own potentialities and the process of self-discovery never end. It is a sad but unarguable fact that most people go through their lives only partially aware of the full range of their abilities. As a boy in California I spent a good deal of time in the Mother Lode country, and like every boy of my age I listened raptly to the tales told by the old-time prospectors in that area, some of them veterans of the Klondike gold rush. Every one of them had at least one good campfire story of a lost gold mine. The details varied: The original discoverer had died in the mine, or had gone crazy, or had been killed in a shooting scrape, or had just walked off think-

ing the mine worthless. But the central theme was constant: riches left untapped. I have come to believe that those tales offer a paradigm of education as most of us experience it. The mine is worked for a little while and then abandoned.

The development of abilities is at least in part a dialogue between individuals and their environment. If they have the ability and the environment demands it, it will surely develop. The young person with excellent athletic skills is likely to discover that ability fairly early. Almost any child with the gift for charming grown-ups will have no trouble discovering that talent. But most abilities are not so readily evoked by the common circumstances of life. The "mute, inglorious Miltons" are more numerous than one might suppose, particularly in an age in which even an articulate Milton might go unnoticed, certainly unrewarded. Most of us have potentialities that have never been developed simply because the circumstances of our lives never called them forth.

Exploration of the full range of our own potentialities is not something that we can safely leave to the chances of life. It is something to be pursued systematically, or at least avidly, to the end of our days. We should look forward to an endless and unpredictable dialogue between our potentialities and the claims of life—not only the claims we encounter but the claims we invent. And by the potentialities I mean not just skills, but the full range of our capacities for sensing, wondering, learning, understanding, loving, and aspiring.

The ultimate goal of the educational system is to shift to the individual the burden of pursuing his own education. This will not be a widely shared pursuit until we get over our odd conviction that education is what goes on in school buildings and nowhere else. Not only does education continue when schooling ends, but it is not confined to what may be studied in adult education courses. The world is an incomparable classroom, and life is a memorable teacher for those who aren't afraid of her.

Excerpted from *Self-Renewal: The Individual and the Innovative Society* by John W. Gardner. W.W. Norton, 1963 (reissued 1995).

Originally published in the May/June 2002 issue of *The Futurist,* pp. 52-53. Used with permission from the World Future Society, 7910 Woodmont Avenue, Suite 450, Bethesda, Maryland 20814. Telephone: 310/656-8274; Fax: 301/951-0394; http://www.wfs.org.

The New Century:
Is It Too Late for Transformational Leadership?

by Elaine Wilmore and Cornell Thomas

Introduction

The principalship has been defined and described in numerous ways. Often current social concerns help to determine the type of school leadership presumed to be most effective. The principalship has been defined and described, for example, by how well learning resources have been managed; whether or not instructional leadership could be noted; how change was managed; and whether or not a safe and conducive environment has been established and maintained. It seems that many of these role definitions are guided by idealized conceptions of what principals should be like rather than on-the-job performance within given circumstances.

Reality tells us, however, that each school has a different set of needs. This reality-based reflection helps us to see that the role of an effective principal varies based on the needs of each particular campus, available resources, and support from the superintendent and school board. Therefore, school leadership can be best measured by the way a principal uses him or herself to help create a school climate characterized by staff productivity, student productivity, and creative thought (Thomas and Walker, 1999).

Two concepts of effective leadership have dominated the literature for the past twenty-plus years. During this period, other notions of leadership have been delineated. Although many of the descriptions provide informative opinions about leadership, has one emerged as a focal point, in an inclusive way to address the diverse range of situations, for the new century? As we enter the next century, how can we best define and describe effective leadership in ways that enhance student achievement and the entire teaching-learning environment? Is there really such a thing as a transformational leader, and if so, how does this leader perform?

Leadership Defined:
The Major Trends Since 1970

The effective-schools movement of the late 1970s and the 1980s described effective principals in terms of instructional leadership. Literature that focused on supporting the effective-schools movement most often stated that efforts to improve the quality of the teaching and learning process must focus on principals (Edmonds, 1979; Lipham, 1981; Cawelti, 1984). Principals are seen in this literature as instructional leaders: individuals who know what effective instruction looks like, how to evaluate it, and how to help teachers improve their instruction. Edmonds (1979) believed that the characteristics of an effective principal include: (1) strong instructional leadership; (2) the ability to lead in the development of a pervasive and broadly understood instructional focus; (3) an orderly and safe school climate conducive to teaching and learning; (4) high teacher expectations; and (5) program evaluations based on varied assessment measures of student achievement.

Discussions of transformation leadership emerged in the 1990s. Leadership in this literature focuses on certain beliefs.

Transformational leaders are expected to:

1. Define the need for change.
2. Create new visions and muster commitment to the visions.
3. Concentrate on long-term goals.
4. Inspire followers to transcend their own interests for higher-order goals.
5. Change the organization to accommodate their vision rather than work within the existing one.
6. Mentor followers to take greater responsibility for their own development and that of others. Followers become leaders, leaders become change agents, and ultimately they transform the organization (Hoy and Miskel, 1996, p. 393).

Transformational leaders are described as values driven. They are committed to the development of learning communities. "Visionary," "change agent," and "expert at dealing with complexity, ambiguity, and uncertainty" are attributes often employed when defining quality leadership. Of primary importance is the level of care principals demonstrate toward their teachers (Schlecty, 1990; Senge, 1990).

Burns (1978) stated that transformational leadership is a process within which "leaders and followers raise one another to higher levels of morality and motivation" (p. 20). He discusses transformational leadership in two stages. Stage one focuses on higher-order psychological needs for esteem, autonomy, and self-actualization. Stage two addresses moral issues regarding goodness, righteousness, duty, and obligation (Burns, 1978).

Movement toward developing what Glickman (1990) calls a "cause beyond self" becomes a primary point of focus. Working together to achieve desired goals is the thread connecting all elements of a learning community.

Leithwood (1992) states, "Transformational leadership is a form of consensual or facilitative power that is manifested through other people instead of over people." Three elements make up this style of leadership:

1. a collaborative, shared decision-making approach;
2. an emphasis on teacher professionalism and empowerment; and
3. an understanding of change, including how to encourage change in others (p. 10).

Sergiovanni (1995) emphasizes a transformational leadership to which—although leadership has the ultimate responsibility and therefore final decision—input and involvement from all individuals within a learning community create optimal opportunities for success. Trying new and other options in classrooms and belief in both teachers and student capital are emphasized.

Sergiovanni thus enhances the notions of transformational leadership previously discussed. Initially, transformative leadership takes the form of leadership by building. Here the focus is on arousing human potential, satisfying higher-order needs, and raising expectations of both leader and follower in a manner that motivates both to higher levels of commitment and performance. Leadership by building responds to esteem, achievement, competence, autonomy, and self-actualizing needs (p. 119).

Transformational leadership embodies, it seems, attributes designed to empower all members of the learning community. Empowerment is defined by Giroux (1988) as "the process whereby teachers acquire the means to critically appropriate knowledge existing outside their immediate experience in order to broaden their understanding of themselves, the world, and the possibilities for transforming the taken for granted assumptions about the way we live." We want to suggest also that empowerment be defined as the obligations and commitments each individual makes to the community and ultimately our society. With these ideals in place empowerment becomes a challenge for individuals. They can participate in determining what is right and good, not just wait to be told what to do and how to respond. In this process, all individuals are afforded opportunities to make many of their own choices in life. People, in these settings, develop an awareness of their abilities to modify and even play significant, positive roles in reconstructing the work and social environment.

There are, however, critically important ideological concepts that must be internalized by members of a learning community in order to maximize opportunities to achieve desired goals. These core concepts can become perceptual barriers that pose often insurmountable challenges toward continued development of the transformational leadership process (Thomas, 1996). The core concepts discussed here are the notions of respect, trust, and caring. These concepts should be revisited as a community of learners evolves within a transformational process. We will provide a rather brief introduction of them.

Individuals must ask themselves whether people must earn their respect, or if respect is initially given. When someone must earn another's respect, the process is often framed by concepts developed from hearsay, partial truths, negative subliminal messages, and skewed interpretations about differences. We all must deal with personal instances of misrepresentation! Respect that emerges from the belief that all individuals have gifts worthy of recognition helps us move beyond this perceptual barrier in less destructive ways. Trust is directly linked to this discussion of respect and the process of building a community of learners. We must internalize the importance of placing trust in others' abilities to enhance a learning community. Members of a learning community must also care for more than the completion of assignments and other work-related outcomes. The transformational leadership process must help individuals begin to care internally for the well-being and happiness of others.

When members of a learning community embrace the notions of respect, trust, and caring, they can avoid many of the perceptual barriers regarding differences as they work within the transformational process. Leadership must understand the importance of these similar concepts and find ways to address them in positive and productive ways.

In an attempt to bring focus to school leadership in one state, the Texas Education Agency (TEA) began studying the literature regarding effective principalship and developed a response. In 1994 the Texas Education Agency published *Learner-Centered Schools for Texas: A Vision of Texas Educators*. This document defines and describes six proficiencies designed to help administrators in Texas public schools become student focused in six areas:

- leadership style
- climate
- curriculum and instruction
- diversity
- Communication
- professional development of faculty and staff

Each factor and its relation to transformational leadership will be discussed.

The Texas Learner-Centered Proficiencies: Learner-Centered Leadership

"Through inspiring leadership, the administrator maximizes learning for all students while maintaining professional ethics and personal integrity." (Texas Education Agency, 1995, p. 11)

Leadership is what transformational principalship concerns itself with (Johnson and Evans, 1997). Without transformational leadership, the school becomes a ship without a sail, a journey without a map, a compass without a pointer. There are principals who are not leaders. Subconsciously, they do not even want to be leaders. They are satisfied to be managers. Content to take care of the "nuts and bolts" of operating a school, they steer clear of true leadership, because real leaders must take risks. Leadership sets them up for possible failure, because real leaders fail almost as often as they succeed (Peters, 1999). The distinction between real leaders and "wannabe" leaders is that real leaders get back up every time they fail. They get back on the horse. They "thrive on chaos" (Peters, 1988). Real leaders are never satisfied with the status quo. They are always seeking to change, to improve, and to reflect on "How can I do this better next time?" There is always a next time.

"Wannabe" leaders are afraid of failure. In truth, they are afraid of change. They would rather stick with what they have, because they at least know what it is—a primary reason so many schools are low performing. Such principals have no vision of excellence, regardless of circumstance, because they have let fear overrule the need for change. Without a specific vision of excellence, how can anyone be expected to inspire greatness in others? How can anyone sell a dream, a vision, or a plan that has not been worked out and committed to in his or her own mind?

The development of vision and its intricate implementation are the keys to successfully creating a transformational leader. First, the administrator must actively work with all facets of the learning community (Giles, 1998). Such facets include students and teachers as well as parents, churches, business leaders, community groups, neighbors, and anyone else who can be talked into helping (TEA, 1995). It is the responsibility of the leader to empower all these people in the development of a school vision and all the steps in its achievement. These people together will work toward assessing what is currently in place. What is successful? What is not? Where are the sacred cows that have never been touched, but need to be eliminated? All this should be done together. The principal's role is to develop leadership skills in others so that he or she is not left alone to carry the whole load—a classic case of multiple heads being better than one.

But the team's work is not yet complete. Its members must have continual active involvement with the school. Program planning, implementation, and assessment should be ongoing. They must never stop. The assessment piece is very important. If new programs are put into place but never assessed, they fall into the same dangers as previous ones. They too become sacred cows. Wrong! Nothing should be immune from inspection, assessment, and modification. Even assessment itself is only half finished if the results are not studied and analyzed for modification and improvement. Not until every student is achieving to the maximum of his or her capability is a transformational leader's work done. The community's work is not done. The team has a moral and ethical responsibility to nothing less.

The days of top-down leadership are gone in favor of a collaborative leadership style that empowers the entire learning community to take ownership in what takes place at school (Behar-Horenstein and Amatea, 1996). Not every child is easy to teach. Not every child sits quietly and does everything he or she is told. In fact, not every student even cares about being in school. These are impossible issues for any one person to solve. It becomes a principal's responsibility to seek input from all stakeholders, help create the specifics of a collaboratively developed school action plan, and achieve a mutually developed mission. Then it becomes everyone's responsibility to make it happen. A transformational leader, one truly committed to transforming a school, must have a clear vision, be able to communicate it, and be able to inspire others to collaborate ethically and professionally for the achievement of all children, even those difficult to teach.

Learner-Centered Climate

"The administrator establishes a climate of mutual trust and respect which enables all members of the learning community to seek and attain excellence." (Texas Education Agency, 1995, p. 12)

Too many people underestimate the importance of climate in creating a results-oriented, productive school. Thinking of climate as the "soft" stuff, they delegate it to lesser importance than solid curriculum, effective instructional strategies, and authentic assessment. But that assumption is not true. Without a positive campus climate, there will not be maximum success or productivity in any area. Developing this positive climate is not easy. It is just as difficult to achieve as anything else and certainly as important (Leithwood, Leonard, and Sharratt, 1998).

Every school has its own unique ethos. No matter how much in common two schools may have, their campus climates and cultures are never duplicated. Even when a principal changes schools and seeks to implement similar strategies and programs in a different place, the effects are never identical. No two schools are ever exactly alike. Schools are made up of people. Not even identical twins are identical in DNA or personality. Neither are two schools. What works in one will not have the same results in any other. It is a transformational leader's role to get to know everything about the school, from the students, to the staff, to the community it serves. What makes it tick? What rings its bells? What does it value? What are the written and unwritten rules and mores (Peterson and Deal, 1994)? If a principal does not take the time to find out, he or she is headed for big trouble. Big trouble is a long way from excellence.

A transformational leader seeks to establish school as a safe place for everyone. A diligent effort must go into building open and respectful relationships, again with all people. The word "all" is paramount through each of the learner-centered proficiencies. This means everyone. "All" means "all," even the hard to teach, hard to deal with, the disenchanted, the ones who do not speak English, and the just plain crazy. Is "all" easy? No. Is "all" necessary? Yes. No one can be left out. The person who is making trouble is the very person to include. Lyndon Johnson used to say he wanted to know who his enemies were so he could keep them close at hand. If certain individuals are creating problems, involve them in the decision-making process. Empower them. Instead of keeping a distance, bring them in close. Slowly and carefully, make them a part of the solution rather than allowing them to become a big part of the problem. The more vocal naysayers are, the more important it is to bring them onto the team. The goal is to keep former naysayers vocal, but as proponents rather than as opponents of the change process. Develop openness. Develop trusting relationships. They will pay off.

Trust is of utmost importance. Without it, a campus is doomed. No organization can achieve maximum effectiveness without it. It is also very fragile. Most people will give others the benefit of the doubt in the beginning. But once trust is broken, it is incredibly hard to rebuild. Transformational leaders know trust is a two-way street, and it must be cultivated carefully.

Once a climate of openness, respect, and trust is established, all stakeholders are free to express themselves safely. The idea that no idea is a bad idea is paramount to campus improvement. Everyone must feel free to share ideas, toss them around, change them, discard them, or whatever. The important thing is that everyone's viewpoint is valued and that everyone feels free to share. In this environment, creative problem solving is utilized. Consensus is developed. Solutions are mutually developed, not driven by just one person. The effect is greater academic and personal growth for all.

Technology is not the "be all, end all" of lifelong learning. Creating an intrinsic desire to know more and be able to use more in the minds and hearts of students as well as teachers is the goal of transformational leaders.

A transformational leader supports innovation. When teachers or groups come up with ideas they want to try, a transformational leader asks questions in a supportive, reflective manner and works as a part of the team to assess and analyze the new ideas. When they are successful, the transformational leader leads the celebration. No success is too small to celebrate. On the other hand, if an idea is not successful, it is still up to the transformational leader to be supportive and, again, ask insightful questions designed to analyze what went wrong and why. The goal is to encourage further innovation, not nip it in the bud due to a bad experience. No one feels worse about an unsuccessful venture than the persons involved. The old style of leadership, filled with reprimands and accusations, will not instill a burning desire in anyone to try again (Behar-Horenstein and Amatea, 1996). An insightful leader supports the idea and intent behind a concept that was not successful, yet always encourages reflection. How can we do it better next time? What specific ways can we improve what went wrong? These strategies will encourage others to try again to be innovative, rather than make them feel worse than they already do. Teachers are more motivated by leaders they perceive as being transformational (Ingram, 1997). Risk taking should be encouraged. Dialogue for improvement should be encouraged. Helping people succeed is the foundation of a great campus climate. Beating people with a stick is not.

Learner-Centered Curriculum and Instruction

"The administrator facilitates the implementation of a sound curriculum and appropriate instructional strategies designed to promote optimal learning for all students." (Texas Education Agency, 1995, p. 13)

This proficiency is the "meat and potatoes" of transformational school leadership. If we do not have effective curriculum and instruction, how can we expect all children to learn, much less learn to their maximum capability? Most people who aspire to enter the principalship are already excellent educators. What else must beginning administrators, as well as practicing administrators, learn in order to become transformational?

Collaboration. Lots of collaboration. A transformational leader makes use of all participants in the learning community to address the learning styles of each student. If individual needs as well as strengths in knowledge, ability to learn, and best ways of learning are not addressed, how can any school realistically expect to maximize learning for every student? Not every student learns in the same way, yet traditional schools treat all students as if they were strictly auditory learners. Surprise. They are not. Does it take time to study what works per student? Of course. Some teachers complain that they do not have that amount of time. The real question for a transformational leader in today's society is: Do we have time *not* to study individual students? No. As long as we keep on doing what we have always done, we will keep on getting what we always have. Are any of us satisfied with that? Collaboration in planning among many players as well as continuous assessment and modification of what we are doing are the keys to improving curriculum and instructional-delivery systems.

Students need to be learning more than "for the test." Students need to be learning for all their tomorrows. Society depends on it. Transformational leaders will be seeking ways to address individual differences within and outside the confines of today's world as we know it. We must be producing students who create lifelong quests for learning and who continue learning when they leave the school. Technology is important in this quest. It creates a vehicle to reconnect many who are disenchanted with traditional instructional-delivery systems. But technology is not the "be all, end all" of lifelong learning. Creating an intrinsic desire to know more and be able to use more in the minds and hearts of students as well as teachers is the goal of transformational leaders. Students with this desire for learning will have no trouble acquiring the right skills as they progress from grade to grade and into the world.

Transformational leaders work with the whole learning community to study and find ways to accomplish this goal within individual schools. The strategies are as unique as the campuses they serve. The Comer School Development Program (Emmons, Hagopian, and Efimba, 1998) and the Industrial Areas Foundation (Giles, 1998) are just two examples of models that utilize community-based models to achieve these goals. There are others. The trick of transformational leadership is to first study the school with input from many different people with different perspectives, then together create an action plan for getting it done.

Learner-Centered Professional Development

"The administrator demonstrates a commitment to student learning through a personal growth plan and fosters the professional development of all staff in the learning community." (Texas Education Agency, 1995, p. 14)

In the highly successful *The Seven Habits of Highly Effective People*, Steven Covey (1990) discusses the importance of "sharpening the saw." He means that for anyone to achieve and maintain maximum effectiveness, he or she must spend time in introspection, looking inside himself or herself, assessing personal strengths and weaknesses, creating an action plan of what to do about it, and then doing it. No matter how good principals are, their bodies, minds, and souls require time for reflection and self-assessment. Principals must have the time to study themselves to determine their own leadership styles (Carr, 1997). What is working? What is not? Specific time must be set apart for this assessment. Purposeful leaders know it cannot be put off until they "get around to it." That may never happen. Just as a car requires regular fuel, maintenance, and tune-ups, so do we. This time for inner reflection is not a frill. It is a requirement for maximum effectiveness. It is particularly true for transformational leaders who are actively involved in risk taking and change efforts that may or may not have full district support (Osterman, Crow, and Rosen, 1997). Believe it or not, some administrators actually *like* the status quo.

Everyone needs time for personal retreat to refocus on goals and priorities as well as to participate in self-assessment and renewal activities (Wilmore, 1999). Without it, even principals with the best of intentions will burn out. Taking time away for professional conferences not only adds to a principal's knowledge base; it also provides important time away from the campus to learn, network, and recharge their batteries.

Biologists tell us all living things must have a time of dormancy in order to sustain life. The same is true with careers and souls. Transformational leadership is time and energy intensive. Administrators must have time to step back, far from the madding crowd, to rest, refocus, and assess both themselves and their schools. Sometimes we cannot see the forest for the trees. Sometimes we get so physically and emotionally tired that a bit of time alone is essential. So take it. Do not feel guilty. Literally, just do it.

Where to go is of secondary importance. Again, professional conferences are an obvious choice. They take principals away from campus for what can be an important developmental activity. They provide the benefit of cognitive growth as well as reconnection with other colleagues and introduction to new ones with similar interests and concerns. Hearing keynote speakers and concurrent sessions led by known experts is another obvious benefit.

Although professional conferences are critical to the growth and development of all leaders, they are not the only avenues of opportunity. In fact, after hurrying from general to concurrent sessions and meeting with friends and colleagues, some leaders return home exhausted. Often a day or weekend in someplace quiet is needed (Wilmore, 1999). In silence we can find introspection and in so doing reconnect with ourselves. Different people find this in different ways. For some it is fishing, hunting, or engaging in golf or tennis. For others it is a day at a library or spa. For others, it is the simple pleasure of time spent quietly in the out-of-doors. Again, where is not important. Refueling your soul is what matters.

Another excellent tool for introspection and reflection for professional development as well as stress reduction and sanity is journal writing (Wilmore, 1998). Keeping a journal is inexpensive and therapeutic. It is private. No one but the writer sees it. It also serves the greater purpose of helping a leader regain perspective. There is something about framing thoughts, concepts, and problems into words and sentences that helps bring them into perspective and provides synthesis. Journal writing can be as simple or elaborate as desired. It can be done on a computer or with a pencil and paper. Format and pretty little books to write in are not important. Venting innermost feelings is. Journal writing takes time and effort to become a habit. But it is a healthy habit in both personal and professional development for all leaders in and out of education.

Beaver Cleaver's class is never coming back. Students will never again look basically alike, sit primly in their seats, and say in unison, "Yes, Miss Landers," to anything the teacher says.

Back at school, a transformational leader allocates time for all faculty and staff to reflect, meet in teams, plan, and develop their own professional growth activities. Their own commitment to professional and personal growth will be a model for others. Teachers and staff will see the importance the transformational leader places on professional and personal growth activities by the way the walk matches the talk. All members of the learning community should employ professional-development plans with specific growth activities built in. Each plan should incorporate professional and personal goal setting as well as allocate time to read professional journals, keep up with relevant research and literature, and visit other schools and business enterprises in the community. We have much to learn from the private sector. Transformational leaders seek to go outside the walls of the school to learn, just as they bring the community into the school. Above all, transformational leaders are committed to personal and professional growth for everyone involved with the school, including themselves.

Equity in Excellence for All Learners

"The administrator promotes equity in excellence for all by acknowledging, respecting, and responding to diversity among students and staff while building on shared values and other similarities that bond all people." (Texas Education Agency, 1995, p. 15)

Transformational leaders know they are no leaders at all without this belief system. They are instead hindrances to the future of a democratic society and should resign immediately. It is one thing to acknowledge differences among people, but quite another to respect them. Beaver Cleaver's class is never coming back. Students will never again look basically alike, sit primly in their seats, and say in unison, "Yes, Miss Landers," to anything the teacher says. Respecting differences as opportunities for learning is a critical component of transformational leadership. But it is not enough. Leaders must go beyond respecting to responding. There is a hierarchy of action here. *Acknowledging* is on the lowest level. *Respecting* is a step up and worlds ahead. *Responding* is the key to appreciating and celebrating differences as well as commonalities that are traits of humankind.

Differences of race, gender, socioeconomic background, or anything else should never be allowed as excuses for lack of student performance. Every student should be held to a high standard of achievement, and every teacher must work to that end. Anything less is discrimination, whether intentional or nonintentional. We must not accept the fact that "Poor Juan," or "Poor Tamika," or "Poor Susie" cannot possibly excel or even learn at grade level because gosh, they just never had a chance. Transformational leaders work with their communities, work with their schools, and find ways to maximize Juan's, Tamika's, or Susie's opportunities. A transformational leader "respects all learners, is sensitive to their needs, and encourages them to use all their skills and talents" (TEA, 1994, p. 9). The status quo is never accepted. Rationalizations are never accepted.

Excellence for all is the goal. Nothing less is permitted in a transformational school. The administrator must be proactive at all times. Because school and community demographics will never be static again, it makes no sense to continue treating school leadership and governance as we have in the past. Administrators must keep a constant eye on issues and problems that schools will face in the future. The goal is to address them before they become problems. All members of the learning community must work together to develop common values. They might be simple in some schools or more elaborate in others. The important thing is that everyone has a part in their development, is empowered in the decision-making, and reaches consensus. All other issues that arise should be held up against these commonly developed values. Is this idea or program congruent with our values, our mission, and where we all agree we want to go? If not, chuck it.

Not every new idea is appropriate for every school. Find the ones that are, communicate them well, and work always toward the common goal of what is best for the students rather than what is easiest to implement. Common values foster unity of purpose, and unity of purpose is essential to school success.

Learner-Centered Communication

"The administrator effectively communicates the learning community's vision as well as its policies and successes in interactions with staff, students, parents, community members, and the media." (Texas Education Agency, 1995, p. 16)

Having a vision is wonderful, but if it cannot be communicated clearly it is not doing the good it should. Learner-centered leaders inspire others. It is impossible to inspire anyone without communication. Both verbal (what we say, how we say it) and nonverbal (what our body relates about what we are saying) communication are essential. We may have developed a wonderful campus vision with exceptional implementation strategies, but if no one knows or cares about it, problems arise. Furthermore, it is also a problem if the communication of the vision is faulty. This is particularly true when dealing with parents, community members, and the media. Transformational leaders know what needs to be said and communicate it effectively. There is power in language. Think about what needs to be said ahead of time. Practice, if necessary. Be careful with the media. They can be your best friends or worst enemies. Their personnel are usually overworked and underpaid. They must work fast to meet deadlines. Misquotations are inevitable. But take the advice of a sage city manager: "Don't pick a fight with someone who buys ink by the barrel." There is power in language. Use it to your advantage.

Nonverbal skills are essential too. Active listening is critical. Give people your full attention, no matter how busy you are. Listen 1,000, not 950, times. The time invested will be productive. Active listening also promotes trust, interest, and concern, which are critical to campus climate and a supportive workplace. Listen with empathy to everyone, including parents, students, teachers, and auxiliary personnel. They are all part of the learning community. They are all part of transforming the school from mediocre to excellent. They deserve empathy and attention regardless of circumstance. Communication with people inside and outside the school is paramount to a transformed school (Johnson and Evans, 1997). It is a leader's responsibility to be prepared, to listen and respond, to work well with media, to have specific outcomes in mind, to articulate the outcomes, and to inspire others to greatness. It is a tall task. A lot is being asked. But no one ever said being a transformational leader was easy.

Conclusion

Today's schools face an array of problems that administrators in the past did not have to address. Besides societal issues, there are important policy and regulatory issues such as the future and effect of school privatization, vouchers, and charter schools. No one can say exactly where such proposals will lead. But one thing is certain. We cannot keep managing schools as if they were independent entities unconnected to the community as a whole. To produce the results necessary, a transformational leader is required to march students and teachers, academically and personally, into the new century with a love and desire for future learning. Anything less we cannot afford. A transformational leader seeks to change schools as we have known them into caring, responsible, knowledge rich, competent, change-oriented centers of the community. These schools are places where all students truly can and will learn.

So is it too late for transformational leadership? Definitely not. To give up on transforming our schools is to give up the American dream of a free and noble society. Giving up on "ideal" is certainly something a transformational leader would never do.

In future schools, leaders must be focused on children, on what is right rather than what is easy. Transformational leaders must lead with care and concern, as well as intelligence and savvy. They must focus on sound and appropriate curriculum and instruction in which all students can achieve to their capacity. They must strive toward continual, lifelong learning for themselves and those they lead. They must have a noble vision, articulate well, and inspire others toward its success. Transformed schools must be safe places, both physically and psychologically.

For this is the American dream.

References

Behar-Horenstein, L. S., and Amates, E. S. (1996). Changing worlds, changing paradigms. Redesigning administrative practice for more turbulent times. *Educational Horizons*, 75 (1), 27–35.

Burns, J. M. (1978). *Leadership*. New York: Harper and Row.

Carr, A. A. (1997). Leadership and community participation: Four case studies. *Journal of Curriculum and Supervision*, 12 (2), 152–168.

Covey, S. R. (1990). *The seven habits of highly effective people*. New York: Simon and Schuster.

Deal, T. E., and Peterson, K. D. (1994). *The leadership paradox: Balancing logic and artistry in education*. San Francisco, Calif.: Jossey Bass.

Emmons, C. L., Hagopian, G., and Efimba, M. O. (1998). A school transformed: The case of Norman S. Weir. *Journal of Education for Students Placed at Risk*, 3 (1), 39–51.

Giles, H. C. (1998). *Parent engagement as a school reform strategy*. (Report No. EDO-UD-98-5). New York: ERIC Clearinghouse on Urban Education. (ERIC Document Reproduction Service No. ED419031)

Glickman, C. (1990). *Supervision and instruction: A developmental approach*. Boston: Allyn and Bacon.

Hoy, W., and Miskel, C. (1996). *Educational administration: Theory, research and practice*. New York: McGraw-Hill, Inc.

Ingram, P. D. (1997). Leadership behaviors of principals in inclusive educational settings. *Journal of Educational Administration*, 35 (5), 11–27.

Johnson, P. E., and Evans, J. P. (1997). Power, communicator styles, and conflict management styles: A web of interpersonal constructs for the school. *International Journal of Educational Reform*, 6 (1), 40–53.

Leithwood, K. (1992). The move toward transformational leadership. *Educational Leadership*, 49 (5), 8–12.

Leithwood, K., Leonard, L., and Sharratt, L. (1998). Conditions fostering organizational learning in schools. *Educational Administration Quarterly*, 34 (2), 243–276.

Peters, T. (1988). *Thriving on chaos*. New York: Alfred A. Knopf.

Peters, T. (1999). *The circle of innovation*. New York: Alfred A. Knopf.

Schlecty, P. (1990). *Schools for the 21st century: Leadership imperatives for educational reform*. San Francisco: Jossey-Bass.

Senge, P. M. (1990). *The fifth dimension: The art and practice of the learning organization*. New York: Doubleday.

Sergiovanni, T. (1995). *The principalship: A reflective practice perspective*. Boston: Allyn and Bacon.

Texas Education Agency. (1995). *Learner-centered schools for Texas: A vision for Texas educators*. Austin, Texas: Texas Education Agency.

Thomas, C. (1996). *Educational equality and excellence: Perceptual barriers to the dream*. Duncanville, Texas: Nellnetta.

Thomas, C., and Walker, P. (1999). "The role of the urban principal in school restructuring." *International Journal of Leadership in Education*, 1 (3), 297–306.

Wilmore, E. L. (1998). Nebuchadnezzar in the land of school administration. *The School Administrator*, 55 (11), 38–39.

Wilmore, E. L. (1998). Reflection through journal writing. In B. Irby and G. Brown (eds.), *Women and leadership: Creating a balanced life*. Commack, N.Y.: Nova Science.

Elaine Wilmore, Ph.D., is the chair of educational administration at the University of Texas at Arlington. Cornell Thomas, Ed.D., is special assistant to the chancellor for diversity and community and former chairman of educational foundations and administration in the school of education at Texas Christian University.

From *Educational Horizons*, Spring 2001, Vol. 79, No. 3, pp. 115-123. © 2001 by Pi Lambda Theta, Bloomington, IN 47407-6626. Reprinted by permission of Elaine L. Wilmore, Ph.D., Special Assistant to the Dean & Associate Professor of Educational Leadership and Policy Studies.

Index

Index

Test Your Knowledge Form

We encourage you to photocopy and use this page as a tool to assess how the articles in *Annual Editions* expand on the information in your textbook. By reflecting on the articles you will gain enhanced text information. You can also access this useful form on a product's book support Web site at *http://www.dushkin.com/online/*.

NAME:

DATE:

TITLE AND NUMBER OF ARTICLE:

BRIEFLY STATE THE MAIN IDEA OF THIS ARTICLE:

LIST THREE IMPORTANT FACTS THAT THE AUTHOR USES TO SUPPORT THE MAIN IDEA:

WHAT INFORMATION OR IDEAS DISCUSSED IN THIS ARTICLE ARE ALSO DISCUSSED IN YOUR TEXTBOOK OR OTHER READINGS THAT YOU HAVE DONE? LIST THE TEXTBOOK CHAPTERS AND PAGE NUMBERS:

LIST ANY EXAMPLES OF BIAS OR FAULTY REASONING THAT YOU FOUND IN THE ARTICLE:

LIST ANY NEW TERMS/CONCEPTS THAT WERE DISCUSSED IN THE ARTICLE, AND WRITE A SHORT DEFINITION:

We Want Your Advice

ANNUAL EDITIONS revisions depend on two major opinion sources: one is our Advisory Board, listed in the front of this volume, which works with us in scanning the thousands of articles published in the public press each year; the other is you—the person actually using the book. Please help us and the users of the next edition by completing the prepaid article rating form on this page and returning it to us. Thank you for your help!

ANNUAL EDITIONS: Education 03/04

ARTICLE RATING FORM

Here is an opportunity for you to have direct input into the next revision of this volume.
We would like you to rate each of the articles listed below, using the following scale:

1. **Excellent: should definitely be retained**
2. **Above average: should probably be retained**
3. **Below average: should probably be deleted**
4. **Poor: should definitely be deleted**

Your ratings will play a vital part in the next revision.
Please mail this prepaid form to us as soon as possible.
Thanks for your help!

RATING	ARTICLE		RATING	ARTICLE
	1. Census 2000: As a Nation, We Are the World			30. The Other Marriage War
	2. An Overview of America's Education Agenda			31. Tales of Suburban High
	3. The 34th Annual Phi Delta Kappan/Gallup Poll of the Public Attitudes Toward the Public Schools			32. Learning With Jazz
				33. Small Class Size and Its Effects
	4. When Improvement Programs Collide			34. Profiles in Caring: Teachers Who Create Learning Communities in Their Classrooms
	5. Personalized Instruction			
	6. Action Research for School Improvement			35. Accountability: What's Worth Measuring?
	7. The Dark Side of Nationwide Tests			36. Early Childhood Education: Distance Learning for Teachers Adds a New Dimension
	8. The Human Face of the High-Stakes Testing Story			
	9. How and Why Standards Can Improve Student Achievement: A Conversation With Robert J. Marzano			37. The Winding Path: Understanding the Career Cycle of Teachers
				38. The Kind of Schools We Need
	10. Standards: Here Today, Here Tomorrow			39. The World Is Your Classroom: Lessons in Self-Renewal
	11. Where's the Content? The Role of Content in Constructivist Teacher Education			
				40. The New Century: Is It Too Late for Transformational Leadership?
	12. Saving Standards			
	13. Welcome to Standardsville			
	14. Is the Supreme Court's Ruling "Good News" for Public Schools?			
	15. Inculcating a Passion for Truth and Learning			
	16. My Morals, Myself			
	17. Humanistic Education to Character Education: An Ideological Journey			
	18. Bullying Among Children			
	19. Creating School Climates That Prevent School Violence			
	20. Discipline and the Special Education Student			
	21. E-Mentality: Is E-Learning Affecting Classroom Behavior?			
	22. Decisions That Have Shaped U.S. Education			
	23. Educating African American Children: Credibility at a Crossroads			
	24. The Evils of Public Schools			
	25. Can Every Child Learn?			
	26. School Vouchers Showdown			
	27. Meeting the Challenge of the Urban High School			
	28. Teaching and the Truth			
	29. Common Arguments About the Strengths and Limitations of Home Schooling			

(Continued on next page)

BUSINESS REPLY MAIL

FIRST-CLASS MAIL PERMIT NO. 84 GUILFORD CT

POSTAGE WILL BE PAID BY ADDRESSEE

McGraw-Hill/Dushkin
530 Old Whitfield Street
Guilford, Ct 06437-9989

NO POSTAGE
NECESSARY
IF MAILED
IN THE
UNITED STATES

ABOUT YOU

Name

Date

Are you a teacher? ☐ A student? ☐
Your school's name

Department

Address   City   State   Zip

School telephone #

YOUR COMMENTS ARE IMPORTANT TO US!

Please fill in the following information:
For which course did you use this book?

Did you use a text with this ANNUAL EDITION? ☐ yes ☐ no
What was the title of the text?

What are your general reactions to the *Annual Editions* concept?

Have you read any pertinent articles recently that you think should be included in the next edition? Explain.

Are there any articles that you feel should be replaced in the next edition? Why?

Are there any World Wide Web sites that you feel should be included in the next edition? Please annotate.

May we contact you for editorial input? ☐ yes ☐ no
May we quote your comments? ☐ yes ☐ no